THEORY
AND TECHNIQUE
OF PLAYWRITING

By John Howard Lawson

Books

THEORY AND TECHNIQUE OF PLAYWRITING
THE HIDDEN HERITAGE
FILM IN THE BATTLE OF IDEAS
FILM: THE CREATIVE PROCESS

Plays

ROGER BLOOMER   THE INTERNATIONAL
PROCESSIONAL   SUCCESS STORY
NIRVANA   GENTLEWOMAN
LOUDSPEAKER   THE PURE IN HEART
MARCHING SONG

Motion Pictures

BLOCKADE   FOUR SONS
ALGIERS   SAHARA
THEY SHALL HAVE MUSIC   COUNTERATTACK
EARTHBOUND   SMASHUP
ACTION IN THE NORTH ATLANTIC

THEORY
AND TECHNIQUE
OF PLAYWRITING

WITH A NEW INTRODUCTION
BY
JOHN HOWARD LAWSON

A DRAMABOOK

HILL AND WANG – NEW YORK

Acknowledgment of permission to quote from Brunetière's *The Law of
the Drama* is herewith made with thanks to the Brander Matthews
Dramatic Museum of Columbia University; from Maxwell Anderson's
Both Your Houses to Maxwell Anderson through Samuel French, Inc.;
from Barrett H. Clark's *European Theories of the Drama* and *A Study
of the Modern Drama* to Barrett H. Clark.

Manufactured in the United States of America

FIRST DRAMABOOK EDITION AUGUST 1960
SECOND PRINTING NOVEMBER 1961
THIRD PRINTING JANUARY 1964
FOURTH PRINTING APRIL 1965
FIFTH PRINTING MARCH 1967
SIXTH PRINTING JANUARY 1968
SEVENTH PRINTING FEBRUARY 1969

CONTENTS

Contents

PART 4
DRAMATIC COMPOSITION

INTRODUCTION

The Changing Years

THIS study of dramatic theory and technique was first published in 1936, in the midst of the social and theatrical upheaval that Harold Clurman calls "The Fervent Years." Today, the arts display less fervor, and far less interest in "social significance." The transition in dramatic thought from *Waiting for Lefty* to *Waiting for Godot* is almost as sweeping as the changes that have taken place among the world's peoples and powers.

There are those who regard the culture of the thirties as dead and best forgotten. The question need not be debated here— except insofar as this book offers testimony to the contrary. My beliefs have not changed, nor has my fervor abated. I can hope that my understanding has ripened. But I see no need to modify or revise the theory of dramatic art on which this work is based.

The theory holds that the dramatic process follows certain general laws, derived from the function of drama and its historical evolution. A play is a mimed fable, an acted and spoken story. The tale is presented because it has *meaning* to its creator. It embodies a vision, poses an ethical or emotional problem, praises heroes or laughs at fools. The playwright may not be conscious of any purpose beyond the telling of a tale. He may be more interested in box-office receipts than in social values. Nonetheless, the events taking place on the stage embody a point of view, a judgment of human relationships. Conceptual understanding is the key to mastery of dramatic technique. The structure of a play, the design of each scene and the movement of the action to its climax, are the means by which the concept is communicated.

The theatre is a difficult art form. No labor of thought can give talent to the untalented or sensitivity to the insensitive. The pattern of a play is as subtle and chromatic as the pattern of a symphony. Theatrical concepts are profoundly, and at best magically, *theatrical,* growing out of the culture of the theatre as part of the culture and history of mankind. Therefore, dramatic craftsmanship encompasses the past from which it has evolved. The artist is not bound by traditional styles. He is more likely to be bound by ignorance, enslaving him to the parochial devices and cheap inventions of "show business." The true creator turns to the theatre's heritage in order to attain freedom, to select and develop modes of expression suited to his need, to give radiance to his vision and substance to his dream.

The history of dramatic thought which constitutes the first part of this book traces the evolution of European theatre from ancient Athens to the twentieth century. I must acknowledge my regret that it deals only with European development, and does not encompass the riches of theatre culture in other parts of the world. Today we are beginning to realize that our dramatic heritage is not limited to the Greeks and Elizabethans and the English and continental drama of the last three centuries. There is a growing recognition in the United States of the power and resources of the theatre in India, China, and Japan. Yet these forms, and those of other lands, are still regarded as quaint and esoteric. Brecht is the only modern dramatist who has utilized Oriental modes as an integral part of his own creative style.

The contemporary stage uses a conglomeration of techniques, ranging from the banalities of the "well-made play" to the splendors of musical comedy; but all this is done eclectically, to achieve an effect, to titillate sensibilities. Broadway uses shreds and patches of theatre experience and related forms of dance, pantomime, and ritual, drawn from all parts of the globe. But there has been no attempt to consider the order and value of stage traditions, their relation to contemporary culture, their potential use in stimulating the theatrical imagination and developing new modes of dramatic communication.

Let us now turn to a more modest historical task—an appraisal of the trend of European and American dramatic thought from the middle thirties to the present. At first glance, we see a kaleidoscope of contradictory tendencies: wider public interest in the theatre is manifested in the growth of "Off-Broadway" production and the activity of community and university theatres; yet all this stir and effort have not stimulated any movement of creative writing. The Stanislavsky method has attained considerable prestige, but it is doubtful whether the art of acting has progressed during these decades. The posthumous presentation of O'Neill's last plays has added to his reputation; Brecht and O'Casey exert a growing influence; there is far more interest in Shakespeare and other classics than there was a quarter-century ago.

Yet statistical evidence and critical judgment agree that the theatre is sick. The number of playhouses available for professional production in the United States dropped from 647 in 1921 to 234 in 1954. The decline continues. There were sixty-five legitimate theatres in New York in 1931 and only thirty in 1959.* The Off-Broadway stage is said to have lost one million dollars during the season of 1958-59.

Each year, critics lament the decline of the art. Early in 1945, Mary McCarthy wrote: "In 1944, the stage presents such a spectacle of confusion, disintegration and despair that no generalization can cover the case." † Fifteen years later, Brooks Atkinson wrote in the *New York Times* of January 3, 1960: "Last year was on the whole banal. This season, so far, is worse. . . . There is nothing creative at the center of things, pushing the theatre into significant areas of thought or feeling."

On May 14, 1959, President Eisenhower broke ground for the new seventy-five-million-dollar Lincoln Center for the Performing Arts in New York City. The Shakespeare festivals at Stratford, Ontario and Stratford, Connecticut attract enthusiastic crowds. There is apparently a need for living theatre in the United States. How does this need relate to the decline of the commercial stage? Why is there "nothing creative at the center of things?"

Burden of Guilt

A group of European playwrights—Giraudoux, Anouilh, Beckett, Ionesco, Genet, Sartre, Camus, Duerrenmatt—have been honored and praised in the United States in recent years. Their collective influence goes far beyond Broadway, and is a major factor in creating the climate of thought that pervades the drama departments of our universities and the experimental work of amateur and professional groups. We must turn to these dramatists for the clearest statement, and often the most imaginative theatrical realization, of ideas which are more confusingly and less imaginatively projected in English and American plays.

The turning point in the development of the modern French theatre is signalized by one play, *The Madwoman of Chaillot*. Its author, Jean Giraudoux, who died in 1944, belonged to the older generation of French intellectuals. His rhetoric and fantasy are derived from ancient sources, combining elements of Racine with nineteenth-century sensibility and twentieth-century wit. But underlying Giraudoux's classicism is his mordant sense of the failure of bourgeois values in the society of his own time. The

---

* *International Theatre Annual,* No. 4, edited by Harold Hobson, New York, 1958.
† Mary McCarthy, *Sights and Spectacles,* New York, 1957.

action of his plays may take place in Argos or Thebes or Troy. But the social milieu is always the narrow middle-class life of the provincial town of Bellac where he was born. There are always the petty officials, the grubby businessmen, the deadening routine that destroys the human spirit.

The conflict between the ideal and the real runs through all of Giraudoux's plays. It is often veiled in fantasy, as in *Ondine,* or sentimentalized in terms of a young girl's search for beauty, as in *The Enchanted* or *The Apollo of Bellac.* But finally, in *The Madwoman of Chaillot,* the roots of the conflict are exposed. The Countess, "dressed in the grand fashion of 1885," is a madwoman because she holds to the old values threatened by the greedy businessmen who are going to tear down the city to find oil under the houses. "Little by little," says the Ragpicker, "the pimps have taken over the world."

The Countess lures the seekers after oil into her cellar, and sends them down into a sewer from which there is no escape. Then she closes the trap door. They are gone forever. The vagabonds, and the poor who have retained their humanity, enter: "The new radiance of the world is now very perceptible. It glows from their faces." The simplicity of this denouement ("They were wicked. Wickedness evaporates") indicates the gap between Giraudoux's hatred of an inhuman society and his dreamlike solution. The final lines turn to sentiment and irony. The Countess tells the young lovers to accept love while there is still time. Then she says: "My poor cats must be starved. What a bore if humanity had to be saved every afternoon."

The indictment of bourgeois society in *The Madwoman of Chaillot* foreshadows the course of European theatre in the years following World War II. But the ironic twist at the end is even more revealing of the mood of the period. The intellectual knows that "the times are out of joint"; the sensitive artist is tortured by awareness of evil. But the evil seems inexorable, and humanity cannot be saved every afternoon.

The mad Countess has strength of will and even optimism. But the will tends to atrophy in the person who sees the immensity of evil but finds no way of combating it. Inability to act creates a feeling of guilt, a loss of all rational values. A world without values is a world in which *action*—the heart of life and drama— has lost meaning. According to Camus, human dignity is achieved through recognition of the "absurdity" of existence: "For one who is alone, with neither God nor master, the weight of days is terrible." * As early as 1938, in *Caligula,* Camus created a drama in which nihilism is the motive-force of the action. Caligula is the symbol of Man without values. In a criminal society, he can exercise his will only by killing and destroying.

Sartre's existentialist philosophy and his creative work attempt to resolve the contradiction between the idea that life is absurd and tragic, and the search for responsibilities that give it purpose. The contradiction between these two irreconcilable concepts is strongly, almost absurdly, demonstrated in *The Respectful Prostitute.* Sartre's unfamiliarity with the small-town life of the American South is evident in the play. But his choice of such a social setting shows his concern with moral values and also his abstract approach, his inability to achieve clarity. The characters seem to be under a spell of absolute evil. Lizzie, the prostitute, tries to save the Negro from lynching. The white Southerner, Fred, pursues the Negro and two revolver shots are heard offstage. When Fred returns to Lizzie, she wants to kill him but cannot. He explains that the Negro was running too fast and he missed him. Then the racist embraces the prostitute and tells her he will put her "in a beautiful house, with a garden"; as she yields to his embrace, he says, "Then everything is back to normal again"; adding as he reveals his identity to her for the first time, "My name is Fred."

The ironic twist as the curtain descends is characteristic of the modern drama. But here the irony is heavy-handed. It tells us that nothing has happened: the threatened violence did not take place. The Negro is not central to the action; he is merely a symbol of the decadence which is more fully expressed in the brutal sensuality of the racist ("Is it true that I gave you a thrill? Answer me. Is it true?"),† and the helplessness of the woman.

There is an existentialist link between *Caligula* and *The Respectful Prostitute.* In both plays, men accept the absurdity and cruelty of their existence and absolve themselves of guilt by denying moral responsibility.

The burden of guilt is carried more gracefully in the plays of Jean Anouilh. These are sentimental lamentations over the dead body of love. There is no development of action because the doom is inescapable. In the plays of youthful passion, such as *Eurydice*‡ or *Romeo and Jeannette,* the lovers meet and cry out against the fate that engulfs them at the final curtain. In *Romeo and Jean-*

---

* *The Fall,* New York, 1957.
† It may be noted, as a matter of technical interest, that the repetition of phrases is often a sign that the emotion is not valid.
‡ Produced in the United States as *Legend of Lovers.*

nette, the only act of will on the part of the lovers is their final
decision to die together. Jeannette's brother and father watch as
the pair walk out across the sands to be engulfed by the tide. Her
brother says: "They're kissing, kissing. With the sea galloping up
behind them." He turns to his father: "You just don't understand
it, do you, you scruffy old Don Juan, you old cuckold, you old
rag bag!"

Here the last twist of irony reveals Anouilh's mode of thought.
The contrast between love's illusion and the "scruffy old Don
Juan" leavens the sentimentality of his more sophisticated plays.
The sophistication is largely strutting and posing, as in *Waltz of
the Toreadors.* If the drama explodes into action, it is so melodramatic that it tears the fabric of the story. Hero's rape of Lucile
in the third act of *The Rehearsal* is preceded by a long scene,
punctuated by pauses, hesitations, philosophic comments, as if the
character could not quite bring himself to the violent action that
his creator demands of him.

The recurrent theme of all Anouilh's plays is simply that our
society destroys love and life. The charge that modern civilization
is a criminal enterprise is made more directly in the work of the
Swiss playwright, Friedrich Duerrenmatt. It is instructive to
compare Giraudoux's last play with Duerrenmatt's *The Visit.*
From the imaginary town of Chaillot to the imaginary town of
Güllen, European dramatic thought has made a significant journey.

In Chaillot, the Madwoman saves the town from corruption
and restores it to decency. In Güllen, Claire Zachannasian finds no
decency; the immorality of the whole population, so different from
the unassuming virtue of the poor people of Chaillot, is the condition of the action. From the moment of Claire's arrival, it is clear
that the community is ready to murder Anton Schill for a billion
marks. Therefore, when she makes her offer at the end of the first
act, the play is over. She says, "I can wait"; the audience can also
wait, but the conclusion is foreordained. There is no suspense,
because all the characters—the rich woman, the victim, the townspeople—are caught in the same web of corruption.

Loss of Identity

The social criticism which gives some force to Duerrenmatt's
plays is muted and divorced from reality in the work of Samuel
Beckett. An unseen power has destroyed the humanity of the characters, who can do nothing but comment, philosophically and
often with comic vigor, on their fate. This is world's end, and

drama's end. The denial of action is the sole condition of the action. Beckett achieves a sort of theatricalism by the denial of all theatrical values. In *Waiting for Godot,* the two hapless wayfarers do not know why they are waiting:

ESTRAGON: What exactly did we ask him for?
VLADIMIR: Were you not there?
ESTRAGON: I can't have been listening.
VLADIMIR: Oh, nothing very definite.

Beckett gets an effect by making fun of conventional dramatic exposition. He also adopts a principle of indeterminacy which denies all dramatic meaning. The first act ends with the appearance of the boy who reports that Mr. Godot cannot come. The same news is brought in the same manner at the end of the play. The action is circular; the lost figures in the twilight are the same at the end as they were at the beginning.

The concept of total futility in Beckett's plays is applied to middle-class life in the work of Eugene Ionesco. In directing his attack against middle-class values, Ionesco is less intellectual and more savage than Beckett. Even the interplay of ideas is lost in Ionesco, because his people are incapable of consistent thought. They have not only lost their will; they have lost their minds. Their personalities have disintegrated, so that they do not know who they are.

The Bald Soprano, which Ionesco calls "an anti-play," opens with Mr. and Mrs. Smith: "We've eaten well this evening. That's because we live in the suburbs of London and because our name is Smith." We soon find that time and human identity are hopelessly scrambled. They do not know whether "Bobby Watson" died yesterday or four years ago, and they talk of dozens of people, wives, husbands, sons, daughters, cousins, uncles, aunts, who are all named "Bobby Watson." The end is an exact repetition of the beginning. Another couple, Mr. and Mrs. Martin, "are seated like the Smiths at the beginning of the play. The play begins again, with the Martins, who say exactly the same lines as the Smiths in the first scene, while the curtain softly falls."

Jean Genet portrays people who have lost their identity. But they are no longer safely encircled by the comforts of the middle-class milieu. They have lost their innocence. Camus made Caligula conscious of his crimes, but Genet's men and women have neither consciousness nor conscience. Even their sex is uncertain. In *The Maids,* the author wishes the two sisters, whose personalities are interchangeable, to be played by male actors. In an introduction to *The Maids,* Sartre remarks that Genet "has managed to transmit to his thought an increasingly circular movement. . . . Genet detests the society that rejects him and he wishes to annihilate it."

Genet sees the world as a nightmare charade. In *The Balcony,* the visitors to the brothel indulge their perverse desires while they play at being archbishops, judges, and generals. Outside a revolution is taking place, and finally the madam of the whorehouse is installed as queen, with the fake dignitaries as religious, civic, and military leaders.

In the closed world of the brothel, people seek any illusion to escape from "the hellish agony of their names." At the end of *The Maids,* Solange says that nothing remains of them but "the delicate perfume of the holy maidens which they were in secret. We are beautiful, joyous, drunk and free!"

It would require a much more detailed analysis of the plays to explore the political and social tendencies underlying the weird concept of freedom which releases the "maids" from their agony. It is sufficient for our purpose to note the breakdown of dramatic structure in the "anti-plays" of Beckett, Ionesco, and Genet. Ionesco claims that "the comical is tragic, and the tragedy of man, derisory. . . . Without a new Virginity of spirit, without a purified outlook on existential reality, there is no theatre; there is no art either." *

The prophet of this new dramatic dispensation is Antonin Artaud, who issued a series of manifestoes in France in the nineteen-thirties. He called for "a theatre of cruelty . . . furnishing the spectator with the truthful precipitates of dreams, in which his taste for crime, his erotic obsessions, his savagery, his chimeras, his utopian sense of life and matter, even his cannibalism, pour out, on a level not counterfeit and illusory, but interior." †

Anger in England

In England the tensions that indicate the breakdown of old certitudes are not as sharply felt as on the continent. The English bourgeoisie hold, somewhat doubtfully and with growing uneasiness, to the fading glories of their great past. It follows that the English theatre is more conventional and less addicted to fantasy and philosophical despair. But the tendencies which we have noted in Europe are also present in Britain.

---

* Ionesco, "Discovering the Theatre," *Tulane Drama Review,* Autumn 1959.
  † Antonin Artaud, *The Theatre and Its Double,* New York, 1958.

Christopher Fry is a more optimistic Anouilh. While the lovers in Anouilh are doomed, the lovers in *The Lady's not for Burning* escape the execution demanded by the stupid townspeople. They look at the town, and Thomas says:

> There sleep hypocrisy, porcous pomposity, greed,
> Lust, vulgarity, cruelty, trickery, sham
> And all possible nitwittery . . .

But the lovers have each other. They look forward, with comfortable foreboding, to a lifetime together. As the curtain descends, Thomas says: ". . . And God have mercy on our souls."

T. S. Eliot, grown old and sanctimonious after his wanderings in the wasteland, has moved from the poetic eloquence of *Murder in the Cathedral* to the desiccated language and stilted situations of his later plays. The faith that illuminates *Murder in the Cathedral* seems to have lost its potency in the dramas that follow it: religion has become a remote answer to the desperation of a declining upper class. Violence shadows *The Family Reunion:* Lord Monchensey returns to his mother's house to admit that he has murdered his wife. There is an atmosphere of indeterminate danger:

> Why do we all behave as if the door might suddenly open, the
>   curtains be drawn,
> The cellar make some dreadful disclosure, the roof disappear,
> And we should cease to be sure of what is real and unreal?

Harry leaves on a vague mission of expiation, "somewhere on the other side of despair." But his address will be "Care of the Bank in London until you hear from me."

Eliot's voluble aristocrats are haunted by the fear that their society is disintegrating. The fear is more stridently articulated, from the viewpoint of the lower middle class, in the school of naturalistic drama inaugurated in 1956 by John Osborne's *Look Back in Anger*. Jimmy Porter, like the same author's George Dillon and all the other angry young men, is caught in a cage of futility. The cage, the shabby attic apartment, is small and isolated from the winds of change which are the ultimate cause of Jimmy's frustration.

Here there is no large speculation on Man's fate, no indictment of the whole society. Jimmy Porter's hysterical talk is divorced from action, and tells us only that he is very sorry for himself.

He is a sentimentalist, basically interested only in love. The action is circular. When Jimmy's wife leaves, she is replaced by Helen. At the beginning of the third act, Helen is leaning over the ironing board, working with a pile of clothes, in exact duplication of Alison's activity at the opening of the play. When Alison returns, Helen leaves, and the game of love goes on. Jimmy and Alison pretend they are a squirrel and a bear (their favorite game), hiding from unknown dangers: "There are cruel steel traps about everywhere." As the curtain descends, they embrace, pooling their despair, hugging their misery.

The first great Greek tragedy that has come down to us shows Prometheus, tortured and bound to his bleak rock, defying the power of the Gods. There is no Promethean defiance and there are no tragic heroes, in Osborne's world. Even despair is reduced to a small gesture. In *The Entertainer,* Osborne describes the people of this nether world: "We're drunks, maniacs, we're crazy. . . . We have problems that nobody's ever heard of, we're characters out of something that nobody believes in. But we're really not funny, we're too boring."

The Castrated Hero

It seems strange that Americans, inhabitants of a proud and prosperous country, can accept the grotesque image of the United States in the plays of Tennessee Williams. Yet his plays are no further removed from reality than the ironic extravaganzas of Anouilh or the nightmares of Genet. The popularity of Williams' work, reaching a vast public in film adaptations, shows that the themes of guilt and lost identity, criminal impulses and profitless despair, evoke an emotional response in the American audience.

Williams' first important play, *The Glass Menagerie,* produced in 1945, tells a story of frustrated love with moving simplicity. The concept that the search for true love is an illusion, harshly shattered by reality, reminds us of Anouilh. But two years later, in *A Streetcar Named Desire,* the conflict between illusion and reality is projected in violent, almost pathological terms. The climax, Stanley Kowalski's rape of Blanche while his wife is in the hospital having a baby, indicates the further course of the author's development, leading to the treatment of homosexuality and cannibalism in *Garden District* (called *Suddenly Last Summer* on the screen) and the frenetic melodrama of *Sweet Bird of Youth.*

The first act of *Sweet Bird of Youth* exhibits his style and technique. The scene is a hotel bedroom. The young adventurer,

Chance Wayne, has brought an aging Hollywood actress to his home town on the Gulf, in order to impress the girl who is his only true love, Heavenly Finley. He intends to force the actress, called Princess Pazmezoglu, to help him get a film job so that he can bring Heavenly to the West Coast with him.

We learn that Heavenly had contracted a venereal disease, which required an operation—making it impossible for her to have children. Her father and brother, holding Chance responsible, are determined to castrate him. The exposition conveying this information begins with a dialogue between Wayne and a young doctor, George Scudder, who performed the operation, and who announces as he leaves that he intends to marry Heavenly. When George has departed, the actress wakes up. She cannot remember whom she is with. She calls frantically for oxygen. After she inhales the oxygen, she demands her pink pills and vodka. Then she wants dope, which is hidden under the mattress. As they smoke the stuff, she becomes sentimental. But Chance tells her that their whole conversation, including the talk of dope, has been taped. He insists that she sign over all her traveler's checks to him.

She agrees. But first he must make love to her: "When monster meets monster, one monster has to give way. . . . I have only one way to forget these things I don't want to remember, and that's through the act of love-making." As the ritual of sex begins, the stage goes dark.

There are several points of technical interest in the opening scene. It is almost all expository, dealing with previous events and with Chance's elaborate plans. The plot is so fully stated that the only suspense lies in watching the way in which the predicted action will unfold. Williams has a habit of exposing the whole course of his story in the first act. This is due in part to the complicated and retrospective situations with which he deals. In *The Rose Tattoo,* in *Garden District,* in *Orpheus Descending,* the present action is determined and made inevitable by past events. In *Cat on a Hot Tin Roof,* the author's two versions of the final act reveal his difficulty in achieving a climax after the detailed presentation of a situation from which there is no escape.*

This aspect of Williams' method is far more than a technical weakness. It goes to the heart of his meaning. We are foredoomed to defeat. We thrash about in a net of evil. The innocence of

---

*The various versions of Williams' plays offer fascinating opportunities for technical study: *Battle of Angels,* produced in 1940, contains the matrix of *Orpheus Descending,* presented in 1957; two short plays are the basis for *Baby Doll;* the sketch, *Time,* shows the origin of *Sweet Bird of Youth.*

young love is in the past: Heavenly was fifteen and Chance was seventeen when they discovered the wonder of a "perfect" sexual experience. (In *Orpheus Descending,* Val tells a curiously similar story of a girl who appeared to him on the bayou when he was fourteen; like Heavenly in the photograph shown by Chance Wayne, she was stark naked and immediately available.)

At the final curtain of *Sweet Bird of Youth,* when Chance's enemies have captured him and the castration is about to take place, Chance comes forward to face the audience: "I don't ask for your pity, but just for your understanding—not even that! No, just for your recognition of me in you, and the enemy, time, in us all!" This is the monstrous message of the play: sexual lust and greed are the conditions of our lives; we are all as ambitious, frustrated, and amoral as Chance Wayne. The reference to "the enemy, time," is false sentiment and false philosophy, suggesting that age and death are the real cause of our defeat. But Chance does not face old age; he faces castration, which symbolizes the failure and degradation of modern man.

Williams tries to give the play a larger social framework by means of the racist speech delivered by Boss Finley at the end of the second act. But this political background has no validity in relation to the central situation, which revolves around Chance and the Princess.[*]

Williams' pessimism is visceral and mindless. The Princess is as ruthless as Claire in *The Visit.* But Claire is a clever woman plotting vengeance for a wrong that was done her. The Princess is a wreck, living on pills, oxygen, and dope. She needs sex and will buy it on any terms. The scene in which she forces Chance to come to bed with her is not merely a sensational device. As the stage darkens, the degradation of both characters is final. He has nothing except his virility; she has nothing except her need of the male. Each personality is reduced to its irreducible minimum, a sex-urge without emotion or joy.

Robert Robinson observes that in Williams' plays "there can be no intimacy, for intimacy is the act of rewarding identity to another . . . other people simply satisfy an appetite. . . ." He adds that "Mr. Williams is a doggedly minor artist." [†] He is minor because those who deny identity to others lose their own sense of life; this is true of the playwright as well as of the characters to

---

[*] Williams confirms this in a recent statement: he feels that the second act is ineffective, because Boss Finley is of no interest to him, and he has prepared a new second act for the published play (*New York Times,* May 1, 1960).

[†] *New Statesman,* London, September 27, 1958.

whom he refuses the gift of living.

There is a long descent from Caligula to Chance Wayne. Jimmy Porter stands between the two. Caligula chooses, consciously and of his own will, to reject moral responsibility. He learns that life without responsibility has no human warmth or dignity. Jimmy Porter, caught in drab frustration, learns the same lesson. The part of Caligula in the New York production of the Camus play was assigned, appropriately, to an actor who had played Jimmy Porter. The new American hero can learn nothing. Even his role as a phallic symbol is a delusion. Castration is the answer to his claim to manhood.

Robert Brustein writes that the modern "inarticulate hero" sees society "as the outside of a prison," which he wishes to enter for warmth and security. Therefore, "much of the acting and writing of the inarticulate hero is not only neurotic but conformist." * Chance Wayne is a thoroughgoing conformist. He is conventional in his longing for lost love, in his exaggerated toughness, his Hollywood ambitions. He wants to *belong,* and even at the end he is asking the audience to like him.

Among the many playwrights influenced by Williams, conformity is advocated more tenderly, as in the plays of Robert Anderson or the more recent work of Paddy Chayefsky. William Inge offers a romantic version of the tough male in *Picnic,* and a farcical portrait in *Bus Stop.* In Inge, the male's aggressiveness is always tamed by a woman, who finds out in her turn that the man is as frightened and lonely as she is.† In *Come Back, Little Sheba,* Doc gets drunk and violent in order to drown his desire for Marie, the young boarder. At the end, he and his wife are together in the love and misery of the bourgeois prison. At the end of *The Dark at the Top of the Stairs,* Cora ascends the stairs, where her husband's naked feet can be seen "in the warm light at the top."

The theme of acceptance and submission is projected in large poetic terms in *J. B.* by Archibald MacLeish. J. B. is a good man and he is rich. But he must undergo a catalogue of horrors. The three "comforters" who try to console him represent psychiatry, religion, and "left-wing materialism." The last, of course, is the most absurd of the three, but all talk in ridiculous clichés. The anti-intellectualism inherent in this caricature of contemporary thought, and the crude violence of the melodrama preceding it,

* *Commentary,* February 1958.
† See Brustein's "The Man-Taming Women of William Inge," *Harper's,* November 1958.

remind us less of the Book of Job than of Tennessee Williams. J. B. discovers that he must accept life blindly. His wife says:

> Blow on the coal of the heart.
> The candles in churches are out.
> The lights have gone out in the sky.
> Blow on the coal of the heart
> And we'll see by and by.

There are, of course, other tendencies in the American theatre. Lorraine Hansberry's *A Raisin in the Sun* opened in March 1958, on the day following the premiere of *Sweet Bird of Youth* at a playhouse a few blocks away. The contrast between the two plays is fascinating; the fact that *both* were greeted with equal acclaim makes one wonder what criteria—if any—determine Broadway success. The enthusiastic applause for *A Raisin in the Sun* may be due in part to the circumstances of its production. Dramas which deal honestly with Negro themes are a rarity in the New York theatre.* When such a play is the first work of a Negro woman, its success has broad meaning, both in the theatre and in the American life of our time.

Lorraine Hansberry's unusual accomplishment involves unusual responsibilities, both for the author and for those who venture to appraise her contribution. The sense of theatre and vivid characterization revealed in her first play demand realistic discussion of its merits and limitations, and its relationship to the further course of her work.

A Raisin in the Sun is impressive in its simplicity, its respect for human values. This is the source of its modest strength; yet it also indicates a lack of depth, an oversimplification of the dramatic event. The structure seems old-fashioned, because many plays have dealt with a similar theme—an inheritance transforms the prospects of a lower-middle-class family, and the money, or part of it, is wasted by an improvident son.

This theme seems to acquire new vitality when it is applied to the problems of a Negro family. But the reverse is also true: the passions and aspirations of the Negro family, the psychological singularity of each person, are minimized by the triteness of the structure. Underlying the conventional technique of the play is a more profound conventionality. The Negro family struggles, as

---

* Among the few important plays by Negro authors to reach Broadway, mention must be made of Langston Hughes' *Mulatto,* and Theodore Ward's *Our Lan'.* Of special interest is Alice Childress' *Trouble in Mind,* produced off Broadway with far less recognition than it deserves.

it must, for a better home in a better neighborhood; but there is no hint that there is anything wrong with the bourgeois world the family seeks to enter. The monstrous evil of racism shadows the play, but it has no dimension of horror. It is symbolized in the only white character, who is an ineffectual racist. But the emotional life of the family centers on the son's foolish anger, his bitter dreams.

Conformity to bourgeois values is the key to the play's viewpoint. It is embodied in the aimless stupidity of Walter's rebellion. It may be unfair to see in him some shreds and patches of Williams' mindless heroes; but Walter's action, his irresponsible loss of the money, have meaning only in relation to his mother's humble common sense, which is rooted in her adherence to an old value: "In my time," she says, "we was worried about not being lynched and getting to the North if we could and how to stay alive and still have a pinch of dignity too."

Thus the difference between *Sweet Bird of Youth* and *A Raisin in the Sun* poses troubling questions. Williams shows bleak decadence, and says there is no escape from it. Miss Hansberry sees a society of simple virtues, in which conformity is desirable and inescapable. This may account for the success of *A Raisin in the Sun*. It is to be hoped that its author possesses the modesty and feeling for art to learn from success as others must learn from failure.

Julian Mayfield has said that many Negro writers are "reluctant to leap head first into the nation's literary mainstream," because it means "identifying the Negro with the American image—that great power face that the world knows and the Negro knows better. . . ." To be sure, the "great power face" is not the true image of America, but Mayfield is justified in describing the mainstream of American culture as characterized by "apathy and either a reluctance or a fear of writing about anything that matters." *

Miss Hansberry, having become part of the mainstream, runs the risk of being immersed in it. But her talent, and the position she has achieved, offer her a unique opportunity to go beyond her first play to deeper insights and larger themes.

The Testament of Eugene O'Neill

When the first edition of this book was published, O'Neill seemed to have retired from the theatre. After 1934, he wrote

---

* *The American Negro Writer and His Roots,* Selected Papers from the First Conference of Negro Writers, March 1959, published by the American Society of African Culture, New York, 1960.

nothing that reached the public, except *The Iceman Cometh,* finished in 1940 and produced six years later. Yet during this long period, O'Neill worked feverishly, destroying much of what he wrote and leaving several plays in manuscript. These plays, staged after his death in 1953, reveal the intensity of his quest for dramatic truth. He was tortured by the artist's need to find some order and reason and beauty in existence.

His conviction that something had gone wrong, in his own troubled heart and in the life of his time, forced him to turn back to a crucial year: in 1912, when O'Neill was twenty-four years old, the world was moving toward a war which would undermine the foundations of "Western civilization"; he had returned from his sea voyages; he had seen the world from the decks of tramp steamers, from dark forecastles and water-front dives. He returned to haunt the New York water front, to read Marx for the first time, to contribute social poems to the old *Masses.* In December 1912, he was stricken with tuberculosis.

In *The Iceman Cometh,* O'Neill tried to create a social allegory of that fateful year. The action is confused and melodramatic, because the *ideas* are beyond the author's grasp. O'Neill could not give order and meaning to his impassioned indictment of a society that destroys human values. Lack of conceptual clarity tends to make dramatic action strained and improbable.* Without clarity, there can be no aesthetic form, no sustained magic.

But O'Neill could understand, with masterful emotion and depth, the disintegration of his own family. In *Long Day's Journey into Night,* he returns again to 1912, to tell, as he has said, "of old sorrow, written in tears and blood." The play is his testament, a last monument to his genius. Through his pity and love for "the four haunted Tyrones," he offers a vision of the whole society which decreed their suffering.

There is terrifying emotional clarity in the long drunken scene in the third act of *Long Day's Journey into Night,* reaching its climax when the father and his sons are interrupted by the mother's appearance carrying her old-fashioned wedding gown of white satin. Under the influence of morphine, she speaks of her girlhood, her desire to be a nun. The play ends with her simple words: "That was in the winter of my senior year. Then in the spring something happened to me. Yes, I remember, I fell in love with James Tyrone and was so happy for a time." The three men remain motionless as the curtain comes down.

O'Neill has left the dark jungle of irrational fears to ascend the

---

* This is true even in Shakespeare—for example, in *Timon of Athens.*

wintry heights of tragedy. Yet in doing so he acknowledges that the long sojourn in the jungle defeated the fulfillment of his genius. Edmund Tyrone, the younger son who is O'Neill himself, tells his father that he doubts whether he has even "the *making* of a poet . . . I couldn't touch what I tried to tell you just now. I just stammered. That's the best I'll ever do. I mean, if I live. Well, it will be faithful realism, at least. Stammering is the native eloquence of us fog people."

Thus O'Neill acknowledges that the grace and majesty, the shining clarity of dramatic poetry, would elude him. Edmund Tyrone tells his father that he "must always be a little in love with death!" But is this muted eloquence of the "fog people"—untouched by the magic of the sun—the only eloquence of which the modern theatre is capable?

The Theatrical Imagination

I use the term "theatrical imagination" to describe the quality of dramatic art that transforms the imitation of an action into a new creative experience, a vision and revelation shared by the performers and the audience. Francis Fergusson suggests "study of the cultural landmarks—the drama of Sophocles and Shakespeare, the *Divina Commedia* of Dante—in which the idea of a theatre has been briefly realized":

> Dante presents his contemporaries with the photographic accuracy of Ibsen and Chekhov; and he presents all of the social and political issues of his time. But the literal realities are also seen in the round, with all the dimensions of meaning, historical, moral and final. . . . The perspectives of dream, of myth, and of the most wakeful reason, which we think of as mutually exclusive, succeed each other in the movement of his poem but do not cancel each other out.*

It may be asking too much to propose that our theatre of Broadway—on and off—aspire to the copious splendor of *The Divine Comedy*. But even the idea of such a theatre is foreign to the contemporary stage.

The two modern playwrights who have done most to restore the theatrical imagination are Sean O'Casey and Bertolt Brecht. Their modes of communication are different; they come from divergent cultures; but they are alike in their sense of history,

---

* *The Idea of a Theatre,* Garden City, N. Y., 1953.

their concern with social and political realities, their dissatisfaction with the dry conventions and emasculated language of today's theatre, their use of forms and techniques derived from the drama's classic heritage.

O'Casey's early plays, growing out of his youthful experience in the Dublin slums and the social struggles that culminated in the 1916 Easter Rebellion, are deceptively simple in plot structure. But the tragicomic naturalism of *Juno and the Paycock* and *The Plough and the Stars* is illuminated by a Shakespearean largeness and humanity. O'Casey's response to the uncertainties that shadowed the world in the late twenties and thirties demanded a broader dramatic setting. Beginning with the antiwar play, *The Silver Tassie,* in 1927, he uses symbolism and rhetoric, dance and song, to create an image of our time.

It has been said that these later dramatic murals lack the compact intensity of the earlier domestic portraits. It is true that O'Casey's exuberant creativity sometimes sets goals that he cannot attain. But even when his rhetoric and his dreams race beyond the dramatic moment, he has enlarged the potentialities of the theatre. In *Red Roses for Me,* the whole movement of the third act takes the form of a ballet. The relationship between the spectacle and the love story of Ayamonn and Sheila is not fully realized, but the dance and the accompanying lyrics carry the action to a higher level and give it an extension that could not be otherwise achieved.

While Elizabethan influences, combined with the rhythms of Irish speech, predominate in O'Casey, Brecht has drawn from a wide range of classical and romantic sources, and most notably from the theatre of the Orient. Brecht's idea of Epic drama originated in the twenties. The best-known and most characteristic work of this period is *The Three-Penny Opera,* completed in 1928. In the early thirties, he became familiar with the Nō plays of Japan. In 1935, on his first visit to Moscow, he saw the Chinese actor, Mei Lan-fang, performing without make-up, costume, or lighting. The aloofness and purity of the actor's style, combined with theatrical fervor and controlled emotion, seemed to confirm Brecht's Epic theory, and to offer a practical technique for its development.[*]

Brecht was neither an imitator nor a traditionalist. The way he transmuted his rather limited knowledge of the Oriental theatre into a new and intensely modern mode of expression is explicitly shown in *The Good Woman of Setzuan* and *The Caucasian Chalk Circle*. But the influence is implicit in all his later plays.

The ribald wit and picaresque satire of *The Three-Penny Opera*

[*] John Willett, *The Theatre of Bertolt Brecht,* New York, 1959.

do not as yet constitute an integrated style—although many styles have been imposed on it in various performances. Brecht showed his dissatisfaction with the play by undertaking a massive reorganization of the material as a novel, in which he attempted to deepen the implications of the story.* The novel is important, because it shows Brecht's determination to find the roots of human psychology in the whole system of circumstances through which the individual moves. This is a better key to Brecht's art than his somewhat didactic exposition of the Epic method.

However we cannot ignore the claim that Epic constitutes a new kind of theatre. Brecht argued that Epic discards "plot" in favor of "narrative"; it makes the spectator a judge and observer, and thus arouses his power of action, which is lulled by the emotional involvement of conventional drama; it makes the human being an object of inquiry instead of taking him for granted; it regards human nature as alterable rather than unalterable; it treats each scene for itself instead of relating one scene to another.†

These views reflect the rebellious mood of the German theatre of the twenties and the rejection of the false values of the commercial stage, with its stuffy emotionalism, its world of bourgeois illusion behind the glare of the footlights. But Brecht draws a false distinction between involvement and judgment, between theatre as magic and theatre as "tribunal." Mordecai Gorelik defines the real problem: Epic style, he says, "changes the value of psychology in the drama. To give one example, it alters the meaning of Stanislavsky's views on character. . . . The Stanislavsky system has a tendency to become introspective and even static. The reason, perhaps, is that the actor's adjustments are in terms of *thoughts* rather than in terms of action." ‡

It is true that the Stanislavsky method, as interpreted by actors and directors in the United States, has become increasingly psychological and Freudian. But in the process, American artists have moved further and further away from Stanislavsky. We can hardly blame the Moscow Art Theatre for the shoddy emotionalism of Kazan's direction.

Brecht's greatest achievement is his probing of character in terms of action and moral values and the pressures of the environment. This does not mean that he opposes or supersedes Stanislavsky. Nor does it mean that the spectator is aloof, nor that the scenes are unrelated. We cannot pause to examine the lessons which

* *Three-Penny Novel,* translated by Desmond I. Vesey, verse translated by Christopher Isherwood, New York, n.d.
† "Notes for Mahagonny," cited, Willett, *opus cit*
‡ *New Theatres for Old,* New York, 1940.

Brecht learned from Oriental drama. It would require a treatise to show how the stylized movement, the lyric symbolism, the narrative flow, the restrained violence, of the theatre of China and Japan, brought a flowering of Brecht's imagination. But the Oriental stage is not a "tribunal," nor do the plays of Asia ignore structure or climactic development. It is a misunderstanding of Japanese culture to suppose that the great puppet plays of Chikamatsu do not involve the spectators in the dramatic events.

Brecht's plays also have structure, climax, and an emotional bond—much closer than the lachrymose "participation" or idle laughter of the usual commercial show—between the performance and the audience. The scope and vividness of Brecht's action tend to assume a narrative aspect; he uses a technique of *montage,* intercutting moods and events, with abrupt contrasts and poetic flights. But, as with any work of art, the unity of the whole is the test of its creative value.

There are weaknesses in Brecht's work as well as in his theory. At his best, he restores the classic dimensions of meaning—historical, moral, and personal—that have been lost in the modern theatre. Mother Courage, toiling through the Thirty Years' War with her cart and her three children, accepts and is part of the degradation of her environment. She sings her "Song of Capitulation"; seeking only to survive, she loses one after another of her children. But at the end, as she pulls her wagon alone, she is an image of the human spirit, corrupted but indestructible.

Mother Courage has moments of superb drama—for example, the scene in which she must deny the corpse of her dead son; or the scene in which the dumb girl beats the drum to warn the city of Halle of the impending attack. Above all, Brecht defines the kind of heroism which is new and yet as old as life—the heroism of ordinary mortals, vacillating, self-seeking, yet indomitable and enduring, capable of love and sacrifice, the heroism which is the hope of the world.

The Dilemma of Arthur Miller

Arthur Miller's serious contribution to the American theatre begins with *All My Sons* in 1947. It was not his first play, but his eighth or ninth. Miller had been struggling to formulate an attitude toward American life, growing out of the ferment of the thirties and the experience of the Second World War. *All My Sons* is a social document, in the manner of the thirties. It reminds us of the two plays by Lillian Hellman which mark the highest development of dramatic thought in that period—*The Little Foxes,* which appeared in 1939, and *Watch on the Rhine,* produced in 1941.

All My Sons lacks the maturity and theatrical invention of the Hellman plays. Its power lies in the clarity with which a simple theme is dramatized. Miller tells us that our society is corrupted by money: "This is the land of the great big dogs, you don't love a man here, you eat him." Both Miller's artistic need and the changing temper of the times in the late forties urged him to go beyond this simple indictment. The corruption was present and increasing, but the issues were becoming more complicated and the democratic fire of the thirties had become a flickering and uncertain flame.

Miller, writing a decade later, says: "I think now that the straightforwardness of the *All My Sons* form was in some part due to the relatively sharp definition of the social problems it dealt with." * Miller was right in feeling that the play is too "straightforward." Joe Keller is not a tragic figure, because his crime and punishment illustrate a thesis and lack psychological depth.

In trying to probe more deeply into the heart of man, Miller found difficulty in relating subjective factors to objective reality. Regarding *Death of a Salesman,* produced in 1949, he says: "The first image that occurred to me . . . was an enormous face the height of the proscenium arch which would appear and then open up, and we would see the inside of a man's head. In fact, *The Inside of His Head* was the first title." †

Miller is too much of an artist to deny reality. The illusions darkening Willy's soul arise from real and destructive social forces. But a man who lives by illusions becomes interesting and tragic only when he is brought face to face with the reality he has ignored. The intensity of the confrontation will determine the tragic element in the drama.

The essence of *Death of a Salesman* is Willy's defeat. His failure as a salesman is established in the first scene; the appearance of action is maintained by the psychoanalytical elements, the family relationships, the enmity between father and sons. The action is retrospective, relating in large part to the past. In abandoning the "straightforward" form of *All My Sons,* Miller shows extraordinary skill in developing a technique that substitutes moods and dreams for external conflict. The finality of illusion is symbolized

* Introduction, *Arthur Miller's Collected Plays,* New York, 1957.
† *Ibid.*

in the ghostly figure of Uncle Ben. At the end, Ben urges Willy to come to the jungle: "It's dark there, but full of diamonds. . . ." Ben disappears, and the stage direction shows that Willy has lost all contact with reality: "He turns around as if to find his way; sounds, faces, voices, seem to be swarming in upon him and he flicks at them, crying, Sh! Sh!" His death, immersed in irrational dreams, achieves pathos, but it cannot touch tragedy.

Miller could not be content to depict Man lost and helpless in a psychological maze. His most impressive play, *The Crucible,* produced in the evil days of McCarthyism in 1953, portrays a man who decides to die rather than compromise with his own conscience.

Yet the conflict between psychological and social factors is unresolved in *The Crucible.* Miller tells us that his "central impulse for writing" the play "was not the social but the interior psychological question, which was the question of that guilt residing in Salem which the hysteria merely unleashed, but did not create." He says he was puzzled by the existence of "such absolute evil in men." * Thus Miller gives some measure of support to the view prevalent in our culture that the criminal conduct of society is an "interior psychological question." It would be difficult to muster historical evidence that Cotton Mather, or Danforth, or any of the other Salem witch-hunters, were motivated by "absolute evil." But we are at present not so much concerned with the historical reality as with Miller's concept of reality and its effect on the structure and meaning of the play.

Miller tells us of his discovery of Abigail Williams' testimony in the records of the witchcraft trials: "Her apparent desire to convict Elizabeth and save John made the play possible for me." It was this aspect of the story that clarified the psychological problem of evil for the playwright: "Consequently the structure reflects that understanding, and it centers on John, Elizabeth and Abigail." †

The triangle does give the play a structure. Abigail, seventeen, "with an endless capacity for dissembling," has been dismissed as the couple's bond-servant because she had an affair with Proctor. When she meets him in the first scene, she is determined to renew the relationship: "John, I am waiting for you every night." Her hatred of the wife motivates her false testimony against Elizabeth. It can be argued that this sexual situation enriches the texture of

* *Ibid.*
† *Ibid.*

the story and avoids the sparse "straightforwardness" of a socially oriented drama.

In a sense, the argument has some weight. We have seen too many plays and read too many books in which social issues, divorced from psychological insights, are presented with artless naïveté. It would be rash to suggest that the betrayal of Marguerite is not central to the first part of Goethe's *Faust*.

But John Proctor is not Faust, and his wrestling with his conscience at the climax would not be different if he had never known Abigail. Yet there is a meaning in Proctor's past sin, and it is expressed in his final scene with his wife: "I cannot mount the gibbet like a saint. It is a fraud. I am not that man. . . . My honesty is broke, Elizabeth; I am no good man. Nothing's spoiled by giving them this lie that were not rotten long before."

Miller wants to show us a man who is not committed, who is prone to sin, without moral certainties. The point is emphasized in the contrast between Proctor and Rebecca Nurse; the old woman has no problem, because she cannot conceive of compromise: "Why, it is a lie, it is a lie; how may I damn myself? I cannot, I cannot."

Proctor's dilemma may be regarded as a reflection of Miller's own inner struggle, between moral conviction and avoidance of commitment, between the heroism of the true artist and the ignoble pressures of the time. When Proctor cries out, "I am no saint," it seems like an echo of the author's distress.

This is a magnificent theme. If Miller had exposed Proctor's consciousness in depth, he might have written a great play. But the study of man's soul demands understanding of the social forces that press in upon him and test his will. The use of the subplot concerning Abigail is largely responsible for Miller's failure to give this added dimension. The author's feeling that the story of the girl "made the play possible" by providing a structure, points to the structural weakness. Proctor's sin with Abigail is a sidelight on his character, but it cannot give any powerful stimulus to the action. It merely adds to the impression that some vague "force of evil" overshadows the Salem community.

Eric Bentley observes that "*The Crucible* is *about* guilt yet nowhere in it is there any *sense* of guilt because the author and the director have joined forces to dissociate themselves and their hero from evil." * This is true because the hero has no relationship to the reality around him; he is merely surprised and eventually

* *The Dramatic Event,* Boston, 1954.

destroyed by it. Since his affair with Abigail cannot supply this connection, the evil that afflicts the town is a mystic absolute. The attempt to dramatize this concept in its impact on Proctor brings down the curtain on the second act. Proctor has learned that his present bond-servant, Mary Warren, has been prompted by Abigail to testify falsely against his wife. As he takes Mary by the throat, almost strangling her, Proctor says:

> Now Hell and Heaven grapple on our backs, and all our old pretense is ripped away—make your peace! (He throws her to the floor . . . turning to the open door) Peace. It is a providence, and no great change; we are only what we always were, but naked now. (He walks as though toward a great horror, facing the open sky) Aye, naked! And the wind, God's icy wind, will blow!

The scene is effective, hysterical, and obscure. Insofar as it relates to Proctor's feeling of horror and unworthiness, the scene should be between him and Abigail. But the substitution of the other girl makes the speech more general and dictates its value as a statement of the condition of the action: Man is "naked" under "God's icy wind." We are reminded of Maxine Greene's description of the "new hero" of modern literature as a man who has no faith in the rational world, who has found "the tragic way of daring to stand up to the uncaring sky." * But this whole idea is contradicted by the climax. Proctor does not stand up to the uncaring sky, but to a specific social situation.

The premise that evil is a curse written on man's soul reappears in *A View from the Bridge,* produced two years after *The Crucible.* We may wonder whether the title suggests the author's suspicion of commitment, his desire to view the human situation from above and afar. The ambivalence of *The Crucible* is repeated in *A View from the Bridge,* but the background story of a man's passion for a young girl has now been brought into the foreground. Eddie Carbone's half-incestuous desire for his niece is the focal point of the action; it motivates the denouement, his death is retribution for his having become an informer.

The difficulty lies in the concept of an inevitable fate driving Eddie to his doom. There could be potent tragedy in a man's fixation on his adopted daughter. But this tragedy of family life is not contrived by destiny. In attributing Eddie's emotional instability to a power beyond his control, the author attempts to give him dignity, but succeeds only in making him absurd.

* "A Return to Heroic Man," *Saturday Review,* August 22, 1959.

Eddie is an existentialist hero, justifying his passion in a world that has ceased to have moral meaning to him. His desire to act, to consummate his love, must make him a criminal. He is related both to the Caligula of Camus and the mindless symbols of masculinity in the plays of Tennessee Williams. The climate of evil which is the condition of the action is invalidated in the climax: we are asked to forgive Eddie for his incestuous love—because he cannot avoid it; and to blame him for becoming an informer—because this action relates to society and must be judged in its social context.

Miller has given us an insight into his conceptual confusion in two different versions of the final speech of the lawyer, Alfieri. When the play was produced in New York, the killing of Eddie by Marco was followed by this epilogue, spoken by the lawyer:

> Most of the time we settle for half,
> And I like it better.
> And yet when the tide is right
> And the green smell of the sea
> Floats in through my window,
> The waves of this bay
> Are the waves against Siracusa,
> And I see a face that suddenly seems carved;
> The eyes look like tunnels
> Leading back toward some ancestral beach
> Where all of us once lived.
>
> And I wonder at those times
> How much all of us
> Really lives there yet,
> And when we will truly have moved on,
> On and away from that dark place,
> That world that has fallen to stones.*

Eddie's fate is explained in Freudian terms: he is driven by impulses going back into the dark past. These inner drives affect all of us, but the time may come when we escape from the ancestral curse.

In the revised version of the play, printed in the *Collected Plays,* Alfieri speaks as follows:

> Most of the time now we settle for half and I like it better. But the truth is holy, and even as I know how wrong he was, and his death useless, I tremble, for I confess that something perversely pure calls to me from his memory—not purely good,

* Printed in *Theatre Arts,* September 1956.

but himself purely, for he allowed himself to be wholly known and for that I think I will love him more than all my sensible clients. And yet, it is better to settle for half, it must be! And so I mourn him—I admit it—with a certain . . . alarm.

Miller has escaped from the Freudian myth to invent a contrary myth of his own: he has reversed the concept of Eddie's guilt and made him "perversely pure." The reference to "settling for half," which appears in the opening line of the earlier version, has been expanded to make Eddie guiltless, and even, in a sense, an admirable figure. It is difficult to understand what is meant by settling for half: would it have been a "compromise" to let his niece marry and to resume a normal existence with his wife? Did he fulfill "himself purely" by calling the immigration authorities to arrest his wife's cousins?

More than five years have passed since the appearance of *A View from the Bridge,* and Miller has not yet produced another play. We may assume that he is wrestling with the problem of dramatic clarity, so cogently exposed in the two endings of his last drama. Miller's dilemma is central to the theatrical culture of our time. Miller has said that pathos comes easily to him, but he wants to achieve the greatness of tragedy. There is pathos in the plight of people driven by fate. But there is neither tragic splendor nor comic vitality in people who have lost their will. False concepts of man's relation to reality inhibit theatrical inventiveness and paralyze the creative imagination.

Today the world is being transformed by heroes whose name is legion. The drama of our time is being enacted by these millions who refuse to accept the "absurdity" of existence, who live, and if necessary die, to give life meaning.

The theatre will be restored to creative life when it returns to the classic function described by Shaw: "The theatre is a factor of thought, a prompter of conscience, an elucidator of social conduct, an armory against despair and darkness, and a temple of the ascent of man." *

May, 1960   JOHN HOWARD LAWSON

* Preface, *Our Theatres in the Nineties,* 3 vols., London, 1932.

PART i

HISTORY OF DRAMATIC THOUGHT

European dramatic thought has its origin in the Greek theatre. Contemporary theories of technique are still based to a remarkable degree on Aristotle's principles. Chapter I undertakes a brief appraisal of the Aristotelian heritage.

Chapter II brings us to the Renaissance flowering of the drama in the sixteenth century. There is no historical justification for this hiatus of eighteen centuries. However, it may be justified in dealing with dramatic theory. For theory in any formal sense was at a standstill during the middle ages. Minstrelsy, rural festivals, and cathedral rites created an enduring theatrical tradition. But the tradition was not subjected to any critical evaluation until the theatre of the Renaissance, and even then theory lagged far behind practice. While the Elizabethans stormed the heavens with their poetry, critical thought ignored the drama or repeated the formal classical rules.

The later seventeenth century, the age of Molière in France and Restoration comedy in England, may be regarded either as the backwash of the Renaissance or as the beginning of the realistic treatment of sex, marriage, and money that was to exert a decisive influence on the further development of the theatre. The change was accompanied by a new approach to dramatic technique; the panorama of Elizabethan action was contracted to fit the picture-frame stage. We conclude the second chapter with this turning point in dramatic thought.

Chapter III deals with the eighteenth century. The bourgeoisie, driving toward the American and French revolutions, produced a rational philosophy, an emphasis on the rights and obligations of the individual, that could no longer be satisfied wtih the money-and-sex situations of seventeenth-century comedy.

The nineteenth century brought the full development of bourgeois society, with its inescapable contradictions and deepening class conflicts. The problem of the middle class, torn between abstract ideals and practical necessities, was elaborated in the philosophy of Hegel. The dualism of Hegel's thought reflected the conflict between the "free" individual and the conditions imposed by his environment, between the soul's aspiration and the subjection of the human will to mean and ignoble ends. The Hegelian dilemma was dramatized in Goethe's Faust.

The problem posed with such intellectual power in Faust *cast its shadow across the later years of the nineteenth century. The shadow moved across the make-believe world of the stage, forcing a choice between illusion and reality.*

The hopes of the middle class in a period of economic growth and competitive opportunity were reflected in the laissez-faire *economics and romantic individualism of the early nineteenth century. As the concentration of economic power reduced the area of* laissez-faire, *conflict no longer appeared as a healthy competition between individuals; it appeared in a threatening light as the cleavage of social classes. The area of conflict in which the conscious will could operate without facing fundamental social issues became constricted. The drama lost passion and conviction.*

Since nineteenth-century thought provides the basis for the technique of the modern play, it is essential to review the period in some detail. Therefore, a slight variation in the arrangement of the text of Chapter IV, with subdivisions under separate headings, seems permissible as a means of clarifying the presentation.

The dramatic culture of the nineteenth century is most completely embodied in Ibsen's work. Having considered the general trend in Chapter IV, Ibsen's specific contribution is analyzed in Chapter V.

CHAPTER I

ARISTOTLE

ARISTOTLE, the encyclopedist of the ancient world, has exercised a vast influence on human thought. But in no field of thought has his domination been so complete and so unchallenged as in dramatic theory. What remains to us of the *Poetics* is only a fragment; but even in its fragmentary form Aristotle's statement of the laws of playwriting is remarkable for its precision and breadth.

One of the most famous principles in the *Poetics* relates to the purgation of the emotions through pity and terror. The passage, in spite of its suggestiveness, offers no accurate explanation of the meaning of "purgation" or how it is brought about. But the passage is significant, because it is the only point at which Aristotle touches on the *psychological* problems (the feelings which bind the writer to his material and which also seem to create the bond between the play and the audience) that puzzle the modern student of the drama. Aristotle's approach is structural: he described tragedy as "the imitation of an action that is complete and whole and of a certain magnitude." * The question of magnitude has caused a great deal of discussion, but Aristotle's explanation is sufficiently clear: "There may be a whole that is wanting in magnitude. A whole is that which has a beginning, middle and end." Dramas which are properly composed "must neither begin nor end at haphazard." He regarded magnitude as a measure which is neither so small as to preclude distinguishing the parts nor so large as to prevent us from understanding the whole. In regard to an object which is too small, "the view of it is confused, the object being seen in an almost imperceptible moment of time. ... So in the plot, a certain length is necessary, and a length which can be easily embraced by the memory." Thus "magnitude" means architectural proportion. "Beauty depends on magnitude and order." He described the "structural union of the parts being such that, if any one of them is displaced or removed, the whole will be disjointed and disturbed. For a thing whose presence or absence makes no visible difference, is not an organic part of the whole."

The unities of time and place are supposed to derive from

---

* All quotations from Aristotle are from S. H. Butcher's *Aristotle's Theory of Poetry and Fine Art* (New York, 1907). Reprinted by permission of The Macmillan Company.

Aristotle, but this is inaccurate.* He made no mention of unity of place, and his only reference to time is the following: "Tragedy endeavors, as far as possible, to confine itself to a single revolution of the sun, or but slightly to exceed this limit." The writers of Greek tragedy frequently failed to observe this limitation. But at a later period, among the Italian and French classicists, the unities became a fetish. Corneille, in a mood of wild radicalism, ventured to say that he "would not scruple to extend the duration of the action even to thirty hours." Voltaire was very emphatic about the unities: "If the poet makes the action last fifteen days, he must account for what passes during these fifteen days, because I am in the theatre to learn what happens." †

Aristotle defined style as avoiding both the commonplace and the magniloquent, "to be clear without being mean." He discussed plausibility, saying that dramatic effect derives from what is probable and not from what is possible. He advised the playwright to construct his plot with consideration for the limitations of the playhouse.

He associated action with a reversal of fortune, a change in social relationships. The action must be such that "the sequence of events, according to the law of probability or necessity, will admit of a change from bad fortune to good or from good fortune to bad." He gave the name of "peripeteia" (revolution) to the sudden intrusion of an event which affects the life of the hero and turns the action in a new direction. Another form of reversal of action is the "anagnorisis" or recognition scene, the finding of friends or enemies unexpectedly.

Aristotle maintained that action, not character, is the basic ingredient of drama, and that "character comes in as a subsidiary to the actions." This is very widely accepted as one of the cornerstones of technical theory. George Pierce Baker says, "History shows indisputably that drama, in its beginnings, no matter where we look, depended most on action." Gordon Craig, rebelling against the wordy theatre of the nineteen hundreds, says that "the father of the dramatist was the dancer." Brander Matthews says: "A wise critic once declared that the skeleton of a good play is a pantomime." Roy Mitchell remarks that "literature crosses the

---

* Lodovico Castelvetro, an Italian critic writing in 1570, is responsible for the first formulation of the triple unities: "The time of the representation and that of the action represented must be exactly coincident... and the scene of the action must be constant." He wrongly attributed this idea to Aristotle, and began a controversy which continued for several hundred years.

† From Barrett H. Clark, *European Theories of the Drama* (New York, 1947).

threshold of the theatre only as the servant of motion." The turbulent poetry of Shakespeare is an example of literature which functions admirably as "the servant of motion."

The simple statement that *action is the root of drama* conveys an essential truth—but the interpretation of this truth is by no means simple. The term must be defined; we cannot suppose that the theatre deals with *any* kind of action. We must therefore distinguish between *dramatic action* and *action in general*. Aristotle made no clear distinction along these lines. Later theorists seem to take the idea of action for granted, and to assume that it means whatever the particular writer would prefer to have it mean. One also finds that action is often viewed in a mechanical, rather than in a living sense. Those who protest (very properly) against the idea of mechanical movement as a dramatic value, are apt to go to the other extreme and insist that character is prior to, and more vital than, action.

There is probably more confusion on this point than on any other aspect of technique—a confusion which grows out of an abstract approach to theatre problems; character and action tend to become abstractions, existing theoretically on opposite sides of a theoretical fence. The inter-dependence of character and action has been clarified by the conception of drama as a *conflict of will,* which has played a prominent part in nineteenth century dramatic thought. Ashley H. Thorndike points out that Aristotle "devoted much attention to the requirements of the plot. He did not, moreover, recognize the importance of the element of conflict, whether between man and circumstance, or between men, or within the mind of man." * This is true. Aristotle failed to grasp the rôle of the human will, which places man in conflict with other men and with the totality of his environment. He viewed the reversal of fortune (which is actually the climax of a conflict of will) as an objective event, neglecting its psychological aspect. He saw that character is an accessory to action, but his conception of character was limited and static: "An action implies personal agents, who necessarily possess certain distinctive qualities both of character and thought; for it is by these that we qualify actions themselves, and these—thought and character—are the two natural causes from which actions spring, and on actions again all success or failure depends.... By character I mean that in virtue of which we ascribe certain qualities to the agents."

Aristotle's view of character as a *collection of qualities* made it impossible for him to study the way in which character functions.

* Ashley H. Thorndike, *Tragedy* (New York, 1908).

Instead of seeing character as part of the process of action, he drew an artificial line between qualities and activities. He also drew a line between character and thought. From a modern point of view, this mechanical way of treating the subject is valueless, and must be attributed to Aristotle's limited knowledge of psychology and sociology. Psychologists have long been aware that character must be studied in terms of activity—the action of stimuli upon the sense organs and the resulting action of ideas, feelings, volitions. This *inner* action is part of the whole action which includes the individual and the totality of his environment. Aristotle was right when he said that "life consists in action, and its end is a mode of action, not a quality." He was therefore right in maintaining that action is basic, and that "character comes in as a subsidiary to the actions." His mistake lay in his inability to understand character as itself a mode of action which is subsidiary to the whole action because it is a living part of the whole.

The theory of the conflict of wills amends, and in no way contradicts, Aristotle's theory of action. A conflict of wills, whether it be between man and circumstance, or between men, or inside the mind of man, is a conflict in which the environment plays an important part. We cannot imagine a mental conflict which does not involve an adjustment to the environment. Action covers the individual and the environment, and the whole interconnection between them. Character has meaning only in relation to events; the human will is continually modified, transformed, weakened, strengthened, in relation to the system of events in which it operates. If we describe a play as *an action,* it is evident that this is a useful description; but a play cannot be defined as a character, or a group of characters.

In spite of his wooden treatment of psychological qualities, Aristotle put his finger on two fundamental truths which are as valid today as when the *Poetics* was written: (1) the playwright is concerned with what people *do;* he is concerned with what they *think* or what they *are* only insofar as it is revealed in what they *do.* (2) The action is not simply an aspect of the construction, but is the construction itself. Aristotle regarded action as synonymous with plot—a view which most later theorists have failed to grasp: "The plot then is the first principle, and, as it were, the soul of the tragedy." This is a valuable key to the problem of unity. Unity and action are generally considered separately, but Aristotle treated them as a single concept. Plot is frequently regarded as an artificial arrangement, the *form* of events as opposed to their *content.* Aristotle ignored such a distinction. In speaking of the whole play as "an action," in regarding the plot (or action, or system of events) as "the soul of the tragedy," he took the first step toward an organic theory of the drama.

In considering the later course of dramatic thought, there is one point in regard to Aristotle which cannot be disregarded, and which may in some measure account for the unique position which he occupies. From the fourth century B.C. to the present day, Aristotle represents the *only* attempt to analyze the technique of the drama in conjunction with a comprehensive system of scientific thought. Many philosophers have written about dramatic art: David Hume wrote an *Essay on Tragedy;* Hegel's formulation of the theory of tragic conflict was of great importance. But these and other philosophers were interested in the theatre only in relation to general esthetics, and gave no thought to its more technical aspects.

The great critics of the drama, in spite of all they have contributed toward our knowledge of its laws, have failed to connect these laws with the science and thought of their period. Goethe made extensive investigations in biology, physics, chemistry and botany; he incorporated the results of these investigations in his plays; but his views of the drama were emotional, unsystematic, and quite divorced from scientific thought.

Goethe and most of his contemporaries agreed that art is emotional and mysterious. Such a view would have been inconceivable to Aristotle, who took the theatre in his stride as part of a rational inquiry into the processes of man and nature.

Aristotle had the advantage of studying the theatre logically. But he could not possibly study it *sociologically*. He made no mention of the social or moral problems which were dealt with by the Greek poets. It never occurred to him that a writer's technique might be affected by his social orientation.

There is a widespread idea that Attic tragedy shows men trapped and destroyed by blind fate, destructive, unrelenting, unforeseen. Fate, as personified by the will of the gods or the forces of nature, plays a major part in Greek drama. But it is not an irrational or mystic fate; it represents definite social laws. The modern idea of destiny tends to be either religious or Nihilistic; it is based either on a belief in the mysterious will of God or on a belief in the inherent lawlessness and purposelessness of the universe. Either of these beliefs would have been incomprehensible to the Greek audience which was moved by the plays of Æschylus, Sophocles, and Euripides.

These were social problem plays. They dealt with the family

as the social unit, and with a system of taboos which govern the family relationship, and whose violation must be punished. A vital part of the system was the belief that moral guilt can be transmitted or inherited. The taboo, the violation, the punishment, constitute the moral law on which Greek tragedy rests. This law does not make the individual helpless or irresponsible; it emphasizes his responsibility, forcing him to face the consequences of his own acts.

In *The Furies,* the last play of the trilogy of the House of Atreus, Æschylus shows Orestes, pursued by the Furies, coming to the Temple of Pallas in Athens, and being judged by the council of citizens for having murdered his mother. Orestes accepts full responsibility, saying that he did the deed of his own will. He defends himself by saying that he was compelled to revenge his father, who had been killed by his mother. But the chorus tells him that Clytemnestra was *less* guilty than he, because the man she murdered was not of her own blood. The votes of the Athenians are equally divided for and against Orestes, but Athena casts the deciding vote and permits him to go free.

There is a more definite irony in Sophocles, and a suggested questioning of man's responsibility for the unconscious violation of social laws. In Euripides, we find that the question of justice, and its relation to problems of the will, has taken on a new and profound meaning. Gilbert Murray says: "Euripides seems at times to hate the revenge of the oppressed almost as much as the original cruelty of the oppressors."

Aristotle took no interest in the development of ideas which led from Æschylus to Euripides, nor in the technical differences in the work of these playwrights. He wrote the *Poetics* one hundred years after the great period of Greek tragedy, but he made no comparison between his own ethical ideas and those of the tragic masterpieces. His approach was thoroughly unhistorical: he mentioned the origins of comedy and tragedy; but he was unaware that these origins determined the form and function of the drama. The simplicity of Aristotle's analysis is possible largely because of the simplicity of the Greek dramatic structure, which centers around a single tragic incident, the climax of a long train of events which are described but not depicted. The original ritual, from which the more mature dramatic form was derived, was a recitation in celebration of past events. "A chorus with a leader," writes Donald Clive Stuart, "sang of a dead hero at his tomb. The fact that the hero of the ritual was dead explains much of the construction of serious tragedy.... Such scenes of narration and lamentation were the nucleus about which other scenes were grouped in later tragedies. ... It is evident that the point of attack (the point in the story where the play begins) had to be pushed back within the play itself." *

This form was historically conditioned; it perfectly suited the social basis of Attic tragedy. The Greek dramatist had no desire to investigate the *causes,* the prior conflicts of will, which led to the violation of family law. This would have involved ethical questions which were outside the thought of the age; it would have led to questioning the whole basis of the moral law. We find a hint of such questioning in Euripides. But the questioning is undeveloped and is given no dramatic formulation. The Greeks were concerned with the *effects* of breaking the moral law, not with the *causes* which led to breaking it.

Being unaware of the underlying social motivation in tragedy, Aristotle also seems to have had no clear idea of the social significance of comedy. Only a few phrases in the *Poetics* refer to comedy; we are told that its subject-matter is that which is ridiculous but neither painful nor destructive. Whatever further comments Aristotle may have made on comic technique have been lost. But it is evident that he made a sharp division between comedy and tragedy, regarding the former as a different type of art, subject to different laws.

"The Aristophanic Comedy," says Georg Brandes, "with its grand and exact technical structure, is the expression of the artistic culture of a whole nation." Today we realize that the principles of construction must be as valid in their application to the plays of Aristophanes as to those of Euripides. In dealing only with tragedy, in regarding comedy as a separate field of inquiry, Aristotle established a precedent which was followed throughout the Renaissance, and which still strongly colors our ways of thinking about the drama.†

Aristotle is the Bible of playwriting technique. The few pages of the *Poetics* have been mulled over, analyzed, annotated, with religious zeal. As in the case of the Bible, enthusiastic students have succeeded in finding the most diverse, contradictory and fantastic meanings in the *Poetics.*

* Donald Clive Stuart, *The Development of Dramatic Art* (New York, 1928).

† For example, Francisque Sarcey wrote in 1876: "The conclusion is that the distinction between the comic and tragic rests, not on prejudice, but on the very definition of drama." Modern critics seldom express the idea in such a clear form, but comedy is often treated as a distant relative of the drama, living its own life, and adhering to different (or at least far less stringent) codes of conduct.

Most of the misinterpretations are due to lack of historical perspective. By studying the Greek philosopher in connection with his period, we are able to test the value of his theories, to select and develop what will serve in the light of later knowledge.

CHAPTER II

THE RENAISSANCE

DURING the middle ages and the first years of the Renaissance, when interest in the drama was quiescent, there was no direct knowledge of Aristotle's writings. The few references to the drama in this period were based on the *Ars Poetica* of Horace. The beginning of Aristotle's influence dates from 1498, when Giorgio Valla's Latin translation of the *Poetics* appeared at Venice. During the sixteenth and seventeenth centuries, Horace and Aristotle were the twin stars of classical tradition. Aristotle was interpreted with narrow formalism, special emphasis being placed upon the alleged inviolability of the three unities.

In order to understand the Renaissance idea of tragedy, we must give some consideration to the work of Horace. The *Ars Poetica*, written between 24 and 7 B.C., is the only work on dramatic theory which has been preserved from ancient Rome. This gives it an historical value which is greater than the intrinsic importance of the ideas which it contains. Barrett H. Clark calls it "on the whole a somewhat arbitrary manual; the greatest importance must be attached to the purely formal side of writing, the dramatist must adhere closely to the five acts, the chorus, and so on; proportion, good sense, decorum, cannot be neglected." * It was no doubt this quality which endeared Horace to the theorists of the Renaissance, who delighted in dogma and decorum.

Horace was a formalist; but there is nothing dry or dull in the presentation of his views. The *Ars Poetica* is like the Roman age in which it was written—superficial, entertaining, crowded with random "practical" observations. Indeed, there is some ground for regarding Horace as the originator of the narrowly "practical" idea of art: "To have good sense, is the first principle and fountain of writing well.... Poets wish either to profit or to delight; or to

* Clark, *opus cit.*

deliver both the pleasures and the necessaries of life." * Horace's easy and diverting way of handling fundamentals is shown in his discussion of unity. He asks whether "a painter should wish to unite a horse's neck to a human head," or whether it is proper that "what is a beautiful woman in the upper part terminates unsightly in a fish below."

However, the essence of Horace's theory is contained in the one word—*decorum*. It is evident that the idea of decorum is meaningless unless we interpret it in connection with the manners of a particular period. But Horace used the word with finality, and drew definite technical conclusions in regard to its application. He said that actions which are "indecorous" are "fit only to be acted behind the scenes." "You may take away from view many actions, which elegant description may soon after deliver."

The idea of decorum was accepted literally during the Renaissance. Jean de la Taille wrote in 1572 that a fit subject for tragedy "is the story of him who was made to eat his own sons, the father, though unwittingly, being the sepulchre of his own children"; *but* "one must also be careful to do nothing on the stage but what can easily and decently be performed." †

The insistence on decorum, directly negating Aristotle's principle of action, had a painful effect on the technique of French tragedy. It caused avoidance of direct conflict, fountains of rhetoric, oceans of dignified lamentation. Corneille, in 1632, rebelled against the rhetorical technique: "Any one who wishes to weigh the advantages which action has over long and tiresome recitals will not find it strange that I preferred to divert the eyes rather than importune the ears." ‡ In spite of these brave words, both Corneille and Racine continued to "importune the ears." The rule against "indecorous" actions was so undisputed that it was not until a century after Corneille that a French dramatist dared to introduce a murder in view of the audience. Gresset (who was influenced by the English theatre) accomplished this feat in 1740. His example was followed by Voltaire, whose *Mahomet* contained a murder which was visual —but as carefully lighted and draped as the nude "visions" in a modern musical revue.

But the living theatre, as it emerged from the womb of the middle ages and grew to abundant strength in the masterpieces of Shakespeare and Calderon, was unaffected by the disputes of the

* Translation by C. Smart, included in Clark's *European Theories of the Drama.*
† Clark, *opus cit.,* translation by Clark.
‡ Translation by Beatrice Stewart MacClintock, in Clark, *opus cit.*

classicists. One may say that the beginnings of the split between theory and practice are to be found at the dawn of the Renaissance. The critics were engrossed in verbal battles over the unities. First in Italy, later in France, tragedy followed the classical formula. The critics thought comedy was outside the realm of art. Modern historians are frequently guilty of the same error, in underestimating the importance of fifteen and sixteenth century comedy.* Yet the comedies which grew out of the moralities and farces of the middle ages contained both the technical and social germs of the later flowering of dramatic art.

Sheldon Cheney says of the French farce of the fifteenth century: "It was the early gross form of later French satirical comedy—that was to bloom so finely when French vulgar comedy and Italian *Commedia dell' Arte* together fertilized the genius of Molière." † It was also the comedy of the fifteenth and early sixteenth century which fertilized the genius of the Elizabethans and the golden age of the Spanish theatre.

The rise of comedy reflected the social forces which were weakening the structure of feudalism and bringing about the growth of the merchant class. *Maistre Pierre Pathelin,* which appeared in France in 1470, is the first play which may be considered realistic in the modern sense, dealing directly with the foibles and manners of the middle class.

But the main development of comedy took place in Italy. The first great name in the history of the Renaissance theatre is a name which is generally not associated with the theatre at all—the name of Machiavelli (1469-1527). Machiavelli's plays are important, but his major claim to a place in dramatic history lies in the fact that he crystallized the morals and sentiments of his time; he applied this system of ideas to the theatre; his influence spread throughout Europe, and had a direct effect on the Elizabethans.

Ariosto and Aretino were contemporaries of Machiavelli. All three helped to free comedy from classical restrictions. Aretino and Machiavelli depicted the life of their time with a brutality and irony which seem startlingly modern. "I show men as they

---

* Modern writers are especially apt to take a moral view toward what they consider the vulgarity of old comedy. Brander Matthews, in *The Development of the Drama* (New York, 1908), dismisses the whole of Restoration comedy in a few lines, including a pointed reference to "dirty linen." Sheldon Cheney describes Machiavelli and Aretino as a picturesque "pair of ruffians." Cheney's book, *The Theatre* (New York, 1929), is by far the best history available; it covers acting and scenic designs, and contains a tremendous amount of reliable information. Cheney's judgments, however, are routine and sometimes careless.

† *Opus cit.*

are," said Aretino, "not as they should be." * This began a new
era in the theatre. The attempt to "show men as they are" follows
a clear line, from Aretino and Machiavelli, to the theatre of Ibsen
and of our own day.

If we examine the *system of ideas* in Machiavelli's prose works,
we find here too a clear line connecting him with the stream of
later middle-class thought. The myth about Machiavelli as a
cloven-footed sinner preaching deception and immorality need not
concern us here. He believed in ambition, in the ability to get there;
he took as his model the man who combines audacity and prudence
in the achievement of his aims. The successful men, politicians,
merchants, leaders of the period of industrial expansion, have conformed to this model. It is absurd to suggest that Machiavelli
ignored ethics: he was deeply preoccupied with moral problems.
Determined to take what he considered a realistic view, he consciously separated ethics and politics—a policy which has been
followed, often much less consciously, by subsequent political
thinkers. He respected the possibilities of middle-class democracy;
he believed that the people are the real nation, but that they cannot
attain practical control, which must therefore be manipulated by
politicians. His foresight in regard to the modern state may be
illustrated by two of his opinions: he formulated the idea of a
national militia as the main strength of the national state—this
later proved to be the case, both in Germany and in France; he
eagerly demanded the unification of Italy—a dream which took
more than three hundred years to accomplish.

A recognition of Machiavelli's significance does not imply that
one accepts his emphasis on the *unscrupulous man* as the most
decisive factor in his writings or in their later influence. This factor
cannot be entirely ignored, because guile and double-dealing *did*
play a considerable rôle in the literature and drama of the centuries following Machiavelli. Maxim Gorki exaggerates this point
when he says of middle-class literature that "its principal hero is a
cheat, thief, detective and thief again, but now a 'gentleman thief.'"
Gorki traces this hero from "the figure of Tyl Eulenspiegel at
the end of the fifteenth century, that of Simplicissimus of the seventeenth century, Lazarillio of Tormes, Gil Blas, the heroes of
Smollett and Fielding, up to *Dear Friend* by Maupassant, Arsene
Lupin, heroes of the 'detective' literature of our days." † There is

* Quoted by Cheney, *opus cit.*
† Speech at Soviet Writers Congress, 1934, included in *Problems of
Soviet Literature* (New York, n.d.).

enough truth in this to make it worth thinking about; but there is enough bias to make it misleading.

The moral structure of Elizabethan drama (the first detailed expression of the ideals of the new era) is not based upon a belief in guile, but on a boundless faith in man's ability to do, to know and to feel. This faith dominated three hundred years of middle-class development; at the end of the nineteenth century, we come to a breaking point—the split between the real and the ideal, between politics and ethics, is as complete in Ibsen as in Machiavelli. But whereas Machiavelli, at the beginning of the era, regarded this split as necessary, Ibsen recognized it as a dangerous contradiction which threatened the stability of the whole social order.

The connecting link between Italian comedy and the flowering of Elizabethan culture is to be found in the *Commedia dell' Arte,* the theatre of improvisation which grew up in the public squares of Italy in the middle of the sixteenth century. The robust power of the *Commedia dell' Arte* affected the dramatic life of every country in Europe.

In England, the drama had grown from native roots. But it began to show Continental influences early in the sixteenth century. This is apparent even in the antiquated comedies of John Heywood. In a critical essay on Heywood's plays, Alfred W. Pollard points out that "we can see even in the less developed group of plays English comedy emancipating itself from the miracle-play and morality, and in the *Pardoner and the Frere* and *Johan Johan* becoming identical in form with the French fifteenth century farce." Pollard mentions the fact that both of these plays seem to be taken directly from French originals, the former from the *Farce d'un Pardonneur* and the latter from *Pernet qui va au Vin.*

The direct Italian influence on Shakespeare and his contemporaries is evidenced in their choice of plots, which came largely from Italian sources. The sudden coming of age of the Elizabethan theatre coincided exactly, as John Addington Symonds tells us, with the point at which "the new learning of the Italian Renaissance penetrated English society." At the same time, voyages of discovery were causing the rapid expansion of England's commercial empire. The awakening of science was closely connected with the awakening of the drama. It is no accident that the first quarto edition of *Hamlet* appeared in 1604, and Francis Bacon's *Advancement of Learning* in 1605. There was also a close connection between the changes in religious thought and the growth of art and science. Alfred North Whitehead says: "The appeals to the origins of Christianity, and Francis Bacon's appeal to efficient causes as against final causes, were two sides of one movement of thought." *

These complex forces created a system of dominant ideas which determined the technique and social logic of Elizabethan drama. Shakespeare is often spoken of as the type of the supremely "timeless" artist; the mirror which he holds up to nature is said to reflect "an eternity of thought," and also "an eternity of passion." On the other hand, there are politically-minded writers who accuse Shakespeare of being "unfair to labor," because he treats members of the working class as buffoons and clowns.†

These two extremes are equally absurd. In selecting lords and ladies as his heroes and heroines, Shakespeare expressed the social viewpoint of his class. These very lords and ladies were rebelling against feudalism and forming the upper layer of a new capitalist society. To assume that Shakespeare's plays reflect passions or ideas which are outside or above the class and period reflected, is illogical —and means ignoring the specific material in the plays themselves. The plays contain a system of *revolutionary* concepts which were beginning to cause a profound upheaval in the structure of society.

Shakespeare was intensely occupied with the problem of personal ambition, both as a driving force and as a danger. This is as vital in Shakespeare's play as the problem of "idealism" in the plays of Ibsen—and for the same reason: it is the key to the special social conditions and relationships with which Shakespeare dealt. He believed passionately in man's ability to *get ahead,* to conquer his environment. He did not believe that this is to be accomplished by force and guile; he viewed *conscience* as the medium of adjustment between the aims of the individual and the social obligations imposed by the environment.

We find the first, and simplest, expression of ambition as the dynamo of civilization in Christopher Marlowe: *Tamburlaine the Great* idealizes the theme of conquest:

> Is it not passing brave to be a King,
> And ride in triumph through Persepolis?

Dr. Faustus deals with the ambition to acquire knowledge:

> But his dominion that exceeds in this
> Stretcheth as far as does the mind of man.

* Alfred North Whitehead, *Science and the Modern World* (New York, 1925).

† One finds this attitude, in all its naïve simplicity, in Upton Sinclair's *Mammonart* (Pasadena, Calif., 1925), in which the world's literature is judged by whether it regards workers as villains or heroes.

Allardyce Nicoll stresses the influence of Machiavelli on the Elizabethans, and points out that this influence is first manifest in the plays of Marlowe: "Their author had drunk deep of a source unknown to the preceding dramatists." * Nicoll remarks on the significant reference to Machiavelli in the prologue to *The Jew of Malta:*

> And let them know that I am Machiavel,
> And weigh not men, and therefor not men's words.
> Admired I am of those that hate me most. . . .
> I count religion but a childish toy,
> And hold there is no sin but ignorance.

The threads of Machiavelli's ideas run through the whole texture of Shakespeare's plays, affecting his method of characterization, his treatment of history, his ideas in regard to morals and politics. Shakespeare saw the struggle between man and his conscience (which is essentially a struggle between man and the necessities of his environment), not only as a struggle between right and wrong, but as a *conflict of will,* in which the tendency to act is balanced against the tendency to escape action. In this he sounded a peculiarly modern note.

The need to investigate the sources of action, to show both the changes in men's fortunes and the conscious aims which motivate those changes, was responsible for the diffuseness of the action in the Elizabethan theatre. Whereas the Greeks were concerned only with the effect of breaking an accepted social law, the Elizabethans insisted on probing the causes, testing the validity of the law in terms of the individual. For the first time in the history of the stage, the drama recognized *fluidity* of character, the making and breaking of the will. This caused the extension of the plot. Instead of beginning at the climax, it was necessary to begin the story at the earliest possible point. Shakespeare's psychology was a clean break with medievalism, pointing directly toward the responsibilities and relationships which would characterize the new economic system. He dramatized the specific concepts on which middle-class life was to be founded: the romantic idea of love in *Romeo and Juliet;* the intensely personal relationship between mother and son in *Hamlet.* "Shakespeare's women," says Taine, "are charming children, who feel in excess and love passionately." These were not "universal" women; they were the women who would decorate the homes of the merchants and traders of the new

* Allardyce Nicoll, *The Theory of Drama* (London, 1931).

social order. They were very *limited* women, forced by society to retain the status of "charming children."

Shakespeare summed up the driving energy of the Renaissance, which combined the thirst for power and knowledge with the Protestant idea of moral citizenship. The Elizabethan drama, says Taine, was "the work and the picture of this young world, as natural, as unshackled, and as tragic as itself." But this young world was going in a very definite direction, developing, as Taine says, "all the instincts which, forcing man upon himself and concentrating him within himself, prepare him for Protestantism and combat." The Protestant idea "forms a moralist, a laborer, a citizen." *

In the later Elizabethan period, political and economic issues began to enter the theatre in more concrete terms. Nicoll speaks of *Arden of Feversham* and *A Woman Killed with Kindness* as "the attempts of unconscious revolutionaries to overthrow the old conventions. . . . Those plays are to be associated with the gradual rise of Parliamentary control and the emergence of the middle classes." †

The great age of the Spanish theatre was contemporary with the Elizabethans. The plays of Lope de Vega and Calderon differed in many respects, both in technique and in social direction, from those of the English dramatists. Since the Spaniards exerted only an oblique influence on the main stream of European dramatic thought, we can dispense with a detailed study of their work. But it is important to note that Spain and England were the only countries in which the Renaissance attained mature dramatic expression. These were the most turbulent, the most alive, the richest nations of the period; they were bitter commercial rivals, both reaching out to conquer all the wealth of the known world. But medievalism had a strong hold on Spain, while England was destined to follow a more revolutionary course. These factors accounted both for the similarities, and the variations, in their dramatic achievements.

We must now turn to the question of dramatic theory. Both in Spain and England, the theatre developed with no conscious regard for rules and no formulated body of doctrine. The only important discussions of the drama in the Elizabethan era are those of Sir Philip Sidney and Ben Jonson. They attacked the current mode and demanded a more rigid technique. In Spain, Cervantes took

---

* H. A. Taine, *History of English Literature*, translation by H. Van Loun (New York, 1886).
† Nicoll, *opus cit.*

up the cudgels for classical tradition; in spite of the gargantuan exuberance of *Don Quixote,* its author was bitterly opposed to what he called the "absurdity and incoherence" of the drama. He considered the plays of his time "mirrors of inconsistency, patterns of folly, and images of licentiousness." *

Lope de Vega, in *The New Art of Writing Plays in This Age* (1609), defended the right of the dramatist to be independent of the customs of the past. His opinions are practical and entertaining. Like many playwrights of the present day, he disclaimed any knowledge of technique, remarking that plays "are now written contrary to the ancient rule," and that "to describe the art of writing plays in Spain ... is to ask me to draw on my experience, not on art." †

This raises an interesting question: if there was no organized dramatic theory in the theatre's most creative period, why should it be needed today? The modern dramatist may well ask: "If Shakespeare could manage without conscious technique, why not I?" For the present it is sufficient to point out that the existence of a conscious technique among the Elizabethans would be a fantastic historical anachronism. While creative effort flowered, critical thought was swaddled in scholasticism. In order to analyze the method of the artist, the critic himself must possess a method and a system of ideas. The Elizabethan critic was unequipped for such an analysis, which would have required a knowledge of science, psychology and sociology several centuries ahead of his time. To ask why Sir Philip Sidney failed to understand Shakespeare's technique is like asking why Newton failed to understand the quantum theory.

It was inevitable that Renaissance theory should be restricted to the exposition of supposedly static laws; those who rebelled against the laws had no method by which to rationalize their rebellion. They were carried along by a dynamic process which was social in its origin; they knew nothing about the logic of this process.

In France, seventeenth-century criticism continued the respectful discussion of Horace and Aristotle. The critical opinions of Corneille, Boileau and Saint-Evremond are of interest chiefly because of their attempt to adapt the principles of Aristotle to the aristocratic philosophy of the time. Corneille (in 1660) declared that "the sole end of the drama is to please." But it was evident that the pleasure derived from the tragedy of the period was of a

---

* From anonymous translation of *Don Quixote* in Clark, *opus cit.*
  † Translation by William T. Brewster, in *Papers on Playmaking, I* (New York, 1914).

mild kind. Therefore we find Saint-Evremond (in 1672) deriding
Aristotle's theory of *purgation:* indeed Saint-Evremond was sure
that the pity and terror occasioned by the violence of Attic tragedy
had a bad effect on the Athenians, causing them to be irresolute in
battle: "Ever since this art of fearing and lamenting was set up at
Athens, all those disorderly passions which they had, as it were
imbibed at their public representations, got footing in their camps
and attended them in their wars." The author concluded that
tragedy should achieve "a greatness of soul well expressed, which
excites in us a tender admiration." *

One can assume that "greatness of soul" was well suited to the
court of Louis XIV, and that the monarch had no desire to set up
an "art of fearing and lamenting" which would produce "disorderly passions" and destroy the morale of his troops.

The tragedies of Corneille and Racine were based on the social
philosophy of the aristocracy. There can be no denying the impres-
siveness of Racine's plays; their power lies in the simplicity with
which static emotions are presented. The structure is a rational
arrangement of abstract qualities. There is no heat of living, no
possibility of change in the lives of the characters. The special
character of the reign of Louis XIV was its absolutism; he was
his own prime minister from 1661 until his death, and all state
business passed through his own hands. The plays of Corneille and
Racine are a dramatization of absolutism. There is no need of
purgation, because passion is purified by detaching it from reality.

But reality was present—the voice of reality spoke harshly and
gaily in the plays of Molière. Molière was a man of the people,
the son of an upholsterer, who came to Paris with a semi-amateur
theatrical company in 1643. His plays grew out of the tradition of
the *Commedia dell' Arte.* From farces which were fashioned
directly on the old models, he passed to plays of character and
manners. Schlegel indicates Molière's importance as the spokesman
of the middle class: "Born and educated in an inferior rank of
life, he enjoyed the advantage of learning by direct experience the
modes of living among the industrious portion of the community—
the so-called Bourgeois class—and of acquiring the talent of imitat-
ing low modes of expression." † Louis XIV, who prided himself
on his paternal interest in the arts, and who liked nothing better
than to take part in a ballet himself, took Molière under his
protection. But even the King was forced to ban *Tartuffe;* there

* From anonymous translation in Clark, *opus cit.,* 165-6, 167.
† All quotations from Schlegel are from his *Lectures on Dramatic Art
and Literature,* translation by John Black (2nd ed., London, 1914).

were five years of controversy before this slashing attack on religious hypocrisy was finally produced.

Restoration comedy in England followed the comedy of Molière, but under very different social conditions. A revolution had already taken place in England (1648). The Royalists, who were exiled in France while Cromwell was in power, were soothed and uplifted by the static emotions of French tragedy. When they returned to England in 1660, "the Royalists," says Edmund Gosse, "came home with their pockets full of tragedies." The reign of Charles II was a period of violent social tension. There was nothing absolute about the position of the "Merry Monarch," whose merriment was always overshadowed by the urgent fear of losing his throne. Restoration comedy reflected the tension of the time: the first of these bitter comedies of manners, *The Comical Revenge, or Love in a Tub,* by George Etheredge, appeared in 1664. The next summer the great plague swept the disease-ridden slums of London, followed by the great fire in the fall of the same year.

The plays of Etheredge, Wycherley, Congreve and Farquhar, were produced before a restricted upper-class audience. But it is a mistake to dismiss them as merely examples of the cynicism of a decadent class. The intellectual currents of the period were so strong, the social conflict so raw and imminent, that the cynicism of these plays turned to stinging realism. Their cynicism cut beneath the surface and exposed the deeper moral issues of the time. Restoration comedy stands, with Molière, at a crucial half-way point between the first stirrings of the Renaissance and the beginning of the twentieth century.

It is also at this crucial half-way point that we find the first critical attempt to understand the theatre in living terms. John Dryden's plays are dry and formalistic, but his critical writings strike a new note. *An Essay of Dramatick Poesie,* written in 1668, is a series of conversations in which the ancient and modern drama are compared, and the plays of France and Spain are contrasted with those of England. Thus Dryden instituted a *comparative* method of criticism. He pointed out the inaccuracy of attributing the unities of time and place to the ancients: "But in the first place, give me leave to tell you, that the unity of place, however it might be practiced by them, was never any of their rules: we neither find it in Aristotle, Horace, or any who have written of it, till in our age the French poets first made it a precept of the stage. The unity of time, even Terence himself, who was the best and most regular of them, has neglected." *

* Dryden, *An Essay of Dramatic Poesy* (Oxford, 1896).

Dryden emphasized the need of fuller characterization: he spoke of plays in which "the characters are indeed the imitation of nature, but so narrow, as if they had imitated only an eye or a hand, and did not dare to venture on the lines of a face, or the proportion of a body."

Dryden made an important, although vague, observation on the relationship between the theatre and the ideas of the period. "Every age," he said, "has a kind of universal genius." Thus the writers of the time need not imitate the classics: "We draw not therefore after their lines, but those of nature; and having the life before us, besides the experience of all they knew, it is no wonder if we hit some airs and features which they have missed ... for if natural causes be more known now than in the time of Aristotle, because more studied, it follows that poesy and other arts may, with the same pains, arrive still nearer to perfection."

This is the first time in dramatic criticism that we find the suggestion of an historical perspective. In this Dryden marks the end of an epoch, and points the way to the analysis of "natural causes" and of "the life before us" which is the function of criticism.

CHAPTER III

THE EIGHTEENTH CENTURY

THE progress of dramatic theory in the eighteenth century is summed up in the work of one man; Gotthold Ephraim Lessing ranks next to Aristotle for the depth and originality of his contribution to technique.

Exactly one hundred years after Dryden's *An Essay of Dramatick Poesie,* Lessing wrote the *Hamburg Dramaturgy* (1767-1769). The tendency toward a scientific approach, toward applying general knowledge to the problems of the theatre (which is shown in a rudimentary form in Dryden's writings) reached fruitful maturity in the *Hamburg Dramaturgy.* Lessing did not create a complete structure of technique; he was not equipped to do so; but he formulated two vital principles which are closely inter-connected: (1) drama must have social validity, it must deal with people whose station in life and social attitudes are understandable to the audience. (2) The laws of technique are psychological, and can only be understood by entering the mind of the playwright.

In the light of these two principles, Lessing was able to see the meaning of Aristotle, and to free his theories from the scholastic dust which had settled heavily upon them. He broke the grip of French classicism on the German stage and introduced the cult of Shakespeare—thus being responsible for the succeeding flood of bad Shakespearian imitations. Historians emphasize Lessing's immediate influence (his fight for naturalness and against French conventions) and pay little or no attention to the ideas which were inherent in his work.

The *Hamburg Dramaturgy* is a collection of dramatic criticisms written during his two years as critic of the new National Theatre in Hamburg.* He described it as "a critical index of all the plays performed." There is no attempt at formal organization of the material. Nevertheless, the two main theses which I have mentioned form a dominant pattern throughout the work. In regard to social validity, Lessing argued that the poet must so arrange the action that "with every step we see his personages take, we must acknowledge that we should have taken it ourselves under the same circumstances and the same degree of passion." Instead of rejecting or misinterpreting Aristotle's purgation by pity and terror, he observes that "we suddenly find ourselves filled with profound pity for those whom a fatal stream has carried so far, and full of terror at the consciousness that a similar stream might also thus have borne ourselves."

We must therefore make "the comparison of such blood-and-thunder tragedies concerning whose worth we dispute, with human life, with the ordinary course of the world."

In denying the validity of aristocratic emotions, Lessing also denied the validity of the aristocrats who were soothed and flattered by sentimental tragedy. He saw no reason that the *dramatis personæ* should be kings and queens and princes; he insisted that the activities and emotions of common people were more important. "We live in an age when the voice of healthy reason resounds too loudly to allow every fanatic who rushes into death wantonly, without need, without regard for all his citizen's duties, to assume to himself the title of a martyr."

Lessing's psychological approach is closely related to his social

---

* The *Hamburg Dramaturgy* is the first example of journalistic criticism, thus setting a standard of excellence which has not, unfortunately, been maintained. Quotations from Lessing are from the translation by E. C. Beasley and Helen Zimmern (London, 1879).

point of view. Since the drama must possess a recognizable social logic, this logic must derive from the playwright's approach to his material: we must examine his *purpose*. "To act with a purpose is what raises man above the brutes, to invent with a purpose, to imitate with a purpose, is that which distinguishes genius from the petty artists who only invent to invent, imitate to imitate." We must test the material psychologically; otherwise, "it imitates the nature of phenomena without in the least regarding the nature of our feelings and emotions."

Lessing went right to the root of the artificiality of French tragedy. He saw that the trouble lay in the emphasis on invention instead of on inner cause and effect. Therefore, instead of avoiding improbability, the French writers *sought after it,* delighting in the marvelous and unexpected. He defined this difference in one of his greatest critical passages: "Genius is only busied with events that are rooted in one another, that form a chain of cause and effect. To reduce the latter to the former, to weigh the latter against the former, everywhere to exclude chance, to cause everything that occurs to occur so that it could not have happened otherwise, this is the part of genius. . . . Wit, on the contrary, that does not depend on matters rooted in each other, but on the similar and dissimilar . . . detains itself with such events as have not further concern with one another except that they have occurred at the same time."

It follows that *unity of action* ceases to be a scholastic term, and becomes a matter of organic growth and movement, which is determined by the playwright's *selection* of his material. "In nature everything is connected, everything is interwoven, everything changes with everything, everything merges from one to another. But according to this endless variety it is only a play for an infinite spirit. In order that finite spirits may have their share of this enjoyment, they must have the power to set up arbitrary limits, they must have the power to eliminate and to guide their attention at will.

"This power we exercise at all moments of our life; without this power there would be no feeling for us. . . . All in nature that we might wish to abstract in our thoughts from an object or a combination of various objects, be it in time or in place, art really abstracts for us."

Lessing's more superficial comments show him continually fighting for honesty and deriding artifice. He ridiculed the habit of killing off the characters in the final act: "In very truth, the fifth act is an ugly disease that carries off many a one to whom the first four acts promised longer life." * He brilliantly exposed the weakness of getting an effect solely by surprise: "Whoever is struck down in a moment, I can only pity for a moment. But how if I expect the blow, how if I see the storm brewing for some time about my head or his?"

The two central ideas which form the framework of the *Hamburg Dramaturgy* are part of the two great streams of thought which flowed through the eighteenth century—the *social* thought which led to the American and French revolutions; and the *philosophic* thought which was turning special attention to the problems of the mind, and which led from Berkeley and Hume to Kant and Hegel.

From Lessing's time to our own, the dominant ideas which have shaped the course of the drama, as well as other forms of literature and art, have been closely related to the ideas of speculative philosophy. For two centuries, philosophy has endeavored to create systems which rationalize man's physical and mental being in relation to the whole of the universe. Perhaps the most exhaustive of these systems have been those of Kant and Hegel. The importance of these attempts lies in the fact that they crystallize in a systematic form the intellectual atmosphere, the habits of mind, the social concepts, which grow out of the life of the period. The same concepts, ways of thinking, intellectual atmosphere, determine (less systematically) the theory and practice of the theatre. In order to understand the playwright's mental habits, we must examine the mental habits of his generation, which are coordinated, more or less completely, in systems of philosophy.

The two streams of thought which influenced Lessing were sharply divergent, although they flowed from the same source. The intensive speculation which marked the intellectual life of the eighteenth century grew out of the scientific investigations of the previous century. The period from 1600 to 1700 was preeminently a time of scientific research, which resulted in a series of discoveries that laid the groundwork for modern science, and upon which the whole development of later speculation was based. Francis Bacon initiated the method of science at the beginning of the century; he was followed by men who achieved epoch-making results in various branches of research: Harvey, Descartes, Hobbes,

---

* This widely quoted observation is not startlingly original. Dryden had said almost the same thing: "It shew little art in the conclusion of a dramatick poem, when they who have hindered the felicity during the four acts, desist from it in the fifth, without some powerful cause to take them off their design." Also Aristotle: "Many poets tie the knot well but unravel it ill."

Newton, Spinoza, Leibnitz, and many others. The most definite achievements of the seventeenth century were in the fields of physics, mathematics, physiology. Out of this new knowledge of the physical universe arose the need for a theory of *thinking and being,* which would solve the riddle of man's mind in relation to the reality of the universe.

Modern philosophy begins with Descartes, whose *Discourse on Method* and *Meditations,* written in the middle years of the seventeenth century, present the first thoroughgoing statement of the point of view of subjectivism or idealism. Descartes argued that "modes of consciousness" are real in themselves, regardless of the reality of the physical world which we perceive through our senses: "But it will be said that these presentations are false, and that I am dreaming. Let it be so. At all events, it is certain that I seem to see light, hear a noise, feel heat; this cannot be false, and this is what in me is properly called perceiving, which is nothing else than thinking. From this I begin to know what I am with somewhat greater clearness and distinctness than heretofore." *

Descartes was also a physicist, and his scientific investigations followed the method of Francis Bacon, and were concerned solely with objective reality; his analysis of the mechanics of the brain was untouched by his interest in "modes of consciousness." Thus Descartes faced in two directions: he accepted the dualism of mind and matter, and failed to understand the contradiction between the conception of physical reality and the conception of an independent mind or soul whose being is subjective, and whose realness is of a different order.

Both the idealists and the materialists drew their inspiration from Descartes. His scientific views were accepted and developed by John Locke, whose *Essay Concerning the Origin of Human Understanding* appeared in 1690. He defined the political and social implications of materialism, saying that the laws of society are as objective as the laws of nature, and that the social conditions of men can be controlled by rational means. Locke laid down the economic and political principles which have been dominant through two centuries of middle-class thought. Among his most noteworthy theories was his belief that the government is the trustee of the people, the state being the outcome of the "social contract." He also believed that the right of property depends on labor, that taxation should be based solely on land. He also fought for religious toleration, and a liberal system of education. Almost

---

* René Descartes, *Meditations,* translated by John Veitch (New York, 1901).

a century later, Locke's ideas found concrete expression in the American Declaration of Independence.

The French materialists of the eighteenth century (Diderot, Helvetius, Holbach) followed the principles of Locke. "Surely," said Holbach, "people do not need supernatural revelation in order to understand that justice is essential for the preservation of society." Their theories led directly to the French revolution.

Idealist philosophy also stemmed from Descartes. In the second half of the seventeenth century, Spinoza endeavored to solve the dualism of mind and matter by regarding God as the infinite substance which interpenetrates the whole of life and nature; according to Spinoza, both man's consciousness and the reality which he perceives or thinks he perceives are *modes* of God's being.

In the *Treatise Concerning the Principles of Human Knowledge* (1710), George Berkeley went further and denied the material world altogether. He held that objects exist only in the "mind, spirit, soul, or myself." * He regretted that "the tenet of the existence of Matter seems to have taken so deep a root in the minds of philosophers, and draws after it so many ill consequences." And again: "Matter being once expelled out of nature drags with it so many skeptical and impious notions, such an incredible number of disputes and puzzling questions."

But the "disputes and puzzling questions" continued. Being unable to accept the complete denial of matter, philosophers were compelled to bridge the gap between the world of spirit and the world of objective fact in one of two ways: (1) We depend only on our sense-data, which tells us all that we can know about the world we live in, and deny the possibility of attaining knowledge of absolute or final truth; (2) we frankly accept a dual system of thought, dividing the facts of experience from the higher order of facts which are absolute and eternal.

David Hume, in the middle of the eighteenth century, developed the first of these lines of reasoning. His agnosticism ruled out metaphysics; he disapproved of dabbling with the unknowable. He trusted only the immediate data of sensations and perceptions. It remained for Kant, whose *Critique of Pure Reason* was published in 1781, to formulate a complete system of knowledge and metaphysics based on the dualism of mind and matter.

It may be objected that the connection between the abstractions of philosophy and the work of the stage is too tenuous to be of any genuine interest. But we shall find that the threads which bind the drama to the general thought of the period are not tenu-

* Chicago, 1928.

ous at all, but are woven into a coherent fabric which reveals the logic of the theatre's development.

Lessing, like many men of his time, combined elements of the conflicting currents of thought which were agitating his generation. He was under the influence of the French materialists, and especially of Diderot, whose opinions on the theatre had been published ten years before the *Hamburg Dramaturgy*. From Diderot came "the voice of healthy reason," the emphasis on social validity. But the intellectual atmosphere of Lessing's Germany was charged with the philosophy of idealism. From this Lessing drew the richness and subtlety of his psychological approach—which would have been impossible for the materialists of the period, whose views on the processes of the mind were undeveloped and mechanistic.

The question of mind and matter has a direct bearing on the dramatic treatment of character and environment. This problem was not clear to Lessing. He considered "the nature of our feelings and emotions" as apart from "the nature of phenomena." Although he saw that "in nature everything is connected, everything is interwoven," he was unable to apply this idea to the growth and change of character. The incompleteness of his theory of the theatre, the lack of a precise technical formulation of his opinions, may thus be accounted for: he was unable to solve the contradiction between the emotions of men and the objective world in which they live. Many of Lessing's essays on theological matters show this dual approach, drawn from the official philosophy of the period.

In summing up and combining these two currents of thought, Lessing foreshadowed the future development of the theatre. In Germany, Lessing's demand for social realism and the treatment of humble themes fell on barren ground; he himself wrote plays of middle-class life; for example, his *Emilia Galotti* is a tragic version of the Cinderella story; but it was the idealist side of Lessing's thought, his emphasis on psychology and on "the nature of our feelings and emotions," which transformed the German stage, leading to the stormy romanticism and nationalism of the "Sturm und Drang" period—which culminated in the masterpieces of Schiller and Goethe.

Lessing's psychological approach was only slightly influenced by transcendentalism. He died in the year in which the *Critique of Pure Reason* was published. Kant described his philosophy as "transcendental idealism." He boldly accepted the contradiction between "finite" matter and "eternal" mind. He distinguished between the facts of experience and the ultimate laws which he regarded as above experience. On the one hand is the world of *Phenomena* (the thing-as-it-appears-to-us) ; on the other hand, the world of *noumena* (the-thing-in-itself). The world of phenomena is subject to mechanical laws; in the world of noumena,· the soul of man is theoretically free because the soul freely obeys the "categorical imperative," which is eternal.

Kant's theories exerted a considerable influence on Schiller and Goethe, affecting their point of view, their treatment of character, their interpretation of social cause and effect. Schiller and Goethe form a bridge between the eighteenth and nineteenth centuries; in view of their significant rôle in the development of nineteenth century thought, they may better be considered in connection with the later period.

Lessing was not alone in demanding a drama of social realism; we find the same trend, appearing at approximately the same time, in England, Italy and France. In England, Oliver Goldsmith wrote gentle comedies dealing with middle-class life. Goldsmith's *Essay on the Theatre,* written in 1772, attacks the unnaturalness of tragedy in words which seem like an echo of Lessing: "The pompous train, the swelling phrase, and the unnatural rant, are displaced for that natural portrait of human folly and frailty, of which all are judges, because all have sat for the picture." * The production of George Lillo's play about a London 'prentice, *George Barnwell,* marked the first appearance of domestic tragedy; both Lessing and Diderot praised *George Barnwell* and used it as a model.

In Italy, Carlo Goldoni changed the course of the Italian theatre; he combined the example of Molière with the tradition of the *Commedia dell' Arte.* He said it was his aim to do away with "high-sounding absurdities." "We are again fishing comedies out of the *Mare magnum* of nature, men find themselves again searching their hearts and identifying themselves with the passion or the character which is being represented." † Goldoni moved to Paris in 1761; he remained there until his death and wrote many plays in French.

France was the storm-center of the political disturbances which were brewing in the last years of the eighteenth century. It was therefore in France that the theatre was most deeply stirred by the impact of new ideas. Diderot, the foremost philosopher of materialism, applied his doctrine to the drama with fiery enthusiasm.

* Clark, *opus cit.*
† H. C. Chatfield-Taylor, *Goldoni, a Biography* (New York, 1913).

Diderot fought for realism and simplicity; but he went further; he insisted that the dramatist must analyze the social system; he demanded a new dramatic form, the "Serious Drama"—"which should stand somewhere between comedy and tragedy." * He attempted to carry out this theory in his own plays, *Le Fils Naturel* (1757) and *Le Père de Famille* (1758).

Diderot's dramatic opinions are far less profound than those of Lessing. But his essay, *De la Poésie Dramatique à Monsieur Grimm,* which accompanied the publication of *Le Père de Famille,* is a landmark in the history of the theatre, both because of its influence on Lessing, and because of the clarity with which the aims of the middle-class drama are stated: "Who now will give us powerful portrayals of the duties of man? What is demanded of the poet who takes unto himself such a task?

"He must be a philosopher who has looked into his own mind and soul, he must know human nature, he must be a student of the social system, and know well its function and importance, its advantages and disadvantages."

Diderot then described the basic problem with which he was dealing in *Le Père de Famille:* "The social position of the son and that of the daughter are the two principal points. Fortune, birth, education, the duties of fathers toward their children, of the children toward their parents, marriage, celibacy—every problem arising in connection with the existence of the father of a family, is brought out in my dialogue."

It is curious that these historic lines are almost completely neglected by historians of the drama: it was to be more than a century before Diderot's dream of the middle-class theatre was to be realized. But we must credit him with having first formulated the purpose and limitations of the modern stage: the middle-class family is the microcosm of the social system, and the range of the theatre covers the duties and relationships on which the family is founded.

Pierre-Augustin Beaumarchais joined Diderot in the fight for the "Serious Drama." He wrote a stinging reply to what he described as "the uproarious clamor and adverse criticism" aroused by the production of his play, *Eugenie.* He insisted on his right to show "a truthful picture of the actions of human beings," as against pictures of "ruins, oceans of blood, heaps of slain," which "are as far from being natural as they are unusual in the civilization of our time." † This was written in 1767, the year

* Clark, *opus cit.,* translation by Clark.
† Clark, *opus cit.,* translation by Clark.

in which the first papers of the *Hamburg Dramaturgy* appeared.

Beaumarchais was more precise than Diderot in defining the social function of the theatre: "If the drama be a faithful picture of what occurs in human society, the interest aroused in us must of necessity be closely related to our manner of observing real objects.... There can be neither interest nor moral appeal on the stage without some sort of connection existing between the subject of the play and ourselves."

This leads to a political thesis: "The true heart-interest, the real relationship, is always between man and man, not between man and king. And so, far from increasing my interest in the characters of tragedy, their exalted rank rather diminishes it. The nearer the suffering man is to my station in life, the greater is his claim upon my sympathy." Beaumarchais also said that "a belief in fatalism degrades man, because it takes his personal liberty from him."

The serious plays of Diderot and Beaumarchais were failures, both commercially and artistically. Embittered by public apathy, and determined to use the theatre as a political weapon, Beaumarchais turned to the farce technique of *The Barber of Seville* and *The Marriage of Figaro*. These exuberant attacks upon the foibles and stupidities of the aristocracy were greeted with great popular approval. In his dedicatory letter for *The Barber of Seville* (1775) Beaumarchais stressed his ironic intention, smiled a little at his own success, and reaffirmed his faith in the realistic theatre: "Portray ordinary men and women in difficulties and sorrow? Nonsense! Such ought to be scoffed at. Ridiculous citizens and unhappy kings, these are the only fit characters for treatment on the stage.... The improbability of the fable, the exaggerated situations and characters, the outlandish ideas and bombast of speech, far from being a reason to reproach me, will assure my success."

The political meaning of these plays was clear both to the government and the public. *The Barber of Seville* was produced after three years of struggle against censorship. Louis XVI took personal responsibility for banning *The Marriage of Figaro;* in this case, five years elapsed before the censors were forced to permit the production. When the play was finally presented at the Théâtre Français on April 27th, 1784, there was rioting in and around the theatre.*

---

* It is characteristic of Beaumarchais that he made a determined stand for the rights of the dramatist, both to control casting and direction and to receive an accurate accounting of box office receipts. He began the fight which led to the organization of powerful authors' trade unions.

Thus the theatre played an active, and conscious, part in the revolutionary rise of the middle-class—which was destined in turn to revolutionize the theory and practice of the drama.

CHAPTER IV

THE NINETEENTH CENTURY

Romanticism

"AT the court of Weimar at midnight on the eve of the new century," writes Sheldon Cheney, "Goethe, Schiller, and a group of writer-friends drank a toast to the dawn of the new literature." *
One hundred years later, in 1899, Ibsen's last play, *When We Dead Awaken,* appeared.

The changes which marked the life and thought of the nineteenth century are often presented under the guise of a battle between *romanticism* and *realism;* romanticism being in the ascendant in the early years of the century, realism finally triumphing and continuing its reign in the popular literature and journalistic drama of our own day. These terms undoubtedly suggest the alignment of the intellectual forces of the period; one may be tempted to treat them as *literary equivalents* of the two streams of thought whose origins we have traced.

However, it is dangerous to adhere too closely to this analogy. Literary critics have juggled romanticism and realism so expertly, and have used them for so many sleight-of-hand tricks, that the two words have become practically interchangeable. This is due to the habit of mind which has, in general, characterized modern literary criticism—the tendency to deal with moods rather than with basic concepts, to ignore the social roots of art, and thus to regard schools of expression as *aggregates of moods,* rather than as social phenomena. Thus the critic is content to suggest the feeling which a work of art seems to convey, and makes no effort to trace the feeling, to pin it down and dissect it. Romanticism is often used to describe such a feeling—one might call it an impression of warmth, of sensuousness, of vigor. But this impression covers a wide variety of meanings: (1) since romanticism developed at the end of the eighteenth century as a revolt against classicism, it often

* *Opus cit.*

indicates freedom from rigid conventions, disregard of form; (2) but it is also used, in quite a different sense, to describe an elaborate or artificial style as opposed to a simple mode of expression; (3) it sometimes denotes works which abound in physical action and picaresque incident; (4) we also find it used in exactly the opposite sense to describe escapism, turning away from physical reality, seeking after *romantic* illusion; (5) again it denotes a quality of the mind—imagination, creativeness as opposed to a pedestrian or pedantic quality; (6) it has a philosophic meaning, indicating adherence to a metaphysical as opposed to a materialist point of view; (7) it is also used psychologically, suggesting a subjective as opposed to an objective approach, an emphasis upon emotion rather than upon commonplace activity.

It is evident that the *aggregate of moods* which has become known as romanticism includes a variety of contradictory elements. How does it happen that literary criticism has made very little effort to reconcile these contradictions? The answer lies in the fact that the majority of critics are unaware that these contradictions exist: the critic who regards art as an irrational personal experience sees nothing surprising in this combination of elements; he feels that *all* art is subjective and metaphysical; he believes that art is woven of the stuff of imagination which is distinct from the stuff of life. Therefore art is necessarily a sublimation, a seeking after Illusion; convinced that reality is drab and unimaginative, he believes that free action can exist only in a dream world; therefore the picaresque material is a means of escape; since art is irrational it must escape from conventional forms; but since it deals with the subtleties of the soul, it must employ elaborate and subtle language.

Thus we have found a useful key to modern criticism and nineteenth-century romanticism. Critical thought (both in the nineteenth and twentieth centuries) has not analyzed romanticism, because it has inherited the system of thought which constitutes romanticism. The essence of this system, the principle that unifies its apparent contradictions, is the idea of the uniqueness of the individual soul, of personality as a final emotional entity. The higher nature of man unites him to the thing-in-itself, the *idea* of the universe. Art is a manifestation both of man's uniqueness and of his union with the ultimate idea.

This conception constitutes the main stream of middle-class thought from the early eighteen-hundreds to the present day. The realistic school, as it developed in the later years of the nineteenth century, did not achieve a clean break with romanticism—it was a new phase of the same system of thought. The realists attempted to face the increasingly difficult problems of social and economic life; but they evolved no integrated conception which would explain and solve these problems. The devil and the angels fought for the soul of Goethe's Faust. Ibsen's Master Builder climbed to the very top of the tower, and as he stood there alone Hilda looked up and saw him striving with some one and heard harps in the air.

The romantic school developed in Germany as a revolt against French classicism; Lessing was chiefly responsible for initiating this revolt. The word, romanticism, has its origin in the picaresque stories of the middle ages, which were called *romances* because they discarded Latin and used the vulgar languages of France and Italy, the "romance" languages. This is important, because it indicates the dual nature of the romantic movement: it wished to break away from stuffy tradition, to find a fuller and more natural life; it therefore suggested comparison with the medieval poets who broke away from Latin and spoke in the language of the people. But the fact that the romantic school was based on such a comparison also shows its regressive character; it looked for freedom, but it looked for it in the past. Instead of facing the problem of man in relation to his environment, it turned to the metaphysical question of man in relation to the universe.

The attitude of romanticism was determined by the alignment of social forces at the beginning of the nineteenth century. Following the stormy upheavals which closed the previous century, the middle class began to consolidate its power; machine production introduced the first phase of the industrial expansion which was to lead to modern trustified industry. The intellectual temper of the middle class was veering toward moderation, self-expression and fervent nationalism. In Germany, the middle class developed less rapidly than in France and England; it was not until 1848 that Germany entered into world competition as an industrial and political power. In the early eighteen-hundreds, German romanticism was a reflection of this very weakness, combining a desire for a richer personal life, a desire to explore the possibilities of the real world, with a tendency to seek a safe refuge, to find a principle of permanence.

Georg Brandes, in *Main Currents in Nineteenth Century Literature,** emphasizes both the nationalism of the period and the romantic tendency to look back toward the past: "The patriotism which in 1813 had driven the enemy out of the country contained two radically different elements: a historical retrospective tendency, which soon developed into romanticism, and a liberal-minded

* New York, 1906.

progressive tendency, which developed into the new liberalism."
But both these tendencies were actually contained *within* romanticism. We have pointed out the dual character of Kant's
philosophy. This dualism found its dramatic embodiment in the
plays of Goethe and Schiller.

Goethe worked on *Faust* throughout his life; he made the first
notes for the project in 1769 at the age of twenty; he completed
the play a few years before his death in 1832. The dualism of
matter and mind is indicated in the technical structure of *Faust*.
The vivid personal drama of the first part ends in Margaret's
death and the saving of her soul. The vast intellectual complexity
of the second part analyzes the ethical law which transcends the
world of physical phenomena.

It is instructive to compare Goethe's treatment of the legend
with Marlowe's use of the same material. No metaphysical con-
siderations entered the Elizabethan's world. Marlowe's thesis is
simple: knowledge is power; it may be dangerous, but it is infinitely
desirable. To Goethe, knowledge is suffering, the agony of the
soul's struggle with the limitations of the finite world. Goethe
believed that evil cannot gain complete possession of the soul,
because the soul does not belong to man; it must, ultimately, be
reunited with the divine will. Marlowe's Helen is an object of
sensual delight. To Goethe, Helen symbolized moral regeneration
through the idea of beauty. At the end of the second part,
Mephistopheles fails to secure Faust's soul, which is carried aloft
by angels. Faust is not saved by his own act of will, but by infinite
law (embodied in the final verses of the Mystic Chorus) which
decrees that the soul is the type of the ideal.*

In a religious sense, this is the doctrine of predestination. One
cannot question the deeply religious character of Goethe's thought.
But his method is scientific and philosophical. He enters all the
complexities of the world of phenomena and the world of noumena.
Faust is a dramatization of Kant's categorical imperative.

Georg Hegel

During Goethe's later years, the range of German thought was
broadened by the philosophic work of Georg Hegel (Hegel died in

---

* This conception, or anything resembling it, cannot be found in Shakespeare's plays. Shakespeare often takes life after death for granted, but
he is never concerned with *attaining* immortality by the release of the
soul. In the soliloquy, "To be or not to be," Hamlet faces death objectively; he says that the fear of death "puzzles the will" and makes
"cowards of us all." Instead of being an ethical necessity, the thought
of union with the absolute makes cowards of us.

1831, and Goethe in 1832). The second part of *Faust* is much influenced by the Hegelian dialectic, the idea of the evolutionary progression of life and thought.

Hegel's philosophy was also dualistic; on the transcendental side he followed in the footsteps of Kant. Kant's "pure reason" resembles Hegel's "absolute idea," which is "the *True,* the *Eternal,* the absolutely *powerful* essence ... the World-Spirit—that spirit whose nature is always one and the same, but which unfolds this its one nature in the phenomena of the World's existence." * In place of Kant's "categorical imperative," Hegel offered the "pre-existence of the logical categories," which are ultimate ideas independent of physical reality. These categories include: being, becoming, quality, quantity, essence, appearance, possibility, accident, necessity, reality.

But in studying the unfolding of "the phenomena of the World's existence," Hegel observed that certain laws of motion are inherent in the movement of things; and that the same laws of motion govern the processes of the mind. He noted that phenomena are not stable and fixed, but are continually in a state of movement, of growth or decay. Phenomena are in a condition of unstable equilibrium; movement results from the disturbance of equilibrium and the creation of a new balance of forces, which is in turn disturbed. "Contradiction," said Hegel, "is the power that moves things." And again: "There is nothing which is not becoming, which is not in an intermediate position between being and not being."

In applying this principle to the movement of thought, Hegel evolved the method of *dialectics,*† which conceives logic as a series of movements in the form of thesis, antithesis and synthesis: the thesis is the original tendency or state of equilibrium; the antithesis is the opposing tendency or disturbance of equilibrium; the synthesis is the unifying proposition inaugurating a new state of equilibrium.

Those who are unaccustomed to philosophic inquiry may find it difficult to estimate the significance of dialectics as a question of formal logic. But if we turn to its practical effect on the study of science and history, the change wrought by Hegel's system of thought is readily apparent. Up to the beginning of the nineteenth

---

* Georg Hegel, *The Philosophy of History,* translation by J. Sibree (New York, 1902).

† The term *dialectic* did not originate with Hegel: Plato used the term to signify the process of argument by which the presentation of two opposing points of view results in bringing to light new elements of truth. But the Platonic idea involved merely the formal presentation of opinions; Hegel's formulation of the laws of the movement of thought constitutes a revolutionary change in philosophic method.

century, science had been concerned solely with the analysis of fixed objects; regardless of whether the object was in movement or at rest, it was studied as a detached thing. Newton's *Principia* had served as a model of the scientific method: the collection and cataloguing of separate facts. In the past hundred years, science has been devoted to the analysis of processes. The fact that *matter is motion,* that there is a continuity of moving and becoming, has been very generally accepted. One cannot say that Hegel succeeded *single-handed* in tearing down the rigidity of the universe; this was due to a whole series of scientific discoveries. But Hegel played a major part in creating a system of thinking, by which these discoveries could be understood in relation to the life of man and the world in which he lives. For several generations, science and philosophy had been feeling their way toward some comprehension of the fluidity of matter. Lessing had expressed this thought fifty years before, when he said that "everything in nature is connected, everything is interwoven, everything changes with everything, everything merges from one to another."

The Hegelian dialectic established the principle of continuity, both factually and rationally. This had an electrifying effect, not only upon the methods of science, but in all fields of inquiry. Georg Brandes speaks of Hegel's method with lyrical enthusiasm: "Logic... came to life again in the doctrine of the thoughts of existence in their connection and their unity.... The method, the imperative thought-process, was the key to earth and to Heaven." *

Neither Hegel nor his contemporaries were able to use his doctrine satisfactorily as "the key to earth and to Heaven." But looking back over a period of one hundred years, we can estimate the importance of the Hegelian method. His *Philosophy of History* is the first attempt to understand history as a process, to view the underlying causes behind disturbances of equilibrium. Earlier historians had seen only a disconnected assortment of phenomena, motivated by the personal whims and ambitions of prominent individuals. There had been no perspective, no tendency to estimate the forces *behind* the individual wills; human motives were represented as static; events which took place in Greece or Rome or in the middle ages were treated simply as events—discontinuous, springing from fixed causes, motivated by fixed emotions.

Hegel substituted the dynamic for the static method of investigation. He studied the evolution of human society. Many of his historical opinions and conclusions are outmoded today; but the historical research of the nineteenth and twentieth centuries has

* *Opus cit.*

been based on the dialectic method. Today the historian is not content with the description of events, the presentation of a sequence of wars, conquests, diplomatic negotiations and political maneuvers. History attempts, with greater or less success, to show the inner continuity, the changing equilibrium of social forces, the ideas and purposes which underly the historical process.

Since the theatre deals with the logic of human relationships, a new approach to logic must have a definite effect upon the drama. Hegel applied the dialectic method to the study of esthetics. His belief that "contradiction is the power that moves things" led him to evolve the principle of *tragic conflict* as the moving force in dramatic action: the action is driven forward by the unstable equilibrium between man's will and his environment—the wills of other men, the forces of society and of nature. Hegel's interest in esthetics was general rather than specific; he made no effort to analyze the technical factors in the dramatic process; he failed to see the vital implications of his own theory.

But the conception of *tragic conflict* stands with Aristotle's laws of action and of unity as a basic contribution to the theory of the theatre. Aristotle's laws had been based on the view that an action is simply an arrangement of events in which the participants have certain fixed qualities of character. Lessing realized that action and unity are organic, that events "are rooted in one another." But Lessing offered no indication of the manner in which this organic process takes place. The law of conflict points the way to an understanding of the process: we can agree with Aristotle that action is basic, that character is "subsidiary to the actions"; but we can see that the actions are a complex movement in which the wills of individuals and the social will (the environment) are continually creating a new balance of forces; this in turn reacts upon and modifies the wills of individuals; the characters cease to be embodiments of fixed qualities, and become living beings who shift and grow with the shifting and growing of the whole process.

Thus the idea of conflict leads us to examine the idea of will: the degree to which the will is consciously directed, and the question of free will and necessity, become urgent dramatic problems. Hegel analyzed free will and necessity as aspects of historical development. Seen in this light, it is clear that, as man increases his knowledge of himself and his environment, he increases his freedom through the recognition of necessity. Thus Hegel anni-hilated the old idea that free will and necessity are fixed opposites —which is contrary to reason and to the facts of our daily experience. Hegel saw free will and necessity as a continually shifting system of relationships—the shifting balance of forces between the will of man and the totality of his environment.

Another philosopher of Hegel's time based his theory of the universe entirely on the idea of a universal will. Schopenhauer's principal work, *The World as Will and Idea,* appeared in 1819. He held that blind will operates throughout nature, and that all the movements of inanimate objects and of men are due to the striving of the will: this is a new version of the "pre-existence of the logical categories"; Schopenhauer substituted the ultimate will for Hegel's ultimate idea. But this is an important difference, and was destined to have a serious effect on future thought. While Hegel believed in a rational universe, Schopenhauer regarded the will as emotional and instinctive. Since man's will is not based on rational purpose, it is not free, but is an uncontrolled expression of the universal will.

The two most important dramatic critics of the early eighteenth century formulated the theory of tragic conflict and its relation to the human will in terms which were very similar to Hegel's. The idea appears in the writings of both Schlegel and Coleridge. In the last decade of the nineteenth century, Ferdinand Brunetière clarified the meaning of the law of conflict as the basis of dramatic action.

The idea of conflict is only one side of our indebtedness to Hegel in the study of technique. The dialectic method provided the social logic on which Ibsen's technique is grounded. Instead of showing a chain of cause and effect, Ibsen showed a complex movement, a system of checks and balances between the individual and the environment. Disturbances of equilibrium furnish the moving force of the action. Ibsen's logic does not depend on *qualities* of character; the motives which activize his characters are woven through the whole fabric of their environment. This is a fundamental change in dramatic construction. We have already observed that Georg Brandes regarded Hegel's logic as "the key to earth and to Heaven." Both Brandes as a literary critic and Ibsen as a dramatic craftsman, derived their method from Hegel's "imperative thought-process."

Hegel made another vital contribution to technical theory; he brushed aside the foggy notions concerning form and content. This question played a big part in the lengthy sham battles between the classicists and the romanticists. Since Hegel regarded art and life as a process, he was able to see the fallacy of the customary distinction between form and content. In commenting on the idea that classical form might be imposed on unclassical material, he said:

"In a work of art, form and subject-matter are so closely united that the former can only be classical to the extent to which the latter is so. With a fantastic, indeterminate material ... the form becomes measureless and formless, or mean and contracted." *

Since Hegel's philosophy is dualistic, his influence on his contemporaries was also dualistic. The contradiction between his method and his metaphysics expressed the contradictions in the thought of his era. Heine hailed Hegel's philosophy as a revolutionary doctrine. But at the same time, Hegel was the official philosopher of the German state. The official side of his philosophy was the metaphysical side, expressing the need for permanence, the desire for the "absolute idea." Although he said that contradiction is "the power that moves things," Hegel believed that his own age marked the end of contradiction and the realization of the "absolute idea."

In both Kant and Hegel, we find metaphysics closely allied with a belief in the permanence of the existing order. In 1784, Kant had written an essay entitled *What is Enlightenment,* in which he declared that the age of Frederick the Great contained the final answer to this question. Forty years later, Hegel said that the Germany of Frederick William III represented the triumph of the historical process: "Feudal obligations are abolished, for freedom of property and of person have been recognized as fundamental principles. Offices of state are open to every citizen, talent and adaptation being of course necessary conditions." †

Hegel's dual influence continued after his death. The years preceding the revolution of 1848 (in which the vestiges of feudalism were finally destroyed) were years of increasing political tension. Hegel's philosophy furnished the ammunition for both sides of the quarrel. The defenders of conservatism and privilege cited Hegel as authority for their claims. But another group of Hegel's disciples led the fight against the existing state. In 1842, the *Rhenische Zeitung* made a considerable stir as the organ of the so-called "Young Hegelians." One of the editors of this newspaper, who was then twenty-four years old, was Karl Marx.

The English Romantic Poets

In these years, the romantic movement in literature and the theatre developed, and, to a large extent, disintegrated. Samuel Taylor Coleridge studied philosophy and physiology at the Uni-

* *Opus cit.*
† *Ibid.*

versity of Göttingen in 1798 and 1799; he drank deep of German metaphysics. On his return to England he translated Schiller (in 1800); and later became the great critical exponent of the romantic school. English romanticism is associated with the names of Byron, Shelley and Keats, all of whom died in the early eighteen-twenties. Byron and Shelley made important contributions to the theatre; but their special significance, in connection with the general trend of thought, lies in the rebellious, romantic individualism to which they dedicated themselves.* Here too we find that the dominant idea is the idea of the unique soul. The freedom so passionately desired is to be achieved by transcending the environment. In *Prometheus Unbound,* Shelley's thought is closely related to the theme of Goethe's *Faust*—the individual escapes the chains of reality by union with the ultimate idea; man must leave himself, "leave Man, even as a leprous child is left," in order to enter the metaphysical world, the region of

> "Man, one harmonious soul of many a soul,
> Whose nature is its own divine control."

In her notes on *Prometheus Unbound,* Mary Shelley says: "That man could be so perfectionized as to be able to expel evil from his own nature, and from the greater part of the creation, was the cardinal point of his system. And the subject he loved best to dwell on was the image of one warring with the Evil Principle." † This was also the image which Goethe immortalized. In *The Cenci,* the soul "warring with the Evil Principle" is embodied in the superb figure of Beatrice Cenci.

The romantic poets were magnificently sincere in their love of liberty. Byron joined the campaign for Greek independence and died at Missolonghi in 1824. In Germany, Heine proclaimed his revolutionary faith with deep fervor. But the idea of freedom remained metaphysical, a triumph of mind over matter. The contact with social reality was vague and lacked perspective. Brandes says of Heine: "The versatile poet's temperament made the momentous struggle for a political conviction hard for him, and he was, as we have already shown, drawn two ways and rendered vague

---

* Shelley and Byron were deeply influenced by the French revolution. Byron's political enthusiasm was chiefly emotional. But Shelley's relationship to William Godwin gave him a thorough familiarity with the ideas of the French philosophers who preceded the revolution. Godwin's most important work, the *Enquiry Concerning Political Justice* (1793) is in large part an elaboration of the ideas of Helvetius.

† Shelley's *Poetical Works,* edited by Mrs. Shelley (Philadelphia, 1847).

in his utterances by feeling himself to be at one and the same time a popular revolutionist and an enthusiastic aristocrat." *

It was natural that the romantic assault on society should be directed far more fiercely against morals and conventions than against property rights. The revolt against the middle-class moral code was of great importance; the fight against narrowness and hypocrisy has continued to our own day; the period of emancipation following the world war echoed the ideas of the dawn of the romantic movement. The battle against convention was waged both in England and Germany; Byron and Shelley refused to accept the restrictions which they considered false and degrading; Goethe and Schiller and their friends made the little town of Weimar the "Athens of Germany"; they also made it a center of sex freedom, sentimental excesses and experimental revisions of the moral code.

Dramatic Criticism

Dramatic theory in the early years of the nineteenth century dealt chiefly with abstractions, and only incidentally with concrete problems of craftsmanship. The reason for this may be found in the nature of romanticism: if one believes in the *uniqueness* of genius, a veil is cast over the creative process; the critic does not wish to pierce this veil; indeed he has a veil of his own, which suggests the uniqueness of his *own* genius. We find no attempt to continue the comprehensive analysis of dramatic principles begun by Lessing.

The first critical spokesman of the romantic school was Johann Gottfried Herder, who was an intimate member of the Weimar circle and died in 1803. Brandes says that Herder was "the originator of a new conception of genius, of the belief namely, that genius is intuitive, that it consists in a certain power of conceiving and apprehending without any resort to abstract ideas." †

Friederich Wilhelm Joseph Schelling developed the same theory and gave it a more philosophic form. He held that the activity of the mind is mystic, and that there is a special gift of "intellectual intuition" which enables genius to transcend reason.

But one figure towers far above the German critical thought of the period. August Wilhelm Schlegel delivered his famous lectures on dramatic art in Vienna in 1808. Schlegel's survey of the history of the theatre is still of abundant interest to the student of the drama; his analysis of Shakespeare is especially penetrating. But

* *Opus cit.*
† *Ibid.*

the shadow of the unique soul lies across his work. He expressed
the philosophy of romanticism with great clarity: in tragic poetry,
"we contemplate the relations of our existence to the extreme limit
of possibilities." These possibilities lead us to the infinite: "Everything finite and mortal is lost in the contemplation of infinity."
Thus we come to the customary dualism of matter and mind:
poetry endeavors to solve this "internal discord," "to reconcile
these two worlds between which we find ourselves divided, and to
blend them indissolubly together. The impressions of the senses
are to be hallowed, as it were, by a mysterious connexion with
higher feelings; and the soul, on the other hand, embodies its fore-
bodings, or indescribable intuitions of infinity, in types and symbols
borrowed from the visible world." *

This theory deserves very careful attention: first, we observe
that it is necessarily subjective. In Schlegel's words, "The feeling
of the moderns is, upon the whole, more inward, their fancy more
incorporeal, and their thoughts more contemplative." Second, we
note the reference to "types and symbols," suggesting the later
methods of expressionism. Third, there is the suggestion that the
playwright deal with "higher feelings," and not with immediate
social problems. Schlegel criticized Euripides for failing adequately
to depict the "inward agony of the soul": "He is fond of reducing
his heroes to the condition of beggars, of making them suffer
hunger and want." Schlegel disapproved of Lessing's precision and
of his social orientation. He accused Lessing of wanting art to be
"a naked copy of nature": "His lingering faith in Aristotle, with
the influence which Diderot's writings had had on him, produced
a strange compound in his theory of the dramatic art." Schlegel
regarded Goethe's *Werther* as a welcome antidote to the influence
of Lessing, "a declaration of the rights of feeling in opposition to
the tyranny of social relations."

Schlegel had very little use for Aristotle, but his discussion of
the *Poetics* contains the most important thing he ever wrote. He
disliked what he called Aristotle's "anatomical ideas." In objecting
to mechanical notions of action, he made a profound observation
on the rôle of the will: "What is action?... In the higher, proper
signification, action is an activity dependent on the will of man.
Its unity will consist in its direction toward a single end; and to
its completeness belongs all that lies between the first determination
and the execution of the deed." Thus he explained the unity of
ancient tragedy: "Its absolute beginning is the assertion of free
will, with the acknowledgment of necessity its absolute end."

* These and succeeding quotations from Schlegel, *opus cit.*

It is unfortunate that Schlegel failed to continue the analysis of unity along these lines; it might have led to a valid technical application of the theory of tragic conflict. But Schlegel's metaphysics was at odds with his technique. Having opened the door to a discussion of unity, he closed it again with surprising abruptness, with the statement that "the idea of *One* and *Whole* is in no way whatever derived from experience, but arises out of the primary and spontaneous activity of the human mind... I require a deeper, more intrinsic, and more mysterious unity than that with which most critics are satisfied."

The critical utterances of Coleridge resemble those of Schlegel; his comments are wise and creative, but every clear-cut issue dissolves in generalizations: "The ideal of earnest poetry consists in the union and harmonious melting down, and fusion of the sensual into the spiritual—of man as an animal into man as a power of reason and self-government." * But the power of reason is only attained "where the body is wholly penetrated by the soul, and spiritualized even to a state of glory, and like a transparent substance, the matter, in its own nature darkness, becomes altogether a vehicle and fixture of light." Coleridge also touched on the question of free will and necessity, but concluded that the solution lay in "a state in which those struggles of inward free will with outward necessity, which form the true subject of the tragedian, shall be reconciled and solved."

Victor Hugo

In 1827, romanticism made a belated, but sensational, entry into the French theatre. Victor Hugo became the standard-bearer of the new movement. His conversion was sudden and was announced with smashing vigor in the preface to his play, *Cromwell,* in October, 1827. Hugo and the playwrights who rallied round him, built their plays more or less on the Shakespearian model, and dominated the French theatre of their generation. The romantic movement in Germany had already passed its prime, and had become artificial and bombastic. Hugo reflected this tendency; his dramas lacked Goethe's depth, and possessed little of Shelley's fervor. But he represents an important link in the romantic tradition; he tried to bring it down to earth, to water down the metaphysical content. He tried to make it *naturalistic;* he began the *Cromwell* preface with a bold announcement: "Behold, then, a

* Coleridge, *Notes and Lectures,* edited by Mrs. H. N. Coleridge (New York, 1853).

new religion, a new society; upon this twofold foundation there must inevitably spring up a new poetry.... Let us throw down the old plastering that conceals the façade of art. There are neither rules nor models; or rather there are no other rules than the general laws of nature." *

But the focal point in Hugo's conception of the romantic drama is the idea of the *grotesque:* "The fact is, then, that the grotesque is one of the supreme beauties of the drama." But the grotesque cannot exist alone. We must achieve "the wholly natural combination of two types, the sublime and the grotesque, which meet in the drama as they meet in life and in creation." It is evident that the grotesque and the sublime are simply other names for the worlds of matter and spirit. Hugo tells us that "the first of these two types represents the human beast, the second the soul." Hugo's thought is precisely that of Schlegel and of Coleridge: the drama projects "that struggle of every moment, between two opposing principles which are ever face to face in life, and which dispute possession of man from the cradle to the tomb."

Hugo is the bridge between romanticism and realism: he shows that one merged into the other without any change of fundamental concept.† This is even more evident in his epic novels than in his cramped and somewhat operatic plays. His idea that it is the function of art to represent the grotesque has had an important bearing on the technique of realism—later this idea was torn from the realists and revived again in the neo-romantic movement of expressionism. Hugo's emphasis on local color is also noteworthy: "The local color should not be on the surface of the drama, but in its substance, in the very heart of the work."

Hugo's political ideas were more concrete than those of the earlier romantic groups. Events were moving rapidly; the alignment of social forces was becoming more definite—Hugo's belief in the rights of man led him into the political arena. During the events following the revolution of 1848, his democratic views clashed with the wave of reaction which swept in after the suppression of the revolution. He was banished from France, and

---

* Clark, *opus cit.,* translation by George Burnham Ives.

† George Sand illustrates the way in which the ideas of romanticism were carried forward and transformed into the rebellious and somewhat sentimental individualism of the middle years of the century. In her early years, George Sand took a great interest in socialism, and played an active part on the side of the extreme Republicans in the revolution of 1848. She dramatized many of her novels, but her sentimental approach to characters and situations did not lend itself to successful dramatic treatment. The brilliant plays of Alfred de Musset also constitute a bridge between romanticism and realism.

remained abroad from 1851 until the fall of the Empire in 1870 permitted his return.

Mid-Century

The period of Hugo's exile marked the final consolidation of capitalism, the victory of large-scale industry, the growth of world commerce which was to lead to modern Imperialism. At the same time, there was a rapid growth in labor organization and a sharpening of class lines. Karl Marx and Friedrich Engels published the *Communist Manifesto* in 1848. In the same year, there were revolutions in France and in Germany, and the Chartist movement created serious disturbances in England. The French and German revolutions resulted in strengthening middle-class rule, but in both cases the working class played a vital rôle. In France the downfall of Louis Philippe in February, 1848, led to the forming of a "social" republic; in June the attempt of the government to disarm the Paris workers and banish the unemployed from the city led to the insurrection of the workers which was crushed after five days of bloody fighting.

In the next twenty years, the American civil war abolished slavery, and made the United States not only a united nation, but a nation whose supply of labor power and raw material were destined to give her world-wide industrial supremacy. Italy also achieved unity. Meanwhile, Prussia under Bismarck was taking the leadership of the German states; the North-German Confederation was organized, and Bismarck prepared methodically for the inevitable war with France.

In these same years, scientific discoveries revolutionized man's knowledge of himself and his environment. Darwin's *Origin of Species* appeared in 1859.

Marx and Engels

In these twenty years, Marx and Engels were shaping the world-philosophy which was to guide the course of the working-class movement. It is often assumed that Marxism is a mechanical dogma, and attempts to reduce man and nature to a narrow economic determinism. Those who hold this view are evidently not familiar with the extensive philosophic works of Marx and Engels, nor with the basis of their economic thought. Marx adopted the method of Hegelian dialectics, but rejected Hegel's metaphysics. It was necessary, according to Marx, to "discover

the rational kernel within the mystical shell." Instead of considering the phenomena of the real world as manifestations of the absolute idea, he said that "the ideal is nothing other than the material when it has been transposed and translated inside the human head." * This means the consistent denial of *final* truth: Engels said: "Dialectical philosophy dissolves all conceptions of final, absolute truth, and of a final absolute state of humanity corresponding to it. For it nothing is final, absolute, sacred. It reveals the transitory character of everything and in everything." †
At the same time, dialectical materialism rejects the mechanistic approach of earlier materialism, which, being unequipped with the dialectic method, had regarded phenomena as fixed and unfluid.

The revolutionary character of this philosophy lies in the denial of permanence, in the insistence on investigation of the processes of society as well as those of nature.

Marxism has exerted a profound influence on nineteenth and twentieth century thought, and has affected every aspect of literature and the drama—occasioning a vast amount of dispute, vilification and mystification. Those who identify the doctrines of Marx with economic fatalism, are naturally led to conclude that these doctrines tend to place culture in an economic straitjacket. Joseph Wood Krutch goes so far as to maintain that Marxism is not content to *control* culture, but aims to *abolish* it. Krutch says: "It is assumed that to break with the economic organization of the past is to break at the same time with the whole tradition of human sensibility." ‡ The Marxist must reach the conclusion, according to Krutch, that "poetry and science and metaphysics—however precious they may once have appeared—are, in fact, mere self-indulgence, and the time devoted to them is time wasted."

If we turn to the writings of Marx and Engels, we find a marked insistence on the importance and diversity of culture. But they vigorously reject metaphysical or transcendental theories of culture; they insist that culture is not a means of attaining union with an absolute idea; it is not a "pre-existent category"; on the contrary, it exists only as a product of human relationships. According to Marx, "It is not the consciousness of human beings that determines their existence, but, conversely, it is their social existence that determines their consciousness." § If we deny the

---

* Karl Marx, *Capital,* Preface to second German edition, translation by Eden and Cedar Paul (New York, 1929).
† Friedrich Engels, *Feuerbach,* edited by C. P. Dutt (London, 1934).
‡ Joseph Wood Krutch, *Was Europe a Success?* (New York, 1934).
§ Karl Marx, Preface to *A Contribution to the Critique of Political Economy,* translation by N. I. Stone (Chicago, 1904).

metaphysical *first cause,* we must necessarily assume that all our cultural processes grow out of the totality of our environment. Marx is well aware of the complexity of man's consciousness: "Upon the different forms of property, upon the social conditions of existence, as foundation, there is built a superstructure of diversified and characteristic sentiments, illusions, habits of thought, and outlooks on life in general." * It is obvious that this superstructure cannot be reduced to a mechanical formula. Furthermore, both social existence and consciousness are a continually inter-acting process: "The materialist doctrine that men are products of circumstances and upbringing and that, therefore, changed men are products of other circumstances and changed upbringing, forgets that circumstances are changed precisely by men and that the educator must himself be educated." †

Thus men's *ideas,* which find expression in philosophy and art and literature, are a vital factor in the historical process. "Men make their own history," said Engels, "whatever its outcome may be, in that each person follows his consciously desired end, and it is precisely the resultant of these many wills operating in different directions and of their manifold effects upon the outer world that constitutes history." But Engels pointed out that these "many wills," however individual they may appear, are not *wills in a vacuum,* but are the result of specific social conditions. We must ask: "What are the historical causes which transform themselves into these motives in the brains of the actors?" ‡

The success of the Russian revolution, and the rapid economic and cultural growth of the Soviet Union, have centered the world's attention on the theories of Marx. The recent achievements of the Russian theatre and motion picture have involved the application of the principles of dialectical materialism to the specific problems of esthetics and technique. As a result, the principle of *socialist realism* has been formulated. *Socialist realism* is opposed to either a subjective or a naturalistic method: the artist cannot be content with an impression or with superficial appearances—with fragments and odds and ends of reality. He must find the inner meaning of events; but there is nothing *spiritual* about this inner meaning; it is not subjective and is not a reflection of the moods and passions of the soul; the inner meaning of events is revealed by discovering the *real* connections of cause and effect which underlie the events; the artist must condense these causes; he must give them their

* Karl Marx, *The Eighteenth Brumaire of Louis Bonaparte,* translation by Eden and Cedar Paul (New York, 1926).
† Marx's *Theses on Feuerbach,* in appendix to Engels, *opus cit.*
‡ Engels, *opus cit.*

proper color and proportion and quality; he must dramatize the "superstructure of diversified and characteristic sentiments, illusions, habits of thought, and outlooks on life in general."

Realism

The realism of the nineteenth century was not founded on any integrated philosophy or system of social causation. The realists were not, in the main, concerned with the underlying trend and historical significance of events; their methods tended more toward documentation, naturalism, classification of appearances.

The father of realism, the greatest, and perhaps least romantic, of realists, was Honoré de Balzac, whose work was done between 1830 and 1850. Only a few years after Hugo proclaimed "a new religion, a new society," Balzac undertook to examine this new society with methodical thoroughness and with a pen dipped in acid. Balzac exposed the decay and corruption of his period. *La Comédie Humaine* reveals the instability of the social order, the contradictions which were leading to the upheavals of the sixties and seventies. Balzac regarded himself as a scientist: "The historians of all countries and ages have forgotten to give us a history of morals." But his science was one of classification rather than of evolution. His attempt to view life with completely dispassionate detachment led to his overwhelming preoccupation with factual detail; his failure to find any integrated social meaning or purpose in the relationships which he analyzed made much of his work descriptive rather than climactic; although he was deeply drawn to the theatre, he seemed unable to use the dramatic form successfully. This is indicated in a striking technical characteristic of his novels—the *exposition* is intricately elaborated, and is often longer than the story itself. Joseph Warren Beach notes that the point at which Balzac's stories begin is "sometimes actually more than halfway through the book." * Beach remarks that the author is clearly aware of this, and quotes the passage from *Ursule Mirouet* in which Balzac announces that the actual plot is beginning: "If one should apply to the narrative the laws of the stage, the arrival of Savinien, in introducing to Nemours the only personage who was still lacking of those who should be present at this little drama, here brings the exposition to an end."

The shadow of Balzac lies across the whole course of later realism. His scientific method, his meticulous naturalism, his ret-

* Beach's *The Twentieth Century Novel* (New York, 1932) is a valuable and exhaustive study of the technique of fiction.

rospective analysis, were imitated both in fiction and in the drama.

But the last thirty years of the century witnessed a serious change in the social atmosphere: the structure of society became increasingly rigid, and at the same time the inner stress became more intense. The one open break in the structure was the Paris Commune, which was drowned in a sea of blood on May 21st, 1871.

The triumphant power of capitalism, the vastness of its achievements, and the inner contradictions which it necessarily produced, determined the character of the culture of the era. The fears and hopes of the romanticists were no longer inspiring; their intemperate craving for emotional expression and personal freedom seemed far removed from an age which had apparently achieved permanence, and had crystallized certain limited but definite forms of personal and political freedom. Thought necessarily turned to a more realistic investigation of the environment. This took the form both of an appraisal of what had been accomplished, and an attempt to reconcile the dangerous inconsistencies which were revealed to even the most superficial observer of the social order.

Émile Zola

In 1873, Émile Zola, who was greatly influenced by the example of Balzac, issued a vivid plea for naturalism in the theatre, in the preface to his play, *Thérèse Raquin*. Curiously enough, there is a striking similarity between what Zola wrote in 1873 and Hugo's romantic proclamation in 1828. "We have come," said Zola, "to the birth of the true, that is the great, the only force of the century." * Where Hugo had spoken of "the old plastering that conceals the façade of art," Zola said that "the decayed scaffoldings of the drama of yesterday will fall of their own accord." Hugo had said that the poet must choose "not the *beautiful,* but the *characteristic.*" Zola said of *Thérèse Raquin:* "The action did not consist in any story invented for the occasion, but in the inner struggles of the characters; there was no logic of fact, but a logic of sensation and sentiment." Hugo defended the grotesque, and demanded local color. Zola said: "I laid the play in the same room, dark and damp, in order not to lose relief and the sense of impending doom."

The similarities in these statements are interesting. But there is also a vital difference. Hugo's ideas of the grotesque and of local color were generalizations. Zola went beyond this—he was willing, not only to talk about the real world, but to look at it. On the

* Clark, *opus cit.,* translation by Clark.

other hand, his statement that there is "no logic of fact, but a logic of sensation and sentiment" shows that his mode of thought is romantic rather than realistic. We also hear echoes of romanticism in Zola's announcement that there are "no more formulæ, no standards of any sort; there is only life itself."

Zola's dramatic work was far less vital than his novels. This was partly due, as in the case of Balzac, to the tendency toward journalistic documentation, and the lack of a defined social philosophy. Nevertheless, *Thérèse Raquin* marks a turning point in the history of the theatre. Matthew Josephson says, "It is admitted now that Zola's efforts to reach the stage stimulated and shook up the theatre of his time, and form the original if crude source of the modern French drama of Brieux, Becque, Hervieu, Henri Bernstein, Bataille, which covers nearly forty years of our time." *

This is true; but it is an understatement. *Thérèse Raquin* does much more than crudely suggest the course of later drama; it embodies the scheme of moral and ethical ideas which were to find expression in the twentieth century theatre, and shows the origin of these ideas. In the first place, there is Zola's awareness of social issues, his feeling that something is wrong with society. This is inevitable, when we consider that *Thérèse Raquin* was written as a novel four years before the Paris Commune, and done as a play two years after that event. Yet Zola moved through the days of the Commune without attaching any deep historical significance to the disorders which he witnessed. On the whole, he was puzzled and annoyed. Josephson tells us that "the whole period seems to have filled Zola with revulsion, instead of having fired his imagination."

We can readily understand this if we examine Zola's ideas at the time. Here is what he wrote in his notes for the *Rougon-Macquart* series: "The time is troubled; it is the trouble of the time that I am painting. I must absolutely stress this: I do not deny the grandeur of the modern effort, I do not deny that we can move more or less toward liberty and justice. I shall even let it be understood that I believe in these words, liberty, justice, although my belief is that men will always be men, good and bad animals according to circumstances. If my characters do not arrive at good, it is because we are only beginning in *perfectibility*." †

Liberty and justice are therefore not a matter of the immediate moment, but of the ultimate perfectibility of man. Thus he turned,

---

* Josephson, *Zola and His Time* (New York, 1928).
† Quoted by Josephson, *opus cit.* The present discussion is based largely on the data presented by Josephson.

as the romantics had turned at the dawn of the century, to the analysis of the heart of man. In *Thérèse Raquin,* his interest is less in the poverty of the poor than in their *emotions.* He spoke of *Thérèse Raquin* as an "objective study of the emotions." What did Zola mean by an objective study? Josephson points to the impression made upon Zola by the experiments of Dr. Claude Bernard, whose studies in the physiology of the nervous system were causing a sensation. Zola was also influenced by Lamarck and Darwin. He wanted to dissect the soul scientifically. But what he shows us is the romantic soul, tortured by animal passions, upheld by the hope of ultimate perfectibility.

Zola believed that the physiology of the nerves determines our actions; this physiology is hereditary; it is impossible to struggle against it. *Thérèse Raquin* is a story of violent sexual emotion. Thérèse is obsessed, her doom is foreordained by her own *"blood and nerves."* Thus passion is an expression of the ego; but passion is also the primary stuff of life. It contains in itself both cause and effect. It is both good and evil. Men are not to attain perfectibility by destroying emotion, but by purifying it. The "absolute idea" reappears as absolute feeling. This conception is derived directly from Schopenhauer's philosophy of the emotional will. But Zola avoided Schopenhauer's pessimism—because he combined the idea of blind will with the idea of a benevolent life force which would eventually transform the wayward emotions of men into a pure, eternal emotion.*

There is abundant proof that this was the essential direction of Zola's thought: the *Rougon-Macquart* series, begun in 1868 as a clinical study, ended in 1893 as a hymn to the "eternally fecundating breath of life."

Zola considered himself a materialist; he used a scientific method which he inherited from Balzac. But his view of science was clouded and sentimental; his physiology and heredity were merely symbols of the universal power of which the soul of man is a fragment. Although he insisted that emotion is "a purely physical phenomena," he treated emotion as being outside body and mind, controlling both. This led him, as Josephson says, to consider "the all-powerful rôle of the sexual act, as the origin and continued

---

* This aspect of Zola's thought shows the influence of Saint-Simon and his followers: at the beginning of the nineteenth century, Saint-Simon advocated a controlled industrial society; he also attacked religious asceticism, maintaining the value of physical emotion, and stating that man and woman constitute the "social individual." Some of Saint-Simon's followers developed this side of his thought to a semi-religious philosophy of emotion. This is especially true of the sensual mysticism preached by Barthelemy Enfantin (1794-1864).

achievement of the act of life.... In *Madeleine Ferat* he showed
'the nostalgia for adultery by a supposed irresistible attraction
which swayed all women during their natural lives toward the
man who had first revealed to them the destinies of their sex.'"
It would have been instructive to hear Dr. Claude Bernard,
working in his laboratory at the College de France, comment on
the *physiological* value of this passage. However banal the passage
may appear, it reveals the type of thinking which, from Zola's
time to our own, has dominated literature and the drama.

Zola's system of ideas, derived from romanticism with naturalistic trimmings, found its dramatic formulation in *Thérèse Raquin*.
Since these ideas underlie the technique and social orientation of
the modern drama, it may be well to sum them up briefly: (1)
awareness of social inequality; (2) use of a drab milieu presented
uncompromisingly; (3) use of sharp contrasts between dullness of
conventional lives and scenes of sudden physical violence; (4)
marked influence of current scientific ideas; (5) emphasis on blind
emotion rather than on conscious will; (6) concentration on sex
as practically the sole "objective" expression of emotion; (7) idea
of sex as a means of escape from bourgeois restrictions; (8) fatalism—the outcome is foreordained and hopeless.

Thérèse is the forerunner of many modern heroines. Although the
social milieu is very different, Hedda Gabler is closely related to
her, and so are all of O'Neill's heroines. Zola turned the scientific
discoveries of Dr. Bernard to his own account, using them to express an unscientific conception of sex fatalism. We find O'Neill
using an equally unscientific version of psychoanalysis for the same
purpose.

The Well-Made Play

Zola was miles in advance of the theatre of his time. He knew it.
He predicted the changes which would take place, and for which
he was in no small measure responsible. Meanwhile, French playwrights devoted themselves with skill and energy to the development of *the well-made play*. As soon as capitalism became solidly
entrenched, there rose the need for a type of drama which would
reflect the outward rigidity of the social system, which would give
orderly expression to the emotions and prejudices of the upper
middle class. The plays of Eugene Scribe, Alexandre Dumas fils
and Victorien Sardou presented prevailing conventions in a *fixed*
form. Their function was similar to that of French tragedy at
the court of Louis XIV.

Scribe's smoothly contrived dramas were turned out with

amazing speed in the days of Louis Philippe, and were symptomatic of the increasing prosperity and mediocrity of the era. Dumas fils, writing in the time of Napoleon III, catered to a society which was not content with the facile sentimentalities of Scribe. He brought the well-made play to maturity, giving it more emotional depth and social meaning. His technique combined the artificiality of Scribe with the analytic method of Balzac. He said that he wanted to "exercise some influence over society." But his analysis was superficial and his ideas were the dregs of romanticism. Montrose J. Moses says of *Camille* that its author "had injected into the romantic play of intrigue and infidelity a species of emotional analysis which was somehow mistaken for an ethical purpose." * This was a real accomplishment; the technique perfected by Dumas fils is used extensively today; it combines an escape into a realm of unbridled sentimentality with an appearance of serious ethical meaning.

Victorien Sardou was a contemporary of Zola's. His first successful play appeared in 1861, the year in which Scribe died. He carried on the Scribe tradition of skillful shallowness. But he also made an essential contribution in emphasizing naturalness and journalistic vitality. While Dumas fils created a theatrical ethics, Sardou was busy creating a theatrical naturalness—which was as fictitious as the ethics of Dumas fils, but which served the same purpose, serving to cloak the escape from reality.

The school of the well-made play produced one critic who has earned an honored place in the history of the theatre. Francisque Sarcey, who was the leader of Parisian criticism from 1860 to 1899, was what may be described as a well-made critic. His opinions, like the plays he admired, were conventional and shallow. But he hit upon one principle of dramatic construction which has made him famous, and which has a bearing, not only on the mechanical works of Scribe and Sardou, but upon the fundamentals of technique. This was the theory of the "scène à faire," which William Archer translates as the "obligatory scene"—a scene made necessary by the logic of the plot. As Archer describes it, "an obligatory scene is one which the audience (more or less clearly and consciously) foresees and desires, and the absence of which it may with reason resent." † The dramatist's task lies, to a great degree, in the preparation of such a scene, in arousing the expectation of the audience and maintaining the right amount of uncertainty and tension.

---

* Moses, *The American Dramatist* (Boston, 1917).
† Archer, *Playmaking, a Manual of Craftsmanship* (New York, 1928).

Sarcey's theory has received a great deal of attention. But it has been treated rather vaguely, and its full value in the analysis of play construction has not been understood. The idea that the plot leads in a *foreseen* direction, toward a clash of forces which is *obligatory,* and that the dramatist must give double consideration to the logic of events and to the logic of the spectator's expectation, is far more than a mechanical formula. It is a vital step toward understanding the dramatic process

Gustav Freytag

We have traced the course of romanticism from Goethe and Schiller, through Hugo, to Zola's emotional realism. This was, in general, a progressive course, building toward the dramatic renaissance at the end of the nineteenth century. At the same time, we must consider another tendency—the tendency to turn back, to cling to the most reactionary aspects of romanticism. Zola faced life with many delusions, but he attacked it crudely and voraciously. There was a parallel movement which turned away from reality altogether, which sought refuge and dignity in a glorification of the soul. Gustav Freytag's *Technique of the Drama,* published in 1863, gave a definite technical formulation to the metaphysical aspect of romanticism. German philosophy at this time was immersed in Kantian "pure reason" and Hegelian idealism. Freytag was an idealist in the dramatic field; he took the official philosophy of Bismarck's Germany, and applied it to the theatre with rigid precision. There is nothing vague about Freytag's metaphysics; he regarded the drama as a static framework in which the romantic soul struts and suffers; his romanticism is narrow, formal and scholastic; he separated form and content, as one might separate the structure of the established church from the ideal which it embodies.

Freytag referred to the soul continually; he spoke of "the rushing forth of will power from the depths of man's soul toward the external world," and "the coming into being of a deed and its consequences on the human soul." * But the soul to which he referred was not the tortured seeking soul of early romanticism. Freytag's soul had money in the bank. The hero, he said, must be an aristocrat, possessing "a rich share of culture, manners and spiritual capacity." He must also "possess a character whose force and worth shall exceed the measure of the average man." The

* All Freytag quotations are taken from Elias J. MacEwan's translation of *Technique of the Drama* (5th edition, Chicago, 1908).

lower classes are outside the realm of art: "If a poet would completely degrade his art, and turn to account ... the social perversions of real life, the despotism of the rich, the torments of the
oppressed ... by such work he would probably excite the sympathy
of the audience to a high degree; but at the end of the play, this
sympathy would sink into a painful discord. ... The muse of art
is no sister of mercy."

This raises the old question of the Aristotelian purgation of the
emotions. Freytag interpreted Aristotle in a way which enabled
him to reconcile the idea of purgation with the avoidance of "painful discord." According to Freytag, the spectator is purified, not
by direct contact *with* pity and terror, but by release *from* these
emotions. The spectator does not share the emotions; on the contrary, he feels "in the midst of the most violent emotions, the
consciousness of unrestricted liberty ... a feeling of security." He
discovers as he leaves the playhouse that "the radiance of broader
views and more powerful feelings which has come into his soul,
lies like a transfiguration upon his being."

These are almost the same words used two hundred years earlier
by the French critic, Saint-Evremond, in discussing the idea of
purgation. Saint-Evremond spoke of "a greatness of soul well-
expressed, which excites in us a tender admiration. By this sort
of admiration our minds are sensibly ravished, our courage elevated,
and our souls deeply affected." *

Freytag agreed with Saint-Evremond that the function of the
theatre is to uplift and soothe; but he added a new note—the idea
of esthetic *escape*. At the court of Louis XIV, the world was
smaller and more absolute. In nineteenth century Europe, "the
social perversions of real life" pressed close around the theatre;
"the consciousness of unrestricted liberty" was more difficult to
attain.

Freytag's book is important in two respects: in the first place,
it is the earliest modern attempt to deal comprehensively with
play-construction as a whole, in technical terms. Freytag had no
feeling for the living quality of a play, because he believed that
this quality is outside the jurisdiction of technique; but he believed
that the form of a play can be defined, and he set about this task
methodically, and with considerable success. In the second place,
Freytag's dual preoccupation with technical form and spiritual content led him to regard dramatic conflict in a purely *subjective* light.
He realized that the drama must deal with action; but the playwright's purpose should be to project "the inner processes which

* From anonymous translation in Clark, *opus cit.*

man experiences from the first glow of perception to passionate
desire and action, as well as the influence which one's own and
others' deeds exert upon the soul." Thus his emphasis is on feeling
and psychological stress, rather than on logical cause and effect.
In approaching craftsmanship from this point of view, and in
regarding action as a symbol of the "processes of man's nature,"
Freytag laid the groundwork for German expressionism.

The Denial of Action

The emphasis on subjective processes does not spring from a
desire to investigate the psychological roots of human conduct. We
have observed that Freytag's interest in the soul was directly connected with a desire to ignore "the social perversions of real life."
Toward the end of the nineteenth century, a school of dramatic
thought developed which carried the theory of subjective drama
to the point of altogether denying the value of action. In *The
Treasure of the Humble* (1896), Maurice Maeterlinck said that
"the true tragic element of life only begins at the moment when
so-called adventures, sorrows and dangers have disappeared....
Indeed when I go to the theatre I feel as though I were spending a
few hours with my ancestors, who conceived life as something that
was primitive, arid and brutal." * Allardyce Nicoll quotes this
opinion with the comment that "this, probably, is the most important piece of creative criticism on the drama that has appeared
for the last century." †

The source of Maeterlinck's thought is clear: he wants to
present "I know not what intangible and unceasing striving of the
soul toward its own beauty and truth." ‡ But, since this striving is
intangible, it brings us into the realm of pure metaphysics, where
the soul ceases to strive: "In most cases, indeed, you will find that
psychological action—infinitely loftier in itself than mere material
action, and truly, one might think, well-nigh indispensable—that
psychological action even has been suppressed, or at least vastly
diminished, in a truly marvelous fashion, with the result that the
interest centers solely and entirely in the individual, face to face
with the universe."

Leonid Andreyev expressed a similar point of view. Barrett H.
Clark says that "Andreyev, adopting a transcendental outlook,
treats normal and abnormal people from a position of almost

---

* From Alfred Sutro's translation (New York, 1925).
† *Opus cit.*
‡ *Opus cit.*

unearthly aloofness." * Andreyev asked: "Is action, in the sense of movements and visual achievements on the stage, necessary to the theatre?" †

The Dramatic Renaissance

At the very time that Maeterlinck wrote of a drama in which even "psychological action has been suppressed," the great plays of the reawakened theatre were being written and produced. Among the plays which had appeared before 1893 were Ibsen's *Hedda Gabler,* Tolstoy's *The Power of Darkness,* Hauptmann's *The Weavers,* August Strindberg's *The Father,* George Bernard Shaw's *Widowers' Houses,* Frank Wedekind's *Spring's Awakening,* and many others.

André Antoine, who was a clerk at the gas company, founded the *Théâtre Libre* in a tiny improvised playhouse in Paris in 1887. Here Ibsen's and Strindberg's plays were performed; here the work of François de Curel and Eugene Brieux was produced for the first time. A similar Free Stage Society was started in Berlin in 1889, and in England in 1891.

The first and great figure of the dramatic renaissance was Henrik Ibsen, whose work covers the whole last half of the century. His first play was written in 1850, *Peer Gynt* appeared in 1867, and *A Doll's House* in 1879. Ibsen was the storm center of the new movement which changed the course of the drama in every country in Europe. In the deepest sense, this was a *realistic* movement; it faced reality with vigor and despairing honesty. But it also included a generous portion of the obscurantism which found extreme expression in Maeterlinck's theories. *The Weavers* appeared in 1892; in the next year, Hauptmann wrote *The Assumption of Hannele,* in which a child's vision of immortality is contrasted with the reality of the world. In Tolstoy, in Wedekind, above all in Ibsen himself, there is a similar unresolved struggle between the real and the ideal.

In order to understand the new movement in the theatre, we must see it as the climax of two centuries of middle-class thought. It grew out of the contradiction which was inherent in the intellectual life of the eighteenth and nineteenth centuries, and which was at the heart of the social structure. This contradiction, in a dialectical sense, was the driving force which moved society forward; the explosive inner disturbances of equilibrium were moving

* Clark, *A Study of the Modern Drama* (New York, 1928).
† Quoted by Clark, *ibid.*

at increasing tempo toward imperialism and world war. Men who thought sensitively and deeply were aware of the conflicting forces which were threatening their world. But the conflict was also in *themselves,* it was rooted in their ways of thinking and believing.

It was natural that great drama should rise out of this conflict. It rose at a time when middle-class society was still vital, moving ahead, able, to some extent, to see itself objectively. But the smoldering tension was near the surface. The theatre reflected both the objective vitality, and the dangerous inner tension.

This gives us a perspective, both on the greatness of the drama in the late nineteenth century, and on its inevitable limitations. The contradiction is sharply indicated in the person of Maeterlinck, who was both a mystic and an accomplished scientist. The dread of action, which Maeterlinck expressed in metaphysical terms, *also* found expression in the plays of the most consistent realist of the time—Anton Chekhov. Mysticism and realism were not merely matters of literary mood: *both* sprang from the imperative thought processes of the era. Chekhov gave objective expression to the same forces which dictated Maeterlinck's philosophy.

We have seen that the romantic contradiction was at the bottom of Zola's naturalism. In many ways, Zola typified the spirit of the century, the direction in which it was moving. The increasing pressure of events led Zola to participate in the Dreyfus case, and brought him to the most courageous moment of his career. He was middle-aged and tired; he had wandered aimlessly through the scenes of the Paris Commune; he had preached naturalism and faith in science and the life force; on January 13, 1898, Zola shouted "I accuse" to the President of France and the general staff of the French army and the whole state apparatus. He was tried, and sentenced to prison, and escaped to England—but his voice echoed round the world.

Zola was one of those who were mainly responsible for the awakening of the theatre in the nineties. He had predicted this awakening for twenty years. He was active in the founding of Antoine's free theatre; Antoine testifies that Zola's theories inspired him and determined the policy of the playhouse. A one-act adaptation of one of Zola's stories was on the first bill; it was through Zola that Ibsen's plays were first brought to Antoine's stage.

Ferdinand Brunetière

Here we face another enlightening contradiction. The most important contribution to modern dramatic theory was made by

Ferdinand Brunetière, who was a sworn enemy of Zola's naturalism. Brunetière was a philosopher as well as a critic; he was deeply conservative; his philosophy tended toward fideism, and led him to embrace the Catholic religion in 1894. As early as 1875, when Brunetière was twenty-six, he attacked Zola for "his brutal style, his repulsive and ignoble preoccupations.... Is humanity composed only of rascals, madmen and clowns?" *

But Brunetière was an original thinker: his opposition to naturalism was far more than a plea for a return to classical tradition. While Freytag merely embalmed the traditions of metaphysical thought, Brunetière proceeded to analyze the problem of free will and necessity. He was right in holding that Zola's materialism was incomplete, that Zola's faith in science was romantic and unscientific, and therefore led to a mechanical fatalism. Brunetière held that fatalism makes drama impossible; drama lies in man's attempt to dominate his surroundings: "Our belief in our freedom is of no small assistance in the struggle that we undertake against the obstacles which prevent us from attaining our object." †

On this basis, Brunetière developed the law of conflict, which had been suggested by Hegel, and applied it to the actual work of the theatre: "What we ask of the theatre is the spectacle of the will striving toward a goal, and conscious of the means which it employs.... Drama is the representation of the will of man in conflict with the mysterious powers or natural forces which limit and belittle us; it is one of us thrown living upon the stage, there to struggle against fatality, against social law, against one of his fellow mortals, against himself, if need be, against the ambitions, the interests, the prejudices, the folly, the malevolence of those who surround him."

Brunetière's historical perspective was limited—but he made a remarkable analogy between the development of the theatre and periods of expanding social forces. He showed that Greek tragedy reached its heights at the time of the Persian wars. He said of the Spanish theatre: "Cervantes, Lope de Vega, Calderon, belong to the time when Spain was extending over all of Europe, as well as over the New World, the domination of her will." Writing in 1894, he felt that the theatre of his time was threatened because "the power of will is weakening, relaxing, disintegrating. People no longer know how to exert their will, they say, and I am afraid

---

* Quoted by Josephson, *opus cit.*
† Brunetière, *The Law of the Drama,* translated by Philip M. Hayden (New York, 1914).

they have some right to say it. We are broken-winded, as the poet
says. We are abandoning ourselves. We are letting ourselves drift
with the current." *

Taine and Brandes

Brunetière is among the few dramatic critics who have hinted
at the connection between social and dramatic development. It is
curious that other writers on the theatre have almost completely
neglected its social implications.† One of the most impressive
aspects of general criticism in the nineteenth century was the use
of a new method, based on the analysis of modes of thought, economic conditions, cultural and political trends. The two greatest
exponents of this school were Hippolyte Taine and Georg Brandes,
whose method stemmed directly from Hegel. Both dealt extensively
with the theatre as a part of general literature; but they made no
attempt to deal with it specifically, as a separate creative form.

Both Taine and Brandes studied literature as a social process.
"Looked at from the historical point of view," wrote Brandes, "a
book, even though it may be a perfect, complete work of art, is
only a piece cut out of an endlessly continuous web." ‡ Taine
started with the assumption that there is "a system in human
sentiments and ideas." He believed that this system is conditioned
by three primordial forces, race, surroundings and epoch:
"Whether the facts be physical or moral, matters little; they
always have their causes." Taine's analysis of causes was colored
by the hang-over of romanticism; like other thinkers of his century,
his materialism was the servant of the unique soul. He therefore
decided that "history is a problem in psychology." Instead of
studying the inter-action of race, surroundings and epoch, he
studied only what he believed to be the psychological effect of
these elements; each epoch, he thought, produced a special dominant type, a *unique soul;* he discovered "a certain ideal model of
man; in the middle ages, the knight and the monk; in our classic
age, the courtier, the man who speaks well." §

Taine and Brandes (and other critics who followed in their

* *Ibid.*
† One example of this type of *unhistorical* thinking may be cited from
Brander Matthews' *The Development of the Drama.* He observes that
romanticism tended "to glorify a selfish and lawless egotism." He concludes that one may assume that there is some connection between
romanticism and the Paris Commune, both being characterized by "unsound and unstable" ideas.
‡ *Opus cit.*
§ Taine, *opus cit.*

footsteps) provided much of the intellectual stimulation for the revival of the theatre. Brandes influenced Ibsen. Zola was Taine's disciple; his search for causes, "physical and moral," his concentration on emotional psychology and upon hereditary types, were largely acquired from Taine.

Spencer and Bergson

During the greater part of the nineteenth century, German philosophic thought had been dominated by Hegelianism. The metaphysical side of his vast dual system of mind and matter had been in the ascendant; but the system had been flexible enough to swallow Darwin's theory of evolution and all the wonders of modern science, all of which were accepted as the physical unfolding of the "absolute idea." In France and England, the tradition of Locke, Hume, Montesquieu and Saint-Simon had continued to exert a profound influence, giving a liberal and social direction to the trend of philosophic thought.

In the last years of the nineteenth century, a marked change took place in the dominant trend of European philosophy. The new movement, which was destined to play a large part in twentieth-century thought, was by no means new. It was, to a considerable extent, a return to the agnosticism of Hume, who had maintained that rational knowledge is "metaphysical," and that we can rely only on our immediate sense-data. In the nineteenth century, there were many variations of Humean thought; among these was the positivism of Auguste Comte, who died in 1857. Herbert Spencer carried on the tradition of positivism. He accepted the positive aspects of modern science; in 1855, four years before the appearance of *The Origin of Species,* he published *Principles of Psychology,* which was based on the theory of evolution. But he agreed with Hume in accepting the doctrine of the unknowable; he called his system "synthetic philosophy."

In the eighteen-nineties, the movement of thought which awakened the drama also caused a disturbance in the philosophic equilibrium; this in turn reacted upon general thought, and caused changes in dramatic logic and method. As long as philosophy remained within the framework of idealism, it was impossible to annihilate the dualism of mind and matter. Men were desperately seeking for a new way of freeing the unique soul from the bondage of reality—which at the same time would justify and explain the immediate maladjustments between themselves and their environment. Hegel's *absolute* was too remote and final for the modern world; Spencer's "synthetic philosophy" was too narrow and limited.

Henri Bergson filled this need. He combined agnosticism and positivism with Schopenhauer's idea of the world as the expression of dynamic and irrational will. Bergson's philosophy was both immediate and mystical; it was agnostic and emotional; it was both skeptical and absolute. Instead of the absolute idea, Bergson spoke of the *élan vital,* "the original principle of life."

In *Time and Free Will,** Bergson expounded the old dualism of mind and matter in a form which brilliantly corresponded to new scientific ideas of time and space. He said that there are two aspects of self: the fundamental self which exists in time, and the self "refracted, broken to pieces," which is the "special and social representation" of the self. "The greater part of the time," said Bergson, "we live outside ourselves, hardly perceiving anything of ourselves but our own ghost, a colorless shadow which pure duration projects into homogeneous space....To act freely is to recover possession of oneself and to get back to pure duration."

The importance of this lies, not in what it means (for I confess that I do not know), but in the fact that it clearly projects the idea of escape by transcending reality; "to act freely" in a world of "pure duration." Our life on earth is a "colorless shadow" of the freedom which might exist in the flow of time.

Bergson's philosophy also had its experimental, *realistic* side; he dealt with the world of immediate sensation (the world of space), as a world of fragments of experience which have only temporary value. In this he followed Hume's agnosticism; his conception of reality as something temporarily perceived and having no absolute rational meaning paralleled the pragmatism of William James.

Both in glorifying the *élan vital,* and in emphasizing reliance on sensation, Bergson's position was anti-intellectual. We have seen that Zola's interest in physiology led him to regard emotion as a thing-in-itself; from this it was a short step to Zola's conception of the "eternally fecundating breath of life." Friedrich Nietzsche, writing in the eighteen-eighties, took up the same cry, extravagantly proclaiming the unique soul. Nietzsche held that reason is valueless; we achieve strength only through passionate intuition. Moral values have no meaning, because they imply the possibility of rational judgments. The life force is "beyond good and evil."

Bergson coordinated these tendencies, divested them of their

* Translation by F. L. Pogson (New York, 1910).

poetic vagueness, covered the contradictions with scientific phraseology, evaded the dangerous social implications, and built a shrine to the *élan vital* behind an impressive philosophic façade.

Bergson's most immediate effect on the literature of his day was upon the symbolists, Mallarmé, de Gourmont and others. But his influence was pronounced in the drama at the turn of the century. The Bergsonian philosophy was clearly reflected in Ibsen's final plays.

It is manifestly impossible to make a detailed examination of the thought-content, the forms and variations, the twists and turns and changes and contradictions, which are revealed in the theatre at the beginning of the twentieth century. I have tried to trace these dominant ideas in their broadest outlines; especially to show their historical origins, and the way in which they have been carried over into the theatre of the present.

We shall examine what the theatre was, and what it had learned in 1900, only through the plays of one man, who stood head and shoulders above his time, and whose work came to a close with the close of the century.

CHAPTER V

IBSEN

IBSEN'S work summarizes and concludes the cycle of middle-class development. His genius mirrored his time so clearly that a brief survey of his plays must seem like a repetition of the tendencies which have been traced in the previous chapter. The threads of *all* these dominant ideas are woven through his plays; he succeeded in dramatizing these tendencies, in making them objective. Being a master craftsman, he exposed the instability of society at its points of maximum tension; he showed the complicated pressure between the apparent rigidity of the environment and the sensibilities and perplexities of individuals.

Ibsen's shadow lies across the modern theatre. His analysis of the middle-class dilemma is so final that it has been impossible to go beyond the limits of his thought—to step beyond these limits would mean to step beyond the boundaries of society as it is now constituted.

The drama today depends chiefly on Ibsen both for its system of ideas and for the technique which is the structural embodiment of those ideas. The student of the contemporary theatre must therefore turn to Ibsen's plays, and to his very revealing note-books, as a constant point of reference, by which one's study of the modern drama may be checked and guided.

Ibsen was born at Skien, Norway, in 1828. His dramatic output covers the last half of the century and falls into three divisions: the first phase begins in 1850, and ends with *Peer Gynt* in 1867; the second phase begins with *The League of Youth* in 1869, and ends with *Hedda Gabler* in 1890; the final phase includes the four plays beginning with *The Master Builder* (1892) and ending with *When We Dead Awaken* (1899).

In the first period of seventeen years, ten plays were written. But the two last of these, *Brand* and *Peer Gynt,* represent the culmination of Ibsen's formative years. *Brand* was written only a year before *Peer Gynt;* both plays show the inner struggle in the author's mind, and indicate the course of his later development.

In *Brand,* the action takes place in a village in the northern mountains; the symbolism of the snowy heights and the threatened avalanche is *precisely* the same as in Ibsen's last play, *When We Dead Awaken.* The first scene of *Brand* shows a wild highland: "The mist lies thick and heavy; it is raining and nearly dark." Brand meets a peasant who warns him of the danger: "A stream has hollowed out a channel under us; we are standing over a gulf, no one knows how deep; it will swallow us up, and you too!" But Brand expresses the deep determination which moves through all of Ibsen's plays—he *must* go on, he must be unafraid. At the end of the play (as at the end of *When We Dead Awaken*) the avalanche sweeps down and Brand is destroyed: "The avalanche buries him; the whole valley is filled."

In *Brand* we find the nostalgia for the south, as a symbol of warmth and a sort of sensual escape, which recurs in many of Ibsen's plays, and especially in *Ghosts.* Brand says, "At home I never saw the sun from the fall of the leaf until the cuckoo's cry." Brand's child dies because he sticks to his duty in the village, and refuses to return to the south to save the boy's life. But these are the outward manifestations of Ibsen's thought. The essence of *Brand* is the unique soul seeking to transcend life. In the first act, Brand says that ever since boyhood he has had "a vague consciousness of the variance there is between a thing as it is, and a thing as it ought to be; between being obliged to bear and finding the burden too heavy."

Ibsen's philosophy is based on the dual philosophy of Hegel.

Brand echoes the idea of the dialectical movement and fluidity of the universe: "Every created thing, we know, has 'finis' written after it; it gets tainted by moth and worm, and in accordance with all law and rule, must give way to a new form." But the answer is furnished by the Hegelian absolute: "But there is something which lasts; the Spirit which was not created, which was rescued at its lowest ebb in the first fresh spring of time, which by confident human faith threw a bridge from the flesh to the spirit's source." It is interesting to note the *dualism* which enters even into Ibsen's conception of the absolute. Though he says that "the Spirit ... was not created," he offers the curious idea that it was dormant, "rescued at its lowest ebb," by man's faith.

Ibsen demands that the wholeness of personality be found, that the bridge between the ideal and the real be created: "Out of these fragments of Soul, out of these lumpish trunks of spirit, out of these heads and hands, a *Whole* shall arise."

In *Brand,* the struggle is intensely subjective. "Within, within! That is the word! Thither is the way. There is the track." But Ibsen sees that inward peace can only be achieved by an adjustment between man and his environment: "A place on the whole earth's circuit, whereon to be wholly himself, that is the lawful right of man, and I ask no other!"

Therefore Ibsen sees what Zola, in spite of his physiology and materialism, was unable to see at the same period: that the question of the soul is tied up with *property relations.* Brand's mother is rich, and she tells him: "You'll get all I have ever possessed; it lies told and measured and weighed."

BRAND: On what conditions?

THE MOTHER: On this one, that you don't squander your life away. Keep up the family, son by son; I don't ask any other reward ... keep your inheritance—if you like, dead and unproductive, provided it's in the possession of the family!

BRAND: And if, on the contrary, I took it into my head to scatter it to the winds?

THE MOTHER: Scatter what has bent my back and bleached my hair during years of toil!

BRAND (*nodding slowly*): Scatter it.

THE MOTHER: Scatter it? If you do that, you scatter my soul to the winds.

Brand answers her with a terrible denunciation. When he was a child he crept into the room where his father lay dead, and he saw his mother steal into the room: "She went straight up to the bed. She set to work routing and rummaging; first she moved the dead man's head, then she pulled out a bundle, then several more: she counted, whispering: 'More, more!'...She wept, she prayed, she wailed, she swore; she got scent of the treasure track—and she found, she swooped like a falcon in an agony of delight, straight upon her prey."

This indicates the direction which Ibsen was to take in his later plays: he saw that social relationships are based on property; again and again he pointed to the corrupting influence of money. But the question of money is a family matter between Brand and his mother; it has only a general connection with the life of the community. It is treated as a corruption which springs from the evil which is in the family itself. It is a part of an hereditary taint.

In *Brand* the dominant theme which is repeated again and again is the *will*—man can save himself *by his own will.* "First you must *will,* not merely what is possible in great or small, not merely where the action carries with it its complement of pain and trouble —no, you must boldly and gladly *will* through a whole series of horrors." Again Brand says: "Rich or beggar, I *will* with all my might; and this one thing suffices." In the final act, when he is bruised and bleeding, he says: "The Will hides itself, weak and afraid." At the end, as the avalanche destroys him, he shouts his question to God: does not "man's Will merit a particle of redemption?"

Ibsen's general emphasis on the will shows the influence of Schopenhauer. This leads to a dual treatment of the will: the problem of social will, the definite struggle with the environment, becomes merged in the problem of redemption, the metaphysical will which exists throughout the universe. Thus we find in *Brand* a strain of anti-intellectualism, of uncertainty, and of the ideas which Nietzsche was later to embody in his superman. Agnes, Brand's wife, suggests that intuition is more potent than reason: "Can I gather all the reasons together, reasonably? Does not a current of feeling come like a scent on a current of wind?" In his final loneliness, Brand feels that he is a superior soul: "A thousand people followed me from the valley; not *one* has gained the heights."

In later plays, and especially in the work of his final years, we shall find Ibsen repeating the uncertainty of Brand: "When I stand before the individual soul and put to him the demand that he should rise, I feel as if I were floating on a fragment of wreckage, storm-tossed on the seas."

But the emphasis on the *conscious will* also runs through all of Ibsen's work, giving it direction and courage. Brand's will is semi-religious; but since it is really *will,* and not *faith,* it keeps forcing him back to reality, back to the struggle with the stubborn world of facts. In the final act, alone before the avalanche overtakes him, Brand faces in a vision the whole world of his time: "I see enemies sally forth to the fight—I see brethren sit meek and cringing under the cap of invisibility. And I see still more— all their shuddering wretchedness—the whimpering of women and the cries of men, and ears deaf to prayer and entreaty.... Worse times, worse visions, flash like lightning through the night of the future! The suffocating British coal-smoke sinks black over the land, smirches all the fresh green, stifles all the fair shoots, sweeps low over the land, mingled with poisonous matter.... The wolf of cunning howls and yelps, menacing the sun of Wisdom upon the earth; a cry of distress sounds northward and summons to arms along the fjord...." The vision of Agnes appears to him and begs him to go with her, to seek the sun and summer, but he refuses: he must *"live* what until now I *dreamt—*make *real,* what is still delusion." The vision tries to hold him back: "That terrible ride amid the mists of dreams—wilt thou ride it free and awake?" And he answers: "Free and awake."

Ibsen remained true to this resolve. He never faltered in the bitter struggle to see reality "free and awake." In the next year he wrote *Peer Gynt,* which represents a different aspect of the problems treated in *Brand. Peer Gynt* is far more vital, more imaginatively realized. While *Brand* deals largely in abstract discussion, Peer goes out into the world, testing reality in a series of picaresque adventures. But what Peer seeks is "to be wafted dryshod down the stream of time, wholly, solely, as oneself." Like Goethe's Faust, Peer gains all the wonders of the world; he becomes rich and finances wars. Then he decides that "my business life is a finished chapter; my love-sports too are a cast-off garment." So it might be a good idea to "study past ages and time's voracity." He asks the Sphinx for its riddle; in answer Professor Begriffenfeldt, a German philosopher, pops up from behind the Sphinx; the professor is "an exceedingly gifted man; almost all that he says is beyond comprehension." Begriffenfeldt leads him to the club of wise men in Cairo, which turns out to be a madhouse. The professor whispers to Peer dramatically: "The Absolute Reason departed this life at eleven last night." The professor shows him the assembly of lunatics: "It's here, Sir, that one is oneself with a vengeance; oneself and nothing whatever besides. Each one shuts himself up in a barrel of self, in the self-fermentation he dives to the bottom—and with the self-bung he seals it hermetically, and seasons the staves in the well of self."

Thus Ibsen paid his respects to the unique soul. But in the end Peer must face *himself;* on the barren heath there are voices around him: "We are thoughts; you should have thought us... We should have soared up like clangorous voices... We are a watchword; you should have proclaimed us... We are songs; you should have sung us... We are tears unshed forever." He meets the Button-Molder with a box of tools and a casting-ladle; the Button-Molder tells him he must be melted up, return to the casting-ladle, "be merged in the mass." Peer refuses to be deprived of himself, but the Molder is amused: "Bless me, my dear Peer, there is surely no need to get so wrought up about trifles like this. Yourself you never have been at all."

Alone, Peer sees a shooting star; he calls out, "Brother Starryflash! To flash forth, to go out and be nought at a gulp."... He goes deeper among the mists... "Is there no one, no one in all the turmoil, in the void no one, no one in Heaven—!"

But the answer which Ibsen provides in *Peer Gynt* is neither the lonely courage of Brand nor the infinite grace which rescued Faust. Peer returns to the home he had left and to the woman who has been waiting: he asks Solveig if she can tell him where he has been "with his destiny's seal on his brow?" She answers: "In my faith, in my hope, in my love." He clings to her as both mother and wife; he hides his face against her, as she sings, "The boy has been lying close to my heart all the life-day long. He is weary now!"

The man escapes, hides away in the womb of the mother-wife. This is a new idea of escape; the woman-symbol typifies the life-force; man finds salvation at his own hearthstone. In the plays of Eugene O'Neill, we shall find the woman-symbol has become *absolute;* she engulfs the man and negates action; she is both evil and good, love and hate; she is both the harlot and the mother of holiness.

Thus Ibsen exposed the contradiction which turns the *life-force* into the *negation of life.*

This was as far as Ibsen could go in studying man in relation to the *generalities* of his environment. If he had clung to the woman-symbol, it would have led him to a negation. But he remembered Brand's determination: "Free and awake!" He made a clean break with the mood of *Brand* and *Peer Gynt.* Two years later (one year before the Paris Commune) he wrote *The League of Youth.* Instead of the mists and snowy mountains, "the action takes place in the neighborhood of the iron-works, not far from a market town in southern Norway." Ibsen turned from philosophy to politics with enormous gusto. Stensgard describes a dream: "I could see the whole curve of the hemisphere. There was no sun, only a vivid storm-light. A tempest arose; it came rushing from the west and swept everything before it: first withered leaves, then men; but they kept on their feet all the time, and their garments clung fast to them, so that they seemed to be hurried along sitting. At first they looked like townspeople running after their hats in a wind; but when they came nearer they were emperors and kings; and it was their crowns and orbs they were chasing and catching at, and seemed always on the point of grasping, but never grasped. Oh, there were hundreds of them, and none of them understood in the least what was happening."

In *The League of Youth,* Ibsen shows the extraordinary skill with which he analyzes character in terms of social pressures. Dr. Fieldbo says of Stensgard: "His father was a mere rag of a man, a withered weed, a nobody. He kept a little huckster's shop and eked things out with pawn-broking; or rather his wife did it for him. She was a coarse-grained woman, the most unwomanly I ever knew. She had her husband declared incapable; she had not an ounce of heart in her." But Fieldbo points proudly to his own conservatism: "My lot has been one that begets equilibrium and firmness of character. I was brought up amid the peace and harmony of a modest middle-class home. My mother is a woman of the finest type; in our home we had no desires that outstripped our opportunities, no cravings that were wrecked on the rocks of circumstances."

The last scene of *The League of Youth* is a biting satire on political compromise. Stensgard tries to marry the storekeeper's widow: "I found on my path a woman of ripened character who could make a home for me. I have put off the adventurer, gentlemen, and here I stand in your midst as one of yourselves." But it is all a mistake; the widow marries someone else, and Stensgard leaves in disgrace:

LUNDESTAD: You'll see, gentlemen! In ten or fifteen years, Stensgard will either be in Parliament or in the Ministry— perhaps in both at once.

FIELDBO: In ten or fifteen years? Perhaps; but then he can scarcely stand at the head of the League of Youth.

HEIRE: Why not?

FIELDBO: Why, because by that time his youth will be— questionable.

HEIRE: Then he can stand at the head of the Questionable League, sir.

. . . .

BRATSBERG (*the owner of the iron-works*): I think so too, my friends; for truly we have been groping and stumbling in darkness; but good angels guided us.

LUNDESTAD: Oh, for that matter, I think the angels were only middling.

In this play, we observe the rudiments of Ibsen's social philosophy: awareness of impending change combined with distrust of political methods. He *knows* that man is a product of his environment, but he cannot see how the environment can be changed without changing the heart of man. He therefore comes back to the theme of *Brand:* the *will* itself must be intensified; but how can this be accomplished when the will is subject to all these corrupting influences? He has cast aside his faith in an eternal life-force; he no longer offers the woman-symbol as an escape. But he finds the conflict between the ideal and the real insoluble, because, like Peer Gynt, he clings to the *inner self.* He wants to find the solution *inside* the man. Ibsen is *never* fatalistic, because his belief in the power of the will is too strong; when he finds the social contradictions too difficult to face, he turns to mysticism; but even this (in the final plays) is achieved by the will rather than by faith. In *The League of Youth* he shows his cynicism in regard to group action, a predilection for Rousseau's *natural man,* and hatred for the complexities of industrial civilization—"the suffocating British coal-smoke" of which Brand had spoken.

Ibsen was deeply stirred by the events following the war of 1870. He wrote in a letter on December 20, 1870:* "Historic events are claiming a large share of my thoughts. The old illusory France is all slashed to pieces; and when the modern matter-of-fact Prussia shall also be cut into fragments we shall have made a leap into the midst of a growing epoch. Oh, how ideas will then come tumbling about our heads. All we have had to live upon up to the present date are crumbs from the revolutionary table of the past century." But his conclusion turns back to the soul: "What is needed is a revolting of the human spirit."

After *The League of Youth,* Ibsen wrote two plays, *Emperor and Galilean* and *The Pillars of Society,* which marked a period of transition. He was feeling his way toward a new orientation.

* Quoted by Georg Brandes in *Creative Spirits of the Nineteenth Century,* translation by Rasmus B. Anderson (New York, 1923).

Ten years after *The League of Youth,* the great cycle of the middle period begins with *A Doll's House.*

I have given special attention to Ibsen's early plays, because in these plays we find the elements which attain mature expression in *A Doll's House, Ghosts, Hedda Gabler* and *The Wild Duck.* The earlier probings of character, the search for the *whole man,* for the integrated will, lead directly to these plays. Peer Gynt looked at the night sky where stars were falling and turned in fear to the protecting arms of the wife-mother. But this was another death; in Europe the rushing wind was sweeping kings and emperors before it. Ibsen tried to understand these forces, but it seemed to him that the root of the trouble lay in the corruption of personal relationships. Since the family was the unit of middle-class society, he turned to dissecting the structure of the family with surgical vigor. It was inevitable that he should turn in this direction: to save the family from destruction, to renew its integrity, was the *only* road to freedom within the limits of middle-class society. The human spirit could not be reborn in a vacuum; if the broad framework of society were to continue unaltered, the individual must find honor and liberty in his most intimate relationships; he must rebuild his own home.

This was infinitely more profound than Zola's emotional materialism. Ibsen knew that people could not be saved by *belief* in science, or *belief* in emotion. If they were to be saved at all, they must be saved by their own will operating under definite conditions imposed by their environment—but here again he faced an insoluble contradiction. He could find no honest outlet for the will that would hold the heart and mind *within* the structure of the family; the life which he analyzed offered no constructive values. All that he was able to show us was bitterness, inertia, moral confusion.

The people of Ibsen's plays are the people of the suburbs of industrial cities. Shaw remarked in 1896 that Ibsen households dot all the suburbs of London: "Jump out of a train anywhere between Wimbledon and Haslemere; walk into the first villa you come to, and there you are!"

Modern plays which constitute pale echoes of Ibsen often show the middle class as hopelessly defeated. Ibsen saw them trying to save themselves. He analyzed the ways in which money pressure reacts upon ethical standards; he showed that the cheap conventions which pass for moral law are not final; but are dictated by the property interests of the community. Ibsen's characters fight for their integrity; but their fight is *ethical* rather than *social;*

they fight against conventions, but not against the conditions from which the conventions are derived. In considering Ibsen, one must consider the close tie which binds him to the romantic individualists of the early nineteenth century. Goethe and Schiller, Heine and Shelley, believed that the freedom of the individual could be attained by the destruction of false moral values. To them this was a *general* truth. Ibsen endeavored to *apply* this idea with painstaking honesty, to make it *work* in the rigid community life of his time.

The first of these plays, *A Doll's House,* sounds the most definite note of hope. But the hope is not immediate; it lies in the ultimate results which may be achieved through Nora's courage in leaving her husband and her home: "I am going to find out which is right: society or myself," says Nora. She has discovered that her husband is a stranger: "It dawned upon me that for eight years I had been living here with a strange man and had borne him three children." Nora's parting words are hopeful; both she and Helmer believe that some day they may be reunited in "a real wedlock."

But neither in *A Doll's House* nor in the dramas which follow it is there more than a hint of how this new life can be achieved.

Ghosts (1881) is often spoken of as a play in which heredity is projected as a blind fate, mercilessly destructive. Critics suggest that this destructive force resembles the Fate which broods over Greek tragedy. This is entirely inaccurate. We have noted that the idea of fate in this mystic sense is foreign to Greek tragedy. It is also foreign to Ibsen. Zola *believed* in heredity; he visualized it as an external force, driving people against their will. There is not a line in Ibsen to suggest acceptance of a hereditary fate—or of any other kind of fate or Nemesis or external force. *Ghosts* is a study of disease and insanity in terms of objective social causation. The sick nostalgia of the middle class echoes in Oswald's terrifying cry: "Mother, give me the sun." Ibsen was far less interested in fate than in the character of Mrs. Alving, and in her heroic struggle to control events. Her failure is due to specific social conditions. Ibsen has very little to say about heredity, and a great deal to say about the immediate causes of the situation. These causes are both external and internal: externally there is money pressure; internally there are lies and illusions. In no play has Ibsen shown the inter-connection of these forces so clearly as in *Ghosts.* Money was the root of Mrs. Alving's loveless marriage; money kept her tied to a life of torture. She says: "I could never have gone through with it if I had not had my work. Indeed I can boast that I have worked. All the increase in the value of the property, all the improvements, all the useful arrangements that my husband got the honor and glory of—do you suppose that he troubled himself about any of them?" Mrs. Alving compares her own case to that of the girl whom her husband betrayed and who was married off by a payment of seventy pounds:

PARSON MANDERS: The two cases are as different as day from night—

MRS. ALVING: Not so different after all. It is true there was a great difference in the price paid, between a paltry seventy pounds and a whole fortune.

Mrs. Alving tries to save herself by building an orphanage to her husband's memory: "I do not wish Oswald, my own son, to inherit a penny that belonged to his father.... The sums of money that, year after year, I have given toward this Orphanage, make up the amount of the property—I have reckoned it carefully—which in the old days made Lieutenant Alving a catch."

This is the essence of Ibsen's thought in regard to property: the individual tries to achieve integrity by an *ethical act*. Ibsen does not stop at this; he sees that the ethical act is itself insufficient: the orphanage burns down. This brings the problem to a head: the burning of the orphanage, at the end of Act II, destroys the social equilibrium for which Mrs. Alving has fought so desperately. In Act III, the question must be faced: *why* has she failed? The answer must either go to the foundations of the property system, or endeavor to explain the situation in terms of personal character. Ibsen's answer is a compromise which is an exact repetition of the theme of *A Doll's House*. The tragedy is not the fault of individuals nor of the property system; the *family* is at fault; the solution lies in "a real wedlock." Mrs. Alving tells her son that both she and Alving were to blame: "This boy, full of the joy of life—for he was just like a boy, then—had to make his home in a second-rate town which had none of the joy of life to offer him,: but only dissipations.... And I brought no holiday spirit into his home either.... I had been taught about duty, and the sort of thing that I believed in so long here. Everything seemed to turn upon duty—my duty, or his duty."

Here again the social basis is indicated—but sentiments and beliefs are stressed: "a real wedlock" can be accomplished by freeing the individual from a false idea of duty. The title of the play refers to "dead beliefs." Mrs. Alving says: "They are not actually alive in us, but they are dormant all the same, and we can never be rid of them. Whenever I pick up a newspaper and read it, I fancy I see ghosts creeping between the lines." Again, Oswald speaks of "those beliefs that are put into circulation in the world," and Mrs. Alving answers, "Ghosts of beliefs!"

Ghosts may be regarded as the climax of Ibsen's career. Whether or not one regards it as his greatest play, there can be no question that it is his *clearest* play, his nearest approach to a constructive social conception. His determination to see reality "free and awake" had carried him to a dangerous crossroads. As Mrs. Alving says: "I only intended to meddle with a single knot, but when that was untied, everything fell to pieces. And then I became aware that I was handling machine sewing."

Ibsen's concern with the structure of the family made him aware of the special poignancy of the woman's problem. In his notes for *Ghosts* he says: "These women of the present day, ill-used as daughters, as sisters, as wives, not educated according to their gifts, prevented from following their inclinations, deprived of their inheritance, embittered in temper—it is these who furnish the mothers of the new generation. What is the result?" *

The plays which follow *Ghosts* show an increasing preoccupation with the psychological analysis of the modern woman. *An Enemy of the People* (1882) returns to politics; but following this the plays of the next eight years deal less with the totality of the environment and more with emotional tensions inside the family. The reason for this is evident in *Ghosts:* Ibsen had gone as far as he dared to go in undermining the foundations of society. He turned away from this to the analysis of the emotional superstructure.

In *The Wild Duck* (1884) we again see the integrity of the family destroyed by false ideals and illusions. Relling says: "Don't use that foreign word, ideals. We have the excellent native word, lies." Gregers asks: "Do you think the two things are related?" Relling: "Yes, just about as closely as typhus and putrid fever." It is the stupidity and selfishness of the male which destroys the Ekdal family. Hialmar Ekdal is of the same breed as Helmer in *A Doll's House,* but he is depicted far more venomously; at the end, after he has driven his sensitive daughter to her death, the conclusion is hopeless. Relling says: "Before a year is over, little Hedvig will be nothing to him but a pretty theme for declamation ... then you'll see him steep himself in a syrup of sentiment and self-admiration and self-pity."

In *Rosmersholm* (1886), Rebecca West can find integrity only in death. Her love for Rosmer leads them both to throw them-

* *The Collected Works of Henrik Ibsen,* v. 12, ed. by William Archer (New York, 1909-12).

selves from the bridge across the mill-race. Here we observe the beginnings of the mysticism which became dominant in Ibsen's final period. The mother-wife of *Peer Gynt* reappears. But she has none of Solveig's holy innocence; she too is trying to save herself by her *will*. She is no longer Nora, the child-wife grown up and going blithely into the world. She is embittered, driven by sex. Rebecca says that she came to Rosmersholm deliberately to get what she could get out of it: "I knew no scruples—I stood in awe of no human tie." She broke up Rosmer's home and his wife killed herself. She wanted him to be "a free man, both in circumstances—and in spirit." But when this is accomplished, she finds that her "will is crippled." Her love has become "self-denying," and the two lovers follow the wife to their doom.

In the last play of his middle period, *Hedda Gabler* (1890), Ibsen makes a brutally honest analysis of the socially maladjusted woman. He says in his notes for *Hedda Gabler* that "it is the want of an object in life that torments her." It was also "the want of an object in life" that tormented Rebecca West, but in *Rosmersholm* Ibsen had neglected to dramatize this factor.

Hedda's intense sexuality, her lack of scruple, her dependence on convention, her fear of anything "ludicrous and mean," her thwarted idealism, her despairing selfishness, make her the archtype of the women whose instability and charm are the chief decorations of the modern drama. Few contemporary playwrights draw the portrait either honestly or accurately. Hedda's bitter tragedy has become what she herself most feared—"ludicrous and mean." Nevertheless, her features are clearly discernible in the pale replica: she is the restless Gilda in Noel Coward's *Design for Living;* she is the furiously romantic Nina in *Strange Interlude.* She is a dozen other heroines who have no object in life besides the pursuit of men and ideals.

The thing that lifts Hedda above the "ludicrous and mean" is the quality of *will;* like all of Ibsen's characters, she knows that she must make her own destiny. When Judge Brack tells her that Lövborg is dead, she says: "It gives me a sense of freedom to know that a deed of deliberate courage is still possible in this world—a deed of spontaneous beauty." What horrifies her (and really destroys her will) is the fact Lövborg did not shoot himself voluntarily. In the twentieth century theatre, the Heddas have lost this distinctive quality. They seek "spontaneous beauty" through feeling, through emotion without will. Ibsen's Hedda shows that she is drifting in this direction, that, like Rebecca in *Rosmersholm,* her will is becoming crippled. And this is the direction of Ibsen's own thought.

William Archer quotes a letter written by Ibsen to Count Prozor in March, 1900: "You are essentially right when you say that the series which closes with the Epilogue (*When We Dead Awaken*) began with Master Solness." It is interesting that, through the whole period from *Brand* to *Hedda Gabler,* Ibsen had lived in Germany (from 1864 to 1891), with occasional visits to Italy. The final cycle of four plays was written after his return to Christiania.

In *The Master Builder* (1892), the first and most powerful of these plays, Ibsen exposed the dilemma which he was facing: Hilda, like Rebecca West and Hedda, is again the woman who seeks emotional freedom for herself, by her own will, regardless of the cost. Solness, the aging master builder, says to her: "Don't you agree with me, Hilda, that there exist special chosen people who have been endowed with the power and faculty of desiring a thing, craving for a thing, willing a thing—so persistently and so—so inexorably—that at last it has to happen?" The scene continues:

SOLNESS: You are the younger generation, Hilda.

HILDA (*smiles*): That younger generation that you are so afraid of.

SOLNESS: And which, in my heart, I yearn toward so deeply.

Hilda tells him that he must climb to the top of the tower which he has built; she says she also wants to go up in a tremendously high tower, where she can "stand and look down on the other people—on those that are building churches and homes for mother and father and the troop of children... and then we will build the loveliest—the very loveliest—thing in the world... castles in the air... they are so easy to take refuge in—and so easy to build too." Solness says that the castle in the air must be real, it must have "a firm foundation under it." A little later he tells Hilda: "Men have no use for these homes of theirs—to be happy in.... See, that is the upshot of the whole affair, however far back I look. Nothing really built; nor anything sacrificed for the chance of building. Nothing, nothing! The whole is nothing.... I believe there is only one possible dwelling place for human happiness—and that is what I am going to build now."

HILDA: You mean our castle?

SOLNESS: The castles in the air. Yes.

HILDA: I am afraid you would turn dizzy before we got half-way up.

His last words to Hilda as he goes to climb to the top of the tower are also Ibsen's valedictory: "On a firm foundation." Hilda

sees him at the top of the tower "great and free again," and at the
end she says: "He mounted right to the top. And I heard harps
in the air."

In *The Master Builder,* Ibsen surveyed his own work and con-
fessed his own confusion. He had analyzed the middle-class family,
and he had found decay and bitterness: "Men have no use for
these homes of theirs—to be happy in." But he was convinced that
happiness is "the lawful right of man." Man must conquer by his
will, but in the modern community the will tends to atrophy and
become sterile. Ibsen had said in 1870 that "what is needed is a
revolting of the human spirit." He had tried to find a way in
which the human spirit could conquer its environment, but he had
found no solution. So the will must transcend the environment,
must achieve the "spontaneous beauty" of which Hedda had spoken.
Ibsen realized that this solution is really an escape: "castles in
the air...are so easy to take refuge in." He saw that Hilda, like
Hedda Gabler, is herself a product of an unhealthy environment.
Hilda is described as like "a bird of prey"; she is seeking emotional
thrills.

Mrs. Solness is one of the most tragic figures in the whole course
of Ibsen's work. She chokes with tears as she speaks of her "nine
lovely dolls," which she had cherished from childhood and had
retained after her marriage, and which were destroyed when their
home was destroyed by fire. (The fire which destroyed the Solness
home is the *same* fire which destroyed the orphanage in *Ghosts.*)
"All the old portraits were burnt on the walls," says Mrs. Solness,
"and all the old silk dresses were burnt, that had belonged to the
family for generations and generations. And all mother's and
grandmother's lace—that was burnt too. And only think—the
jewels, too! And then all the dolls—." Solness says of her: "She
too had a talent for building...for building up the souls of little
children, Hilda. For building up children's souls in perfect balance, and in noble and beautiful forms. For enabling them to soar
up into erect and full-grown human souls. That was Aline's
talent. And there it all lies now—unused and unusable forever—
of no earthly service to anyone—just like the ruins left by a fire."

So the Master Builder turns to "castles in the air," to an act of
will which he recognizes as emotional and irrational: and as he
climbs to his death, his last despairing words are: "On a firm
foundation."

So the cycle of thought which began with *Brand* returns to its
point of departure: in *When We Dead Awaken,* we are again lost
in the northern mists; again the avalanche sweeps down to destruc-

tion. Brand's will to desert dreams and to see life "free and awake," ends in a dream which escapes life. The personal will ends in Bergson's *élan vital* which is impersonal and outside the world of space. At the end of *When We Dead Awaken,* Rubek and Irene face the dual universe: "All the powers of light may freely look on us—and all the powers of darkness too." But even here, Ibsen's powerful sense of the *continuity* of life is present: "Both in us and around us life is fermenting and throbbing as fiercely as ever!" So they climb higher:

> RUBEK: We must first pass through the mists, Irene, and then—
> IRENE: Yes, through all the mists and then right up to the summit of the tower that shines in the sunrise.

As the thunder of ice and snow engulf them, the voice of Maia, the earth spirit, is heard singing triumphantly below in the valley.

In all the later plays, we note the emphasis on sexual emotion; love is "beyond good and evil"; it heals and destroys. The triangle situation becomes the central theme. The social forces in this situation are disregarded, and the emotional aridity of the home, the need for emotional inspiration, are stressed.

The modern theatre owes an especially large debt to Ibsen's final period: the triangle treated not as a *situation,* but as a psychic problem; the intense sexuality partially sublimated; the bitter aridity of family life; the weakened will, the sense of foreboding; the idea of the *superior* man and woman who have special feelings and special potentialities; the mystic solution, to gain one's life by losing it—these concepts find unlimited repetition in the drama today. However, these ideas grow out of the whole range of Ibsen's development; the threads which we have traced through the course of his work are the threads of which modern dramatic thought is woven.

These thoughts were not peculiarly Ibsen's; they were the dominant ideas of an epoch, which he dramatized and carried forward. But he went forward to the brink of an abyss—because the epoch was one of increasing instability. Historically and philosophically, the nineteenth century was moving toward a breakdown of equilibrium. This is essential to any understanding of Ibsen's influence. In a recent essay,* Joseph Wood Krutch assumes that Ibsen and Shaw represent, not the *end,* but the *beginning* of a movement, intellectually and dramatically. Krutch says of the new drama: "From having constituted a stagnant back-

* *The Nation,* September, 1935.

water it was to become a roaring torrent in which the most advanced and vertiginous ideas were to sweep onward.... The premises of a newer drama had been established and, logically, the next task of the dramatist was to create that drama." This is an example of literary wish-fulfillment. Splendid technical lessons are to be derived from Ibsen, but a forward movement of the drama based on Ibsen's ideas is a logical impossibility, because his ideas do not "sweep onward." The use of material derived from Ibsen was bound to become increasingly repetitious and uncreative—and this is exactly what has happened.

Ibsen's social philosophy never went beyond the limits of early nineteenth-century romanticism; he searched for the right to happiness and for the triumph of the individual will; this led him to a devastating analysis of social decay. But there is not a socially constructive idea in the vast range of his work. He attacked conventions and narrow moral standards; but as a substitute he offered time-worn generalities: we must be true to ourselves, we must expose lies, we must fight hypocrisy and sentimentality and stupidity. Ibsen saw the world he lived in with blinding clarity— but what he wrote, in the last analysis, was its epitaph.

Ibsen inevitably evolved a technique which is the counterpart of his social philosophy. His method of thinking is the method of Hegelian dialectics. The references to Hegel in his work are numerous. In *Brand,* the contradictions which the hero faces are dramatized in terms of a variable balance of forces breaking and reëstablishing equilibrium. This accounts for the surprising dramatic power of a play which is basically a discussion of abstract ideas. But even as early as *Brand,* we discover that Ibsen made only a limited use of this method; he used it to present the flow of social forces which react upon the characters; but the characters themselves are not fluid. The reason for this is obvious; the dominant idea of the unique soul prevented Ibsen from seeing the whole inter-connection between character and environment. The integrity of personality for which he was seeking was static; if it were achieved (in the terms in which Ibsen conceived it), it would be achieved by conquering the fluidity of the environment. In *Peer Gynt,* Peer's adventures cover a life-time; yet in all his seeking it is only the fluid world around him which changes. The reason that Peer is never able to *be* himself is because the self for which he is looking is an abstraction.

In *The League of Youth,* Ibsen adopted a method which he followed throughout his career: he accepted the fact that man's consciousness is determined by his environment and investigated the environment with meticulous care. But he continued to assume that, once the character has been formed, it must seek its own integrity in the fulfillment of itself. Thus, in all the plays following *The League of Youth,* the characters are produced by the environment, but they undergo no change or growth during the course of the drama.

This determines the distinctive technical feature of the great plays of the middle period. Instead of developing the action gradually, the plays begin *at a crisis.* The period of preparation and increasing tension is omitted. The curtain rises on the very brink of catastrophe. Clayton Hamilton says: "Ibsen caught his story very late in its career, and revealed the antecedent incidents in little gleams of backward looking dialogue.... Instead of compacting his exposition in the first act—according to the formula of Scribe—he revealed it, little by little, throughout the progress of the play." *

This constituted a break, not only with the formula of Scribe, but with the whole romantic tradition. It seems like a truism to say that the playwright's selection of a point of departure (and also the number and kind of events which he selects for inclusion in the dramatic framework) is of prime importance in the study of technique. Yet this truism is very generally neglected.

Ibsen was not the first dramatist to begin the action at a crisis. This had been characteristic of Attic tragedy, and of the Renaissance drama which imitated the Greeks. In each case, the form selected was historically conditioned. Greek tragedy was retrospective and dealt with the crisis resulting from the violation of fixed laws. In the Renaissance, the living theatre, growing out of the turbulent new life of the period, immediately broke away from this form. But the aristocratic theatre continued retrospective: Corneille and Racine dealt with *eternal* emotions, and had no interest in the social causes which might condition these emotions.

Shakespeare viewed social causation objectively. He was passionately interested in *why* men did what they did. He therefore spread the action over a wide chain of events. Goethe used the same method to narrate the subjective adventures of the soul. In *Peer Gynt,* the romantic soul is still free and adventurous in seeking its own salvation; the action covers a whole life from youth to old age. But the social dramas deal with the final psychological crisis within the middle class family. This forced Ibsen to create a more compressed technique. He was dealing with people fighting against a fixed environment; laws and customs had become

* Hamilton, *Problems of the Playwright* (New York, 1917).

rigid. Ibsen limited himself chiefly to investigating the *effects* of this environment. He was interested in causes—but to investigate these causes thoroughly, to dramatize them before his own eyes and the eyes of the audience, would be to accept a responsibility which he *could not accept*. In dealing only with the crisis, Ibsen evaded the danger of a too close examination of the forces which made the crisis inevitable.

We therefore find that the play in which Ibsen approached a direct attack upon the social system is the play in which the events leading up to the crisis are most graphically dramatized (in dialogue and description). In *Ghosts,* these retrospective crises are almost as impressive as the play itself. Mrs. Alving's desperate attempt to escape from her husband in the first year of their marriage, the scene in which she offered herself to Manders and was forced to return to her home, her fight to save her child, Alving's affair with the servant girl—these incidents are as powerfully and carefully constructed as the scenes of the play.

If Ibsen had continued the social analysis begun in *Ghosts,* one can predict with certainty that the construction of the next play would have been broadened to include a wider range of events. A further analysis of causes would have been impossible without a broader technique. But Ibsen turned to subjective psychology; he continued to present only the final crisis, to show the balance of forces only at a moment of maximum strain.

Ibsen's conception of character as static, endeavoring to impose its will on a fluid environment, is the chief technical fault in his plays. This may be described as a failure to strike a correct balance between free will and necessity. In the last mystic period, free will and necessity dissolve into one another, and both are lost. Ibsen's nearest approach to a character that *grows* is Nora in *A Doll's House.* But Nora's development is toward a knowledge of herself rather than toward a change in herself. In the later dramas, the characters become increasingly detached from their environment, and increasingly fixed. In *John Gabriel Borkman* and *When We Dead Awaken,* the environment has faded to a twilight grey.

The retrospective technique tends to weaken the force of action; this is especially true of French classical tragedy, in which oratory and narrative took the place of movement. In Ibsen's middle period, the driving force of the will and the movement of social contradictions keep the action full-blooded and vigorous. But in the last plays, the crisis itself is diluted; introspection takes the place of retrospection.

In following Ibsen's system of thought, the modern theatre has also followed his technique. His ideas and methods have not been taken over integrally or with conscious purpose, but piecemeal and often unconsciously. His compression of the action, beginning at the denouement and revealing the past in brief flashes, has *not* been followed by contemporary playwrights. It requires a master craftsman to handle this construction effectively; and its tightness and concentration of emotion are foreign to the mood of the modern theatre. Ibsen dealt with the disintegration of society; therefore he was forced to limit himself to as much of the social pattern as he could handle. The modern drama accepts Ibsen's mood and philosophy, but often neglects his deeper implications. It accepts his mysticism—which it decorates with ethical comments taken from his earlier plays, much as one might select a towering pine tree in a lonely forest and hang it with brittle Christmas tree ornaments.

Since the playwright today tends to deal with superficial emotions, and since it is assumed that these emotions have no social roots, the action tends to be diffuse; the movement has none of the fulness of the Elizabethan action; since the commercial theatre is both an escape and a sedative, it serves somewhat the same purpose as the theatre of Scribe and Sardou; to some extent, the modern play resembles the synthetic pattern invented by Scribe and amplified by Sardou. But the intellectual atmosphere has changed greatly since the middle of the nineteenth century. Therefore the old pattern has been modified and its inner construction renovated. Ibsen provided the technical basis for this change; his way of building a scene, the dry naturalness of his dialogue, his method of characterization, his logical counter-balancing of points of view, his use of under-statement and abrupt contrast, his sharp individualization of minor characters, his use of humor in tragic situations, his trick of making the drabness of middle-class life dramatic—these are only a few of the many aspects of Ibsen's method which have become the stock-in-trade of the modern craftsman.

In Ibsen the course of dramatic thought which began with Machiavelli, reached completion. But Ibsen himself looked toward the future. Even in the cold mists which shroud the end of *When We Dead Awaken,* he felt life "fermenting and throbbing as fiercely as ever." In the theatre of the twentieth century we shall find superficial polish, intellectual aridity, stale emotions; but we shall also find new trends, new creative forces. The theatre is not unmindful of the tradition to which Ibsen devoted his life—to see reality "free and awake."

PART 2

THE THEATRE TODAY

The eighteen-nineties witnessed the emergence of independent theatre movements in a number of European cities. Antoine's Théâtre Libre in Paris, the Freie Bühne in Berlin, the Independent Theatre in London, the Abbey in Dublin, the Moscow Art Theatre, proclaimed a new faith in the drama's integrity and social function.

These groups described themselves as free or independent, because they were determined to escape from the cheap conventions and tawdry standards of the professional stage: "The movement which includes the reform of the modern theatre and the revival of the drama in five European countries—and more recently in America—found its origin outside the established commercial playhouses." *

The fact that the movement developed outside the commercial domain provides a clue to its origin and character. It received its most potent stimulus from Ibsen; Ghosts *was the opening play at three of the theatres of protest, and it was among the early productions at a fourth. The dramatic revolt did not have deep roots among the people. It reflected the growing social awareness of the more sensitive and perceptive members of the middle class. The regular stage appealed chiefly to a middle-class audience: the well-fed gentry in the more expensive seats and the suburban families and clerks and students in the galleries came to the playhouse for surcease and illusion. Ibsen cut through the web of illusion, and exposed the rotten foundations on which the family life of the bourgeoisie was built.* Ghosts *was bitterly attacked and reviled, but it created an*

---

* Anna Irene Miller, *The Independent Theatre in Europe* (New York, 1931).

intellectual ferment that was given direction by the increasing social tensions of the last decade of the nineteenth century. The emergence of the little theatres coincided with the economic crisis that began in 1890 and the growth of imperialist rivalries among the European powers.

The dramatic revolt achieved its greatest vitality in Ireland and Russia. In these countries, the discontent of the bourgeoisie merged in deep currents of social protest: the group in Dublin became the custodians of a revitalized national culture, reaching maturity in the plays of Synge and O'Casey. In Russia, the Moscow Art Theatre drew strength and inspiration from the resistance to Czarist oppression, asserting a creative realism that exerted a salutary influence on the development of the Soviet theatre and film.

The fears and uncertainties that gripped European intellectuals did not have their full impact on Americans until the outbreak of the first world war. The news of the European holocaust brought the independent theatre movement to America, with the almost simultaneous formation in 1915 of the Provincetown Players, the Neighborhood Playhouse, and the Washington Square Players. The last of these, effecting an adroit combination of art and business, became the Theatre Guild in 1919.

The basic problem that confronts modern man is the efficacy of the conscious will. We have noted that the problem was at the root of Ibsen's thought: in his last years, which were the dying years of the century, Ibsen mourned the death of the will; the creative spirit seemed to dissolve in dreams that "lose the name of action."

As Ibsen wrote his valedictory—"When we dead awaken, what do we really see then? ... We see that we have never lived"—the world stood at the threshold of an era of war and destruction without parallel in history. What could the theatre offer, what could it say of man's will and fate, as the years thundered their warning? Could it do nothing more than report, prosaically, without the hope and passion of true tragedy, that man's will had atrophied, that his capacity for "enterprises of great pith and moment" had turned to brutality and confusion?

Chapter I deals with certain influential trends in modern thought that deny man's ability to exert any rational control over the conditions of his existence. One of the early and widely popularized formulations of the trend is to be found in the pragmatism of William James. The cultural influence of pragmatism is most clearly indicated in the novel. James's "world of pure experience" is the world of fragmentary sensation and irrational impulse that we find in the work of Dos Passos, Farrell, Faulkner, Saroyan, and many other modern writers. In these stories, as Charles Humboldt observes, "the individual makes his appearance on the stage of the novel in full retreat from the demands of reality. . . . One can ultimately reconstruct him from the scattered fragments of his sighs, memories, interests and reactions." *

The contemporary theatre resembles the novel in its acceptance of a "world of pure experience," in which moods and fears replace courage and consistent struggle to achieve rational goals.

Chapter II continues the study of the pattern of modern thought, showing that the dualism of spirit and matter, subjective and objective, has a long history. In the period of expanding capitalism, the conflict between the individual and his environment was dynamic and seemed to hold the possibility of ultimate adjustment. But today the social situation forbids a partial escape or temporary retirement into the sanctuary of the spirit. The negation of the will moves to mystic absolutes—or to cowardly acceptance of life as a via dolorosa *of suffering and despair.*

Having defined the pattern of ideas, we return, in Chapter III, to the specific application of these ideas to the

* "The Novel of Action," in *Mainstream* (New York, Fall, 1947).

technique of playwriting. George Bernard Shaw is selected as the most important transitional figure in the course of dramatic development from Ibsen to Eugene O'Neill. In Shaw, the social conscience seeks meaningful expression. But his characters cannot translate the demands of conscience into action, and the will is exhausted in conversation.

It would give a misleading impression of the complexity of the theatre's twentieth century growth to jump directly from Shaw to O'Neill. Chapter IV endeavors to bring together the main threads of critical thought and technical practice, indicating the close relationship between the dominant social philosophies of the time and the development of dramatic theory.

Chapter V considers O'Neill as the most distinguished, and in a fundamental sense the most typical, dramatist of the contemporary American stage. We are especially concerned with O'Neill's conception of the conscious will, and its effect on the structure and technique of his work. O'Neill's genius, his integrity, his determination to go to the heart of life give him impressive stature. Yet his work is the symbol of a defeat which goes far beyond the playwright's personal problem to the problem of his age. In 1926, a play by John Dos Passos showed death as a garbage man collecting tortured humanity as refuse. Two decades later, O'Neill's portrayal of death as an ice man repeated the adolescent pessimism of the earlier Dos Passos play.

The study of O'Neill enables us to reach certain conclusions regarding the technique of the modern American drama. These conclusions are summarized in Chapter VI. Four plays by different authors, with different themes and backgrounds, are selected for analysis. We find that the underlying modes of thought are similar and thus produce striking similarities in structure and dramatic organization.

CHAPTER I

CONSCIOUS WILL AND
SOCIAL NECESSITY

THE law of tragic conflict, as formulated by Hegel, and developed by Brunetière, lays special emphasis upon the exercise of the will. Brunetière demanded "the spectacle of the will striving toward a goal"; at the same time, the greatest dramatist of the nineteenth century used the conscious will as the basis of his philosophy and technique. In 1894, the year in which Ibsen wrote *John Gabriel Borkman,* Brunetière complained that "the power of will is weakening, relaxing, disintegrating."

An understanding of the rôle of the conscious will in the dramatic process is necessary to an understanding of the trend of the modern theatre. In seeking the precise meaning of the term *conscious will,* we receive very little assistance either from Brunetière or from those who have discussed his theory. It is assumed that we all know what is meant by the *exercise of conscious will,* and that deeper implications of the idea need not concern the student of the drama. Brander Matthews notes that Brunetière "subordinates the idea of struggle to the idea of volition." William Archer touches lightly on the philosophic problem: "The champions of the theory, moreover, place it on a metaphysical basis, finding in the will the essence of human personality, and therefore of the art which shows human personality raised to its highest power. It seems unnecessary, however, to apply to Schopenhauer for an explanation of whatever validity the theory may possess." *

From what we know of Brunetière's philosophic opinions, there can be no doubt that he was influenced by Schopenhauer, and that his conception of the will had metaphysical implications. But there is nothing metaphysical about his statement of the theory—"to set up a goal, and to direct everything toward it, to strive to bring everything into line with it," is what men actually *do* in their daily activity. This is as far as Brunetière goes; indeed, he remarked, in outlining the theory, that he had no desire to "dabble in metaphysics." It would be convenient if we could follow his example. But we have already proved that there is a close

* Archer, *opus cit.*

connection between philosophy and dramatic thought; if we are to get to the root of the dramatic process, we must examine this connection as closely as possible.

If we use the phrase, *exercise of conscious will,* simply as a fancy way of describing the manner in which men habitually carry on their activities, it would be much better not to use it at all. Dramatic and literary criticism are saturated with terms derived from science and philosophy and applied in a vaguely *human* way which devitalizes them. *Exercise of conscious will* has a deceptively scientific ring: are we using it to give a scientific flavor to a loose definition of the drama, or has it a precise meaning which limits and clarifies our knowledge of dramatic laws?

Broadly speaking, philosophers are concerned with how far the will is *free;* psychologists endeavor to determine how far the will is *conscious.* (In both cases, the question of what the will *is,* or whether there is any such thing, must also be faced.) The main task of experimental psychology has been to ascertain how consciousness receives stimuli, and how consciousness produces activity. In recent years, the whole approach to the subject has undergone startling changes. This has affected the theatre; the modern drama lays *less* emphasis on conscious will than the drama of any previous epoch: by this I mean that character is not studied primarily from the point of view of setting up a goal and striving toward it, but from the point of view of emotional drift, subconscious determinants, psychic influences, etc.

This puts the conscious will in a new light. The crux of the matter is the word, *conscious.* It is curious that Brunetière seems to think this word is self-explanatory. To be sure, the idea of will suggests awareness of an aim toward which the exercise of will is directed. But if this is self-evident, why should the idea of consciousness be introduced as a special adjunct of the will? If *conscious* will means anything, it means that there is a distinction between voluntary and involuntary acts, and that dramatic conflict deals with acts which are voluntary. But what *are* voluntary acts? How accurately can they be distinguished? What about acts which spring from subconscious or unrealized desires? What about the Freudian complexes? What about behaviorism? What about conditioned and unconditioned responses?

The modern stage has taken for its special province the actions of people who *don't know what they want.* Hamlet is aware of his own vaccilation; Tartuffe seems to be aware of his own deceit. But the drama today deals very generally with the psychic problems of people who are not aware. In Sidney Howard's *The Silver*

Cord, Mrs. Phelps tries to destroy her sons' lives under the guise of mother love; in Clifford Odets' *Awake and Sing,* Henny is in love with Moe, but she thinks she hates him. Eugene O'Neill deals with psychic motives and influences which spring from the subconscious. One cannot say that these plays exclude conscious will; but the conflict does not seem to be based primarily on striving toward a known and desired end.

Viewed historically, the conceptions of will and consciousness have been closely associated with the general stream of thought as it has already been traced from the Renaissance to the nineteenth century. The philosophers who have contributed most vitally to the discussion of free will and necessity are Spinoza, Hegel, and Schopenhauer. William James points out that Spinoza's pantheism bears a very close relationship to modern conceptions of monism— an emotional acceptance of the substantial *oneness* of the universe. Spinoza regarded all activity, subjective and objective, as a direct manifestation of God's being. Since he was one of the most logical of thinkers, Spinoza carried this belief to its logical conclusion: he made no compromise with the unique consciousness. If God is everything, there can be no will opposed to God. Man is part of nature and the necessity to which he is subject is absolute. "A child believes it desires milk of its own volition, likewise the angry boy believes he desires revenge voluntarily, while the timid man believes he voluntarily desires to flee." There can be no *accident:* "A thing is called accidental merely through lack of inner understanding." Spinoza's statement of determinism is logical and final—unlike later philosophers, Spinoza had no hesitation in accepting his own conclusions.

In Hegel, we find for the first time the idea that free will and necessity are not fixed opposites, but are continually in a state of unstable equilibrium. History shows that man seldom achieves what he wills; even when he thinks he has achieved his aim, the newly established state of equilibrium is temporary, and a new disturbance of equilibrium brings results which are contrary to the original intention. On the other hand, there is no final necessity, because the various and contradictory aims which men pursue cause continuous changes and modifications in their environment.

This conception corresponds fairly obviously to at least the outward facts of experience. But it gives no comfort to the metaphysicians: it denies both the *unique* soul (which implies absolute free will) and *eternal* truth (which implies absolute necessity). We have seen that neither Hegel nor the men of his period were able to dispense with the soul and the hope of its ultimate union with a higher power.

In maintaining that the will is universal and irrational, Schopenhauer formed a link between Spinoza and Bergson. Instead of following Spinoza's single-minded logic, Schopenhauer used the will as a means of denying logic: will is divorced from consciousness; impulse is more dynamic than thought. In Bergson we find this idea developed in the *élan vital*. In Zola, in Nietzsche, in the last plays of Ibsen, and in a large portion of the drama and fiction of the late nineteenth century, we find the literary development of this idea. Instead of religious mysticism, we have a mysticism of sensation, a mysticism with a physiological shape.

It is significant that Schopenhauer's emphasis on emotion as a thing-in-itself led him to the most bitter pessimism: he held that "the will to be, the will to live, is the cause of all struggle, sorrow, and evil in the world.... The life of most men is but a continuous struggle for existence,—a struggle in which they are bound to lose at last.... Death must conquer after all." * He therefore felt that the only way to happiness is inertia, the passive contemplation of the futility of things: "The best way is total negation of the will in an ascetic life." This combination of pessimism and emotionalism is a characteristic feature of modern culture.

At this point we must turn from philosophy to psychology— which is exactly what the main stream of modern thought has done: William James' essay, *Does Consciousness Exist?* was published in 1904. Alfred North Whitehead says with some reason that this essay "marks the end of a period which lasted for about two hundred and fifty years." † James began that famous essay by saying: "I believe that 'consciousness' when once it has evaporated to this estate of pure diaphaneity, is on the point of disappearing altogether. It is the name of a non-entity, and has no right to a place among first principles. Those who still cling to it are clinging to a mere echo, the faint rumor left behind by the disappearing 'soul' upon the air of philosophy." James maintained that there is "no aboriginal stuff or quality of being, contrasted with that of which material objects are made, out of which our thoughts of them are made." ‡ Consciousness, he said, is not an entity, but a *function*.

This is a tremendously vital contribution to psychology. It estab-

---

* Quoted by Walter T. Marvin, in *The History of European Philosophy* (New York, 1917).
† Whitehead, *opus cit.*
‡ William James, *Essays in Radical Empiricism* (New York, 1912).

lishes a new method of psychological study. It seems to make a direct attack upon the romantic idea of the unique soul. But when we examine what James means by *consciousness as a function,* we find that this function without entity is all-inclusive: "Our normal waking consciousness, rational consciousness as we call it, is but one special type of consciousness, whilst all about it, parted from it by the filmiest of screens, there lie potential forms of consciousness entirely different." *

These "potential forms of consciousness" sound suspiciously like Bergson's *élan vital;* having saluted "the disappearing 'soul,'" James created a *function* which is a fluid sort of soul, part of "that distributed and strung along and flowing sort of reality we finite beings swim in." Instead of a dual universe, we have a pluralistic universe: the world, said James, is "a pluralism of which the unity is not fully experienced yet." How can this unity conceivably be experienced? Here the unique soul makes its reappearance. In a "world of pure experience," the *feeling* of uniqueness or of oneness is just as valid and useful as other feelings. In *The Varieties of Religious Experience,* James speaks of the value of the mystic sense of union: "The man identifies his real being with the germinal higher part of himself.... *He becomes conscious that this higher part is conterminous and continuous with a More of the same quality, which is operative in the universe outside of him, and which he can keep in touch with, and in a fashion get on board of and save himself when all his lower being has gone to pieces in the wreck."*

The only thing which holds this "world of pure experience" together is "the will to believe." James is vigorously anti-intellectual: "I found myself compelled to *give up* logic, fairly, squarely irrevocably.... I prefer bluntly to call reality if not irrational, then at least non-rational, in its constitution." † If reality is non-rational, the finite beings who swim in reality have no real need of reason to keep them afloat. They feel, but they can neither plan nor foresee.

Pragmatism is partly responsible for the greatness of William James as a psychologist. This was exactly what was needed at the beginning of the twentieth century to free psychology from previous superstitions. Pragmatism led James to concentrate brilliantly on the immediate sense-data. But it also led him to a curious *mechanical spiritualism* which has affected psychology ever since

* William James, *The Varieties of Religious Experience* (New York, 1928).
† William James, *A Pluralistic Universe* (New York, 1909).

his time. On the mechanical side, James sees that the sense-data are physiological: he says of the body, that "certain local changes and determinations in it pass for spiritual happenings. Its breathing is my 'thinking,' its sensorial adjustments are my 'attention,' its kinesthetic alterations are my 'efforts,' its visceral perturbations are my 'emotions.' " * But pragmatically, what we actually seem to experience is thinking, attention, efforts, emotions. Therefore pragmatic psychology is based on "spiritual happenings" (because this is the way experience *feels*) ; these "spiritual happenings" are *really* "kinesthetic alterations" and "visceral perturbations" which are not directly experienced. The realm of our experience has only a fleeting, temporary contact with causation; and real causation is outside our experience. For pragmatic purposes, causality "is *just what we feel it to be.*" Since James takes this view of causality, he must inevitably take the same view of the human will.

What we feel is a *sensation* of will: "In this actual world of ours, as it is given, a part at least of the activity comes with definite direction; it comes with desire and sense of goal; it comes complicated with resistance which it overcomes or succumbs to; and with efforts which the feeling of resistance so often provokes." † Activity includes "the tendency, the obstacle, the will, the strain, the triumph or the passive giving up."

James speaks of "a belief that *causality* must be exerted in activity, and a wonder as to how causality is made." He gives no answer to this question; whatever this causality might be, it has no connection with free will: "As a matter of plain history, the only 'free will' I have ever thought of defending is the character of novelty in fresh activity-situations." Even if there were a principle of free will, he says, "I never saw, nor do I now see, what the principle could do except rehearse the phenomena beforehand, or why it ever should be invoked." ‡

In modern psychology, we have the absolutely mechanical point of view represented in behaviorism, and the psychic approach represented in psychoanalysis. Although they seem to be irreconcilably opposed, these two schools have important points of resemblance.

The attempt to discover the machinery of emotions and sensations is by no means new. Early in the seventeenth century, Thomas Hobbes defined sensation as "a mode of motion excited in the physiological organism." In the middle of the nineteenth century,

* *Essays in Radical Empiricism.*
† *Ibid.*
‡ *Ibid.*

Wilhelm Wundt held that voluntary actions are the complex or developed form of involuntary acts. The great Russian scientist, I. P. Pavlov, has contributed greatly to the knowledge of conditioned responses. Slowly, by painstaking experimentation on animals, Pavlov is working toward what he describes as "a general system of the phenomena in this new field—in the physiology of the cerebral hemispheres, the organs of the highest nervous activity." Pavlov suggests that "the results of animal experimentation are of such a nature that they may at times help to explain the hidden processes of our own inner world." * Pavlov's method is scientific, seeking to reveal facts without mixing them with beliefs or illusions.

Behaviorism, however, is both pragmatic and narrowly mechanical. Without adequate experimental data along physiological lines, John B. Watson denies both consciousness and instinct, and arbitrarily selects *behavior* as the subject of psychology. What we call instinct, says Watson, is simply "learned behavior." † "What the psychologists have hitherto called thought is in short nothing but talking to ourselves." Our activities consist of stimulus and response. There are internal and external responses. "Personality is the sum of activities that can be discovered by actual observation of behavior over a long enough period to give reliable information."

The trouble with all this is that no observation of human behavior along these lines has ever been undertaken. One cannot draw conclusions in regard to stimulus and response, one cannot decide that thought is "nothing but talking to ourselves," unless these assumptions are proved through experimental study of the physiology of the nervous system. The work accomplished by Pavlov on animal reflexes is merely a tentative beginning. Watson offers us, not a science, but a belief. Knowing that the mind is matter organized in a certain way, he takes a leap in the dark and jumps to the conclusion that mind does not exist. This corresponds to one aspect of pragmatism—the dependence on immediate experience. Although he is dealing with the mechanics of the brain, Watson pays only scant attention to *mechanics,* and is chiefly preoccupied with *habits*—because this is the appearance of our behavior, the way it looks and feels, as we experience it pragmatically.

It would seem evident that the will can have no part in a psychological system which deals only with stimuli and responses. Watson goes a step further than James: he not only abolishes the

* Pavlov, *Conditioned Reflexes* (London, 1927).
† Watson, *Behaviorism* (New York, 1925).

will, but also abolishes responsibility. To be sure, he holds out the hope that we may eventually control behavior by changing the stimuli; but this would have to be done by thought; if thought is an automatic response, it is impossible to change the thought until the stimulus is changed. Thus we find ourselves in the charmed circle of fruitless experience.

Behaviorism is mechanized pragmatism. Psychoanalysis is emotional pragmatism. Here too there is a groundwork of genuine scientific research in a difficult and little explored field. Freud's experiments in psychopathology are epoch-making. But psychoanalysis takes us from rational experiment to a world which bears an interesting resemblance to William James' "world of pure experience." "Consciousness," says Freud, "cannot be the most general characteristic of psychic processes, but merely a special function of them." The essence of psychoanalysis, according to Freud, is "that the course of mental processes is automatically regulated by 'the pleasure principle': that is to say we believe that any given process originates in an unpleasant state of tension and thereupon determines for itself such a path that its ultimate issue coincides with a relaxation of this tension; i.e., with avoidance of pain or production of pleasure." * There is obviously no will in this; tension and the avoidance of pain are *automatic;* they are nothing more nor less than stimulus and response. However, according to the Freudian theory, pleasure and pain not only strike the consciousness from the outer world, but also from within, from the subconscious in which memory-records are accumulated. These memory-traces cover not only the history of the individual, but go back to primitive racial memories, "the savage's dread of incest," ancient taboos and tribal customs. "Faulty psychic actions, dreams and wit are products of the unconscious mental activity..." says A. A. Brill. "The aforementioned psychic formations are therefore nothing but manifestations of the struggle with reality, the constant effort to adjust one's primitive feelings to the demands of civilization." †

This gives us the key to psychoanalysis as a system of thought: man's soul (the subconscious) is no longer a manifestation of the absolute idea, or of the life-force; it is a reservoir into which are poured the feelings and sentiments of himself and his ancestors. This is a "world of pure experience" which is well-nigh infinite; the unique soul, which sought union with the universe, has now succeeded in swallowing a large part of the universe.

* Sigmund Freud, *Beyond the Pleasure Principle,* translated by C. J. M. Hubback (London, 1922).

† In his introduction to Sigmund Freud, *Totem and Taboo,* translation by A. A. Brill (New York, 1931).

The important feature of this conception is its retrospective character. Instinct turns back to the past; not only is the will inoperative, but the primitive feelings must be controlled and adjusted. In *Beyond the Pleasure Principle,* Freud accepts this backward-looking tendency as his main thesis: "An instinct would be a tendency innate in living organic matter impelling it toward reinstatement of an earlier condition. . . . If then all organic instincts are conservative, historically acquired, and are directed toward regression, toward reinstatement of something earlier, we are obliged to place all the results of organic development to the credit of external, disturbing and distracting influences." It is the "repression of instinct upon which what is most valuable in human culture is built."

This is a complete reversal of all previous theories of the relationship between man and his environment. The environment is creative, the man is conservative; the external influences build, the man tears down. The unique soul can reach no further indignity than this; its fight for freedom has turned to a fight for its own dissolution. The subconscious is the last refuge of the unique soul, the ultimate hiding place in which it can still pretend to find some scientific justification.

What has here been said does not constitute a sweeping indictment of the discoveries of psychoanalysis. On the contrary, it seems certain that elements of the psychoanalytic theory of the subconscious are provably true. One may say the same thing, with even greater certainty, of the theory of behaviorism. In both fields, experimental work, in a scientific sense, has been tentative, feeling its way toward clearer knowledge. One must distinguish between the experimental value of these theories and their meaning as *systems of thought.** We are dealing with them here as systems. It is in this form that they enter the general consciousness and affect man's conception of his own will and of the social necessity with which his will is in conflict.

Behaviorism and psychoanalysis offer a specialized and one-sided interpretation of the relationship between man and his environment. In one case, reflexes occupy the whole stage; in the other case, memory-records are placed in a spotlight. But both systems are similar in important respects: (1) they are anti-intellectual; reason might conceivably sort out the reflexes or memory-records (although it is hard to see how this jibes with the fundamentals of

---

* This is true in many fields of modern speculation. For example, one must distinguish between Bertrand Russell as a mathematician and Bertrand Russell as a philosopher.

either scheme), but the *process* is emotional or mechanical, and reason, if it enters into the system at all, enters as a wily but unimpressive servant of emotions or reflexes; (2) both systems place a Chinese wall between man and the totality of his environment; the wall can be scaled or broken through; but meanwhile there can be no satisfactory contact between man and the realities which may lie on the other side of the wall, because his "learned behavior" or his inhibitions and complexes make his will powerless; since "learned behavior" or inhibitions and complexes are obviously conditioned by the total environment, the only way in which anything can *happen* to these elements is by lively inter-action between them and the environment. But the terms of both psychoanalysis and behaviorism prohibit this inter-action. In apparently attempting to create an adjustment with the environment, these systems *prevent* any successful conflict with it. (3) Both systems use what William James called "the principle of pure experience" as "a methodical postulate." Conclusions are based on a certain grouping of observed experiences (dreams or responses to stimuli) and not on any general examination of causation. For example, psychoanalysis examines the mental life of man at a certain period in a certain environment by studying the man's "world of pure experience" at this point; historical or social causation is considered only as it achieves a fleeting contact with this point of experience; a wider system of causation is ruled out because it would introduce factors outside the immediate sense-data. This seems strange in a theory based on the analysis of subconscious traces of personal and racial history. But Freud specifically tells us that these traces are *unhistorical:* "We have found by experience that unconscious mental processes are in themselves 'timeless....' They are not arranged chronologically, time alters nothing in them, nor can the idea of time be applied to them." * The subconscious resembles Bergson's realm of "pure duration."

One point stands out sharply in this discussion: consciousness and will are linked together. To undervalue rational consciousness means to undermine the will. Whatever consciousness may or may not be, it functions as the point of contact between man and his environment. The brain is matter organized in a certain manner. Man is a part of reality, and continually acts and is acted upon by the total reality of which he is a part. It needs no metaphysics to explain this *real* relationship, nor to lend dignity to man's rôle as a conscious entity. Man's success in changing and controlling his

* *Beyond the Pleasure Principle.*

world is sufficient evidence of his capacity. In this sense, such terms as consciousness, or soul, or ego, are both proper and useful.

In conventional psychology, a distinction is often made between three aspects of will: conation, will and volition. Conation is the broadest term, covering the theoretical element from which the will is supposed to originate, such as "the will to live." Will, in the narrower sense, is the combination of intellectual and emotional elements which bring the *desire to act* to the level of consciousness. Volition describes the immediate impulse which initiates bodily activity.

The distinction is not entirely satisfactory; but it may serve to illustrate what is meant by will in the dramatic sense. Conscious will, as exercised in dramatic conflict, is to be distinguished from conation or simple volition. Conation (at least as it is at present understood) is more metaphysical than scientific. The immediate impulse is a matter of the connection between the brain and the nervous system. But the dramatist is concerned with the emotional and mental organization of which the activity is the end-state. This supplies the social and psychological logic which gives the drama meaning. Where the organization of the conscious will is not dramatized, the action is merely *action-at-any-price,* the writhing and twitching and jumping and bowing of dummy figures.

As the link with reality, the conscious will performs a double function: the consciousness receives impressions from reality, and the will reacts to these impressions. Every action contains these two functions: man's consciousness (including both emotion and intellect) forms a picture of reality; his will works in accordance with this picture. Therefore his relationship to reality depends on the accuracy of his conscious impression and the strength of his will. Both these factors are variable, just as there is a continuous variation in the strength and quality of the forces with which the individual is in contact. No one would be so rash as to suggest that men *ever* achieve anything approaching full knowledge of the reality in which they move; the possible web of cause and effect is as wide as the world and as long as history. Every action is a part of this web of cause and effect; the action can have no *separate* meaning outside of reality; its meaning depends on the accuracy of the picture of reality which motivated the action, and on the intensity of the effort exerted.

At this point the playwright's conscious will must also be considered; his emotional and intellectual picture of reality, the judgments and aims which correspond to this picture, the intensity of his will in seeking the realization of these aims, are the determinants in the creative process. The dramatist is no more able to draw a *final* picture of reality than are the characters in his play. The total environment which surrounds the characters is not as wide as the world or as long as history; it is exactly as wide and as long as the playwright's conscious will can make it. Even this is only an approximation of the whole process: the conscious wills of all those who take collective part in the production of a play modify the dramatic content; then the conscious will of the audience comes into the process, further changing the content, applying its own judgment of reality and its own will to accept or reject the whole result.

We cannot undertake to explore this labyrinth of difficulties; we are dealing here with the playwright's task in selecting and developing his material. His material is drawn from the world he lives in. He attempts to present this world in *action*. The play is a series of actions, which the playwright attempts to unite in a single organic action. These actions grow out of the relationship between individuals and their environment—in other words, the relationship between conscious will and social necessity. The playwright's experience in conflict with his own environment determines his way of thinking; his experience and his thought are associated with the group-experience and group-thought of his class and time. Changes in the social structure produce changed conceptions of will and necessity. These are changes in the basic thought-pattern by which men seek to explain and justify their adjustment to their environment. These patterns constitute the playwright's dramatic logic, his means of explaining and justifying the lives of his characters.

CHAPTER II

DUALISM OF MODERN THOUGHT

THE movements of thought discussed in the foregoing chapter are a continuation of the old dualism of mind and matter. So far, we have summed up this dualism in terms of behaviorism and psychoanalysis: one system conceives of human conduct in terms of mechanical necessity; the other system depends on subconscious and psychic determinants. It has been pointed out that both systems are based on similar postulates. But it is also evident that they represent divergent tendencies; many thinkers regard this contradiction as the eternally unsolvable problem of philosophy. The problem appears throughout the course of European thought—but the form in which the issue is presented changes radically with every change in the structure of society. In the middle ages, the dualism of mind and matter was regarded serenely as fixed and irrevocable. The destruction of feudalism destroyed this conception. In the early days of the Renaissance, the expansion of new social and economic forces caused the problem to be temporarily forgotten. In the period of Shakespeare and Bacon, the dualism of body and spirit played very little part either in scientific or philosophic thought. The problem reappears—in its modern dress—in the work of Descartes in the middle of the seventeenth century. Its reappearance coincided with the growth of new class alignments which were to cause serious dislocations in the existing social order. Poets and philosophers have presented this dualism in the guise of a struggle between man and the universe. But the real conflict has been between man's aspirations and the necessities of his environment. The dualism of mind and matter, and the accompanying literary dualism of romanticism and realism, has reflected this conflict.

The modern form of this dualism must therefore be examined, not only in psychological terms, but in its broadest social meaning.

The modes of thought with which we are dealing are those of the urban middle class. This class, more than any other group in modern society, combines reliance on immediate sensation with spiritual aspirations. Commercial and moral standards, although they vary widely for individuals, are low for the group. But money provides leisure-time in which to cultivate esthetic other-worldliness. A double system of ideas is therefore a natural development simply as a matter of convenience. Practical, or pragmatic, thought provides a partial adjustment to the needs of the everyday world, including business and personal morality. Spiritual esthetic thought offers (or seems to offer) a means of escape from the sterility of the environment. These systems of thought are contradictory—but when we examine them, not as logical abstractions, but as expressions of the needs of human beings, we find that *both* systems are necessary in order to live at all under the given conditions, and that their inter-dependence is complete. The trend toward mechanical materialism is continually balanced by the trend toward escape-at-any-price from the very conditions which are the product of narrow materialism. When this attempted escape is thwarted, when freedom of the will cannot be achieved under the specific circum-

stances, an *unreal escape must be invented.* Mysticism, in one of its
many manifestations, provides such a means.

We find the root of twentieth century dualism in William James.
He presents the contradiction in a form which especially corresponds to the mental habits created by the needs and pressures of
modern civilization. James' belief in reality as "created temporarily
day by day" necessarily led him to imagine a deeper reality "not
fully experienced yet." In *The Varieties of Religious Experience,*
he described mystic experience as a sensation of unity: "It is as
if the opposites of the world, whose contradictoriness and conflict
make all our difficulties and troubles, were melted into unity."
Since "contradictoriness and conflict" are aspects of reality, it is
evident that mystic experience transcends reality. Since it solves
"our difficulties and troubles," the sense of unity also conveys a
sense of security, a sense of balance between ourselves and our
environment, which is not offered by empirical experience. This
explains the double movement of modern thought toward a narrower materialism and toward a more remote spiritualism; as men
attempt to adjust themselves *pragmatically* to an increasingly
chaotic environment, they inevitably seek refuge in a mysticism
which is increasingly emotional and fatalistic.

It may be objected that I am here using mysticism in a vague
sense. James warns against employing the term as one "of mere
reproach, to throw at any opinion which we regard as vague and
vast and sentimental, and without a basis in either fact or logic." *

The Baldwin Dictionary of Philosophy and Psychology † gives a
similar warning: "Mysticism is sometimes used, by writers of an
empirical or positivistic bias, as a dislogistic term or opprobrious
epithet." This authority defines mysticism as "those forms of
speculative and religious thought which profess to attain an immediate apprehension of the divine essence, or the ultimate ground of
existence." From the same source, we learn that "thinkers like
Novalis, Carlyle and Emerson, whose philosophic tenets are reached
by vivid insight rather than by 'the labour of the notion,' often
exhibit a mystical tendency." Writing in the twelfth century, Hugo
of St. Victor said: "Logic, mathematics, physics teach some truth,
yet do not reach that truth wherein is the soul's safety, without
which whatever is is vain." ‡

It is precisely in this sense that mysticism may be described as a
dominant trend of modern thought. Mysticism is characterized by

* *Varieties of Religious Experience.*
† New York, 1905.
‡ Quoted in H. O. Taylor, *The Medieval Mind,* v. 2 (London, 1927).

the *immediacy* of apprehension, by the dependence on *vivid insight* rather than on logic, and by the *finality* of the truth so apprehended. Mystical *tendencies* need not be confused with a system of thought based exclusively on "immediate apprehension" of truth—no such system could exist or be imagined, because it would deny the basic laws of thought. Mystical *tendencies* may be found in many periods and in many kinds of speculation. These tendencies must be examined critically in order to determine their living value under specific conditions. Twentieth century mysticism is not to be reproached because it is "vague and vast and sentimental." On the contrary, its apparent vagueness and vastness must be brushed aside in order to understand its social meaning.

Ibsen's genius revealed the social groundwork of modern mysticism. He showed how it originated from earlier religious and philosophic speculations (in *Brand* and *Peer Gynt*), how it is molded by social necessity (in the plays of the middle period), and how it reappears in a new form as an emotional compulsion (in *When We Dead Awaken*). In other words, Ibsen began with metaphysics; then he realized that the conflict between the real and the ideal must be fought in the social arena. Appalled by the gap between man's will and the world he lives in, unable to find a rational solution and unable to find comfort in the doctrines of earlier philosophy or religion, Ibsen was forced to create a solution to meet his need. Since the need grew out of his psychic confusion, the mysticism which he created was the image of his own mental state.

The dominant ideas of the twentieth century show a repetition and acceleration of this process. The instability of the social order makes a successful escape impossible; it is only in periods of comparative calm that men can find genuine satisfaction in the contemplation of eternity. Medieval mysticism reflected the security and wealth of monastic life in the middle ages. Today what is required is not reflection, but immediate emotional relief from an intolerable situation. The denial of reality is not sufficient—*something* must be substituted for reality. The substitution naturally takes the form of wish-fulfillment, a dream world in which emotion is raised to the nth power and achieves its own liberation. But the emotions which fill this dream world are the emotions which constitute the middle-class man's real experience: sexual desire, the feeling of personal and racial superiority, the need for permanent property relationships, the sense of the necessity (and therefore the holiness) of pain and suffering. This is the *truth* which is attained by the "immediate apprehension" of the mystic. "Immediate apprehension" simply means that the emotions are not tested by the logic of reality.

In its extreme form, this process is pathological. Psychic disorders spring from a maladjustment to reality; the maladjustment is accentuated when the patient tries to make his misconception *work* in terms of the real world. The mystic's escape from reality brings him right back to reality in terms of a distorted social philosophy. Historically, this tendency developed throughout the nineteenth century. In the eighteen-eighties, Nietzsche spoke of the world as the dream of "a suffering and tortured God." Nietzsche's view of life as "an immense physiological process" and his emphasis on pure emotion, cover ground with which we are already familiar: "It is true we love life; not because we are wont to live, but because we are wont to love." But Nietzsche went further than this: he attempted to apply the idea of *pure emotion* to the real problems of the society in which he lived; he showed that this meant the destruction of ethics and all standards of value—except *force*. The future would belong to "exceptional men of the most dangerous and attractive qualities." Whatever these qualities might be, they would require neither reason nor self-control: "Considered physiologically, moreover, science rests on the same basis as does the ascetic idea; a certain *impoverishment of life* is the presupposition of the latter as of the former—add, frigidity of the emotions, slackening of the tempo, the substitution of dialectic for instinct. ...Consider the periods in a nation in which the learned man comes into prominence; they are the periods of exhaustion, often of sunset, of decay." * This is the complete reversal of the struggle for learning, the growth of reasoning, which has guided and inspired the development of civilization. Machiavelli's man of guile and force becomes the Nietzschean superman, who is an emotional fool.

Modern mysticism could not go beyond this: it simply remained to elaborate the social implications of the idea in ominously *practical* terms. This has been accomplished by Oswald Spengler whose monumental work, *The Decline of the West,*† purports to show "the forms and movements of the world in their depth and final significance." He correctly describes contemporary middle class society as "Faustian civilization." He echoes the clichés of metaphysics: "The bright imaginative Waking-Being submerges itself in the silent service of Being." He reminds us of Bergson when he

* *The Complete Works of Friedrich Nietzsche,* edited by O. Levy (New York, 1911-24).
† Translation by Charles Francis Atkinson (New York, 1932).

says that "Time triumphs over Space." But the essence of Spengler lies in the way in which he presents the old conflict between the real and the ideal; he describes it as "the conflict between money and blood." This is a new version of the contradiction between pragmatism and emotional mysticism. "Money is overthrown and abolished only by blood. *Life* is alpha and omega, the cosmic onflow in microcosmic form." This, according to Spengler, is "the metaphysic and mysticism which is taking the place of rationalism today." It is a mysticism of blood, of force, of callous fatalism: "Masses are trampled on in the conflicts of conquerors who contend for the power and the spoil of this world, but the survivors fill up the gaps with a primitive fertility and suffer on...." "It is a drama noble in its aimlessness, noble and aimless as the course of the stars." He says that "the very élite of the intellect that is now concerned with the machine comes to be overpowered by a growing sense of its Satanism (it is the step from Roger Bacon to Bernard of Clairvaux)."

Spengler's work is striking because of the extreme brutality with which he states his case. No such brutal (and obviously political) formulation is accepted by the majority of modern thinkers. Yet the direction is the same; the drama of man's fate is aimless—as long as very definite aims are assured by the "primitive fertility" of the masses. "For what are we, my brother?" asks Thomas Wolfe. "We are the phantom flare of grieved desire, the ghostling and phosphoric flickers of immortal time, a brevity of days haunted by the eternity of the earth . . . the strange dark burden of our heart and spirit." *

In Wolfe's novels, the leading characters are exceptional people, whose emotions and sensitivities are above those of the average person. Being haunted by the "brevity of days," they think and act pragmatically, dominated by their immediate impulse. They make no attempt to justify themselves rationally, but explain their conduct in terms of eternity. They follow the "phantom flare of grieved desire" because they live for the moment and have no rational purpose in life. But this is never admitted; neurotic conduct due to specific social conditions is explained as a "strange dark burden." †

* Wolfe, *Look Homeward, Angel* (New York, 1930).
† It must be emphatically pointed out that Wolfe is not here being accused of agreement with Spengler or with the brutalities of fascism. Wolfe's emphasis on "immortal time" and "the eternity of the earth" shows his intense desire to *avoid* social issues, his unwillingness to accept the cruelty and decadence of his environment. But this mode of thought has social origins and social implications which must be faced.

Thus ideas which appear "vague and vast" turn out to serve a very useful purpose—in justifying irrational, brutal or impulsive conduct. The conception of impulse as the basis of human behavior is elaborately intellectualized in the philosophy of Pareto. He analyzes sociology as the "undulations in the various elements constituting social phenomena." The pattern of these undulations is based on *sentiments* which take the form of six residues. Pareto's residues are preconceived categories similar to the categorical imperatives devised by Kant. But Kant's imperatives were forms of "pure reason." Pareto's residues turn out to be forms of *non-logical conduct*. In short they are nothing more nor less than an attempt to systematize the "phantom flare of grieved desire" in the modern man's "brevity of days." This brings Pareto, by a circuitous route, to the point reached by Spengler: the sum-total of non-logical conduct is a drama of blood and force, sublime, timeless—and financed by international bankers.

Patterns of ideas are designed to meet definite needs. The laws of thought are so rational that the mind is forced to invent a double pattern in order to conceal and justify maladjustments which would otherwise appear crudely illogical. The most amazing thing about the human mind is that it simply cannot tolerate lack of logic.* Whenever a method of reasoning is inadequate, men devise what they call a primary law to cover the inconsistency. Today a large section of society depends on a pragmatic method of thinking.† This forces the mind to turn to mysticism for a more complete explanation. As soon as the mystic explanation is accepted, the laws of thought drive the mind to apply this explanation, to make it *work*—which brings us right back to pragmatism again.

The special character of pragmatism as a method is its *acceptance of the immediate perception of contradictions as absolute*. The dialectic method follows the movement of contradictions in their change and growth. The movement is continuous, and results from the inter-action of causes and effects which can be traced and understood. To the pragmatist, no system of causation can have

---

* This is not as amazing as it seems, because our conception of logic is based on the way we think.

† In *The History of European Philosophy,* Walter T. Marvin says of pragmatism that "it has made its presence felt in almost every department of western intellectual life. In art and literature it makes its presence evident in a rebellion against any fixed principles such as formalism and in the general artistic doctrine that the individual should throw off the authority of tradition and frankly put in the place of this authority his own likes and dislikes.... Other places in which pragmatism is nowadays especially noticeable are in moral theory, jurisprudence, politics and educational theory."

more than an immediate perceptual value. From this point of view, Pareto is right in saying that "non-logical conduct" must be accepted at its face value; if we ignore a wider system of causation, our perception of conduct reveals only its non-logical aspect; it *looks* non-logical. But we also perceive that "non-logical conduct" *always* has two sides to it; it always represents a contradiction. Since the pragmatist fails to investigate the prior conditions which led to this contradiction, or the changes which will bring about a solution, he must accept the contradiction at its face value; he must make himself as comfortable as he can on the horns of a perpetual dilemma.

The pragmatic tendency in contemporary liberalism is responsible for the charge that liberals vacillate and straddle on all issues. This is by no means true of the great tradition of liberalism, nor is it altogether true of its more distinguished modern representatives. John Dewey may be cited as an example of the influence of pragmatic methods on modern liberalism. Dewey's principle of sensationalism (a philosophy based on the validity of the immediate sense-data) descends directly from the radical empiricism of William James. Dewey courageously faces what he calls "the confusion of a civilization divided against itself." He analyzes this conflict in terms of the immediate balance of forces; he tries to construct a solution out of the elements as he perceives them at a given moment of time; he discusses "the problem of constructing a new individuality consonant with the objective conditions under which we live." *

But he can reach no conclusion, because he sees individuality as consisting of certain elements, and objective conditions as consisting of certain other elements—which constitute our immediate experience. But the relationship of these elements *changes* before Dewey can finish writing a book about them. He then proceeds to analyze them *again* in terms of immediate experience. But his method gives him no adequate means of analyzing the wider system of causation which governs these changes.

The acceptance of opposites as final can be found in all departments of contemporary thought. The ideas which have here been traced in their philosophic form, can also be traced in scientific thought, or in business and advertising, or on the editorial pages of American newspapers. For example, yellow journalism echoes the philosophy of Spengler; liberal journalism adheres strictly to pragmatism. Editorials are devoted to formulating accepted contradictions: on the one hand, democracy is a perfect form of government;

* John Dewey, *Individualism Old and New* (New York, 1930).

on the other hand, democracy cannot be expected to work; on the one hand, war is destructive; on the other hand, war is inevitable; on the one hand, all men are created free and equal; on the other hand, certain races are manifestly inferior; on the one hand, money destroys spiritual values; on the other hand, money-success is the only reliable test of character.

The dual system of ideas, of which pragmatism and mysticism constitute as it were the positive and negative poles, expresses a basic contradiction which includes a complex system of major and minor contradictions throughout the social structure. The modern man uses this double system in order to achieve a partial adjustment to the world in which he lives; his pragmatic experience continually upsets his adjustment; but mysticism gives him the illusion of permanence.

It would be absurd to assume that the modern man simply accepts this mode of thought in a fixed form. Thought is dynamic; it expresses the continually changing balance of forces between man and his environment.

This is important in considering the theatre. The drama reflects the pattern of contemporary ideas. But the playwright does not conform to this pattern automatically; the pattern is fluid, and the playwright's use of it is fluid. To conceive of the acceptance of ideas as static or final would be an example of the *absolutism* we have been discussing. A system of ideas is not a "strange dark burden," which men carry against their will. The playwright, like any other human being, fights to adjust himself to his environment. His scheme of thought is the weapon he uses in this fight. He cannot change his ideas as he would change a suit of clothes. But insofar as his ideas prove unsatisfactory in the course of the struggle, he endeavors to modify or discard them. The conflict is also within himself; he is trying to find ideas that work, to achieve a more realistic adjustment to the world he lives in.

A play embodies this process. If the playwright's scheme of thought is irrational, it distorts the laws of the drama, and inhibits his will to create meaningful action. He must either conceal this weakness by obscurantism or pretense; or he must overcome it by the slow labor of thought. This conflict proceeds in the mind of the playwright and in the world of the theatre. It leads to a new balance of forces, and a new creative direction.

CHAPTER III

GEORGE BERNARD SHAW

SHAW is both the most eminent critic and the most important English-speaking dramatist of the period following Ibsen. A number of his finest plays (including *Candida, The Devil's Disciple* and *Mrs. Warren's Profession*) were written in the last decade of the nineteenth century. His most serious critical work also belongs to this period. It is often said that Shaw uses the drama merely as "a means to an end." The *end* to which Shaw dedicates the drama is the end to which Ibsen proclaimed his allegiance, and to which all great drama has invariably been dedicated—to see reality "free and awake." Shaw understood the greatness of Ibsen's plays; he saw that dramatic conflict is necessarily social conflict; he realized that if the theatre of his time were to live and grow, it must deal uncompromisingly with the struggle between man's conscious will and his environment. This was contrary to the popular and critical opinion of the nineties, which associated art with esthetic moods and emotions. Writing in 1902, Shaw explained that he was aiming at deeper and more fundamental emotional values: "The reintroduction of problem, with its remorseless logic and iron framework of fact, inevitably produces at first an overwhelming impression of coldness and inhuman rationalism. But this will soon pass away... it will be seen that only in the problem play is there any real drama, because drama is no mere setting up of the camera to nature: it is the presentation in parable of the conflict between Man's will and his environment." * It follows that it is the "resistance of fact and law to human feeling which creates drama. It is the *deux ex machina* who, by suspending that resistance, makes the fall of the curtain an immediate necessity, since drama ends exactly where resistance ends." †

These passages illustrate Shaw's clarity as a critic. Considered in the light of his later life and work, his statement of the law of conflict becomes a tragic admission of his own failure. The myth has been widely circulated that Shaw's preoccupation with social problems has caused him to neglect the problems of dramatic art.

* Shaw, Apology from *Mrs. Warren's Profession* (New York, 1905).
† *Ibid.*

This is consoling to neo-romantic critics; but if we examine Shaw's plays, we find that his difficulty lies in his inability to achieve a rational social philosophy. Unable to face or solve the contradictions in his own mind, he has been unable to dramatize the "remorseless logic and iron framework of fact" which he described as the conditions of dramatic conflict.

In his earliest, and most creative, period, the influence of Ibsen is most pronounced. Shaw depicted the maladjustments of English middle-class life in terms which were borrowed from Ibsen's social dramas. But even in these plays, Shaw's limitations are manifest. Ibsen's remorseless logic shows the enormous power and complexity of the social structure. Shaw's tendency is to look for an easy solution, to suggest that *immediate* reforms can be accomplished through man's inherent honesty. In *Widowers' Houses* (1892) and in *Mrs. Warren's Profession* (1898), we are shown the social forces which underlie specific evils; but we are reassured by the suggestion that these forces can be controlled as soon as men are aroused to combat the evil. The problem is not so much the release of the will, as simply the exercise of the will in the proper direction.

Shaw's position is clearly shown in his critical discussions of Ibsen. "The Quintessence of Ibsenism," according to Shaw, is "that conduct must justify itself by its effect upon happiness and not by conformity to any rule or ideal; and since happiness consists in the fulfillment of the will, which is constantly growing, and cannot be fulfilled today under the conditions which secured it yesterday, he [Ibsen] claims afresh the old Protestant right of private judgment in questions of conduct." * This passage throws more light on Shaw's social philosophy than on Ibsen's. Ibsen exposed the falseness of the ideals which ruled the society of his age; he looked desperately for a solution which would permit the fulfillment of the will. But only in Ibsen's earliest plays (particularly in *Brand*) do we find the idea that the exercise of the will is its own justification. In *Peer Gynt,* he went forward to the realization that *to be oneself* is insufficient. Shaw's statement that "happiness consists in the fulfillment of the will" reminds us of Peer Gynt's fevered search for happiness in terms of his own ego; it suggests that the will is not a means, but an end. The root of Shaw's philosophy lies in the assertion of "the old Protestant right of private judgment in questions of conduct." The retrospective phrasing of this thought, "the old Protestant right," is by no means accidental; the essence of the thought is retrospective; it goes back to the early days of the bourgeois revolution, when the attainment of middle class freedom was

* Shaw, *The Quintessence of Ibsenism* (New York, 1913).

regarded as an *absolute* conquest, guaranteeing the fulfillment of the unique soul. Shaw demands, as Shelley demanded at the beginning of the nineteenth century, that this guarantee be made good without further delay. He assumes that all that is needed is the destruction of false moral values. Ibsen also began with this assumption; but he went beyond it. Shaw accepts the assumption as final.

This means the substitution of *good will* for *free will*. In Ibsen's social plays, the essence of the tragedy lies in the fact that good will is not enough, and that "private judgment in questions of conduct" cannot function apart from social determinants. Hedda Gabler and Rebecca West are women of strong will, who endeavor as best they can to exercise their "right of private judgment." This leads them to inevitable disaster. Shaw says of Hedda that "she is a pure sceptic, a typical nineteenth century figure," and that she "has no ideals at all." How can this be reconciled with Hedda's neurotic hatred of the "ludicrous and mean," her seeking after "spontaneous beauty," her idealizing "a deed of deliberate courage"? Shaw misunderstands Hedda because he is chiefly impressed by her *personality,* and only slightly concerned with the "iron framework of fact" which surrounds her. He regards her (at least potentially, insofar as she wishes to be so) as a *free woman;* he mistakes what Ibsen himself called "want of an object in life" for "pure scepticism." This indicates an important difference in dramatic method: *want of an object in life* is a dramatic problem which goes to the root of the relationship between man and his environment; the conscious will must face the real world, must find an object in life or die. On the other hand, *pure scepticism* is an abstract quality of the mind which has no meaning until it is brought into conflict with the real world.

In *Candida* (1895), Shaw gives us the first of his remarkable portraits of women. Ibsen's women (as Ibsen tells us in his notes) are "prevented from following their inclinations, deprived of their inheritance, embittered in temper." Candida, like all of Shaw's women, is genuinely *free;* not only is she able to follow her inclinations, but she has an instinctive rightness of judgment and emotion which transcends the problems with which she is faced. Forced to choose between two men, Candida turns to her husband because he is the man who needs her most. It is significant that her choice, although it may be assumed that it is not based on "conformity to any rule or ideal," is strictly conventional.

In *Man and Superman* (1903), Ann Whitefield is instinctively right in her biological urge toward the man of her choice; there is no insurmountable obstacle between her will and the world in which she lives. She is not, like Hilda in *The Master Builder,* a "bird of prey," because she is free to conquer circumstance and fulfill her desires within the framework of society.

The vitality of Shaw's early work springs from his early insistence on the theatre's historic function—the presentation of man's struggle against the "fact and law" of his environment. His emphasis on social factors did not lead him to ignore dramatic laws. On the contrary, his critical writings in the eighteen-nineties are rich in detailed technical observation. He held no brief for an abstract theatre; he knew that dramatic conflict must be emotional and alive. In 1898, he wrote of the crude melodramas of the period: "All the same these bushwhacking melodramatists have imagination, appetite and heat of blood; and these qualities, suddenly asserting themselves in our exhausted theatre, produce the effect of a stiff tumbler of punch after the fiftieth watering of a pot of tea."* This observation may be applied with equal truth to the dexterous and rowdy dramas of the nineteen-twenties and nineteen-thirties—*Broadway, Chicago, The Front Page,* and many others

Shaw said of James M. Barrie: "He has apparently no eye for human character; but he has a keen sense of human qualities. . . . He cheerfully assumes, as the public wishes him to assume, that one endearing quality implies all endearing qualities, and one repulsive quality all repulsive qualities." † This exposes the core of Barrie's weakness as a dramatist. It also exposes the basic weakness in the technique of characterization in the modern theatre. Character can only be understood in terms of an active relationship between the individual and the world in which he moves. As soon as character is *detached* from environment, it becomes a quality or group of qualities which are assumed to imply a series of other qualities.

This is the essential defect in Shaw's work. He understood Barrie's weakness, but he failed to realize that he himself dealt only in *qualities.*

Shaw's treatment of character is based on his belief that the best qualities of human nature must, in the long run, triumph over the environment. In philosophic parlance, the best qualities of human nature correspond to Kant's ethical imperatives, or Hegel's pre-existent categories. We have observed that both these philosophers derived their conception of absolute truth from contemporary social and ethical values. Shaw's best qualities of human nature, which he accepts as *imperative,* are the qualities of the English upper

* Shaw, *Dramatic Opinions and Essays* (New York, 1907).
† *Ibid.*

middle class. He endeavors to show us these qualities in conflict with the environment. But these qualities have been made by the environment; a change in the environment can only be accomplished in conjunction with a change in accepted standards of conduct. Here Shaw faces a dilemma: the essential faith of the English upper middle class is faith in its ability to control the environment, and in the ultimate perfectibility of human nature in terms of upper middle-class values. Shaw shares this faith; at the same time, he sees that the environment is hopelessly decadent. Shaw has repeatedly attacked the stupidities of the English social system; he has bitingly satirized the men and women who tolerate these stupidities. But his most revolutionary demand has been that these people be *true to themselves,* that they return to the ethical imperatives which they themselves have invented.

This accounts for the progressive weakening of dramatic conflict in Shaw's later plays, for the increasing lack of "imagination, appetite and heat of blood." Shaw assumes that his characters can change their environment if their conscious will is sufficiently aroused. He therefore shows them planning and discussing, exchanging opinions about possible changes which *do not happen.* This makes a technique of pure talk—and the consequent negation of action—inevitable. There is not a grain of truth in the idea that the long conversations in Shaw's plays are designed to elucidate complex ideas. What the talk actually accomplishes is to blur very simple ideas. The characters talk at random in order to conceal their inability to talk or act with definite purpose. The juxtaposition of contradictory ideas in Shaw's essays and plays springs from the contradiction in his own position: he attacks conventions and demands that people be more conventional; he attacks ideals and indulges in flights of pure idealism.

In Shaw's later plays, the gap between character and reality widens. The more diffuse technique shows an increasing lack of precision in social thought. At the same time, the author becomes less interested in dramatic theory: the prefaces become increasingly concerned with generalities. The customary dualism of the modern mind becomes more pronounced. Non-logical conduct is emphasized; the characters move according to whim; immediate impulse takes the place of logic. At the same time, a final solution which transcends logic is suggested; the individual will must be merged in the will-to-live, the life-force.

Peer Gynt asked the riddle of the sphinx, and was answered by an insane German professor. In *Caesar and Cleopatra* (1899), Shaw's Caesar faces the sphinx and discovers the inscrutable guile of the child-woman, Cleopatra. The first period of Shaw's development ends with *Man and Superman* in 1903. His portraits of women show his changing point of view. Candida's grave simplicity is intuitive; but it also has intellectual scope. Cleopatra is depicted as a child; but Shaw's treatment of the character as having universal feminine qualities of childishness and guile is extremely significant. In *Man and Superman,* we see the results of this tendency: Ann Whitefield *thinks* physiologically; her pursuit of Jack Tanner is dictated by her "blood and nerves."

In *Man and Superman,* we also find the beginning of technical disintegration. Shaw says that the third act of this play, "however fantastic its legendary framework may appear, is a careful attempt to write a new book of Genesis for the Bible of the Evolutionists." * He also describes this act as a discussion of "the merits of the heavenly and hellish states, and the future of the world. The discussion lasts more than an hour, as the parties, with eternity before them, are in no hurry." † Shaw's interest in the soul leads him to neglect the fundamentals of dramatic conflict.

Getting Married (1908) is a pragmatic discussion of the *practical* problems of marriage; the technique is pure conversation, without a trace of conflict between the individuals and their environment. The plays of the next few years are more conventional in form: *Fanny's First Play, Androcles and the Lion, Pygmalion, Great Catherine.* The social content is also more conventional, and indicates acceptance of the contemporary world of experience. The dramatic conflict is definite, but lacks depth.

The world war shattered Shaw's illusions, forced him to reconsider the principles of human conduct which he had taken for granted, and brought him new inspiration. In *Heartbreak House* (1919) he confesses the bankruptcy of his world, and faces the "iron framework of fact" with bitter courage. But in *Back to Methuselah* (1921), he regresses to an exact repetition of the point of view presented in *Man and Superman* (in the discursive discussion of the philosophy of evolution in the third act) eighteen years earlier: the whole course of history is covered, not as a conflict between man's will and the iron necessities of his environment, but as a gradual unfolding of the human spirit; evolution is an instinctive process; the life-force moves toward a future in which action and accomplishment are no longer necessary; the future, as Shaw sees it, fulfills Schopenhauer's idea of happiness

---

* Quoted by Clark in *A Study of the Modern Drama.*
† From a printed note written by Shaw, and quoted by Clark, *ibid.*

in the denial of the will, the passive contemplation of truth and beauty.*

In *Saint Joan* (1923), the child-woman is guileless, divinely inspired, defying the pragmatic reasoning of men who trust worldly experience. In this play, the "old Protestant right of private judgment" is completely identified with the purity and depth of Joan's instinct. Like Peer Gynt, Shaw returns to the woman-symbol.

From this point, the break with reality is inevitably accelerated, and the technical disintegration is also rapid. In *Too True To Be Good* and *The Simpleton of the Unexpected Isles,* the structure of the action is entirely pragmatic; the characters follow their immediate whim, and any system of causation outside the momentary impulse is disregarded. In these plays, Shaw for the first time accepts mysticism, not in the form of an evolutionary life-force, but as an immediate irrational means of salvation. The negation of the will is no longer a matter of future development; man's will is inoperative here and now; man cannot be saved by his own efforts, because his efforts are aimless; even his instinct is no longer to be trusted; he is literally a simpleton lost in the unexpected isles; his only hope lies in childlike faith, in an emotional denial of reality.

The extreme confusion of Shaw's final plays is by no means characteristic of the modern theatre. But the basic tendencies which have led to this confusion are in evidence in the great majority of contemporary plays. Many of the lessons which the modern playwright has learned from Ibsen have been learned by way of Shaw. The modern dramatist admires Ibsen's concentrated technique, his social analysis, his method of characterization. But he transforms these elements much as Shaw transformed them: the technique is diluted, events are watered down so as to include a variety of generalized comment; at the same time, abstract social awareness is substituted for specific social meaning. In place of the presentation of social cause and effect *in action,* we have a running commentary covering social and ethical observations which are detached from the events. In place of Ibsen's analysis of the conscious will, we have the presentation of character in terms of qualities.

* Shaw's conception of social change is based on the theories of Fabian socialism, which he was largely instrumental in elaborating. The immediate source of these theories may be found in the opinions of Samuel Butler and Sidney Webb, which in turn are derived to a considerable extent from Lamarck.

CHAPTER IV

CRITICAL AND TECHNICAL TRENDS

BEFORE proceeding to a more detailed study of the theatre today, it may be well to review the trend of dramatic theory. The critical thought of the twentieth century has produced nothing which can compare with the vigor and precision of Shaw's critical writing in the eighteen-nineties. In general, modern criticism is based on the theory that the drama deals with *qualities* of character. These qualities have final value, and are the only moving force in dramatic conflict. The environment is the arena in which these qualities are displayed. A man is a bundle of characteristics, which are intuitive rather than rational. The playwright's skill is also intuitive, and gives him an intuitive insight into the qualities of human nature. Man's deepest and most spiritual values are those which most completely transcend the environment. The great artist shows us men with timeless emotions.

This theory appears in various forms throughout contemporary critical thought—and has also been formulated in technical methods and systems. Its most creative development is to be found in the method of Constantin Stanislavski. V. Zakhava, Director of the Vakhtangov Theatre in Moscow, says that "Stanislavski's theatre concentrated all its intention and art upon the inner life of the acting characters, upon the psychologic, subjective, side of their behavior. The soul of the hero, his inner world, his psyche, his 'inner experiences,' his 'spiritual essence'—this is what absorbed the actors and directors of that theatre. ... The actor in such a theatre is indifferent as to the occasions which employ his feeling." * The aim of art is "an idealistic individualism which views the human psyche as an insulated and self-sufficient value; a 'universally human' morality as the ethical base out of which character is built." Zakhava points to the influence of Bergson's philosophy upon Stanislavski's theory.

Yet Stanislavski was tremendously successful in developing a "natural-psychological" technique of acting. This was due to the fact that his actual system of discovering the "spiritual essence"

* V. Zakhava, "Stanislavski's Method" in *New Theatre* (August, 1935).

of his characters was neither intuitive nor spiritual; but was based on scientific experimentation and analysis. In practice he found that "to work upon a role is to seek for a relation." This means that the actor must find the point of contact between his subjective feeling and objective experience. Stanislavski also discovered, says Zakhava, "that feeling will not come of itself; that the more an actor orders or pleads with himself to cry, the less chance there is of his doing it. 'Feeling has to be enticed.' The decoy for feeling, he finds, is thought, and the trap is action. 'Don't wait for feeling, act at once.' Feeling will come in the process of action, in the clashes with the environment. If you ask for something, and you do it with an awareness that you really need it, and then you are turned down—the feeling of offense and vexation will come to you spontaneously. Don't worry about feeling—forget it." *

Thus feeling becomes a meaningless abstraction, and the core of Stanislavski's work becomes the analysis of the conscious will. The *relation* which determines the feeling is the actor's consciousness of reality; the actor must *think,* and what he thinks about is his environment; his awareness of a need causes action, which is an act of will.

Stanislavski developed his method largely in conjunction with the production of the plays of Anton Chekhov at the Moscow·Art Theatre. Chekhov's plays served as the laboratory in which Stanislavski's experiments were carried out. Chekhov dramatized the tragic futility and aimlessness of the Russian intelligentsia at the turn of the century; the action of his plays seems aimless; the neurotic intensity of Ibsen's characters seems to be replaced by neurotic inertia. But the power of Chekhov lies in the precision with which he exposes the social roots of this inertia. One may say that Chekhov's interest is rather in character than in society as a whole. But his interest in character is an interest in *how it works.* No playwright has ever been less concerned with qualities of character, or less respectful of the "spiritual essence" of personality. In dealing with diseased wills, he probes to the core of the disease; just as a physician may study the inefficient operation of the patient's physical organs, Chekhov studies the inefficient operation of the will. Just as the physician must find the causes of physical maladjustment, Chekhov seeks out the social causes of psychic maladjustment.

For this reason, the conversation in Chekhov's plays is never discursive in the manner of Shaw. Shaw's characters discuss the social system; Chekhov's characters *are* the social system. Like

* *Ibid.*

Shaw's people, they are almost incapable of action. But the playwright enters their conscious will and shows us the causes, the experiences and pressures, which determine their inactivity. The past lives of the characters are presented in detail. We are shown the exact degree to which they are conscious of their problem, and the direction in which the sick will seeks a solution. In *The Cherry Orchard,* Ephikhedof says: "I am a man of cultivation; I have studied various remarkable books, but I cannot fathom the direction of my preferences; do I want to live or do I want to shoot myself, so to speak. But in order to be ready for all contingencies, I always carry a revolver in my pocket. Here it is."

All the characters in *The Cherry Orchard* are shown attempting to express their will. The drama lies in the inadequacy of their acts in relation to the rigidity of the environment. Madame Ranevsky counts the money in her purse: "I had a lot of money yesterday, but there's hardly any left now. Poor Barbara tries to save money by feeding us all on milk soup; the old people in the kitchen get nothing but peas, and yet I go on squandering aimlessly... (*dropping her purse and scattering gold coins; vexed*). There, I've dropped it all!" When the tramp enters slightly drunk, she hastily gives him the remaining money. It is evident that Chekhov has made Madame Ranevsky's aimlessness objective, and has exposed the exact degree of will and consciousness of which she is capable.

Chekhov resembles Proust in his ability to objectivize moods and sensibilities in terms of social meaning. Both writers show that *exceptional* sensibilities and emotions do not transcend the environment, but are directly caused by the environment and are the product of *exceptional* maladjustments.

Chekhov provided Stanislavski with perfect material for psychological study; the creative interpretation of Chekhov's characters could not proceed along subjective or idealistic lines. The author's indication of social determinants is so precise that it offers a broad field for the analysis of *relations* of character and events. Stanislavski had the painstaking honesty of the great artist. Carefully testing and comparing the data obtained in the work of production, he succeeded in formulating many of the elements of a definitive acting technique. But each step in this process brought him farther away from the esthetic subjectivism which had been his starting point. Unable to solve this contradiction, Stanislavski was unable to reach an integrated conception of the theory and practice of his art. The split between theory and practice, between the esthetic aim and the practical result, tended to widen. This is evident in the modern use of the "natural-psychological" method. The practical aspects of the method become increasingly narrow and unimaginative; the interpretation of character becomes a matter of accumulating factual details; these details tend to become illustrative rather than dynamic; since the accumulation of minor data fails to reveal the "spiritual essence" of character, it is assumed that the inner life of the character transcends the sum of its activities and must be realized by esthetic intuition.

The methods of Chekhov and of Stanislavski, both in writing and in production, were valid only for a limited range of social relationships. Chekhov's technique expressed the life of a section of the Russian middle class; his detailed analysis revealed the possibilities of action, the furtive and incomplete actions, of people whose existence had become largely negative. Today the American and English drama deals with a vastly different environment, a world of complex emotionalism and febrile contradictions. When the modern playwright approaches this material in terms of minor incidents and nuances, the result is to obscure rather than illuminate the meaning of the action. This is especially true when the minor incidents are used simply to pile up qualities of character, which are unrelated to the total environment. (*Craig's Wife* by George Kelly, illustrates this tendency.) A world of unimportant detail can be as unreal as a world of vast and foggy aspirations.

The main movement of twentieth century dramatic thought follows a middle course between the naturalism of Chekhov and the abstract treatment of character which we find in Shaw. Both in his plays and his critical writings, John Galsworthy represents this conservative middle course. Galsworthy declares emphatically that the portrayal of character is the sole aim of dramatic art: "The dramatist who hangs his characters to his plot, instead of hanging his plot to his characters, is guilty of cardinal sin." * Galsworthy's emphasis on character is similar to Shaw's; it springs from his belief in the permanence and final value of the standards of character which are accepted in his own class and time. But the technical structure of Galsworthy's plays is solid and economical; this is due to the solidity and economy of Galsworthy's own opinions; he is serenely unaware of the contradictions exposed by Ibsen and others. The actions of his characters are direct, because the author sees no difficulties which obstruct or paralyze the will.

The majority of critical opinion regards Galsworthy's plays as remarkable examples of unprejudiced observation. Clayton Hamil-

* Galsworthy, *The Inn of Tranquillity* (New York, 1912).

ton speaks of his "Olympian impartiality of mind in considering a social thesis—that God-like lack of special sympathy in regard to his characters." * This simply means that Galsworthy gives honest expression to the prejudices of his own class; it happens that his critics share these prejudices, and are eager to agree that "Olympian impartiality" is on the side of their own social point of view.

Barrett H. Clark praises *Strife* for its impartiality: "Throughout the first scene of the second act, the characters are laid bare with admirable clear-sightedness and detachment of vision. If the poor are in a bad condition, it is to a certain extent the fault of their pride and dogged tenacity." † Galsworthy's thesis in *Strife* is that industrial conflict can and must be solved by the good will and sportsmanship of the parties concerned; both sides are at fault in failing to exercise these qualities. The strike has resulted in futile waste, which has no social cause beyond the stubbornness of individuals. This is made clear in the final lines:

> HARNESS: A woman dead, and the two best men broken!
> TENCH (*Staring at him, suddenly excited*): D'you know, Sir —those terms, they're the *very same* we drew up together, you and I, and put to both sides before the fight began? All this— and—and what for?
> HARNESS (*in a slow grim voice*): That's where the fun comes in!

In *Loyalties,* Galsworthy consistently applauds the rightness and delicacy of the aristocratic loyalties which operate against the Jew, De Levis. De Levis is falsely accused of theft and ostracised; but in the final act, when the real thief has been discovered, the settlement with De Levis is treated merely as a legal matter, while the last and most emotional scene in the play is between the thief, Dancy, and his wife, Isabel, showing the decency of his motives and the intensity of his suffering. De Levis is simply eliminated, while Dancy commits suicide rather than face dishonor.

Faced with the storm and stress of the modern period, Galsworthy turns back to the settled system of property relations which marked the Victorian era. The definiteness, the technical austerity of his plays, springs from the depth of his conservatism. The action is concentrated; there are no loose ends and no unsolved problems. There is careful avoidance of colorful details or of emotional excesses. William Archer says of Galsworthy that

---

* *Opus cit.*
† Clark, *A Study of the Modern Drama.*

"even the most innocent tricks of emphasis are to him snares of the evil one." *

Galsworthy's work is the most mature example of the major tendency in dramatic theory and practice during the first two decades of the twentieth century: the more conventional drama depended on retrospective values and a restrained technique. But since dramatic conflict has a social origin and social meaning, it has become increasingly difficult to project this conflict in terms which no longer correspond to contemporary realities. The attempt to create new dramatic values has led to a series of disturbances and experiments. Most of these have lacked clarity, and have attempted to change the theatre by a sort of "palace revolution"— to dictate new policies by decree, rather than in response to popular needs and demands.

Expressionism is a blanket term which covers a variety of experimental movements. In a technical sense, expressionism is defined by Barrett H. Clark as follows: "It is not enough to record what seems to be the actual words and acts of A; his thoughts, his subconscious soul, and his acts are *summarily* presented by means of a symbolic speech or act—aided by scenery or lighting." † This indicates the essentially neo-romantic character of expressionism. The general tendency of the experiments of recent years has been retrospective; in a loose sense, one may speak of all these experiments as containing elements of expressionism, because all have characteristics derived from early nineteenth century romanticism: moral freedom, social justice, emotional release, are not seen as problems involving an adjustment to the environment, but as visions of the unique soul. In the more subjective expressionist plays, symbols take the place of action—the twentieth century soul is emotional, witless, neurotic and introspective.

But expressionism also contains progressive elements—a passionate assertion of will, a defiant attempt to find more genuine ethical values and to rebel against an oppressive code of social laws. The expressionist has frequently re-discovered the real world, and shown us flashes of a new joy and honesty in the drama. The technique of expressionism reflects the confusion of a rebellion without a defined objective. In most cases, the construction is loose, based on pragmatic reasoning, substituting non-logical conduct for progressive action, symbolized moods taking the place of rational acts. But here the expressionist finds himself at a difficult crossroads: having cut loose from the safe limitations of the draw-

---

* *Opus cit.*
† *A Study of the Modern Drama.*

ing room play (which represents an accepted form of pragmatic reasoning), he finds he must throw away even the *pretense* of logic—or else fight his way to a logic which covers the wider range of character and incident to which he has committed himself. In the former case, the treatment of the expressionistic symbols becomes psychopathically personal or foolishly vast (as in *Him,* by E. E. Cummings, or *Beyond* by Walter Hasenclever). The latter course leads to a new analysis of the expressionistic symbol; the symbol can no longer be vague, it must prove itself in terms of actuality; it must summarize the real relationship between the individual and understandable social forces.

O'Neill's adoption of a free technique was the result of a rebellion against his environment, which led him to mysticism— which in turn brought him back to a ponderous but conventional technique. Other writers (notably, Ernst Toller and Berthold Brecht in Germany) have developed the method of expressionism in the direction of increased social awareness.

A similar rebellion of a mixed character and with ill-defined objectives, has taken place in the scenic structure of the stage. Adolphe Appia and Edward Gordon Craig are chiefly responsible for the birth of a genuine art of stage design. This has not only changed the appearance of the stage, but has wrought a corresponding change in the life and movement of the drama. The actor moving in the crudely painted settings of the nineteenth century was necessarily influenced by his background; the setting constitutes the immediate environment of the persons on the stage; as characters, their consciousness and will are conditioned by this environment. In creating a world of light and shadow, of solid masses and integrated structural forms, Appia and Craig have given the actor a new personality. But their attempt to *release* the actor is unsuccessful, because the freedom which they demand is an esthetic freedom which has no dramatic meaning. The actor's new personality is the unique soul, softly lighted and projected against a background of beautiful abstractions. Craig regards *art* as a categorical imperative; the artist is, at least potentially, the *whole man* capable of transcending his environment by the uniqueness of his gifts.

Craig's esthetic confusion has made his career both tragic and impressive. His integrity has led him to fight consistently for a living theatre. His estheticism is akin to Stanislavski's; but he lacks Stanislavski's scientific open-mindedness. He has been unable to understand the forces which prevent the fulfillment of his purpose, and which operate both in himself and his environment. His designs remain sombre and abstract, avoiding what Freytag called "the social perversions of real life." Craig's approach has never been metaphysical; he has been aware that the drama must deal with physical action; he has therefore tried to achieve an esthetic reality; he has tried to *objectivize* beauty as an independent phenomena. Since this task is impossible, it has led him to regard beauty as an emotional experience. He wrote in 1911: "The Beautiful and the Terrible. Which is which will never be put into words." * One might suppose that Craig would take the next step—acceptance of "the Beautiful and the Terrible" as mystic substitutes for action. But his intense and practical love of the theatre has prevented his acceptance of a mystic escape. In 1935, we find him undaunted in his fight for "the only true and healthy theatre," which he still conceives unrealistically as "the theatre where nature dictates and interprets life through the genuine and noble artist." His dreams remain unrealized, but he can look at Russia and see that there the fulfillment of these dreams is being attempted. "The Russian Theatre," he says, "seems to be years in advance of all other theatres. It is the one theatre that does not sulk or put out its tongue at art or progress." †

Many of Craig's ideas of design have been adopted by the modern theatre. Since these ideas do not go to the root of the dramatic problem, they have not brought truth and health to the ailing theatre. But they have enriched the stage, and have indicated the possibilities which are as yet untouched. American scenic designers devote vast technical facility and imagination to the service of retrospective romanticism and stuffy illusion. When these talents are turned to genuinely creative tasks, to the presentation of the world of men and things in all its beauty and power, the theatre will live again.

While workers in the theatre have made chaotic attempts at experimentation and reform, dramatic theory has remained peculiarly aloof, accepting the dramatic *status quo* as inevitable, and expressing neither fears nor hopes in regard to the development of the art. Modern criticism is largely pragmatic—which means that it is largely uncritical. The pragmatic approach precludes either historical or contemporary comparison. The critic may have a scholarly awareness of the traditions of the stage, but he cannot consider the possibilities of the modern drama in the light of these traditions. He is concerned with what *is*. He notes the sensations

* Edward Gordon Craig, *On the Art of the Modern Theatre* (Boston, 1911).
† *New York Times*, February 3, 1935.

produced by a work of art; as long as he remains pragmatic, he cannot be expected to form a judgment either of craftsmanship or of ethical purpose. These are matters which, as the critic often observes, can be settled only by *time*. The critic apparently means *finite* time, and not the "pure duration" of which Bergson spoke. If art can really be rationally understood within finite time, one would suppose that the best way to understand it would be by historical study of its development. But we discover that the critic's conception of history is also pragmatic: time tests the permanence of the impression produced by a work of art; this is simply *an extension of the first impression,* forming a stream of impressions which show that the work retains its appeal. This is a pragmatic proof of value; but the real value, according to the accepted view of modern criticism, is timeless; it exists only in a world of "pure duration." This is, obviously, outside the sphere of the critic's speculations.

Many of the more thoughtful contemporary critics endeavor to create a system of esthetic values by a frank return to the ideals of the past century. Joseph Wood Krutch and Stark Young express opinions which are comparable with those expressed by Schlegel and Coleridge a century ago. Like the earlier critics their approach is untechnical; they are sympathetic toward art which expresses a social point of view, but they believe it is the function of the artist to uncover the eternal aspirations which underlie the specific social content.

In these writers we observe the trend toward a denial of reality in a liberal and restrained form, combined with many elements of culture and liberalism which are still valid. But the emphasis on timeless values and the confused hatred of the machine age lead many modern thinkers to a more extreme position. John Masefield believes that "tragedy at its best is a vision of the heart of life," by which "a multitude can be brought to the passionate knowledge of things exalted and eternal." * This is an echo of Maeterlinck's "striving of the soul toward its own beauty and truth." † But Masefield adds a new factor—the idea of violence: "The heart of life can only be laid bare in the agony and exaltation of dreadful acts. The vision of agony, of spiritual contest, pushed beyond the limits of dying personality, is exalting and cleansing." ‡ Ludwig Lewisohn's belief in emotion as a final value leads him in the same direction. He complains that "Modern

---

* Masefield's note in *The Tragedy of Nan* (New York, 1909).
† *Opus cit.*
‡ *Opus cit.*

tragedy does not deal with wrong and just vengeance, which are both, if conceived absolutely, pure fictions of our deep-rooted desire for superiority and violence." *

Spenglerian mysticism takes a more practical form in the dramatic opinions of George Jean Nathan. Nathan regards art as an emotional experience which only the privileged few are able to enjoy. He derides the taste of the mob; he discusses the present-day theatre with brutal cynicism. The essence of art, he believes, is irrational: "All fine art, as a matter of fact, not only insults the intelligence, it deliberately spits in the eye of intelligence.... Nothing is so corruptive of drama as hard logic." † Nathan's cynicism melts to sentimentality when he talks of the beauty of true art: "Great drama is the rainbow born when the sun of reflection and understanding smiles anew upon an intelligence and emotion which that drama has respectively shot with gleams of brilliant lightning and drenched with the rain of brilliant tears. Great drama, like great men and great women, is always just a little sad." ‡

We turn with relief from this world of sentiment and unreason, to the saner atmosphere of technical discussion. Contemporary studies of the drama are sharply divided between esthetic criticism of a general nature and works which deal with the problems of craftsmanship. This division is unsatisfactory: general criticism becomes a collection of random impressions or metaphysical opinions; at the same time, technical analysis becomes narrow, divorced from general culture.

Modern studies of technique make no attempt to develop a broad theoretical groundwork or historical perspective. George Pierce Baker begins his *Dramatic Technique* with the statement that "It does not deal with theories of what the drama, present or future, might or should be. It aims to show what successful drama has been in different countries, at different periods, as written by men of highly individual gifts." In the course of his work, Baker makes no distinction between these periods; the ultimate truth of art lies in the "highly individual gifts" which defy analysis. The only test of drama, according to Baker, is pragmatic —the ability to arouse "responsive emotion." As far as deeper values are concerned, he tells us that "the permanent value of a play, however, rests on its characterizations." §

* Lewisohn, *The Drama and the Stage* (New York, 1922).
† Nathan, *House of Satan* (New York, 1926).
‡ Nathan, *The Critic and the Drama* (New York, 1922).
§ Baker, *Dramatic Technique* (New York, 1919).

124   *Theory and Technique of Playwriting*

Brander Matthews says: "The rules laid down tentatively or arbitrarily by the theorists of the theatre are but groping efforts to grasp the undying principles which we can seize only unsatisfactorily, which exist in the passions and sympathies of the human race." * If this is true, one can reasonably demand that the theorist at least attempt to analyze the rules of the drama in terms of human passions and sympathies. Matthews makes no such effort, because he accepts these principles as fixed and requiring no discussion. He is more concerned with the history of the theatre than with modern playwriting. His point of view is more retrospective than pragmatic; he resembles Freytag, both in the definiteness of his technical opinions, and in his feeling that beauty is associated with ethical purpose and nobility of soul. In dealing with the history of the drama, his only reference to social forces is the occasional mention of shocking disorders or loose morals.

William Archer is emphatic in his denial of basic values in art: "The only really valid definition of the 'dramatic' is: any representation of imaginary personages which is capable of interesting an average audience in a theatre.... Any further attempt to limit the content of the term 'dramatic' is simply the expression of an opinion that such-and-such form of representation will not be found to interest an audience; and this opinion may always be rebutted by experiment. In all that I have said, then, as to the dramatic and the non-dramatic, I must be taken as meaning: 'Such and such forms and methods have been found to please and will probably please again. They are, so to speak, safer and easier than other forms and methods.'" † This, as always in pragmatic reasoning, involves the acceptance of an immediate contradiction as absolute. In our experience, we know that a third-rate moving picture may reach a wider average audience (if one can admit that there is such a thing as an average audience) and receive a more enthusiastic response, than a play of Chekhov's. The methods used in creating the motion picture are undoubtedly "safer and easier" than those used by Chekhov. There is no strictly experimental way of judging between the two works of art; in order to make a distinction between them, one must "limit the content of the word 'dramatic.'"

The technical approach of these writers is rhetorical rather than functional. The play is not treated as a creative process which must be investigated, but as an exercise in composition concerning which certain tentative rules of grammar and syntax may be sug-

* Matthews, *The Principles of Playmaking* (New York, 1919).
† *Opus cit.*

gested. Baker treats "number and length of acts," "arrangement for clearness, emphasis, movement," much as these subjects are treated in text books on composition. Archer's treatment of "the routine of composition," "dramatis personæ," " 'curiosity' and 'interest,' " is very similar.

Realizing that these rhetorical formulations lack precision, theorists have occasionally attempted to build *practical* systems of playwriting with the aid of rigid mechanical rules. An Italian writer, Georges Polti, has decided with aggressive finality to limit the drama to "thirty-six dramatic situations." The theory is said to have been originated by Carlo Gozzi in the eighteenth century. Polti bases his contention on "the discovery that there are in life but thirty-six emotions." * The most interesting thing about the theory is the reference to *emotions* as if they were identical with *situations:* instead of attempting to classify types of action, Polti offers us a crude catalogue of types of "non-logical conduct." The emotions which he mentions are so vague and contradictory that he might as well have decided on only six emotions, or upon thirty-six thousand. Among the thirty-six brands which he selects are the following: (number 18) "involuntary crimes of love"; (number 20) "self-sacrificing for an ideal"; (number 21) "self-sacrificing for kindred"; (number 22) "all sacrificed for passion." †

A far more significant attempt to study play-architecture as an engineering problem, has been made by W. T. Price, whose work has been amplified and clarified by his pupil, Arthur Edwin Krows. The latter's book, *Playwriting For Profit,* ‡ is one of the ablest modern works on dramatic technique. This is due to the fact that the author's approach, within narrow limits, is thoroughly logical. But it is a dry logic, based on preconceived rules; it is simply an elaboration of what Archer calls "the routine of composition."

Krows feels that the theory on which his book is based is an all-important contribution to the craft of playmaking. He gives Price full credit for the theory, describing him as "one of the greatest dramatic theorists who ever lived." When one turns to Price's work, one finds it difficult to understand this enthusiastic estimate. His books, *The Technique of the Drama,* and *The Analysis of Play Construction and Dramatic Principles,* are honest, long, careful, and singularly pedestrian. He maintains that a play is a *proposition:* "Proposition is the touchstone of structure . . . it is the

---

* Georges Polti, *The Thirty-Six Dramatic Situations,* translated by Lucile Ray (Franklin, Ohio, 1924).
† *Ibid.*
‡ New York, 1928.

only way to obtain Unity." Price describes a proposition as "a statement in terms to be demonstrated. You have its counterpart in any proposition in Euclid. Q. E. D.... the proposition is the least common denominator of the action." It is, he says again, "a brief logical statement or syllogism of that which has to be demonstrated by the complete action of the play." *

Krows' treatment of this idea is basically the same—but it is much less stilted. "Proposition is the microcosm of a play; and it is therefore possible to work out from it the required elements." He regards "the required elements" as the three *clauses* into which a proposition is divided: conditions of the action, causes of the action, and result of the action. His study of the law of conflict is extremely instructive; he especially emphasizes the way in which the conflict begins, because "whichever side was the first aggressor would sacrifice sympathy." The nature of the "precipitating act" must therefore be carefully considered.

This exposes the weakness of the method: as soon as Krows raises the question of sympathy, he confronts problems which are outside the scope of his theory. One is faced with the necessity of examining standards of conduct, variations in these standards, and the movement of social forces by which these standards are determined. Without such an examination, the suggestion that we investigate the "precipitating act" is merely a phrase. Krows offers no satisfactory definition of the beginning, development or end, of a dramatic conflict. His conception of the three required elements is confused: there is no clear distinction between the conditions of the action and the causes of the action. In analyzing *Romeo and Juliet,* he describes the conditions of the action as follows: Romeo and Juliet, whose families are in deadly strife, meet and fall in love. The cause of the action is their marriage. The result of the action is a problem; will their marriage turn out happily and reunite their families? It is evident here that all three of the elements of the proposition are muddled: the *cause* of the action is the *result* of the conditions; the *result* is a question, and throws no light on the movement of events by which this question is solved.

In general, the Euclidean *proposition* is valid as far as it goes. It bears at least a superficial resemblance to the framework of thesis, antithesis and synthesis which underlies the dialectic process. But the essence of the dialectic method is the study of the movement of contradictions. The Euclidean proposition is static, and

* W. T. Price, *The Analysis of Play Construction and Dramatic Principles* (New York, 1908).

therefore does not touch the livingness of the play. To attempt to solve the life of a play in terms of proposition is like attempting to solve the life of a man by saying that he is an atheist and beats his wife. This information may be of value; but its value depends on a variety of conditions and results. In order to understand the simplest human action, we must understand the system of social causation in which it is placed.

In emphasizing the logic of construction, Price and Krows perform a useful service. But they fail because they assume that the playwright's mind is *empty of content,* that he has no prejudices or aims—and that the material with which he deals is also empty of content, unrelated to time or place. They accept the contemporary theatre at its face value and offer advice in regard to contemporary problems; but since the modern playwright's logic is not Euclidean, and since his technique is based entirely on his prejudices and sentiments, their theory turns out to be extremely abstract, and only distantly related to the practical work of the dramatist.

This brings us back to the truth proclaimed by Shaw in the first years of the twentieth century: now, as then, the stale theatre of irrational sentiment and nostalgic repetition can only be saved by "the reintroduction of problem, with its remorseless logic and iron framework of fact." Critical and technical thought has been uncreative during the twentieth century, because it has ignored the traditional function of dramatic art. In the nineteen-thirties, increased social tension has increased the confused and erratic trends in the middle-class theatre. At the same time, the drama has been stirred by the rise of a new social consciousness, a determination to deal with the living world of conflict and change.

To many critics, this seems like a destructive movement; to the jugglers of riddles and dealers in platitudes, the world of illusion is more precious than the world of reality. Clinging to the romantic idea of the unique artist, they ignore the nineteenth century origins of this idea, and maintain that it has been the *eternal* function of art to transcend reality.

It is natural that the critic should cling to this idea—because it is his means of maintaining his adjustment to his environment. An art which creates conflict out of the lives and passions of living men does much more than invade the privacy of soul which the critic cherishes: it also upsets his relationship to his environment, and forces a revaluation of the social beliefs on which that relationship is based.

In *What is Art?*, Leo Tolstoy wrote: "We think the feelings of people of our day and class are very important and varied; but in reality all the feelings of people of our class amount to but three very insignificant and simple feelings—the feeling of pride, the feeling of sexuality, and the feeling of weariness of life." Tolstoy pointed to "the impoverishment of subject-matter" which has resulted. Art, "having only a small circle of people in view, lost its beauty of form and became affected and obscure.... Becoming ever poorer in subject-matter and more and more unintelligible in form, the art of the upper classes, in its latest productions, has even lost all the characteristics of art, and has been replaced by imitations of art." *

In *Individualism Old and New,* John Dewey endeavors to analyze the relationship between the modern man and his environment. I think the analysis is unsatisfactory, due to the limitations of the author's method, and his lack of historical perspective. But the final paragraphs of this book contain a richly suggestive statement of the problem—which applies directly to the modern theatre: " 'The connection of events,' and 'the society of your contemporaries' as formed of moving and multiple associations, are the only means by which the possibilities of individuality can be realized.

"Psychiatrists have shown how many disruptions and dissipations of the individual are due to his withdrawal from reality into a merely inner world. There are, however, many subtle forms of retreat, some of which are erected into systems of philosophy and are glorified in current literature. 'It is in vain,' said Emerson, 'that we look for genius to reiterate its miracles in the old arts; it is its instinct to find beauty and holiness in new and necessary facts, in the field and roadside, in the shop and mill.' To gain an integrated individuality, each of us needs to cultivate his own garden. But there is no fence about this garden: it is no sharply marked-off enclosure. Our garden is the world, in the angle at which it touches our own manner of being." †

---

* London, 1930.
† I have omitted the final sentence of Dewey's book, and have therefore been guilty of changing his meaning. The final sentence, which follows what I have quoted, indicates his pragmatic acceptance of the immediate present, and the accompanying denial of a system of causation which can be known and guided: "By accepting the corporate and industrial world in which we live, and by thus fulfilling the precondition for interaction with it, we, who are also parts of the moving present, create ourselves as we create an unknown future."

CHAPTER V

EUGENE O'NEILL

EUGENE O'NEILL'S career is of special significance, both because of the abundant vigor and poetic richness of his earlier dramas, and because of the confusion which devitalizes his later work. In a sense, O'Neill's case is not typical, because his preoccupation with the subconscious and with the destiny of the soul seems to be of a special kind and intensity. But this also accounts for the special importance of his work: he reveals the ideas which affect the modern theatre in their most intense form.

Shaw's social thought is based primarily on the liberalism of the days prior to 1914. O'Neill's philosophy reflects the period which followed the world war. This has caused him to ignore, to a remarkable extent, the role of conscious will in dramatic conflict. This is of great interest from a technical point of view. O'Neill has made a consistent and impassioned attempt to dramatize subconscious emotions. He frequently uses the terminology of psychoanalysis, and this terminology is often employed in discussions of his work.

But psychoanalysis as a method of psychological investigation has no bearing on O'Neill's plays. His interest in character is metaphysical rather than psychological. He attempts a complete escape from reality; he tries to sever contact with the world by setting up an inner kingdom which is emotionally and spiritually independent.

If we enter O'Neill's inner world and examine it critically, we find ourselves on very familiar ground. O'Neill's philosophy is a repetition of past ideas. In this, he follows the line suggested by Freud, the line of regression, a flight to the past. There is no co-ordinated system in O'Neill's thought; but it is not difficult to trace the origin of his ideas and to establish their general trend. His plays bear a definite resemblance to the plays of Ibsen's final period. The conception of emotion as an ultimate force is repeatedly stressed. But there is a difference: in the last and most mystical of Ibsen's plays, *When We Dead Awaken,* he shows us man and woman facing the universe with unbroken courage; their will has become impersonal and universal; but the man and woman are still together and still determined to join their will to the universal will; to climb "right up to the summit of the tower that shines in the sunrise."

O'Neill's mysticism goes beyond this. There is no drama of O'Neill's in which an intense love relationship between man and woman is presented as creative or satisfying. The deepest emotional drive in his plays is always based on the father-daughter, mother-son relationship. His use of the Freudian formula serves to negate any conscious struggle on the part of his characters. Their passion is necessarily evil, because it is incestuous; yet it is unavoidable, because it is the condition upon which they are born. His characters are emotional but sterile. In Ibsen's *When We Dead Awaken,* Rubek and Irene face the dual universe with courage and consciousness. O'Neill's later plays contain no character who possesses either of these qualities.

While Ibsen presents emotion as a means of salvation, O'Neill can find no salvation outside of religion. At the close of *Days Without End,* John kills his disbelieving self: "Life laughs with God's love again." In other plays, emotion is shown as destructive (as in *Mourning Becomes Electra*), or as a mad struggle against the power of the machine (as in *Dynamo*).

This gives us a somewhat confused picture of O'Neill's confusion. But we can clarify these tendencies accurately in terms of general philosophy: we begin with psychoanalysis, which supplies us with the Oedipus Complex (and its variations) and the subconscious. O'Neill has no use for these in their modern semi-scientific forms, so he goes back to earlier modes of thought. The Oedipus Complex becomes the universal physiological impulse, which originates in Schopenhauer, and is the basis of Zola's "blood and nerves" materialism. The subconscious becomes the *soul* of early nineteenth century romanticism. This is a repetition of the earlier dualism: the "blood and nerves" fight the spiritual ego, just as God and the Devil fought for the soul of Faust. Goethe saw this conflict clearly according to the thought of his time: Goethe accepted dualism, he accepted Hegel's *absolute idea* as a satisfactory solution of man's relationship to the universe. But O'Neill cannot accept this—because acceptance would mean acknowledging both sides of the dualism. O'Neill insists on escaping from the corporeal side altogether. So again he goes back to earlier forms of thought, and again he finds his allegiance divided. In its extreme form, his mysticism is as final as that of Hildegard of Bingen or Hugo of St. Victor in the twelfth century, or of St. Theresa in the six-teenth. But this brings the author no relief, because it is based on a way of life and a pattern of thought which the modern man can neither understand nor assimilate. So he doubles back to the middle of the seventeenth century and combines personal mysticism with Spinoza's pantheism which is impersonal and deterministic. This is as far as O'Neill's thought can go, and his nearest approach to a rational philosophy is to be found in passages which suggest Spinoza's conception of God as one substance inter-penetrating life and nature: "Our lives are merely strange dark interludes in the electrical display of God the Father!" * But O'Neill cannot remain faithful to this idea, because it would mean accepting the material world. The passage just quoted illustrates the difficulty. Our lives are "dark interludes"; "the electrical display" is outside our lives. So O'Neill adopts a partial pantheism (which is a contradiction in terms), a universality from which the universe as we know it objectively is excluded. This leads him back to Schopenhauer, whose emotional pessimism he adopts in its most extreme form.

The special character of this circle of ideas is the consistent dualism of pragmatism and mysticism. In terms of action, this means the combination of non-logical conduct with the attempt to explain this conduct in terms of the most sublime vagaries about time, space and eternity. The cult of the sublime in modern literature and drama is invariably accompanied by the denial of standards of rational or responsible behavior; this is so inevitable that it almost takes the form of a mathematical equation: the emphasis on eternal beauty and truth is in exact proportion to the need to justify conduct which may properly be called sub-human because of its aimlessness, brutality or cowardice.

The behavior of O'Neill's characters is irresponsible, because they have no conscious will. Spinoza denied free will, because he believed in reason and causation as absolute. O'Neill is anti-intellectual, so that in abolishing will and consciousness he finds himself in a vacuum. Medieval mystics believed in the will, and also to some extent in consciousness, as a means of attaining knowledge of God. The wave of anti-intellectualism, from Schopenhauer to William James, began by denying consciousness, but accepting will in the form of intuition or emotional drive. This was the position taken in Nietzsche's prose poems or in Ibsen's last plays. Pragmatism admitted the idea of will (the will to believe, and the feeling of will as an aspect of immediate experience), but the

---

* From the final act of *Strange Interlude*. Note that this closely parallels Thomas Wolfe's "phantom flare of grieved desire, the ghostling and phosphoric flickers of immortal time," quoted in a previous chapter.

function of the will was so limited as to be almost inoperative.

O'Neill clings to the will to believe; but his system of thought leaves no room for either will or belief. In his plays, the life-force is no part of life; even emotion is negative, working in man's own heart to accomplish his destruction. O'Neill, and many of his contemporaries, conceive of fate in a manner which has no parallel in any previous period of world literature or drama. In all previous epochs, man has been depicted exerting his will against objective forces. The modern fate is both in man and outside him; it paralyzes his mind; his consciousness and his will and his emotions are his worst enemies. It has often been said that "whom the Gods would destroy, they first make mad." This is not a denial of the will, it is an assertion that man's will is his only weapon against the hostility of his environment. The Gods cannot overcome him until he is *made mad;* he is able to fight until some power outside himself destroys his mind and purpose. But the modern fate presupposes madness as man's natural state. It is not a curse which descends upon him and weakens him at a decisive moment of struggle (a sudden breaking down of the will under pressure which is common in human experience); it is a precondition, which makes the struggle useless, because even the *desire* to struggle is aimless.

If O'Neill's plays conformed literally to these ideas, they would not be plays at all. But his work possesses the power and drive of a fine mind and a burning sincerity. The author's creative consciousness and will are in conflict with the sterile thinking which destroys both art and life. This inner struggle is evident in his repeated efforts to dramatize the subconscious. This has led to his interest in the problem of dual personality; he tries to use the physical man as a means of showing us the subconscious man in whom he is chiefly interested. In three plays, he has invented devices for this purpose. In *The Great God Brown* masks are used; in *Strange Interlude* the asides are ostensibly used for the same purpose. In *Days Without End,* the split between the two selves is complete, and two actors play the two parts of the same man.

The most interesting of these, as far as the conscious will is concerned, is *The Great God Brown.* In the other two plays, the asides and the split personality are merely ways of showing what the characters *think* and *want*—which are aspects of the conscious will. In *The Great God Brown,* O'Neill has seriously set himself the task of building a play in which *the conscious will plays no part at all.* The play deserves careful study, because it is the only instance in dramatic history of a sustained attempt along these lines by a competent craftsman. O'Neill's statement of his purpose reminds us of Maeterlinck's desire to present the "intangible and unceasing striving of the soul toward its own beauty and truth." O'Neill says that he wishes to show the "background pattern of conflicting tides in the soul of Man." This pattern is "mystically within and behind" the characters. "It is Mystery— the mystery any one man or woman can feel but not understand as the meaning of any event—or accident—in any life on earth." *

Feeling is accepted as the fundamental principle of drama. The "conflicting tides" can have nothing to do with either conscious purpose or logic. Environment is discarded as a factor, because the mystery applies to "any event—or accident—in any life on earth." Evidently the use of masks is intended by the author to show us what is "mystically within and behind" the characters. But this brings us to the first difficulty: the masks do not, and cannot, show us anything of the sort. When a character's mask is off, we see his real self, the conscious desires which he is concealing from other persons—but we cannot see anything else, because neither the character nor the audience can attain consciousness of anything else. O'Neill seems to realize this difficulty, and he is determined to overcome it. He chooses the only means by which it might conceivably be overcome; he goes beyond dual personality and shows us that the "background pattern of conflicting tides" is not individual, but really universal. In a word, the soul has only a partial individuality: it follows that the masks, and the personalities behind the masks, are to some extent interchangeable.

Here we face another difficulty: making character interchangeable does not change the character: we are still concerned with conscious motives and aims—to shift them from one person to another may confuse us, but it cannot introduce a new element. In *The Great God Brown*, Dion Anthony represents two personalities. Both of these personalities are abstract: one side is the pagan acceptance of life; the other is the "life-denying spirit of Christianity." Brown also represents two personalities. As the play proceeds all four of these personalities are scrambled. Dion dies in Act III, Brown steals his mask, and decides to appear to Margaret, Dion's wife, as the real Dion: "Gradually Margaret will love what is beneath—me! Little by little I'll teach her to know me, and then I'll finally reveal myself to her, and confess that I stole your place out of love for her." Then he kisses the mask of Dion: "I

* Prefatory note to Eugene O'Neill's *The Great God Brown* (New York, 1926).

love you because she loves you! My kisses on your lips are for her!" (It is to be noted that, at this point, a fifth personality, that of Margaret, is scrambled with the other four). But this is not all. Brown, masquerading as Dion, pretends that he (as Dion) killed Brown (the real Dion). So the police come and kill Brown thinking he is Dion.

The play proves that men without will and environment are not men. As far as the plot has any meaning at all, it is based on relationships which are factual and even obviously melodramatic. It takes no dual, or plural, personality to explain that Brown loves Dion's wife and wants to take his place. There is no mystery in a situation in which a man is killed because he is mistaken for another man. There is no *additional* meaning, no "background pattern" which conforms to the author's intention; the disorganized expressions of purpose which slip from the characters almost in spite of themselves, are all that distinguish them from lumps of clay. This is evident in the lines quoted: Brown talks about what he, as a person, will *do* in relation to other people.

The Great God Brown has genuine poetic power; it presents O'Neill's confused philosophy with fervor and honesty. The play is undramatic because the philosophy is undramatic. The poetry, as such, has nothing to do with the characters. Like their personalities, the poetry is interchangeable. The play has beauty because, in spite of its confusion, it represents the author's consciousness and will. But it lacks clarity or dramatic truth, because the author's conscious will is concentrated on a refusal of reality.

O'Neill's mode of thought, which is manifested in its most extreme form in *The Great God Brown,* determines the technical arrangement of all his plays. His denial of reality is a denial of logic. This makes unified dramatic development impossible. In the plays following *The Great God Brown,* O'Neill does not persist in his effort to depict only the "conflicting tides in the soul of man"; he tries desperately to find some means by which he can *apply* his philosophy to the living world.

Strange Interlude is the most important work of O'Neill's later period. Although there are mystic overtones in this play, the plot-structure is rational, and the characters are modern men and women whose problems grow out of definite conflict within a definite environment.

I have already suggested that Nina Leeds is a replica of Hedda Gabler. It may be objected that Nina is more unconventional, less inhibited, more modern, than Ibsen's heroine. To be sure, there is a superficial difference, because the conduct in each case is conditioned by the conventions of the period. But in their attitude toward these conventions, the two women are remarkably similar. Both are free of moral scruples; but both are dominated by fear of conventional opinion, and are never guilty of defying conventions. Hedda sends a man to his death and burns his manuscript without a qualm of conscience; but she is terrified at the idea of a scandal. Nina has no conscience in pursuing her emotional needs; but she never has the courage to speak the truth. Both women have unusually dull husbands; both regard love as a right with which nothing can interfere; both have father complexes; both are driven by a neurotic craving for excitement; both have what O'Neill calls "a ruthless self-confidence"; both have a strong desire for comfort and luxury, which motivates their acceptance of conventionality; at the same time, both are super-idealists, hating everything which is "ludicrous and mean."

Hedda fights to find an outlet for her will. Unable to accomplish this within the restrictions of her environment, she dies rather than submit. Nina never faces her problem in this definite form. Like Shaw's Candida, she is able to achieve a sufficiently satisfactory adjustment within her environment. But Candida expressed her will through a free choice. Nina lives in an emotional trance; she never chooses or refuses; her "ruthless self-confidence" does not involve any choice of conduct; it is her way of justifying her pursuit of emotional excitement, which leads her to accept every sensation which is offered. In Act II, Nina confesses "giving my cool clean body to men with hot hands and greedy eyes which they called love." Throughout the play, her actions involve no independent decisions; she lives for the moment, and follows any suggestion which makes a momentary impression.

The story of *Strange Interlude*, expressed in its simplest terms, is the story of a married woman who has a child by a man who is not her husband. The plot is a very common one in the modern theatre. Two plays which offer an interesting basis of comparison are Philip Barry's *Tomorrow and Tomorrow* and Paul Hervieu's *The Nippers*. The three dramas present an identical point of view. In the final scene of Hervieu's play (produced in 1895), the woman says to her husband: "We are only two miserable beings, and misery knows none but equals." At the close of *Strange Interlude,* Nina says, "—to die in peace! I'm so contentedly weary of life." And Marsden answers, speaking of himself as "dear old Charlie...who, passed beyond desire, has all the luck at last."

Hervieu treats the situation as a social problem which must be faced. The characters are forced to adjust themselves to their environment under conditions which they themselves have created. The play develops to a climax in which the wife confesses the truth.

In both *Tomorrow and Tomorrow* and *Strange Interlude,* one looks in vain for any point of open conflict. In both plays, the husband never discovers the truth. In *Tomorrow and Tomorrow,* Gail Redman calls Dr. Hay, her child's father, to save the boy's life by an operation. The cure is successful, there is a short love scene, and the doctor leaves her forever. The tension created by the mother's fear for her child's life has no logical connection with the problem of the child's parentage. Dr. Hay speaks of Gail's special emotional quality: "She wears her rue with a difference." He also says that "emotion is the only real thing in our lives; it is the person; it is the soul." Since emotion is an end-in-itself, it need not express itself through the conscious will, and need have no connection with the actual activity of the character. Gail has neither the honesty to tell her husband the truth, nor the courage to join her lover, but her emotion is her soul, and is therefore its own justification.

In *Strange Interlude,* we find the same conception of emotion. Marsden speaks of "dark intermingling currents that become the one stream of desire." Nina speaks of her three men: "I feel their desires converge in me!...to form one complete beautiful male desire which I absorb." It is evident that Nina, like Barry's heroine, "wears her rue with a difference."

This emphasis on pure emotion is a pragmatic application of the mysticism of *The Great God Brown* to the conduct of living people. This accounts for the plot-structure of *Strange Interlude.* The action rests chiefly on a sense of foreboding, the threat of horrors which never materialize. In the first three acts, Nina marries the dull Sam Evans, and intends to have a baby. She learns that there is insanity in her husband's family. We then discover that these three acts have been exposition to prepare for the real event: since the threat of insanity prevents Nina from having a child by her husband, she selects Dr. Darrell as the prospective father. We watch eagerly for the consequences. But one may say, literally, that there are no consequences. In Act V, Nina wants to tell her husband and get a divorce, but Darrell refuses. In Act VI, Darrell threatens to tell Sam, but Nina refuses. In Act VII, the activity centers around the child (who is now eleven); the boy's suspicions threaten to upset the apple cart. But in the next act (ten years later) everybody is on the deck of a yacht in the Hudson river watching Gordon win the big boat race: "He's the greatest oarsman God ever made!"

Now let us consider the asides. It is generally assumed that these serve to expose the inner secrets of character. This is not the case. Nine-tenths of the asides deal with plot and superficial comments. The characters in *Strange Interlude* are very simply drawn; and they are not at all reticent in telling their inmost feelings in direct dialogue. For instance in Act III, Mrs. Evans says: "I used to wish I'd gone out deliberately in our first year, without my husband knowing, and picked a man, a healthy male to breed by, same's we do with stock." Coming from an elderly farm woman, one would reasonably expect this to be an aside, but it is direct dialogue. Mrs. Evans' asides (like those of the other characters) are devoted to such expressions as "He loves her!...He's happy! ...that's all that counts!" and "Now she knows my suffering... now I got to help her."

Then are we to conclude that the asides are a whim, a seeking after sensation? Not at all. They serve a very important structural purpose: they are used to build up a sense of foreboding. Again and again there are comments like Darrell's in Act IV: "God, it's too awful! On top of all the rest! How did she ever stand it! She'll lose her mind too!" But the asides have a much deeper use; in every scene, they foretell what is about to happen, and blunt the edge of conflict. What might be a clear-cut scene is diluted by needless explanations and by annotating the emotions.

Thus we discover that both the asides and the length of *Strange Interlude* are dictated by a psychological need—to delay, to avoid coming to grips with reality. The function of the asides is to cushion the action and make it oblique. And this same obliqueness creates the need of spreading the story over nine long acts.

Strange Interlude reaches no climax and no solution. But the final scene contains a fairly thorough summing up of the author's position. It is not enough simply to point out that the play ends on a note of frustration. Frustration is negative, and tends to become merely poetic whimpering. The sense of frustration which we find in O'Neill is based, as we have seen, on a complex system of ideas. The social application of these ideas is of the utmost importance.

The ninth act begins with a scene between the two lovers, Madeleine and Gordon: the essence of this scene is the idea of repetition; the saga of love and passion will be repeated. Marsden enters and offers a rose to Madeleine, saying mockingly: "Hail, love, we who have died, salute you!" One expects the playwright to follow this line of thought, but he turns sharply away from it. The action suddenly concentrates on Gordon's bitterness against his mother, his feeling that she never really loved the man whom he regarded as his father. Nina, tortured for fear Darrell will tell the boy the truth, asks her son a direct question: "Do you think I was ever unfaithful to your father, Gordon?" Gordon is "shocked and horrified... he blurts out indignantly: Mother, what do you think I am—as rotten-minded as that!" Here is the germ of a vital idea—if the conflict between mother and son were developed. But O'Neill cuts it short at this point. Gordon leaves, soliloquizing as he goes: "I've never thought of that!... I couldn't! ... my own mother! I'd kill myself if I ever even caught myself thinking...!" Gordon, who represents the new generation, leaves the stage with these negative words. Darrell then asks Nina to marry him and she refuses: "Our ghosts would torture us to death!"

Thus the idea of the repetition of life turns to the negation of life. In all this, O'Neill disregards one simple fact—that Nina has built her life on a lie, and that this accounts for all her troubles. And her son, as he leaves the stage, tells us that he is just as cowardly as his mother: "I've never thought of that!... I couldn't!"

Here we see the conception of an absolute fate as it concretely affects a dramatic situation. The fact that both mother and son evade the truth is not regarded as personal cowardice, but as destiny. Gordon does not face his mother and defeat her—as he would be forced to do in life. He coddles his illusion and goes away on his honeymoon. Since feeling transcends fact, it follows that one preserves the quality of one's feeling even when it means denying or avoiding reality.

The last scene of *Strange Interlude* contains a welter of unfinished ideas which indicate the playwright's feverish uncertainty. There are references to religion, science, womanly intuition, "mystic premonitions of life's beauty," the duty "to love, that life may keep on living," etc. The pain of the author's search lends dignity to his confusion.

However confused or sublime a playwright's thought may appear, it exhibits his own attitude toward his environment. Nina's aimless and deceitful life is called beautiful because it is lived for emotion. The last act tells us that the eternal aim of life is to repeat the saga of emotion. But Nina's emotions are those of a woman to whom security and leisure are guaranteed. Her emotional life is dependent on the social structure. Everything which she feels or thinks is designed to preserve the permanence of her environment. This accounts for her intense conventionality, and for her conviction that deceit is socially necessary. Again and again, she tells us that all she seeks is happiness; her idea of happiness is erotic. She has no interest in other people, no desire to exert an influence on her environment. She pretends desperately to be a woman without an environment, because this is the only condition under which she can exist at all. If she came into contact with reality, her whole world of leisure and sentiment would fall to pieces. Her insistence on emotion is an insistence on a *fixed social system*.

This meaning is increasingly evident in the trilogy, *Mourning Becomes Electra,* which follows *Strange Interlude.* O'Neill's mysticism leads him back to the world of reality; he is not satisfied with showing the passive drift of emotion, as in *Strange Interlude.* One must go beyond this; one must show activity—this leads to a neurotic vision of reality dominated by blood and force.

In *Mourning Becomes Electra,* O'Neill illustrates the Spenglerian conception of the modern intellect "overpowered by a growing sense of its Satanism." Here violence is not a necessity of the action; it is an end in itself. Charmion Von Wiegand points out that "more normal alternatives of action were open to all the characters than the one they chose of murder and blood or which their author chose for them." * It is evident that the characters have no choice whatever; the author's choice of murder and blood springs from the need to justify cruelty and violence as the normal conditions of our existence. The writer's fear of life springs from disturbances and pressures in his environment; since the lack of equilibrium in the environment is due to a process of change, the first step is to invent an eternity ("the electrical display of God the Father") in which change is meaningless; since one cannot invent an eternity out of nothing, the author invents it out of his own experience; his eternity is a crystallization of the environment in what appears to be a permanent form. Ibsen showed us the decay of the middle-class family as part of a system of causes and effects. The causes were increasing tensions in the social structure; the effects were the substitution of lust and greed, hate and egotism, for more normal emotions. This is the environment against which O'Neill rebels and from which he wishes to escape. But he tries to build a world of abstract emotion out of the very emotions from which he is escaping; an eternity of lust and greed, hate

* Charmion Von Wiegand, "The Quest of Eugene O'Neill," in *New Theatre* (September, 1935).

and egotism. In *Strange Interlude,* emotion is abstract, a rarefied desire for happiness; therefore Nina's lust and greed, hate and egotism, are sentimentalized and take the form of aspirations. Nevertheless, these are the only emotions of which she is capable. But the playwright cannot stop at this point; he is driven by the need to remedy the maladjustment between himself and his environment; he must go back and try to *explain* the world in terms of lust and greed, hate and egotism. This task was begun in *Desire Under the Elms,* and continued in *Mourning Becomes Electra.*

Mourning Becomes Electra is a much more realistic play than *Strange Interlude.* The action is less diffuse and better integrated. But the movement of events, in spite of its violence, evades progression. The characters have no goal toward which they are moving. Having no attainable social aims, it is impossible for them to have attainable dramatic aims.

The idea of *repetition* as an emotional commentary on the blindness of the life-force occurs throughout O'Neill's work. This idea plays an important part in the concluding scene of *Strange Interlude.* It occurs in its poetic form in Cybel's lines at the end of *The Great God Brown:* "Always spring comes again bearing life! Always again!... spring bearing the intolerable chalice of life again." In *Mourning Becomes Electra,* repetition is the basic structural pattern. The length of the triple scheme has no justification dramatically, because it involves no development of the action. The length is dictated by the need to prove that repetition is socially inevitable. In this connection, one may recall the remark of William James that there is nothing the principle of free will could do "except rehearse the phenomena beforehand." The activity of O'Neill's characters is a rehearsal of preconceived patterns; the will plays no part except as a repetition-compulsion, which gives what James called a "character of novelty to fresh activity-situations."

An understanding of the social direction of O'Neill's thought clarifies the connection between *Mourning Becomes Electra* and the two plays which follow—*Ah Wilderness* and *Days Without End.* O'Neill being one of the most sensitive and most genuine artists of our time, is horrified by the picture of reality which he himself has drawn. Unwilling to accept "the intolerable chalice of life" on these terms, he turns in two directions: to the consolations of religion, and to the regularities of small-town life in the pre-war era. These plays do not present a positive denial of force and cruelty as emotional values; such a denial would require the courageous analysis of reality which is the function of the artist. *Ah Wilderness* and *Days Without End* are negative and nostalgic; the social thought resolves itself into the wish that religious finality or tender family sentiments might be substituted for the real world.

These plays are therefore among the weakest and most repetitious of O'Neill's works. The structure of *Ah Wilderness* is based on threats of activity which are never realized. The play deals with the pain of adolescence; Richard Miller resembles O'Neill's other characters in that he has neither consciousness nor will in regard to his environment. (Compare *Ah Wilderness* with Wedekind's powerful play, *Spring's Awakening*). Richard's adolescent struggle is merely a dreamy unawareness of an environment which is essentially *friendly*. The suggestions of action never materialize: Richard does not cohabit with the prostitute; his calf-love for Muriel is exactly the same at the end as at the beginning. The love scene on the beach could just as well be placed in Act I as in Act IV. In fact, one can take any scene in the play and transfer it to another position without creating the slightest dislocation in the play's structure. Suppose the play opened with the dinner-table scene which is now in Act II? Would there be any appreciable difference? The scene in which the father tries to advise his son about the facts of life (Act IV) might logically follow the discovery of the passionate poetry in Act I.

In *Ah Wilderness*, O'Neill returns to the conventional pseudo-naturalism which is the accepted technique of the contemporary drama. But the change is a superficial one. The pattern of ideas which determines the structure of *Ah Wilderness* is the same pattern which we find in *The Great God Brown, Strange Interlude, Mourning Becomes Electra*. We shall find this pattern repeated, with variations and modifications, throughout the modern theatre. Few current plays go very deeply into the realm of the subconscious; few deal with space and time and eternal sorrow. But the playwright's treatment of his material is based on a philosophy which duplicates O'Neill's. This is not a matter of general attitudes toward life; it is the way the playwright's mind actually works; it affects every situation he conceives and every line he writes.

CHAPTER VI

THE TECHNIQUE OF THE
MODERN PLAY

"A PLAY lives by its logic and reality," says John W. Gassner. "Conceptual confusion is the disease that halts its pace, dulls its edge, and disturbs its balance." * As has been noted, the disease is a nervous disorder, growing out of the playwright's maladjustment to his environment. The technical symptoms, as diagnosed in the case of O'Neill, are the following: (1) the characters are governed by whim or fate, rather than by conscious will; (2) psychic generalizations are substituted for specific acts of will; (3) the action is illustrative rather than progressive; (4) moments of conflict are diffused or retarded; (5) the action tends to follow a pattern of repetition.

Ibsen avoided preparation, beginning his plays at a crisis, illuminating the past in the course of the action. This retrospective method has now been carried to a further extreme; the crisis is diluted, and the backward looking or expository material is emphasized. What Freytag called the "erregende moment" or firing of the fuse, is unconscionably delayed. William Archer once wondered what *The School for Scandal* would be like "if it consisted of nothing but the screen scene and two laborious acts of preparation." The modern play often consists of elaborate preparation for a crisis which fails to take place.

It is not my purpose in the present chapter to prove this point by a complete survey of the dramatic field. It is enough for the present to select a few plays of contrasting types, and to show the influence of similar modes of thought and the resultant similarity of structural characteristics. The detailed discussion of technique in later chapters will include the more specific analysis of a number of additional examples.

The following plays cover widely differing themes and backgrounds, and are among the most distinguished products of the English-speaking stage: *The Petrified Forest,* by Robert Sherwood;

* John W. Gassner, "The Drama in Transition," in *New Theatre* (August, 1925).

Both Your Houses, by Maxwell Anderson; *Design for Living,* by Noel Coward; *The Silver Cord,* by Sidney Howard.

In *The Petrified Forest,* the pattern of ideas with which we have been dealing is projected in a very direct form. Alan Squier is a tired intellectual who confesses that he has no purpose in life: "I'm planning to be buried in the Petrified Forest. I've been evolving a theory about that that would interest you. It's the graveyard of the civilization that's being shot from under us. It's the world of outmoded ideas of Platonism—Patriotism—Christianity—Romance—the economics of Adam Smith." This is a clear statement of the problem, and we must admire Sherwood's courage in putting the question so uncompromisingly. But the statement of a problem is not sufficient; the dramatist must show the working out of the problem as it affects the shifting balance between man and his environment. This Sherwood fails to do—indeed, he makes no attempt to do so, because he forewarns us that Squier is a man whose conscious will has atrophied. It is the function of the dramatist to show us why, how and in what degree the will is inoperative: Chekhov succeeded in exposing the conscious wills of men and women whose lives are *almost* devoid of purpose. Squier resembles many of Chekhov's characters; his futile idealism reminds us of Trophimof in *The Cherry Orchard,* who says: "The vast majority of the educated people that I know seek after nothing, do nothing, and are as yet incapable of work. . . . They are all serious, they all have solemn faces; they only discuss important subjects; they philosophize."

Yet the difference between Chekhov and Sherwood is the difference between dramatic art and dramatic attrition. Sherwood's approach to his material is as static as the point of view of his hero. The conception underlying the play is as follows: men are drifting toward a doom over which they have no control; if we are to be saved at all, we must be saved by the instinctive rightness of our feeling (exemplified in the love story between Gabby and Squier); but in this world of chaos, the only men who are able to act with instinctive decision and purpose are men who are desperate and evil (as typified in the gangster). Thus Sherwood's thought follows the time-worn circle: the philosophy of blood and nerves leads to pessimism; the denial of reason leads to the acceptance of violence.

The only definite action in *The Petrified Forest* is the killing which takes place at the end of the play. The gangster and the intellectual have an intuitive bond between them, an understanding which has no rational basis. In the final scene, the gangster, as he is escaping, turns and empties his machine gun into Squier as a *favor to him,* because he instinctively realizes that this is what the other man genuinely desires. This violent whim justifies the gangster; it is accepted as what Hedda Gabler called "a deed of spontaneous beauty."

From a structural point of view, the deed is neither climactic nor spontaneous, because it is a *repetition-situation.* Every element of this climax has been presented in the early part of the first act, and has been repeated throughout the play. The first act conversation between Gabby and Squier reveals the sense of futility, the girl's artistic aspirations, the dawning love between them—and the fact that death offers the only solution. "Let there be killing!" says Squier in Act I. "All evening long, I've had a feeling of destiny closing in." When destiny *does* close in, it simply repeats the pattern of human relationships and social concepts with which we are already familiar.

The plot-structure centers around Squier and Gabby. Their relationship undergoes no change. They feel drawn to each other from the moment they meet; but this has no effect on them or their environment. Gabby wants to study art and Squier wants to die; these conscious wishes form the thread which integrates the action; but blind fate contrives the solution without the exercise of will on the part of either of the characters.

The play is not a study of an intellectual's mind and will, facing a problem which he must solve, or die. The play is based on the preconception that struggle is useless. Social causation is disregarded, and absolute necessity governs Squier's puzzled mind and the gangster's brutal whim. Squier makes this clear:

> squier: Do you realize what it is that is causing world chaos?
> gabby: No.
> squier: Well, I'm probably the only living person who can tell you. It's Nature hitting back. Not with the old weapons— floods, plagues, holocausts. We can neutralize them. She's fighting back with strange instruments called neuroses. She's deliberately afflicting mankind with the jitters. Nature is proving that she can't be beaten—not by the likes of us. She's taking the world away from us and giving it back to the apes.*

As has been pointed out in the case of O'Neill, this conception is socially conditioned; it involves the acceptance of man's fate on

---

* Brooks Atkinson speaks of this as "an observation worth making in the presence of intelligent people" (*New York Times,* March 17, 1935).

any terms which Nature (blind necessity, operating in us and around us, causing events in which we take part but over which we have no control) may dictate. Cruelty and violence seem to play a necessary part in Nature's scheme. Since emotion is absolute, it includes both good and evil; the life-force operates through love and violence, sentiment and cruelty, sacrifice and sadism. We find this dualism in the final scenes of *The Petrified Forest*. Squier finds love: "I think I've found the thing I was looking for, I've found it here, in the Valley of the Shadow." As he dies, Gabby says to him, "I know you died happy.... Didn't you, Alan? *Didn't you?*" Love has no positive value; it gives Squier no wish to live, and no strength for further conflict; it is a mystic escape, which gives him the *immediate* sense of union with a power higher than himself. It also sanctifies the needless act of violence which causes his death.

If we turn to an earlier play of Sherwood's, we find that the system of ideas is identical, and produces an identical arrangement of events. *Waterloo Bridge* takes place in London during the world war. The play opens with a chance encounter between an American soldier and an American girl who has become a prostitute. The love story of Roy and Myra is in every respect similar to the later story of Squier and Gabby. Here again we have the repetition of the pattern of sentiment, futility and doom. Roy is more defiant than Squier, but the final scene offers salvation through blood as the only solution. Roy says:

> ...The war's over for me. What I've got to fight is the whole dirty world. That's the enemy that's against you and me. That's what makes the rotten mess we've got to live in.... Look at them—shooting their guns into the air, firing their little shells at something they can't even see. Why don't they turn their guns down into the streets and shoot at what's there? Why don't they be merciful and kill the people that want to be killed?

Roy asks for the very fate which Squier, in the later play, receives from the gangster's bullet. But Myra convinces him that he must *accept* the war:

> ROY (*passionately*): You're good! I know it—I'll swear it before God.
> MYRA: All right, then, prove it to Him. Prove to Him that I didn't break your life in two. Let Him see that I sent you back to the lines, to fight the war, make Him know that...

Thus Roy achieves an *immediate* feeling of the goodness of love, and Myra is sure that he will be content to die (the exact equivalent of Gabby's lines in *The Petrified Forest:* "I know you died happy.") Roy goes, leaving Myra alone on the bridge; she looks up into the sky and an enemy plane drones overhead.* The pragmatic acceptance of *what is,* regardless of reason or volition, brings with it the intimation of an unreal world, in which emotion is purified and goodness is intuitively *known.*

Both Your Houses is a realistic and spicily written account of graft in the conduct of the national government. Here there are no questions of an eternal character, no references to God or destiny or nature, no violent and unresolved emotions. Alan McLean is a political idealist who seeks definite remedies for definite abuses.

In this case, the individual's will is pitted against social necessity. No metaphysical necessity is introduced as a final force against which struggle is vain. One would therefore suppose that the inter-action between the individual and the environment would be dynamic and progressive. But when we examine the construction of *Both Your Houses,* we find that this is not the case. The state-ment of the problem is static, and the conflict contains no element of progression.

Anderson states the theme of his play with admirable clarity. But here, as in *The Petrified Forest,* the mere statement of a proposition is insufficient. *Both Your Houses* contains a burning indictment of American political methods; but this indictment lies in the dialogue, and not in the action; the movement of the play consists in the repetition of human relationships and points of view which are fully presented at the beginning. We are told imme-diately in the first act that the deficiency bill for the Nevada dam is crooked—Solomon Fitzmaurice says: "Fishy! My God, a little honest smell of fish on that bill would hang over it like an odor of sanctity." Alan's determination to fight the bill is also clear in the opening act; he announces that the projects included in the bill are "wasteful, useless, extravagant, ridiculous—." Sol explains to him:

> ... Don't you know about the government of the United States?... You can't do anything in Congress without arranging matters. Everybody wants something, everybody's trying to put something over for his voters, or the folks he's working for.... You all come up to this Congress fighting mad, full of juice and high purpose—just like him.... Yes, and it happened to me too, and I was shocked and I started making radical remarks. Why,

---

* The same pattern of ideas, culminating in the same air-raid, is re-peated by Sherwood in *Idiot's Delight.*

before I knew where I was, I was an outsider. So I began to play ball, just to pacify the folks back home. And it worked. They've been re-electing me ever since—and re-electing a fat crook because he gets what they want out of the treasury, and fixes the Tariff for 'em and sees that they don't get gypped out of their share of the plunder.*

This first act statement covers the whole theme of the play. The same material is repeated in the second act, and the final situation is a further repetition. The language of the closing scene is more intense, but nothing new is introduced, because nothing new has developed in the course of the action. At the end, Sol *again* explains that the Washington system is a system of plunder: "We can't have an honest government, so let 'em steal plenty and get us started again." He *again* points to the apathy of the public: "As a matter of fact, the natural resources of this country in political apathy and indifference have hardly been touched."

The dramatic construction is illustrative and not functional. The hero's battle against corruption is a matter of his opinions, and involves no solid human situation in which his conscious will is tested under the pressure of events. The author tries to remedy this weakness by the introduction of a subsidiary human-interest plot: Simeon Gray, the heroine's father, is in danger of a jail sentence if the appropriations bill is defeated. This situation has no connection with the theme, except insofar as it illustrates the fact that even an honest politician may become dishonest under sufficient pressure. Since this fact is obvious, and since it has already been clearly stated in Sol's first act analysis of Washington politics, the revelation of Simeon Gray's guilt in Act II is merely an artificial means of bolstering up a weak situation. But McLean's struggle against graft is in itself so static, that the most decisive moments of the drama are inevitably concerned with the sub-plot: Act II ends with Gray's confession; Scene 1 of Act III ends with a scene between Marjorie and McLean in which she pleads with him to save her father and he refuses to change his course.

McLean's point of view in the final scene, after he has been defeated in his fight against the politicians, shows the conceptual confusion which obstructs the action:

... How can one speak treason about this government or Congress? It's one vast, continuous, nation-wide disaster!... And I'm not a red! I don't like communism or fascism or any other political patent medicine!... More people are open-minded nowadays than you'd believe. A lot of them aren't so sure we

* I have combined several of Sol's speeches in Act I, Scene 2.

found the final answer a hundred and fifty years ago. Who knows what's the best kind of government? Maybe they all get rotten and have to be replaced.... It takes about a hundred years to tire this country of trickery—and we're fifty years overdue right now. That's my warning. And I'd feel pretty damn pitiful and lonely saying it to you if I didn't believe there are a hundred million people who are with me, a hundred million people who are disgusted enough to turn from you to something else. Anything else but this.*

This is simply an intensified repetition of the problem stated in the first act. It is a literary statement, because it does not face the dramatic or human implications of the problem. These words are supposed to sum up what McLean has learned during the course of the play; but what he has learned has been purely illustrative, and therefore has no emotional validity in terms of character.

If we analyze McLean's position, in an effort to discover what it means in relation to his consciousness and will, we find a contradiction which is at the root of McLean's conflict with his environment: from a political standpoint, the contradiction is between a final belief in the *status quo* (the machinery of democracy as it at present operates) and a final determination to change it. McLean declares his faith in democracy—no political patent medicines; he will appeal to a hundred million people. But the only type of democracy with which McLean has had any experience, and which has molded his point of view, is the very system he wants to change.

In a broader sense, this is a contradiction between free will and necessity, between the principle of permanence and the principle of change. In order to change the world in which he lives, McLean must use his conscious will; but the first difficulty which confronts him is that he himself is the product of this world; *his* aims and prejudices and illusions are created by the environment and contribute to the permanence of the environment. Thus in order to release his will, to act meaningfully and with purpose, he must attain a new consciousness of his environment; he must decide what it *is* and how he wants to change it.

This problem contains the stuff of intense dramatic conflict: but McLean's final speeches merely hint at the problem. The tone of his declaration suggests decision; but what it actually contains is a confession of a maladjustment between himself and his environment; the maladjustment is so serious that he is unable to face the contradiction in his own mind or reach any decision. His only

---

* Again several speeches have been telescoped.

comfort is the feeling that a hundred million people are as disgusted as he is, and are ready to turn to something else—"Anything else but this"! This is not a rational conception of change,
and it does not satisfy the individual's need for rational activity.
McLean must satisfy this need in himself; a similar need exists
among the hundred million people of whom he speaks.

This is not a matter of political opinion; it is a matter of the
character's emotional life. If we consider McLean carefully, we
find that we do not know him as a *person*. He is a young man with
qualities and opinions, just as Shaw's characters are persons with
qualities and opinions. The play ends, as many of Shaw's plays
end, on a question. But it is not a *complete* question; McLean
does not ask: "How can I live and achieve integrity under these
conditions"? This would be an admission of his maladjustment
and a genuine tragic dilemma. But McLean's reasoning is both
pragmatic and final; he denies the possibility of a rational solution— "Who knows what's the best kind of government?" But
he is convinced that the future is safe in the hands of men whose
qualities and opinions correspond to his own. If a majority of the
people agree with McLean, the country will be saved even though
none of them has any conviction as to "the best kind of government." This is obviously nonsense; the very condition against
which McLean is fighting is brought about by the apathy or
uncertainty of people as to "the best kind of government." The
first problem which he must face, before he can convince others
or himself, is *what kind of government he wants*.

This illustrates the close connection between social analysis and
the analysis of character. The answer to this question is the only
adequate test of McLean's character; it involves emotional decision
and introspection; it involves the courage to face the "iron framework of fact" and determine his own course in regard to it; the
way in which he meets this test reveals his faults and virtues, his
consciousness and will as a suffering and aspiring human being.
Failure to ask this question makes his character and problem so
thin that the whole center of the play must be padded out with
an irrelevant sub-plot.

Solomon Fitzmaurice is by far the most human character in
Both Your Houses; he has been emotionally affected by his environment, and has been forced to adjust himself to definite needs and
pressures. For this reason, he is the only person in the play who
talks in terms of social reality.

Writing in the last century, Ibsen displayed an understanding
of democratic politics which is more modern than Anderson's treat-

ment of the subject. *An Enemy of the People* and *The League of Youth* expose the personal and social forces which underlie the mechanism of government and which operate in a somewhat similar manner in Washington today. Ibsen bases his analysis of social causes and effects on the conviction that *ideals* are valueless and meretricious—because they are the by-products of the social system itself. In *An Enemy of the People,* Ibsen draws a great portrait of a liberal fighting for honest politics; but Dr. Stockmann learns two things—that public opinion can be controlled by money, and that "the liberals are the most insidious enemies of freedom." Dr. Stockmann himself remains a liberal at the end, but his position is understandable and poignant because we see him making new decisions and facing new forces. A study of Ibsen throws a great deal of light on *Both Your Houses,* and on the specific difficulties which McLean faces. Anderson has failed to touch these difficulties (which are the core of his play), because his mode of thought is retrospective and idealistic.

Anderson's method is based on the belief that qualities of character are of final value and must triumph over a hostile environment. He takes no interest in social causation, because he assumes that the environment can be changed whenever people wish to change it. Thus ideals (the same ideals which Ibsen found so reactionary and dangerous) become the basis of the drama. This is evident in Anderson's historical plays, which interpret history as a conflict of the passions and whims of exceptional people. The fate of nations is decided by persons who know no necessity beyond their own emotional needs. Since the emotions are timeless, man's relationship to the universe is substituted for his relationship to his environment; emotional drift is substituted for rational causation.

If we turn back and re-examine the quoted portions of McLean's final appeal from this angle, we find that it is an expression of *feeling;* McLean makes no decision as to any future course; he makes no estimate of the vastness of the problem or the possible difficulties. The appeal lacks intellectual toughness; it is neither concrete nor individual; the things that McLean says might be (and often have been) said by any honest man—or, for that matter, by any dishonest politician. One hears similar statements from all sides in every political campaign.

McLean is as helpless as the intellectual in *The Petrified Forest;* Squier is a pessimist, because he regards necessity as absolute; McLean is an optimist, because he disregards necessity completely. Both points of view are unrealistic; in both cases, the solution does not depend on man's relation to the real world, but only on his feelings and thoughts.*

In a later play, Anderson goes back to the founding of the Republic and examines the ideals which motivated the founders of the nation. *Valley Forge* repeats the basic conception of *Both Your Houses;* it therefore follows exactly the same plot construction. Here again we have the contradiction between absolute faith in the machinery of democracy and the conviction that democracy fails to work. Washington weighs this problem in static terms. He admits that "the government's as rotten as the sow-belly it sends us." But he is opposed to the suggestion of a dictatorship; he shares McLean's opinion that the people have complete control; he says: "Whether it gets better or worse it's your own, by God, and you can do what you please with it."

All of this is presented fully in the first act. No attempt is made to examine the social forces that caused the revolution, that affected Washington and all the men of his time, and determined the form of government which they built. The action repeats the problem presented in the first act. The middle portion of the drama is padded with an irrelevant sub-plot; Robert Benchley refers to this as "the spurious heart-interest," provided by the introduction of "Mistress Morris, dressed as a British officer, on a Viennese-operetta mission to Washington with a coy suggestion that he forget business for a minute or two and revive an old amour." † The playwright offers no explanation of this incident beyond the observation of one of his characters (Howe): "What a strange, mad thing is a woman's heart!" But the explanation lies, not in Mary's wayward heart, but in the fact that a diversion is necessary to keep the play from dying of sheer exhaustion. Washington's character is so devitalized and over-simplified that something outside his real interests must be introduced to humanize him. This indicates, as in the case of Shaw, that emphasis on character as a thing-in-itself leads to a fatal weakening of the character's living meaning—the character can only be understood when we understand *what he is up against,* the totality of his environment.

It is often said that the difference between comedy and other forms of drama lies in the treatment of characterization, comedy

*In *Winterset,* this connection of ideas is strikingly revealed. In this play, Anderson develops a final situation which is identical in every respect to the situation in *The Petrified Forest.* The chaos of the modern world is resolved in the combination of sentiment and violence; romantic love is justified and transfigured by an act of brutal destruction.

† *The New Yorker,* December 29, 1934.

152 Theory and Technique of Playwriting

being distinguished by its devotion to pure characterization.
According to this theory, comedy requires a less integrated plot
and less careful organization of the material. Barrett H. Clark
says: "The best comedies... have plots which in the final analysis
are simply threads utilized by the dramatist to hold together his
gallery of portraits." * If this were true, the principles of dramatic
action could not be applied to comedy, and it would be necessary
to consider comedy as a separate form of art. This would be difficult, because it would take the wisdom of Solomon to tell where
comedy ends and drama begins. Fortunately, there is not the
slightest justification for the theory; ancient comedy is especially
distinguished by the complexity of its plot-structure. The best
comedies, both ancient and modern, are those in which the action
is progressive and tightly knit.

Design for Living is an unusually apt example of the use of
repetition as a substitute for progression. Noel Coward has built
his play around the idea of repetition, and has handled the design
of repeated situations with great skill. But his selection of this
theme springs from a social philosophy which denies the rôle of
the conscious will, and which regards pragmatic sensation as the
only test of conduct.

The repetition-compulsion is as strong in Coward's plays as it is
in those of O'Neill. Everything that Gilda says sounds like an
epigrammatic version of Nina Leeds. She resembles Nina in her
aimless thirst for emotion, her excessive sentimentality, combined
with ruthless disregard of anything but her own feelings. Like
Nina, she requires three men; like Nina, she marries the conventional man whom she considers a fool.

In the first act, Gilda is living with Otto. She spends the night
with his best friend, Leo. In the morning Otto discovers them
together, and leaves them together. In the second act, she is living
with Leo and spends the night with Otto. Now it is she who goes
away, leaving the men together. In the third act, she has married
the faithful friend, Ernest, and the two men come and take her
away. If one maps out the social framework of this story, and
endeavors to reconstruct the untold incidents which have a bearing
on the plot, one finds that the author has left out almost everything
that might explain or justify the action. What motivated Gilda's
first decision to be unfaithful to Otto? Why did she marry
Ernest? Why did the two men come to take her away from
Ernest? What will their triple relationship be like after their

* Clark, *A Study of the Modern Drama.*

final departure together? Homosexuality is an essential element in the story, but it is only hinted at.

The author has neglected this framework of cause and effect, because he believes that human behavior is irrational. Why and wherefor are of no consequence. The feeling of the moment is beautiful because it is momentary. Thus the people inevitably come back, again and again, to the feeling already experienced, to renew the momentary sensation—and the only *design for living* is a design of neurotic repetition. These people are completely sentimental (because they depend entirely on feeling), and completely cynical (because their feelings are continually proved contradictory and valueless). Being deprived of conscious will, they are victims of fate, which dictates the twists and turns of feeling which constitute their lives.

It may be objected that this is a very solemn way to attack a mad comedy. But the play would be far more comic if it were more incisively developed. Far from revealing character, Coward's brilliant lines serve to conceal character. There is no differentiation between the two men. They are exactly alike; and Gilda is exactly like both of them. One can take very little interest in whether Gilda loves one man or the other or both, because all three of them have the same whims and sentiments.

> OTTO: Do you have many rows?
> GILDA: Quite a lot, every now and then.
> OTTO: As many as we used to?
> GILDA: About the same.

The triple characterization is superficial, because the author shows us only impulses, and fails to expose motives. We have no idea how Gilda would react to any fundamental problem, because we do not see her tested in any situation which requires decision; she drifts; she speaks of "Good old romance bobbing up again and wrapping our crudities in a few veils." One wonders what she would do in a dramatic situation—that is, a situation in which her impulse could *not* find an easy outlet, because of conflict with unavoidable needs and pressures.

Coward's inability to project a sustained characterization is particularly marked in the treatment of Ernest. In the first two acts, he is depicted as the sympathetic friend. In the final act, he unaccountably turns out to be an old fool. There is no reason for the change beyond the arbitrary exigencies of the plot. One can only agree with Ernest when he remarks in the last scene: "I never could understand this disgusting three-sided erotic hotch-potch."

Coward, being a skillful showman, is no doubt aware of his own limitation. Indeed, he mentions it amusingly in *Design for Living;* Leo, the playwright, complains that the critics call his plays thin: "I shall write fat plays from now onwards. Fat plays filled with very fat people!" But as we have seen, even a play which is as fat as *Strange Interlude* may be thin and repetitious in conception.

Sidney Howard's play, *The Silver Cord,** treats a psychological problem with scientific care. Howard deals with a woman who is driven by subconscious impulses of which she is unaware; there is nothing metaphysical about these impulses. Here we have an approach to the subconscious which is in complete contrast to O'Neill's approach. *The Silver Cord* therefore offers an excellent opportunity for the study of the rôle of the conscious will as it relates to the analysis of subconscious motivations.

Mrs. Phelps has two sons whom she adores so neurotically and selfishly that she inevitably tries to destroy their lives. She succeeds in separating Robert from the girl to whom he is engaged and in tying him to her apron-strings forever. She tries to break up David's marriage, but David's wife, Christina, has a mind and will of her own. She forces David to choose between the mother and herself, and in the end he chooses his wife. The dramatic conflict in this story is clear-cut; the family relationships are typical of the well-to-do middle-class family.

One's first impression of the play is that the characters are over-simplified; the portrait of Mrs. Phelps seems exaggerated and one-sided. The exaggeration does not lie in the fact that she is brutally intent on controlling the lives of her sons. This emotional fixation is understandable. But we are puzzled because *the way she goes about it* seems excessively direct. One wonders how a woman could be so unaware of the horrible things she is doing, and the horrible motives which are behind her conduct. This brings us to the crucial question—the question of conscious will. We do not know how far Mrs. Phelps is conscious of her own motives, how far she is sincere or insincere, how she justifies herself in her own mind. Without this knowledge we are unable to judge her character at all. The author presents her as a woman driven by the furies of the subconscious. She makes no decisions, because her course is fixed in advance. Her actions are not progressive, but are illustrative and spontaneous. For example, she kisses her sons with an emotion which suggests sexuality; she cannot bear having David share the

---

* This is one of Howard's earlier plays. His later achievements as a playwright are more mature, and are discussed in later chapters. Chapter 1 of Part IV is devoted to a detailed analysis of *Yellow Jack.*

bedroom with his own wife. Even when Hester, Robert's fiancee, is drowning in the icy pond, she tries to call her sons back when they go to save the girl. The dramatic meaning of these acts lies in the degree of consciousness and will which accompanies the acts. Unless we know this, there is no progression and no conflict.

This is apparent in the final act, in which the struggle between the young wife and the mother comes to a head. Christina tells Mrs. Phelps what we already know—that she is guided by emotions which are destructive. But there is no development because the two women simply state opposing points of view. The girl's denunciation is a static summing up of the theme: "You're not really bad people, you know, you're just wrong, all wrong, terribly, pitifully, all of you, and you're trapped.... I rather fancy myself, now, as a sort of scientific Nemesis. I mean to strip this house and show it up for what it really is." She calls Mrs. Phelps "a type of self-centered, self-pitying, son-devouring tigress, with unmentionable proclivities suppressed on the side."

This speech exposes the inadequacy of the play's social logic. The fact that these people are *trapped* tells us very little about them—we want to know how they react to being trapped. Mrs. Phelps apparently reacts by being a "son-devouring tigress." If this is true, we can hardly excuse her on the ground that she is not bad, but only pitifully wrong. She has become bad, and we must investigate the causes. Middle-class family life does not turn all mothers into "son-devouring tigresses." Then there must be differences in character and environment which determine the actions of Mrs. Phelps. These differences can only be expressed in terms of conscious will. If Mrs. Phelps is completely unconscious and unwilling, there is no excuse for calling her a "man-eating tigress."

At the end of the play, Mrs. Phelps is left alone with Robert; she talks to him about mother-love, "her voice growing stronger as that deeply religious point of view of hers comes to her rescue":

> ...And you must remember what David, in his blindness, has forgotten. That mother love suffereth long and is kind; envieth not, is not puffed up, is not easily provoked; beareth all things; believeth all things; hopeth all things; endureth all things... at least, I think *my* love does.
>
> ROBERT (*engulfed forever*): Yes, mother.

What does the author mean by mentioning a "deeply religious point of view" in the final moments of the play? There is not a line in the course of the drama which suggests that Mrs. Phelps has a deeply religious point of view. Can we believe that this speech at the end is an honest speech? After Christina's attack and her other son's desertion, the Bible quotations sound like hypocrisy. But we have no way of judging. As we look back over the whole action, we realize that we have never *known* Mrs. Phelps at all, because the conscious will has been obscured by a "scientific Nemesis."

This does not infer that there is any limitation upon the playwright's choice of theme, or his point of view toward his material. The objection to *The Silver Cord* is based on the contention that the author's understanding of *his own purpose* is not sufficiently thorough. The mother-son relationship furnishes a vital theme. Howard's approach is influenced by the theories of psychoanalysis. These theories have thrown a new light on the emotional complexes involved in such a situation. The playwright need not limit himself to a superficial examination of these complexes. He can study them as deeply as if he were a physician actually practicing psychoanalysis. But he must deal with the subconscious in the way in which the physician deals with it: he must find out how the psychic impulses affect the *organization of the will;* if the physician can bring nothing to consciousness, he can have no effect upon the patient. His work consists in analyzing and changing the individual's adjustment to his environment. Memory traces, if and when they are brought to consciousness, show past adjustments to earlier environments.

The error lies in treating the subconscious as a "scientific Nemesis"—or any other sort of nemesis. In this sense, it is a meaningless abstraction, because it is outside our rational understanding of character and environment. In *The Silver Cord,* Howard indicates the incest-wishes which underlie the mother's fixation on her sons. He presents these as explanatory comments on the action. Surely, one may say, the dramatist is permitted to explain human behavior; if the drama deals with cause and effect, it ought to delve as deeply as possible into psychic causation. To be sure! But the whole scheme of causation (including the incest-wishes, and their possible origin in the pre-history of the race) lies in the contact between the individual and the environment. This means that the incest-wishes can be presented dramatically in two ways: the idea of incest may be forced into consciousness, so that the individual must face the conflict and reach a decision as to his conduct. Or the idea of incest may be traced as an *objective* feature of the environment. This is an infinitely more difficult task. It means going deeply into the social and economic conditions, the pattern of human relationships in childhood and family life, the

ideas and sentiments which affect that pattern, the ideas and sentiments which have made incest an objective possibility in this environment. It is conceivable (if the dramatist were skillful enough
and wise enough) that this aspect of the environment could be
traced far back into the past. In his social plays, Ibsen handles
psychic factors in this manner. To some extent, it must be admitted
that Howard uses this method in *The Silver Cord*. He shows that
objective causes exist. But he makes no attempt to dramatize these
causes, to show their impact on the characters, or to use the conscious will as a point of reference in determining the scope of the
individual's conflict with the environment.

The foregoing discussion seems to paint a distressing picture of
the modern drama. It may be well to remind the reader that the
purpose of this investigation is clinical. In tracing the course of
group-ideas and social concepts as they are manifested in structural technique, one is not concerned with the theatre's glamour
or its more superficial charms. A man may say that a woman is
beautiful, and that her appearance in evening dress makes his
heart beat faster. It may also happen that this beautiful woman
suffers from liver trouble, anemia, nervous indigestion and a
persecution mania.

A diagnosis of the theatre's diseases need not include a description of its appearance in evening dress. Such a diagnosis can give
little comfort to the sentimental theatre-lover. But to those who
love the theatre not only for what it is, but for its unlimited
possibilities of power and beauty, the only acceptable standards of
value are the most rigorous standards. If one approaches the contemporary drama pragmatically, it is very easy to assume that its
diseases are unavoidable. The only way in which one can judge
the drama's weaknesses or its possibilities is through the application
of positive standards of value, drawn from the theatre's history and
tradition. Viewed historically, the drama today is passing through
a retrospective period. William Lyon Phelps gravely assures us
that "No form of art has shown more striking or more rapid
development in America than the art of the playwright." * It is
true that a retrospective trend is often accompanied by a considerable development of dexterity and smoothness. Indeed, this
is a *necessity* in order to conceal the lack of fresh themes or
meaningful social concepts.

But the development of an art means the broadening of its
intellectual scope, emotional depth, poetic richness, technical

* Introduction to *The Pulitzer Prize Plays* (New York, 1935).

variety and structural grace. The only modern American plays which have displayed these qualities in any marked degree are the plays of Eugene O'Neill's early period, the last of which, *The Hairy Ape,* appeared in 1922. O'Neill's failure to achieve mature stature as a dramatist is not a purely personal failure; it is due to unfavorable conditions which have affected all the writers of the period.

The patterns of thought which I have described are to be found in the work of every contemporary playwright;* they are the product of his education, background, habits of living, social contacts.

But the ferment of new ideas is today excitingly evident. The needs of the serious artist force him to break the mold of outworn ideas, to *think creatively*. This is a difficult task and involves a serious inner conflict. In order to think creatively, one must understand the function of one's art and the principles which govern the creative process.

---

* It goes without saying that my own plays exhibit these tendencies in their most malignant form: *Nirvana* and *The Pure in Heart* are swamped in mysticism; the ending of *The Pure in Heart* exhibits the typical combination of sentiment and violence. *Gentlewoman* follows a pattern of repetition in the presentation of a static relationship.

PART 3

DRAMATIC STRUCTURE

The study of the history of dramatic theory and technique indicates that the playwright's approach to situation and character is determined by the ideas which are prevalent in the playwright's class and time. These ideas represent a long process of cultural development; modes of thought inherited from previous generations undergo constant change and adaptation, reflecting the movement of economic forces and class relationships.

The form which the playwright utilizes is also historically evolved. The European theatrical tradition has its fountainhead in Greece: when the first actor, Thespis, appeared in the sixth century B.C. as an answerer to the choral passages in the ancient rites performed in honor of Dionysius, the drama emerged as the representation of a story in pantomime and dialogue. With the development of the play structure, it was possible to formulate laws of technique. It was already evident in the Attic theatre that drama deals with actions of men and women, and that the system of events must have some sort of design or unity. The two general principles of action as a reversal of fortune and structural unity to round out the action and define its limits were established by Aristotle.

These principles were lost in medieval Europe, because the drama as a planned and acted imitation of an action ceased to exist, and its place was taken by rural festivals, religious ceremonies, and minstrelsy. These were forms of dramatic communication, but they did not have a plot structure in the Aristotelian sense. The Renaissance reappearance of the play as an acted story coincided with the rediscovery of Aristotle and acceptance of his theories.

However, the theatre of Shakespeare and Lope de Vega and Calderon had a scope and freedom of movement that transcended the Aristotelian formula. The drama reflected the awakening of a new faith in the power of science and reason and the creative will of man. The development of capitalist society brought an increasing emphasis on the human personality, and the rights and obligations of the individual in a comparatively fluid and expanding social system. The drama focussed attention on psychological conflict, on the struggle of men and women to fulfill their destiny, to realize conscious aims and desires.

The theatre of the later nineteenth century was characterized, as Brunetière observed in 1894, by a "weakening, relaxing, disintegrating" of the will. Although the independent theatre movement at the turn of the century brought greater maturity and social consciousness to the European and American stage, it did not recapture the secret of the creative will.

We are not attempting to define abstract and eternal laws of dramatic construction. We are concerned with principles that are applicable to the theatre of our time, illuminating the relationship between contemporary forms and the tradition from which they have evolved.

We therefore begin with a definition of the nature of drama as it has developed in the modern period. Its most essential and inescapable characteristic is the presentation of a conflict of will. But the statement is too general to have any precise meaning in terms of dramatic structure. Chapter I seeks to provide a more specific definition of the law of conflict, considering consciousness and strength of will as factors in creating dramatic movement and bringing the action to a meaningful climax.

What, then, do we mean when we speak of action? The question is posed in Chapter II. In a sense, any event may be described as an action—a prize fight, picketers marching, the operation of a riveting machine, a world war, an old lady falling off a street car, the birth of quintuplets. Obviously, these things, in a raw and unorganized state, do not constitute dramatic action that meets the requirements of effective stage presentation. If we restrict the term to events that take place within the framework of a play, we still find that the word covers a perplexing confusion of incidents. Everything that happens on the stage, entrances and exits, gestures and movements, details of speech and situation, may be classified as action.

We must discover the functional or structural quality of dramatic action. We find this quality in the progression that moves the play toward a climax. The action explodes in a series of ascending crises. The preparation and accomplishment of these crises, keeping the play in constant movement toward an appointed goal, is what we mean by dramatic action.

Having reached this point, it is evident that we cannot proceed further without analyzing the over-all structure of the play. Discussion of conflict and action has only a limited meaning as long as it relates to scenes and situations. We keep referring to a goal or crisis toward which the play is moving. But what is this goal and how is it related to the events that lead to it? We are forced to return to the Aristotelian problem of unity. What holds the system of events together? What makes it complete and organic?

Chapter III, "Unity in Terms of Climax," marks the climactic point toward which we have been progressing in the survey of theatre history and technique. The climax of a play, being the point at which the struggle of the conscious will to fulfill its aim reaches its greatest intensity and maximum scope, is the key to the play's unity. It is the root-action, determining the value and meaning of all the events that have preceded. If the climax lacks strength and inevitability, the progression must be weak and confused, because it has no goal; there is no ultimate test which brings the conflict to a decision.

The next two chapters deal with the playwright's method of selecting and arranging the sequence of events leading to the climax. Here we begin to relate the dramatic form more closely to the social philosophy on which it is based. The root-action expresses the dramatist's convictions concerning man's social destiny, the individual's mastery of his fate or his inability to cope with "the slings and arrows of outrageous fortune." The antecedent action is an exploration of causes which involve social and psychological judgments.

The exploration of causes leads the dramatist beyond the area covered by the structure of the play. The lives of the characters are not circumscribed by the events that take place before the audience. These people have histories. The room which is open to the footlights is part of a house, which is on a city street or a country lane, with a landscape, a town, an expanse of people and events, a world, around it. We can say that this extension of the stage action is imagined and taken for granted. But the most effective plays are those in which the outer framework, the system of events not seen by the audience, is most fully explored and realized. The people of such a play have the dimension of reality, they have a life of their own, they come out of a background that we can feel and understand.

Therefore, it is necessary to deal with the process of selection from two aspects: in Chapter IV, it is studied in terms of the stage-action. Chapter V analyzes the larger framework, in which the inner action of the play moves and from which it derives its deepest reality.

CHAPTER I

THE LAW OF CONFLICT

SINCE the drama deals with social relationships, a dramatic conflict must be a *social* conflict. We can imagine a dramatic struggle between man and other men, or between man and his environment, including social forces or forces of nature. But it is difficult to imagine a play in which forces of nature are pitted against other forces of nature.

Dramatic conflict is also predicated on the exercise of conscious will. A conflict without conscious will is either wholly subjective or wholly objective; since such a conflict would not deal with the conduct of men in relation to other men or to their environment, it would not be a social conflict.

The following definition may serve as a basis for discussion. The essential character of drama is social conflict in which the conscious will is exerted: persons are pitted against other persons, or individuals against groups, or groups against other groups, or individuals or groups against social or natural forces.

The first impression of this definition is that it is still too broad to be of any practical value: a prize fight is a conflict between two persons which has dramatic qualities and a slight but appreciable social meaning. A world war is a conflict between groups and other groups, which has deep social implications.

Either a prize fight or a war might furnish the materials for a dramatic conflict. This is not merely a matter of compression and selection—although both compression and selection are obviously necessary. The dramatic element (which transforms a prize fight or a war from potential material of drama into the actual stuff of drama) seems to lie in the *way* in which the expectations and motives of the persons or groups are projected. This is not a matter solely of the use of the conscious will; it involves the *kind* and *degree* of conscious will exerted.

Brunetière tells us that the conscious will must be directed toward a specific goal: he compares Lesage's novel, *Gil Blas,* to the play, *The Marriage of Figaro,* which Beaumarchais made from the novel. "Gil Blas, like everybody else, wants to live, and if possible to live agreeably. That is not what we call having a will. But Figaro wants a certain definite thing, which is to prevent

Count Almaviva from exercising on Susanne the seigneurial privilege. He finally succeeds—and I grant, since the statement has been made, that it is not exactly through the means which he had chosen, most of which turn against him; but nevertheless he has constantly willed what he willed. He had not ceased to devise means of attaining it, and when these means have failed, he has not ceased to invent new ones." *

William Archer objects to Brunetière's theory on the ground that, "while it describes the matter of a good many dramas, it does not lay down any true differentia, any characteristic common to all true drama, and possessed by no other form of fiction." † Archer's objections seem to be chiefly directed against the idea of *specific volition:* He mentions a number of plays in which he feels that there is no genuine conflict of will. He contends that *Oedipus* and *Ghosts* do not come within the limits of Brunetière's formula. He evidently means that the clash of wills between *persons* is not sufficiently defined in these dramas. He says: "No one can say that the balcony scene in *Romeo and Juliet* is undramatic, or the 'Galeoto fu il libro' scene in Mr. Stephen Phillips' *Paolo and Francesca;* yet the point of these scenes is not a clash, but an ecstatic concordance, of wills." ‡

This confuses a conflict between persons with a conflict in which a conscious and definite aim has been set up in defiance of other persons or social forces. To be sure, the "clash of wills" in the balcony scene in *Romeo and Juliet* is not between the two persons on the stage. It would be absurd to suggest that the dramatist arbitrarily confine his art to the presentation of personal quarrels. Brunetière never maintains that any such direct opposition is required. On the contrary, he tells us that the theatre shows "the development of the human will, attacking the obstacles opposed to it by destiny, fortune, or circumstances." And again: "This is what may be called *will,* to set up a goal, and to direct everything toward it, to strive to bring everything into line with it." § Can there be any doubt that Romeo and Juliet are setting up a goal and striving "to bring everything into line with it?" They know exactly what they want, and are conscious of the difficulties which they must meet. This is equally true of the tragic lovers in *Paolo and Francesca.*

Archer's use of *Oedipus* and *Ghosts* as examples is of considerable interest, because it shows the trend of his thought. He says

---

* Brunetière, *opus cit.*
† Archer, *opus cit.*
‡ *Ibid.*
§ Brunetière, *opus cit.*

that Oedipus "does not struggle at all. His struggles insofar as that word can be applied to his misguided efforts to escape from the toils of fate, are all things of the past; in the actual course of the tragedy he simply writhes under one revelation after another of bygone error and unwitting crime." *

Archer's objection to the law of conflict goes far deeper than the question of *specific acts of volition:* although he disclaims any interest in the philosophic implications of the theory, his own point of view is essentially metaphysical; he accepts the idea of an absolute necessity which denies and paralyzes the will.

Archer neglects an important technical feature of *Oedipus* and *Ghosts.* Both plays employ the technique of beginning at a crisis. This necessarily means that a large part of the action is retrospective. But this does not mean that the action is passive, either in retrospect or in the crucial activity included in the play's structure. *Oedipus* is a series of conscious acts, directed toward sharply defined ends—the acts of men and women of strong will determined to prevent an impending danger. Their acts lead directly to a goal they are striving to avoid; one cannot assume that the exercise of the conscious will presupposes that the will accomplishes its aim. Indeed the intensity and meaning of the conflict lies in the disparity between the aim and the result, between the purpose and the achievement.

Oedipus is in no sense a passive victim. At the opening of the play he is aware of a problem, which he consciously strives to solve. This leads him to a violent conflict of will with Creon. Then Jocasta realizes the direction in which Oedipus' search is moving; she is faced with a terrible inner conflict; she tries to warn Oedipus, but he refuses to turn back from what he has *willed;* come what may, he must trace his own origin. When Oedipus faces the unbearable truth, he commits a conscious act: he blinds himself; and in the final scene with his two daughters, Antigone and Ismene, he is *still* facing the purport of the events which have crushed him; considering the future, the effect of his own acts upon his children, the measure of his own responsibility.

I have already stated that *Ghosts* is Ibsen's most vital study of personal and social responsibility. Mrs. Alving's life is a long, conscious fight to control her environment. Oswald does not accept his fate; he opposes it with all the force of his will. The end of the play shows Mrs. Alving faced with a terrible decision, a decision which strains her will to the breaking point—she must decide whether or not to kill her own son who has gone insane.

* Archer, *opus cit.*

What would *Ghosts* be like if it were (as Archer maintains it to be) a play without a conscious struggle of wills? It is very difficult to conceive of the play in this way: the only events which would be partly unchanged would be Oswald's insanity and the burning of the orphanage. But there would be no action whatsoever leading to these situations. And even Oswald's cry, "give me the sun," would of necessity be omitted, since it expresses conscious will. Furthermore, if no exercise of conscious will were concerned, the orphanage would never have been built.

While denying that conflict is invariably present in drama, Archer does not agree with the Maeterlinckian theory which denies action and finds dramatic power in a man "submitting with bent head to the presence of his soul and his destiny." Archer is well aware that the theatre must deal with *situations* which affect the lives and emotions of human beings. Since he disapproves of the idea of a conflict of will, he suggests that the word, *crisis,* is more universally characteristic of dramatic representation. "The drama," he says, "may be called the art of crises, as fiction is the art of gradual developments." * While this is not an inclusive definition, there can be no question that the idea of *crisis* adds something very pertinent to our conception of dramatic conflict. One can readily imagine a conflict which does not reach a crisis; in our daily lives we take continuous part in such conflicts. A struggle which fails to reach a crisis is undramatic. Nevertheless we cannot be satisfied with Archer's statement that "the essence of drama is crisis." An earthquake is a crisis, but its dramatic significance lies in the reactions and acts of human beings. If *Ghosts* consisted only of Oswald's insanity and the burning of the orphanage it would include two crises, but no conscious will and no *preparation.* When human beings are involved in events which lead to a crisis, they do not stand idly by and watch the climax approach. Human beings seek to shape events for their own advantage, to extricate themselves from difficulties which are partially foreseen. The activity of the conscious will, seeking a way out, creates the very conditions which precipitate the crisis.

Henry Arthur Jones, in analyzing the points of view of Brunetière and Archer, tries to combine them by defining a play as "a succession of suspenses and crises, or as a succession of conflicts impending and conflicts raging, carried on in ascending and accelerated climaxes from the beginning to the end of a connected scheme." †

* *Ibid.*
† Introduction to Brunetière's *The Law of the Drama.*

This is a richly suggestive definition. But it is a definition of dramatic *construction* rather than of dramatic *principle*. It tells us a great deal about construction, particularly in the mention of "ascending and accelerated climaxes." But it does not mention the conscious will, and therefore throws very little light on the psychological factor which gives these climaxes their social and emotional significance. The meaning of the situations lies in the degree and kind of conscious will exerted, and in how it *works;* the crisis, the dramatic explosion, is created by *the gap between the aim and the result*—that is, by a shift of equilibrium between the force of will and the force of social necessity. A crisis is the point at which the balance of forces is so strained that something cracks, thus causing a realignment of forces, a new pattern of relationships.

The will which creates drama is directed toward a specific goal. But the goal which it selects must be sufficiently *realistic* to enable the will to have some effect on reality. We in the audience must be able to understand the goal and the possibility of its fulfillment. The kind of will exerted must spring from a consciousness of reality which corresponds to our own. This is a variable factor, which can be accurately determined by an analysis of the social viewpoint of the audience.

But we are concerned not only with the *consciousness* of will, but with the *strength* of will. The exercise of will must be sufficiently vigorous to sustain and develop the conflict to a point of issue. A conflict which fails to reach a crisis is a conflict of weak wills. In Greek and Elizabethan tragedy, the point of maximum strain is generally reached in the death of the hero: he is crushed by the forces which oppose him, or he takes his own life in recognition of his defeat.

Brunetière concludes that strength of will is the only test of dramatic value: "One drama is superior to another drama according as the quantity of will exerted is greater or less, as the share of chance is less and that of necessity greater." * One cannot accept this mechanical formulation. In the first place, there is no way to measure the quantity of will exerted. In the second place, the struggle is relative and not absolute. Necessity is simply the totality of the environment, and is, as we have observed, a variable quantity, depending on social concepts. This is a matter of quality as well as quantity. Our conception of the quality of the will and the quality of the forces to which it is opposed determines our acknowledgment of the depth and scope of the conflict. The highest dramatic art is not achieved by pitting the most gigantic will

* *Opus cit.*

against the most absolute necessity. The agonized struggle of a weak will, seeking to adjust itself to an inhospitable environment, may contain elements of poignant drama.

But however weak the will may be, it must be *sufficiently strong* to sustain the conflict. Drama cannot deal with people whose wills are atrophied, who are unable to make decisions which have even temporary meaning, who adopt no conscious attitude toward events, who make no effort to control their environment. The precise degree of strength of will required is the strength needed to bring the action to an issue, to create a change of equilibrium between the individual and the environment.

The definition with which we begin this chapter may be re-examined and re-phrased as follows:

> *The essential character of drama is social conflict—persons against other persons, or individuals against groups, or groups against other groups, or individuals or groups against social or natural forces—in which the conscious will, exerted for the accomplishment of specific and understandable aims, is sufficiently strong to bring the conflict to a point of crisis.*

CHAPTER II

DRAMATIC ACTION

THE definition which concludes the preceding chapter serves as a starting point for the discussion of action. The major crisis which brings the unified dramatic conflict to a head is not the only crisis in the play: dramatic movement proceeds by a series of changes of equilibrium. Any change of equilibrium constitutes *an action*. The play is a system of *actions,* a system of minor and major changes of equilibrium. The climax of the play is the maximum disturbance of equilibrium which can take place under the given conditions.

In discussing Aristotle, we noted the importance of his treatment of action, not as a quality of construction, but as the essence of construction, the unifying principle at the core of the play. So far we have not developed this point; we have examined the forces which create dramatic conflict; but we have not shown how these forces take a definitive form; the statement that a play is a system of actions leading to a major change of equilibrium is a generalization, but it gives us very little clue to the structure of the system;

it does not show us how the beginning, middle and end of the system are determined.

In this sense, the problem of action is the whole problem of dramatic construction and cannot be considered as a separate question. However, it is well to give some consideration to the meaning of *action as a quality*. This is important because it is the only side of the problem which is considered in technical studies of the drama. We are told that a bit of dialogue or a scene or an entire play has the quality of action, or lacks the quality of action. Since it is generally agreed that this quality is essential to drama, it must be very closely related to the *principle of action* which unifies the whole structure.

The present chapter deals only with action as a quality which gives impact, life and color to certain scenes. St. John Ervine says: "A dramatist, when he talks of action, does not mean bustle or mere physical movement: he means development and growth." Ervine regrets that people are slow to understand this: "When you speak of action to them, they immediately imagine that you mean *doing things*." * There can be no question that action involves "development and growth"; but one can sympathize with those who cling to the idea that action means *doing things*. If the conscious will does not cause people to do things, how does it make itself manifest? Development and growth cannot result from inactivity.

George Pierce Baker says that action may be either physical or mental provided it creates *emotional response*. This is of very little value unless we know what constitutes an emotional response. Since what moves us in any action is the spectacle of a change of equilibrium between the individual and the environment, we cannot speak of any action as being exclusively mental or exclusively physical; the change must affect *both* the individual's mind and the objective reality with which he is in contact. Such a change need not involve bustle or violence, but it must involve *doing something,* because if nothing is done the equilibrium would remain static. Furthermore, the change of equilibrium does not happen mechanically, at a given *point;* it is a process which includes the expectation of change, the attempt to bring the change about, as well as the change itself.

How are we to apply this principle to a particular scene or group of scenes?

Brunetière defines action by going straight back to his point of departure—the exercise of the conscious will. He says that the use of the conscious will serves to "distinguish action from motion or

* *Opus cit.*

agitation." But this is arguing in a circle. The conscious will is a necessary reference point in studying action, but it cannot be confused with the action itself. We examine the conscious will in order to discover the origin and validity of the action. But we do not see or hear the conscious will. What we see and hear is a physical event, which must be defined in terms of seeing and hearing.

Brunetière explains what he means by action—as distinguished from motion or agitation—by an illustration which is far from convincing: "When you have two men earnestly intent on opposite sides of some issue vital to themselves, you have a contest or play, interesting, exciting or absorbing to watch." * I think we have all seen the two men of whom Brunetière speaks. They are frequently visible in life, and they are also often to be found behind the footlights, "intent on opposite sides of some issue vital to themselves." To assume that therefore "you have a contest or play," is, to put it mildly, optimistic.

A debate is not an action, however conscious and willing the participants may be. It is equally obvious that a vast amount of commotion may result in an infinitesimal amount of action. A play may contain a duel in every scene, a pitched battle in every act— and the spectators may be sound asleep, or be kept awake only by the noise.

Let us begin by distinguishing *action* (dramatic movement) from *activity* (by which we mean movement in general). Action is a kind of activity, a form of movement in general. The effectiveness of action does not depend on what people do, but on the *meaning* of what they do. We know that the root of this meaning lies in the conscious will. But how does the meaning express itself in dramatic movement? How are we to judge its objective realization?

Is it possible that intense meaning may be expressed in the dialogue of two persons who sit facing each other and who never move during a considerable scene? Hamlet's soliloquy, "To be or not to be," is dramatically effective. Is it action? Or should it be criticized as a static element in the play's development?

Action may be confined to a minimum of physical activity. But it must be noted that this *minimum,* however slight, determines the meaning of the action. Physical activity is *always* present. To be seated in a chair involves the act of sitting, the use of a certain muscular effort to maintain the position. To speak involves the act of speaking, the use of the throat muscles, movement of the lips, etc. If a tense conflict is involved, the mere act of sitting

* *Opus cit.*

or speaking will involve a proportionately greater physical effort.

The problem of action is the problem of finding the characteristic and necessary activity. It must involve physical movement (however slight) of a given quality and conveying a given degree of expressiveness. In this connection, a study of the art of acting is of special value to the playwright. The methods of Stanislavski and Vakhtangov, in spite of their limitations, are of tremendous value to the actor, because they assist him in finding the precise physical activity which expresses the emotional direction, habits, purposes, desires, of the character. The actor seeks to create the character in terms of meaningful and living movement.

The playwright's problem is similar: he must find action which intensifies and heightens the conflict of will. Thus, two persons facing each other, not moving and speaking quietly, may offer the exact degree of activity in a given scene. But the important thing in the scene is not the slightness of the movement, but the quality of it—the degree of muscular tension, of expressiveness. Even though the scene may appear to be static, its static element is negative. The positive element is movement.

Then what about speech? Speech is also a form of action. Dialogue which is abstract or deals with general feelings or ideas, is undramatic. Speech is valid insofar as it describes or expresses action. The action projected by the spoken word may be retrospective, or potential—or it may actually accompany the speech. But the only test of what is said lies in its concreteness, its physical impact, its quality of tension.

The idea that speech can simply reveal a mental state is illogical: the *act* of speaking objectivizes the mental state. As long as the action remains in the mind, the audience knows nothing about it. As soon as the character speaks, the element of physical activity and purpose is present. If the speech is cloudy and lacks concreteness, it will give us only a slight impression of consciousness and purpose and will be a bad speech. Nevertheless we ask: *why* is this man speaking? What does he want? Even if he assures us that his mental condition is completely passive, we cannot believe him: we *still* want to know why he is talking and what he expects to get out of it.

There is also another important characteristic of action: this may be called its fluidity. It is evident that action by its nature cannot be static. However, if activity is repeated, or if its connection with other activity is not indicated, it may well give a static impression. Action (as distinguished from activity) must be in *process of becoming;* therefore it must rise out of other action, and must lead to other, and different, action. Each change of equilibrium involves prior and forthcoming changes or equilibrium. This means also, that the timing of any action, the length of time in proportion to the amount of activity, must be considered.

The situation in which two people sit facing each other and talk quietly may now be judged in the light of several definite questions: Are they *merely* sitting? Or is their sitting expressive of a certain stage of conflict? Does their sitting represent a change in their relationship to each other or to their environment? Are they sitting because they are afraid to move? Or does the sitting give one or the other an advantage in a struggle? Is the sitting intended to exasperate or frighten or disturb the other party? Or are both waiting for news, or for an event, so that they sit in order to console or strengthen one another?

The most serious question in regard to this scene is one which can only be answered by viewing its progression in connection with the scenes which precede and follow it, and in connection with the play as a whole. The scene, in the various forms in which it has been described, contains the expectation of a change in equilibrium. If two people sit facing each other because they are afraid to move, or because they wish to exasperate or frighten the other party, or because they are waiting for news, the element of tension is undoubtedly present. But we must ask whether this tension leads to anything? The scene must actually achieve a change of equilibrium, both in relation to previous and following scenes and in relation to the movement within the scene itself. If the scene does not produce such a change, the tension is false and the element of action is lacking. Progression requires physical movement; but it also lies in the movement of the dialogue, in the extension and development of action through the medium of speech.

Hamlet's soliloquy can be considered in this light. His speech expresses an imminent change of equilibrium, because he is deciding whether or not to take his own life. This represents a new phase in Hamlet's struggle, and leads immediately to another phase, because the soliloquy is broken by the meeting with Ophelia. The language makes the conflict objective, offering the problem in sharply defined images. The physical activity expresses the tension: a man alone on the stage, solitary, facing death. But the aloneness flows immediately from, and to, other action. If the action of the soliloquy were maintained too long, it would become static.

Note the position of the suicide soliloquy. It is preceded by the scene in which the King and Polonius plan to have Ophelia meet Hamlet apparently by accident, while his enemies spy on the encounter: it is followed by the hotly emotional scene between Ophelia and Hamlet, in which he realizes that she is betraying him: "Are you honest?... Are you fair?... Get thee to a nunnery: why wouldst thou be a breeder of sinners?"

Hamlet is often spoken of as a *subjective* play. Hamlet's will fails him and he finds it difficult to achieve the tasks which are forced upon him. But his attempt to adjust himself to the world he lives in is presented in vigorously objective terms: he finds that he cannot trust his friends, Rosencrantz and Guildenstern, that even the woman he loves is deceiving him. So he turns desperately to another phase of the problem, to probe the truth in regard to his mother and his uncle, to prove and prove again the fact which tortures him. This is dramatized in the violent activity of the play within the play. Then, knowing the truth beyond all doubt, he is forced to face the unbearable implications of the truth—in the scene with his mother. Here again objective activity accompanies the mental conflict: Polonius is killed; Hamlet compares the portraits of his dead father and his living uncle; the ghost enters to warn Hamlet of his "blunted purpose," to counsel him to better understand his mother: "O, step between her and her fighting soul." This line is an extremely pertinent example of action-dialogue. Although the idea is psychological, it is expressed in terms of action. It presents an image, not of some one feeling something, but of some one doing something.

Dramatic action is activity combining physical movement and speech; it includes the expectation, preparation and accomplishment of a change of equilibrium which is part of a series of such changes. The movement toward a change of equilibrium may be gradual, but the process of change must actually take place. False expectation and false preparation are not dramatic action. Action may be complex or simple, but all its parts must be objective, progressive, meaningful.

This definition is valid as far as it goes. But we cannot pretend that it is complete. The difficulty lies in the words "progressive" and "meaningful." Progression is a matter of structure, and meaning is a matter of theme. Neither problem can be solved until we find the unifying principle which gives the play its *wholeness,* binding a series of actions into *an action which is organic and indivisible.*

CHAPTER III

UNITY IN TERMS OF CLIMAX

"IT is a matter of no small difficulty," wrote Corneille in 1660, "to determine what unity of action is." * Corneille continued: "The poet must treat his subject according to 'the probable' and 'the necessary.' This is what Aristotle says, and all his commentators repeat the words which appear to them so clear and intelligible that not one of them has deigned any more than Aristotle himself to tell us what the 'probable' and the 'necessary' are."

This indicates both the scope of the problem and the direction in which the solution must be sought. The playwright's choice of theme is guided by his conception of the *probable* and *necessary;* the determination to achieve a probable end arouses the conscious will; the "iron framework of fact" sets a necessary limit upon the action of the will. Aristotle spoke simply of "a beginning, a middle and an end." It is obvious that a play which begins by chance and ends because two and one-half hours have passed, is not a play. Its beginning and its end, and the arrangement of the parts in a related design, are dictated by the need of realizing the social conception which constitutes the theme.

[The general principle that unity of action is identical with unity of theme is beyond dispute.] But this does not solve the problem— because the conception of unity of theme is as abstract as the conception of unity of action. [In practice, real unity must be a synthesis of theme and action, and we must find out how this combination is achieved.]

Many practical playwrights feel that construction is a matter of shrewd application of a simple formula: Frank Craven (as quoted by Arthur Edwin Krows) suggests: "Get 'em in hot water and get 'em out again." Emile Augier advises the dramatist to "soak your fifth act in gentle tears, and salt the other four with dashes of wit." Bronson Howard speaks of playwriting as "the art of using your common sense in the study of your own and other people's emotions."

Lope De Vega, writing in 1609, on *The New Art of Making Plays in This Age,* gave a brief but useful summary of construction:

---

* Clark, *European Theories of the Drama.*

"In the first act set forth the case. In the second weave together the events, in such wise that until the middle of the third act one may hardly guess the outcome. Always trick expectancy." *

According to Dumas the Younger, "Before every situation that a dramatist creates, he should ask himself three questions. In this situation, what should I do? What would other people do? What ought to be done? Every author who does not feel disposed to make this analysis should renounce the theatre, for he will never become a dramatist." Since this is sound practical advice, it also has a sound theoretical foundation. These three questions are of basic importance, involving the playwright's point of view, the psychology of the characters, and the social significance of the situation.

But Dumas sets no definite limits to the possibilities of "what ought to be done?" A social analysis along these lines might be applied to a series of diffuse and disorganized situations. Dumas does not ask: how was the situation created in the first place? What led the dramatist to remember or imagine this situation, and to select it as a part of his dramatic structure? In this question— covering the process by which the theme is conceived and developed in the playwright's mind—lies the essence of unity.

If we turn to more theoretical discussions of technique, we find that the origin and growth of the theme is either ignored or treated as a mystery. In outlining his theory that "the drama may be called the art of crises," Archer tells us that "a dramatic scene is a crisis (or climax) building to an ultimate climax which is the core of the action." The dramatic scenes are held together by sustained and increasing tension. "A great part of the secret of dramatic architecture lies in the one word, tension; to engender, maintain, suspend, heighten and resolve a state of tension." †

George Pierce Baker says that sustained interest in a play depends on "clearness and right emphasis" ... and "a third essential quality, movement ... a straining forward of interest, a compelling desire to know what will happen next." And again, "there should be good movement within the scene, the act and even the play as a whole." ‡

Freytag, with his customary grandeur, describes dramatic structure as the "efflux of will-power, the accomplishment of a deed and its reaction on the soul, movement and counter-movement, strife and counter-strife, rising and sinking, binding and loosing." §

Does this throw any light on what Aristotle called "the struc-

* Brewster translation, *opus cit.*
† *Opus cit.*
‡ *Opus cit.*
§ *Opus cit.*

tural union of the parts"? Tension, the "straining forward of interest," "movement and counter-movement," are qualities of action; but they do not necessarily imply an action which is organic and complete within itself. If Aristotle is correct in saying that unity of the parts must be "such that, if any one of them is displaced or removed, the whole will be disjointed and disturbed," there ought to be some definite test of unity, by which we can judge and discard "a thing whose presence or absence makes no visible difference."

It is often thought that unity can be mechanically achieved through the physical concentration of the material: the action must be centered on one individual or closely associated group of individuals, or upon a single incident or narrowly limited group of incidents. But attempts of this sort defeat their own purpose. Aristotle settles the matter with his customary lucidity: "For infinitely various are the incidents in one man's life which cannot be reduced to unity; and so, too, there are many actions of one man out of which we cannot make one action."

The dramatist cannot "make one action," either by limiting the scope of the play's movement, or by dealing with "one man's life." Many plays attain the most intense thematic concentration in handling a multiplicity of events and characters. For example, *The Weavers*, by Gerhart Hauptmann, introduces different groups of people in each act. The third act shows us a new set of characters at the village inn. The fifth act takes us to old weaver Hilse's workshop at Langen-Bielau, introducing Hilse and his family who have played no part in the previous development of the action. But the play gives the effect of harmonious and unified construction. On the other hand, *Both Your Houses,* which deals with a single slight anecdote, is unnecessarily diffuse.

The Russian motion picture, *Three Songs About Lenin,* covers a vast field of activity, including incidents from Lenin's career, the work and lives of the Soviet masses, and the effect of his death upon people in all parts of the Soviet Union. Yet this picture is compact, clear, orderly in construction.

The unifying force is the *idea;* but an idea, however integral it may be, is in itself undramatic. By an apparently miraculous transformation, the abstraction in the playwright's mind comes alive! St. John Ervine says that "a play should be a living organism, so alive that when any part of it is cut off the body bleeds!" * How is this living entity produced? Does the creator breathe the breath of life into his creation through the intensity of his own feeling? Is the

* *Opus cit.*

livingness of it emotional rather than anatomical? Or is the creative
process *both* emotional and deeply rational?

In Schlegel's critical writings, we find the contradiction between
the inspirational theory of art and the deep logic of the creative
process revealed in its clearest form. Schlegel demanded "a deeper,
more intrinsic, and more mysterious unity." He was right in saying
that unity "arises out of the primary and spontaneous activity of
the human mind." But he confused the issue by adding that "the
idea of *One* and *Whole* is in no way derived from experience."
How can anything be known or experienced, except through the
primary activity of the human mind?

Although he declared that unity is beyond rational knowing,
Schlegel himself touched the heart of the problem and pointed the
way to a precise understanding of the way in which *the idea of
dramatic unity is derived from experience.* Unity of action, he said,
"will consist in its direction toward a single end; and to its completeness belongs all that lies between the first determination and
the execution of the deed ... its absolute beginning is the assertion
of free will, with the acknowledgment of necessity its absolute
end." *

This seems to place the scope of the action within definite limits:
but the *absolute beginning* and the *absolute end* are merely fictions
unless we are able to reach a workaday understanding of the meaning of free will and necessity as they operate in our experience. As
long as these concepts remain on a metaphysical plane, the limits
of the probable and the necessary are the limits of the universe.
This was the difficulty which Schlegel was unable to solve.

We have observed that the relationship between free will and
necessity is a continuously shifting balance of forces: this continuity
of movement precludes the idea of absolute beginnings or endings;
we cannot conceive of an assertion of free will which is genuinely
free; this would be an unmotivated decision in an untouched field
of experience. When the will is asserted in a certain direction, the
decision is based on the sum-total of the necessities which we have
previously experienced. This enables us to form a more or less
correct picture of future probabilities, which governs our course of
action. Then the beginnings of an action are not determined merely
by the feeling that the will must be asserted; the beginning of the
action is rooted in necessity just as firmly as the end—the end constitutes the testing, the acceptance or rejection, of the picture of
necessity which motivated the beginning.

This leads us to a genuinely organic conception of unity: the

* *Opus cit.*

movement of the drama does not move loosely between the opposite poles of free will and necessity: the determination to perform an act includes the picture of *how the act will look and what its effect will be* when performed: there is no dualism of the probable and the necessary; probability is what we imagine necessity to be before it happens.

Therefore every detail of the action is determined by the *end* toward which the action is moving. But this end is no more *absolute* than the beginning: it does not represent necessity in any final form: by necessity we mean the laws that govern reality; reality is fluid and we cannot imagine it in any final form. The climax of the play, being the point of highest tension, gives the fullest expression to the laws of reality as the playwright conceives them. The climax resolves the conflict by a change of equilibrium which creates a new balance of forces: the necessity which makes this event inevitable is the playwright's necessity: it expresses the social meaning which led him to invent the action.

The climax is the concrete realization of the theme in terms of an event. In practical playwriting, this means that the climax is the point of reference by which the validity of every element of the structure can be determined.

It is sometimes possible to state the theme of a play in a single phrase: for instance, *Wednesday's Child,* by Leopold Atlas, deals with the sufferings of a sensitive boy whose parents are divorced; this is an adequate statement of the theme which forms the unifying motif of the drama. It is obvious that every scene of the play contributes to the picture of the adolescent boy's suffering.

The action preserves the unity of theme: but does this mean that the movement of the play is so closely knit that every turn of the action is inevitable, that the removal of any part would cause the whole to be "disjointed and disturbed"? We cannot answer this question by referring to the play's subject-matter or purpose: the same theme might have been presented by another arrangement of incidents. One might invent dozens, or hundreds, or thousands of incidents, which would all have a direct bearing on the sufferings of a sensitive child of divorced parents.

If we turn to the climax of *Wednesday's Child,* we have an adequate means of testing the play's development: we no longer ask vague questions about the theme. Rather we ask: What happens to the boy? What is the final statement of his problem in terms of action? The playwright *must* have embodied his living meaning, his consciousness and purpose toward the lives of his characters, in the climactic event. Does every scene build toward this final statement? Could any event be omitted without disjointing and disturbing the ending?

The last scene of *Wednesday's Child* shows Bobby Phillips wearing a uniform in a military school, unutterably lonely but bravely determined to keep a stiff upper lip. This is a genuinely touching conclusion, but we immediately observe that the climax itself is not completely realized. If the climax is the test of the play's meaning, the climax must be clear enough and strong enough to hold the play together: it must be *an action,* fully developed and involving a definite change of equilibrium between the characters and their environment.

The atmosphere of a military school and its social implications must have a very direct bearing on Bobby Phillips' character. Since the author has introduced the military school, he must face what it means; it represents a new stage in the relationship between Bobby Phillips and his environment. In order to give this situation dramatic meaning, we must understand it in connection with the totality of the boy's previous experience. The author does not project this problem: if we go back to earlier scenes, we find that the action is *not* built in terms of the conclusion; it is built in terms of the relation of the boy to his parents; every scene does *not* inevitably lead to the figure of the lonely child in a military uniform. The ending is a way out, a trick of bringing down the curtain. The fault does not lie in the fact that the ending is inconclusive. It is proper, and sometimes brilliantly effective, to end a play on a question-mark. But we must know what the question-mark means: we must see how it arises out of the given social relationships, and to what alternatives it will lead. When the playwright asks a question, he must have an integrated point of view toward his own question: otherwise, the question leads in *all* directions, and the action is diffused instead of being concentrated.

The conceptual confusion exposed at the close of *Wednesday's Child* causes the play to become weaker as it proceeds. The first three scenes are tremendously exciting, because the author has succeeded in these scenes in presenting the child's consciousness and will in relation to his environment. The masterly introductory scene in the Phillips' dining room exposes the family conflict in intense action; we see the burden on the child's mind and we see the web of necessity from which the parents are trying to extricate themselves. The second scene, in a corner of the back lot, shows the boy's poignant struggle to adjust himself among the other children in the neighborhood. The third scene brings the struggle of the parents to a climax; we are aware of the child overhearing the scene; we see the problem through his consciousness and will.

From this point the progression is clouded. Destiny takes control of the action; the pathos of the child's position and the difficulties of a solution are presented in terms of emotional drift: the social problem, which is powerfully dramatized in the first three scenes, is repeated in a static situation in the courtroom scene which closes the first act. In the second act, the problem of the parents is emphasized; they are well-meaning but helpless; good will is substituted for will operating toward a conscious goal; their kindly intentions have no dramatic value because the real trouble lies in the fact that they have ceased to be interested in the child: since this is a passive attitude, it cannot create meaningful progression. The scenes of the second act simply repeat the parents' problem, accompanied by the repetition of the boy's bewilderment and need. The dramatist assumes that necessity is absolute and that there is no remedy for the situation. For this reason, the action becomes *less* convincing; we are not sure whether or not a satisfactory adjustment could have been created between the boy and one or the other of his divorced parents, because the conscious wills of the characters are not exerted toward such an adjustment. On the other hand, if it is assumed that the child is unwanted, the dramatist makes a mistake in devoting the greater part of his second act to proving this negative conclusion; he should rather analyze the boy's conscious will in his lonely attempt to adjust himself to new facts. The final scene shows the boy's loneliness, but it shows it negatively, as an *emotion,* because we have not entered deeply enough into his mind to know how his consciousness and will react to the new environment.

Perhaps a word of explanation is needed as to the use of the term, *climax.* The reader may doubt whether the scene in the military school may properly be called the climax of *Wednesday's Child.* The climax is often regarded as a central point in the action, followed by the "falling action" which leads to the denouement or solution. A detailed analysis of "Climax and Solution" will be found in a later chapter. For the present, it is sufficient to point out that the term *climax* is used as covering the final and most intense stage of the action. This is not necessarily the final scene; it is the scene in which the final phase of the conflict is reached. I believe the military school in *Wednesday's Child* represents the highest stage of the boy's struggle, and must therefore be regarded as the climax.

The centering of the action upon a definite goal creates the in-

tegrated movement which is the essence of drama: it gives new
meaning to the "clearness and right emphasis" and the "straining
forward of interest" of which Baker speaks. It gives practical
application to Archer's statement that the "ultimate climax" is
"the core of the action."

The principle of unity in terms of climax is not a new one; but,
as far as I am aware, it has not been clearly analyzed or applied.
The nearest approach to a logical statement of the principle may
be found in John Dryden's *Essay on Dramatic Poesie:* "As for
the third unity, which is that of action, the ancients meant no other
by it than what the logicians do by their *finis,* the end, or scope, of
any action; that which is first in intention and last in execution." *

Many playwrights have pointed to the necessity of testing the
action in terms of the ending. "You should not begin your work,"
said Dumas the Younger, "until you have your concluding scene,
movement and speech clear in your mind." Ernest Legouve gives
the same advice: "You ask me how a play is made. By beginning
at the end." Percival Wilde is of the same opinion: "Begin at the
End and go Back till you come to the Beginning. Then start."

The advice to "begin at the end" is sound as far as it goes. But
the author who attempts to apply this advice as a cut-and-dried
rule will get very meager results; the mechanical act of writing the
climax first cannot be of any value unless one understands the
function of the climax and the system of cause and effect which
binds it to the play as a whole.

The laws of thought which underlie the creative process require
that the playwright begin with a root-idea. He may be unconscious
of this; he may think that the creative urge springs from random
and purposeless thoughts; but disorganized thought cannot lead to
organized activity; however vague his social attitude may be, it is
sufficiently conscious and purposive to lead him to the volitional
representation of action. Baker says that "a play may start from
almost anything; a detached thought that flashes through the mind;
a theory of conduct or of art which one firmly believes or wishes
only to examine; a bit of dialogue overheard or imagined; a setting,
real or imagined, which creates emotion in the observer; a perfectly
detached scene, the antecedents and consequences of which are as
yet unknown; a figure glimpsed in a crowd which for some reason
arrests the attention of the dramatist, or a figure closely studied;
a contrast or similarity between two people or conditions of life;
a mere incident—noted in a newspaper or book, heard in idle talk,

* *Opus cit.*

or observed; or a story, told only in the barest outlines or with the utmost detail." *

There is no doubt that a playwright *may* start with any of these odds and ends of fact or fancy. He *may* complete an entire play by spontaneously piecing together bits of experience and information, without ever attaining the slightest understanding of the principles which underlie his activity. But whether he knows it or not, the process is not as spontaneous as it appears. The "bit of dialogue," or "figure glimpsed in a crowd," or detailed story, do not appeal to him by chance; the reason lies in a point of view which he has developed as a result of his own experience; his point of view is sufficiently definite to make him feel the need of crystallizing it; he wants to find events which have a bearing on the picture of events which he has formed in his mind. When he finds a "bit of dialogue" or a "figure glimpsed in a crowd" or a story, he is not satisfied that this proves or justifies his point of view —if he were satisfied, he would stop right there, and would not be moved to further activity. What he seeks is the most complete volitional representation of the root-idea. The root-idea is abstract, because it is the sum-total of many experiences. He cannot be satisfied until he has turned it into a living event.

The root-idea is the beginning of the process. The next step is the discovery of *an action* which expresses the root-idea. This action is the most fundamental action of the play; it is the climax and the limit of the play's development, because it embodies the playwright's idea of social necessity, which defines the play's scope and purpose. In searching for this root-action, the author may collect or invent any number of ideas or incidents or characters; he may suppose that these are of value in themselves; but logically he cannot test their value or put them to work until he has found the fundamental event which serves as climax. The meaning of any incident depends on its relationship to reality; an isolated incident (in a play or in life) assumes a meaning for *us* insofar as it appeals to our sense of what is probable or necessary; but there is no final truth as to probability and necessity; the system of incidents which constitutes a play depends on the *playwright's* sense of what is probable and necessary: until he has defined this, by defining the goal and scope of the action, his efforts can have neither unity nor rational purpose.

While the laws of living movement go forward from cause to effect, the laws of volitional representation go *backward,* from effect to cause. The necessity for this lies in the fact that the repre-

* *Opus cit.*

sentation is volitional; the playwright creates from what he has known and experienced, and therefore must think back over his knowledge and experience to seek out causes which lead to the goal which his conscious will has selected. Thus the concentration on the crisis and the retrospective analysis of causes which we find in much of the world's greatest drama (Greek tragedy and Ibsen's social plays) follow the logic of dramatic thought in its most natural form. The extension of the action in the Elizabethan theatre grows out of a wider and less inhibited social point of view, which permits a freer investigation of causes. The dramatic system of events may attain any degree of extension or complexity, provided the result (the root-action) is clearly defined.

There can be no doubt that many playwrights construct the preliminary action of a projected drama without knowing what the climax will be. To some extent, a dramatist may be justified in doing this, because it may be his best means of clarifying his own purpose. But he should be aware of the principles which guide his effort, and which are operative whether or not he is conscious of them. In developing preliminary incidents, he is seeking for the root-action; uncertainty in regard to the root-action indicates uncertainty in regard to the root-idea; the playwright who feels his way toward an unknown climax is confused as to the social meaning of the events with which he is dealing; in order to remedy this conceptual confusion he must be aware of it; he must seek to define his point of view, and to give it living form in the climax. He is justified in writing preliminary material at random only if he knows *why* he is writing at random; much of this preliminary material will prove useful, because it springs from the confused point of view which the playwright is endeavoring to clarify; but when the playwright has cut through his confusion and discovered the meaning and scope of the action, he must subject his work to a rigorous analysis in terms of climax. Otherwise, the conceptual confusion will persist; the action will be spotty or disorganized; the connection between the events and the climax will be obscured. It may happen, as in the case of a surprising number of modern plays, that the author has inadvertently omitted the climax altogether.

In using the climax as a reference point, we must remember that we are dealing with living stuff and not with inorganic matter. The climax (like every other part of the play) is a movement, a change of equilibrium. The inter-relation of the parts is complicated and dynamic. The climax serves as a unifying force, but it is not static; while the play is built in terms of the climax, every event, every element of the action, reacts upon, remolds and revitalizes the climax itself.

This is clear if we think of the playwright as a person performing an act: to act without conscious purpose is irrational; to change one's purpose while one is trying to accomplish it shows weakness and confusion; also, that the purpose was not sufficiently analyzed before the act was undertaken. If it turns out that the purpose cannot be accomplished, then the act must be abandoned. (The playwright can show the failure of his characters, but he cannot show his own failure to write a play.) But every step in the performance of the act adds to one's understanding of one's own aim and modifies its meaning and desirability.

Archer says of Ibsen's notebooks: "Nowhere else as far as I am aware, do we obtain so clear a view of the processes of a great dramatist's mind." * Ibsen's creative method, as he reveals it in the notebooks, shows that he proceeds from the root-idea to the root-action; the development of the play consists in bringing every incident into line with the climactic event. Ibsen's first step is the statement of the theme in abstract terms. The social concept underlying *Hedda Gabler* has already been mentioned. Ibsen states the problem carefully and concretely: "Hedda's despair is that there are doubtless so many chances of happiness in the world, but that she cannot discover them. It is the want of an object in life which torments her." † He then proceeds to develop a series of brief outlines and snatches of dialogue. This material covers the whole course of the play; its evident purpose is to find the physical action which expresses the theme.

When Ibsen has thus succeeded in creating his theme dynamically, he proceeds to his third task, which he describes (in a letter to Theodor Caspari) ‡ as "more energetic individualization of the persons and their modes of expression." This process of revision is certainly a process of "individualization"; but it can be more technically described as the process whereby the author coördinates every incident of his play with the crisis which is to follow. We find the early drafts of *Hedda Gabler* omit certain things which are vital to a full understanding of Hedda's suicide. Mademoiselle Diane is not mentioned in the first version; Hedda's jealousy of Mrs. Elvsted's lovely hair, "I think I must burn your hair off, after all," is a later development. Both the jealousy motif and the reference to Mademoiselle Diane are *essential* to the develop-

---

* Introduction to v. 12 of *The Collected Works of Henrik Ibsen.*
† Ibsen, *opus cit.*, v. 12.
‡ Quoted by Archer in his introduction to the notebooks (v. 12, *ibid.*).

ment of the climax. Since Hedda's suicide must be the result of
her certainty that there are no available chances of happiness, every
moment of the action must contribute to her frustration and
desperation. It is significant that Ibsen's early plans seem to have
called for the manuscript being destroyed by Tesman instead of by
Hedda. This would throw the whole conflict out of balance; it
would make Tesman a more active person, and Hedda more
passive. The whole tendency of Ibsen's original plans was to give
Tesman a more dynamic rôle. It was Tesman who lured Lövborg
to Judge Brack's party. This might have contributed to a more
interesting relationship between husband and wife; but a development along these lines would make Hedda's fevered search for
happiness less dramatic; it would not conform to Ibsen's root-idea
as he had outlined it. Hedda's despair is not due to the fact that
her *marriage* is unhappy; it is due to the fact that "there are
doubtless so many chances of happiness" which she is unable to
discover. The circumstances of Hedda's suicide, following the news
of Lövborg's death and the threats of Judge Brack, express this
root-idea. All of Ibsen's revisions are designed to intensify and
clarify the suicide.*

In the first plans, both Tesman and Mrs. Elvsted show far more
knowledge of the relationship which has existed between Hedda
and Lövborg. In the first act of the play as finally completed, Mrs.
Elvsted says, "A woman's shadow stands between Eilert Lövborg
and me." Hedda asks, "Who can that be?" and Mrs. Elvsted
replies, "I don't know." But in the earlier version, Mrs. Elvsted
answers directly: "It is you, Hedda." This knowledge on the part
of Mrs. Elvsted and Tesman might have great dramatic value in
the development of the play; the only test by which this element
can be accepted or discarded is its effect on the climax. Ibsen uses
this test: if people *know* about Hedda and Lövborg, it brings her
problem to an earlier and different issue; it means that, at an
earlier point in the action, her conscious will must be concentrated
on protecting herself and on solving this issue. But Ibsen wishes
to show that Hedda's conscious will is *not* centered on her relationship to Lövborg or to her husband; "it is the want of an
object in life which torments her." Ibsen projects this problem
in concrete dramatic terms, because he shows that Hedda is conscious of the problem, and is straining her will to the utmost to
find a solution. In order to show the scope of this struggle, it is
better to keep Mrs. Elvsted and Tesman in ignorance of the past

* All material here referred to, covering Ibsen's earlier versions and
plans, is to be found in the notebooks (*opus cit.,* v. 12).

"comradeship" with Lövborg. This gives Hedda more opportunity to explore the possibilities of happiness in her environment. The circumstances of her death are therefore more inevitable and more fully understood.

The same process is followed in the development of Ibsen's other plays. In an early version of *A Doll's House,* the second act ends on a note of dull despair: Nora says, "... no, no, there is no going back now. (*Looks at the clock*) Five... seven hours till midnight. Then twenty-four hours till the next midnight. Twenty-four and seven? Thirty-one hours to live. (*She goes out. Curtain*)." In the later form, Nora's hectic dancing of the tarantella is introduced. Then the men go into the dining room, Mrs. Linde follows, and Nora is alone: "Five o'clock. Seven hours till midnight. Then the tarantella will be over. Twenty-four and seven? Thirty-one hours to live." Then Helmer calls her from the doorway: "Where's my little skylark?" Nora goes to him with her arms outstretched: "Here she is! (*Curtain*)." This ending of the second act is clearly a great improvement simply as a matter of dramatic strategy. But the invention of the tarantella, and especially the ironic lines between husband and wife at the end of the act, bear a direct relation to the ending of the play.

The desperate dancing of the tarantella finds an answer, a solution, in the desperate blunt honesty of Nora's departure. The lines which close the second act in the earlier draft suggest hopelessness, suicide, futility. These lines do not build the tension which reaches its breaking point in the historic slamming of the door when Nora goes free. The lines which close the second act in the later version are perfectly designed as preparation for the scene which ends the play: "Where's my little skylark?" is directly linked to the final lines:

> NORA: Ah, Torvald, the most wonderful thing of all would have to happen.
> HELMER: Tell me what that would be!
> NORA: Both you and I would have to be so changed that— Oh, Torvald, I don't believe any longer in wonderful things happening.
> HELMER: But I will believe in it. Tell me? So changed that—?
> NORA: That our life together would be a real wedlock. Goodbye.

These lines, expressing the essence of the playwright's social meaning, serve as a point of reference by which every scene, every movement and line, of the play may be analyzed and judged.

CHAPTER IV

THE PROCESS OF SELECTION

THE principle of unity in terms of climax does not solve the creative process of playwriting. It is the *beginning* of the process; the climax does not provide an automatic selector by which events are sorted and arranged. How does the selection proceed? How is tension sustained and increased? What is the immediate causal connection between the scenes? How about emphasis and arrangement? How does the dramatist decide the precise order, or continuity, of events? How does he decide which are the big scenes, and which of secondary importance, and the links between them? How does he decide the length of scenes, the number of characters? How about probability, chance and coincidence? How about surprise? How about the obligatory scene? How much of the action must be represented on the stage, and how much may be shown in retrospect or in narrative form? What is the exact relationship between *unity of theme* and *unity of action* in the play's progression?

All of these twelve questions must be studied and answered: the questions are closely inter-connected, and relate to problems which may be grouped under two heads: problems of the selective process, and problems of continuity (which is a later and more detailed stage of the selective process).

Having defined the principle of unity, we must next proceed to find out *how it works:* we must trace the selection and arrangement of the material from the root-idea to the complete play.

A dramatist *creates* a play. However, one cannot think of the play as being created out of nothing, or out of the abstract oneness of life, or out of the great unknown. On the contrary, the play is created out of materials which are very well known—materials which must be familiar to the audience; otherwise the audience would have no way of establishing contact with the events on the stage.

It is not strictly accurate to speak of a dramatist as a person who invents incidents. It is more satisfactory to consider his task as a process of selection. One may conceive of the playwright as some one who enters a huge warehouse, crammed with a supply of possible incidents; theoretically, the contents of the warehouse is unlimited; for each playwright, his field of choice is limited by the extent of his knowledge and experience. In order to select creatively, he must possess a high order of imagination; imagination is the faculty of combining mental-images derived from knowledge and experience so as to give these images fresh meanings and fresh potentialities. These meanings and potentialities appear to be new, but the newness lies in the selection and arrangement.

"Every play," writes Clayton Hamilton, "is a dramatization of a story that covers a larger canvas than the play itself. The dramatist must be familiar not only with the comparatively few events that he exhibits on the stage, but also with the many other events that happen off-stage during the course of the action, others that happen between the acts, and innumerable others that are assumed to have happened before the play began." * If we examine this statement carefully, we find that it suggests two problems which are of fundamental importance in analyzing the selective process. In the first place, what are these other events which are assumed to have happened? Theoretically, anything and everything may be assumed to have happened. "The principle would seem to be," says Archer, "that slow and gradual processes, and separate lines of causation, should be left outside the frame of the picture." † This is unquestionably true, but again we are in the dark as to what these "slow and gradual processes" are. Are they simply what the playwright *mentions* in the course of the action, or are they any "separate lines of causation" which the audience chooses to invent? The fact that the action takes place within a larger framework of events is unquestionable; the extent and character of this larger framework must be determined. In the second place, Hamilton speaks of "a dramatization of a story" as if the story, including all the events which may be assumed to have happened, were already in existence, instead of being in process of *becoming*. The mistake (a common one in all technical studies of the drama) lies in confusing the making of the play with the thing to be made. This is based on the notion that the playwright has a certain story to tell and that technique consists in the skillful arrangement of an existing story.

The dramatist may frequently limit his field of selection by constructing his play around a known event; he may dramatize a novel or a biography or an historical situation. The ancient

* *Opus cit.*
† Archer, *Playmaking, a Manual of Craftsmanship.*

theatre dealt with stories which already existed; the Greeks used religious myths and semi-historical fables; the Elizabethans drew largely upon romances and histories which had been told many times. This in no way changes the nature of the process: insofar as the dramatist only transposes material from one medium to another, he is merely a literary hack: for example, dialogue may be taken verbatim from a novel; this task is not completely uncreative, because it requires the ability to select and arrange the speeches. But the creative dramatist cannot be satisfied with the repetition of dialogue or situations: having selected a novel or a biography or an historical event, he proceeds to analyze this material, and to define the root-action which expresses his dramatic purpose; in developing and remolding the material, he draws on the whole range of his knowledge and experience.

Shakespeare used history and fable as foundations on which to build the architecture of his plays; but he selected *freely* in order to create a firm foundation; and he built *freely,* following the dictates of his own consciousness and will.

The process of selection cannot be understood if we assume that the events to be selected are already *known.* As far as the process is creative, no part of the story is ready-made; everything is possible (within the limits of the playwright's knowledge and experience) and nothing is known. People find it curiously difficult to consider a story as something which is in process of *becoming:* confusion on this point exists in all textbooks on playwriting and is a stumbling block to all playwrights. If the playwright regards his story as a fixed series of events, he is unable to test the development in relation to the climax. He will deny that this is possible. He will argue somewhat as follows: How can we know anything about the climax until we know its causes? And when we know the causes, we know the play. "I intend to build a play," says this imaginary dramatist, "about a situation which I find touching and noteworthy. I am not prejudiced; I am interested in life as it is; I shall investigate the causes and effects which lead to and from the significant situation which I have chosen. This situation may or may not be the climax; I shall work this out when I come to it, and shall draw no conclusions until I have weighed all the factors."

This is the logic of a journalist and not of a creator. One cannot deal with a situation creatively simply by reporting it. As soon as the playwright touches the situation creatively, he transforms it; regardless of its origin, it ceases to be a fact, and becomes an invention. The author is not tracing a group of fixed causes;

he is selecting any causes he wants to select, drawn from every-thing he has known or thought since the day of his birth. It is absurd to maintain that the creator invents a situation, then in-vents the causes which are supposed to lead to the situation; and out of this arrangement of his own invention, he draws con-clusions as to the meaning of what he has invented.

Galsworthy says, "The perfect dramatist rounds up his charac-ters and facts within the ring-fence of a dominant idea, which fulfills the craving of his spirit." * The dramatist who is far from perfect will also be led, consciously or unconsciously, to fulfill "the craving of his spirit" in his choice of events.

Most people think that the playwright is limited as to the choice of dramatic events ("it must be so hard to think of situations"), but that he is completely free in his interpretation of them. Of course it *is* hard to think of situations, and this depends on the power of the writer's imagination; but his choice of events is rigidly controlled by his dominant idea. The field of selection is comparatively free; it is the dominant idea which holds the writer down and inhibits him and prevents him from investigating the whole field of possibilities.

Obviously it is desirable that the process of selection cover as wide a field as possible. On the other hand, the wider the field the greater the difficulties. Any event, however simple, is the result of the action of enormously complex forces. The more *freely* the dramatist investigates these forces, the more difficult it becomes to reach a decision on the significance of the various contributing events.

In order to proceed rationally in covering as wide a field as possible, the dramatist must have a definite objective: a general investigation of causes and effects without a clear point of ref-erence is inevitably vague. If the dramatist has worked out the root-action fully and in detail, he moves far more freely and firmly through the complexity of possible causes. Plays with an inadequate climax generally exhibit an over-simplified development of causation: having no complete point of reference, the author has nothing to guide him in the selection of events, and is forced to deal only with the simplest causes in order to avoid hopeless confusion.

Lessing described the selective process with brilliant psychological insight: "The poet finds in history a woman who murders her husband and sons. Such a deed can awaken terror and pity, and he takes hold of it to treat it as a tragedy. But history tells him no

* *Opus cit.*

more than the bare fact and this is as horrible as it is unusual. It furnishes at most three scenes, and, devoid of all detailed circumstances, three improbable scenes. What therefor does the poet do?

"As he deserves this name more or less, the improbability or the meager brevity will seem to him the greatest want in this play.

"If he be in the first condition, he will consider above all else how to invent a series of causes and effects by which these improbable crimes could be accounted for most naturally. Not satisfied with resting their probability upon historical authority, he will endeavor to construct the characters of his personages, will endeavor so to necessitate one from another the events that place his characters in action, will endeavor to define the passions of each character so accurately, will endeavor to lead these passions through such gradual steps, that we shall everywhere see nothing but the most natural and common course of events." *

This retrospective analysis is a process of transforming social necessity into human probability: the root-action is the end of a system of events, the most complete statement of necessity: the previous events *seem* to be a mass of probabilities and possibilities, but when these are selected and arranged, we observe the rational movement of needs and purposes which make the final situation inevitable.

There is often an element of improbability in a climactic situation—because it represents the sum of the author's experience of social necessity, and is therefore more intense and more final than our day-to-day experience. The selection of previous events is designed to justify this situation, to show its meaning in terms of our common experience.

We have now answered the second of the points raised in regard to Clayton Hamilton's description of the selective process: the field of investigation is not a *known* field in a narrow sense; it is as wide as the playwright's whole experience. But the system of causes which he is seeking is specific, and is related to a defined event. Furthermore, he is not looking for a chain of cause and effect, but for causes, however diverse, leading to *one effect*. This system of causes is designed to show that the end and scope of the action is inevitable,† that it is the rational outcome of a conflict between individuals and their environment. But we have not yet touched on the question of the larger framework: is the playwright select-

---

* Lessing, *opus cit.*

† Of course, this is not a final inevitability. When we speak of social necessity and inevitability, we use the terms as signifying the author's conception of reality. The play does not go beyond this conception.

ing only the action which takes place on the stage? Or is he selecting a wider system of action? If the latter is the case, how is the
wider system limited? Where does it begin and end? This is the
basis of the whole process of selection. In order to understand the
process, we must have a picture of the whole canvas of events with
which the playwright is dealing; we must know what he needs in
order to complete the inner and outer framework. This means
that we must return to the root-action (the beginning of the
process) and gain a clearer idea of its use in the co-ordination of
the action as a whole.

It may be well to select a specific event as an example of a
root action: suppose we take as our starting point a situation which
is characteristic of the modern drawing room play—a wife commits suicide in order to remove herself from an unbearable triangle
situation, and to give freedom to her husband and the woman he
loves. This event occurs in *The Shining Hour* by Keith Winter.
Why has the author selected this incident? We are sure that it
has not been chosen because it is colorful or startling. It has been
chosen because it is the point of highest tension in an important
social conflict.

The mere fact that a woman commits suicide under these circumstances is not sufficient to give the situation value as a root-
action. The situation must be constructed and visualized in detail. In examining the situation, in determining *why* it has been
chosen, the dramatist begins inevitably to search out the prior
causes; at the same time he clarifies his own conception—he makes
sure that the event adequately embodies his social point of view,
that it means what he wants it to mean. He is not dramatizing
the event because of its isolated importance; in fact, it *has no
isolated importance*. It has a moral meaning, a place in the framework of society. It raises many broad problems, particularly in
regard to the institution of marriage, the relationship of the
sexes, the question of divorce, the right of self-destruction. It
must be borne in mind that these problems are not to be considered
abstractly; they have no value as generalized comments, or as
points of view expressed by the various characters. The event is not
isolated: it is connected with the whole of society; but it is also
not an abstract symbol of various social forces; it dramatizes these
social forces as they affect the consciousness and will of living
persons.

In other words, the playwright is not dealing with individuals
without an environment, or with an environment without individuals—because neither of these things is dramatically conceivable.

People sometimes speak of love or jealousy as "universal" emotions: suppose we are told that the wife's suicide is due to a simple combination of love and jealousy, and that there are no other factors. It is obvious that this is so "universal" that it is meaningless; as soon as we attempt to examine the woman as a *person* in order to understand the reasons for her act, we are forced to investigate all the environmental and psychological factors. To say that her act is due to *pure* passion is as fantastic as to say that it is due to *pure* respect for the British divorce laws.

The more we think about the woman as a *person,* the more we are forced to defend or accuse her, to find that her act is socially justified or socially reprehensible. We do this because we are social beings; we cannot think about events without thinking about our own relationship to our own environment. The analysis suggested by Dumas is not only desirable, it is unavoidable. We must ask: "What should I do? What would other people do? What ought to be done?" The playwright has chosen the situation as a means of volitional representation; his examination of it is not non-partisan; its meaning is determined by his will.

One's attitude toward such a situation might be stated in very abstract terms as follows: (a) Emotion is the only meaning of life; or (b) bourgeois society shows signs of increasing decay. Here we have two different modes of thought which lead to different interpretations of any social event. If we apply these attitudes to the case of suicide, we have: (a) the wife dies as an act of glorious self-sacrifice so that the two lovers may have their shining hour; (b) the suicide is the neurotic result of the woman's false conception of love and marriage, which finds its roots in the decay of bourgeois society.

I do not mean to insist that the author's approach need be so simply formulated, or follow such an obvious pattern, as the examples cited. Social attitudes may be very diverse and very individual. (The most serious charge against the modern theatre is its use of frayed familiar patterns of thought, and the lack of what Ibsen called "energetic individualization"). But however individual the author's point of view may be, it must be intellectually clear and emotionally vital (which is another way of saying that it must be fully conscious and strongly willed). If this is the case, the root-action takes a definite and detailed form: the way in which the woman dies, the reactions of the other characters, the surrounding circumstances, the place and time, are dictated by the author's dominant idea. He does not choose a subject and superimpose a meaning on it. Any meaning that is superimposed is worthless dramatically. He does not draw a lesson from the event; one may more correctly say that he draws the event from the lesson. (The lesson which he wishes to draw is itself based on the sum-total of his experience.)

The structure of the root-action does not so much depend on the previous histories and activities of the characters as upon the relationship of individuals to their environment at a given moment of supreme tension: if this moment is visualized, it tells us so *much* about their characters that we are far better able to reconstruct their previous activities. If the conscious wills of the characters are exposed under pressure, we know them as living suffering human beings. The playwright cannot express his dominant idea through types or persons with simplified qualities. The creator does not stand aside and observe the situation he has created. He is as closely involved as if the woman were his own wife; she is a complex being because she has been selected by the author (just as his wife has been selected) on account of her importance to *him*.

There is nothing abstract about the ending of *A Doll's House*. Nora's struggle with her husband is vividly emotional, highly personalized. Yet this event derives from Ibsen's desire to say something of historic importance about the emancipation of women. Since he understands the problem clearly, he is able to present it at its boiling point, at the apex of conflict. Does the climax achieve its strength *in spite of* what Ibsen wants to say, or *because of it?* Could he have expressed his social meaning through puppets? He found the expression of his theme so perfectly in Nora's departure that, as Shaw says, "The slam of the door behind her is more momentous than the cannon of Waterloo or Sedan." *

Let us now turn to the climax of *The Shining Hour* and consider it as a reference point in the play's action. The suicide takes place at the end of the second act.† A barn catches fire accidentally and the woman throws herself into the burning barn. The third act deals with the effect of the event on the two lovers, and their final decision that their love is great enough to surmount the tragedy. The author's attitude is colored by romanticism, but he is not whole-heartedly romantic. At moments he gives us a clear psychological insight into the neurotic side of his characters; but he ends up with the rather muddled idea that one must have courage and it's all for the best.

---

* *Dramatic Opinions and Essays.*
† My use of a second-act situation as the root-action of *The Shining Hour* is explained in the chapter on "Climax and Solution."

It is clear that the author has something definite to say; this accounts for the vitality of the situation (he has felt his subject too strongly to let it peter out in conversation). But he has not analyzed or digested his own conception; this accounts for the fact that the suicide is fortuitous, and the third act is lengthy and anti-climactic.

We do *not* feel that the wife's death is the only way out, that she is trapped by forces which have exhausted her strength, that there is no other escape.

If we go back to the earlier scenes of *The Shining Hour,* we find that the development of the action is not built around the wife at all, but about the man and the other woman. The play is, as its title suggests, an intense love story. Are we then to conclude that the playwright has either written the wrong play or the wrong climax? This is literally the case. Since the interest is concentrated on the lovers, this interest cannot build to an action in which the lovers, however deeply affected, play a passive role. The suicide does not change the relationship between the lovers; it simply shocks them; at the end of the play they go away together, which they could also do if the wife were alive and well.

Although the lovers dominate the play, the wife's death is by far the most eventful incident in the course of the action. It may properly be called the root-action because it embodies the author's dominant idea in a meaningful event. The meaning is confused, but it is none-the-less discoverable. The idea of sacrifice is all-important: the author does not prepare the suicide, because he regards the spontaneous emotional act as its own justification. Death is an emancipation; she frees herself from an intolerable situation, but she also frees herself in an absolute sense. Thus the effect of the act on the lovers is also double; it not only frees them physically, but metaphysically. The underlying mental pattern follows the prevailing trend which we have analyzed at some length. Keith Winter agrees with Philip Barry that "emotion is the only real thing in our lives; it is the person; it is the soul." The immediate sensation of emotion is justified because it is part of a larger stream of emotion, the Bergsonian *élan vital,* the stream of consciousness and unconsciousness. The lovers in *The Shining Hour* have no choice. The wife also has no choice. In Barry's *Tomorrow and Tomorrow,* emotion is negated and sacrificed; at the same time, the fact that the wife and her lover *feel* as they do is sufficient; their self-denial enriches their lives. In *The Shining Hour* the same conception finds a more dramatic formulation. The suicide (an act of supreme negation) releases the lovers, and affords a justification of their love. This mysticism is an evasion of the social problem: the real necessity of the death lies in the fact that it lessens the responsibility of all the persons concerned. The triumph of emotion permits the social order to remain unchallenged. Sacrifice is a way out without asking questions or disturbing existing conventions. The neurotic discussions in the final act, the confused emotionalism, are typical of a situation in which nothing has been solved and in which there has been no genuine progression.

The technical result of this clouded conception is the apparent dualism of the play's action. The play takes the form of a series of love scenes, in which the wife seems to play the part of a troublesome intruder. The climax seems to have been invented solely because of its effectiveness as a dramatic explosion, and not because of its value in terms of theme. However, a careful analysis reveals, as always in these cases, that the structural form is the product of the playwright's social purpose.

This brings us back (after a long, but necessary digression) to the process of selection. The trouble in *The Shining Hour* springs from failure to use the climax as a reference point in the development of the action. This climax, as the playwright has visualized it, could not serve as a reference point. The incident is dramatic enough and effective enough; but it is presented as an emotional evasion of a problem, and not as the inevitable result of a social conflict. If a situation is not *caused* by social forces, it is quite useless to attempt to trace social causes which are apparently nonexistent. To be sure, we can trace the *emotional* causes; but emotions, in this general sense, are vague quantitatively and qualitatively; when one detaches feeling from social causation, one also detaches it from reason; if feeling springs from the soul, it may be aroused by *any* external event or by none, and there is no need to define its origin in terms of *events*.

The use of the root-action in the process of selection depends on the degree to which it dramatizes the social meaning of an event; it must show a change of equilibrium involving the relationship between individuals and the totality of their environment. If it does not show such a change, it cannot aid the dramatist in an investigation of earlier stages of the conflict between these characters and their environment. The social meaning of the root-action may be both physical and psychological. For example, the burning of the barn in *The Shining Hour* is accidental; the suicide is also largely unpremeditated. If the physical event, the fire, were given a social meaning, it would cease to be accidental, and would enable us to trace a prior series of events. The burning of buildings in Ibsen's plays (in *Ghosts* and *The Master Builder*) indicates the extraordinary significance which can be attached to such an incident. The psychological condition which immediately precedes the suicide lends itself to the most complex social analysis. Suppose the act is the consummation of a suicide-wish which has been previously expressed: it becomes imperative to trace the origin of this wish, the external conditions which had awakened it and the social basis for these conditions. On the other hand, suppose the act is chiefly the result of the romantic idea of self-sacrifice; there must have been a long conflict in which this romantic idea struggled against the realities of an unfavorable environment. The suicide follows a long period of change and compromise and adjustment; the woman has twisted and turned and suffered in the attempt to escape disaster.

The ending of *A Doll's House* illustrates an action which combines intense individualization with historic scope. When Helmer says, "No man sacrifices his honor, even for one he loves," Nora replies, "Millions of women have done so." We know that this is true, that Nora is not alone, that her struggle is part of a larger social reality.

This is the answer to the question of the larger framework: the concept of necessity expressed in the play's root-action is wider and deeper than the whole action of the play. In order to give the play its meaning, this scheme of social causation must be dramatized, it must extend beyond the events on the stage and connect these with the life of a class and a time and a place. The scope of this external framework is determined by the scope of the playwright's conception: it must go back far enough, and be broad enough, to guarantee the inevitability of the climax, not in terms of individual whims or opinions, but in terms of social necessity.

Even the worst plays have, to a confused and uncertain degree, this quality of extension. It is a basic quality of volitional representation. It gives us the key to what one may call the predominant physical characteristic of an action. An action (the whole play, or any of the subsidiary actions of which it is composed) is a contradictory movement. This contradiction may be described as extension and compression.

From a philosophic point of view, this means that an action embodies both conscious will and social necessity. If we translate this into practical terms, it means that an action represents our concentrated immediate will to get something done; but it also embodies our previous experience and our conception of future probability. If we consider an action as a disturbance of equilibrium, we observe that the laws of its movement resemble those of a combustion engine: compression produces the explosion, which in turn produces an extension of energy; the degree of extension corresponds to the degree of energy. One may compare the compression to the emotional tension generated; the extension is the social upset which results from the release of the tension.

The principle of extension and compression is of the utmost importance in studying the mechanics of dramatic movement. For the present, we are concerned with it as it affects the play's organic unity. This principle explains the relationship of each subsidiary action to the system of events; each action is an explosion of tension which extends to other actions throughout the play. The root-action possesses the maximum compression, and also the maximum extension, unifying the events within the system.

But the play as a whole is also an action, which possesses *as a whole* the qualities of compression and extension: its explosive energy is determined by its unity as a whole; and again, the degree of extension, embracing a wider system of causation, corresponds to the degree of energy produced.

The process can be clarified if we consider it in relation to the exercise of conscious will. Every act of will involves direct conflict with the environment; but the act is also placed in a whole scheme of things with which it is directly or indirectly connected and with which the act is intended to harmonize. The individual's consciousness reflects this wider scheme with which he wants to bring himself into harmony; his volition undertakes the struggle against immediate obstacles. The stage-action of a play (the inner system of events) embraces the direct conflict between individuals and the conditions which oppose or limit their will; we observe this conflict through the conscious wills of the characters. But each character's consciousness includes his *own* picture of reality with which he wants ultimately to harmonize his actions. If there are a dozen characters in the play, a dozen pictures of ultimate reality might be included or suggested: all of these conceptions touch the social framework (the outer system of events) in which the play is placed: but the only test of their value, the only unifying principle in the double system of causation, lies in the author's consciousness.

The root-action is the key to the double system: since it embodies the highest degree of compression, it also has the widest range of extension. It is the most intense moment of a direct conflict with immediate obstacles: the events which take place on the stage are limited to this direct conflict. The beginning of this conflict is, as Schlegel pointed out, "the assertion of free will." But this assertion is far from being, as Schlegel said, an "absolute beginning." The determination to fight obstacles is based on what one thinks probable—a picture of future necessities which is derived from one's experience of past and present necessities. The climax sums up the results of this conflict, and judges it in regard to the whole scheme of things.

There is often a great deal of uncertainty as to the exact meaning of cause and effect: we assume that the whole question of the rational connection of events is disposed of by a casual reference to cause and effect. I earlier remarked that a play is not a chain of cause and effect, but an arrangement of causes leading to *one effect.* This is important because it leads to an understanding of unity: if we think of indiscriminate causes and effects, the reference point by which unity can be tested is lost. It is useful to consider the root-action as the one effect which binds together the system of causes. But this is merely a convenient formulation. Any action includes both cause and effect; the point of tension in an action is the point at which cause is transformed into effect. The extension of the action is not only its driving force in producing results, but also its dynamic relation to its causes. The scope of its result is the scope of its causes. The root-action is an explosion which *causes* a maximum change of equilibrium between individuals and their environment. The complexity and force of this *effect* depends on the complexity and force of the *causes* which led to the explosion. The extension of the inner action is limited to the causes which lie in the conscious wills of the characters. The extension of the outer action is limited to the social causes which constitute the framework of fact within which the action moves. For purposes of analysis, we view this double system of events as a system of *causes:* as it actually appears on the stage it appears as a system of *effects.* We do not see or hear the exercise of the conscious will; we do not see or hear the forces which constitute the environment. But the dramatic meaning of what we see and hear lies in its causes: the total effect (as projected in the root action) depends on the totality of causes.

Having considered the theory which underlies the playwright's approach to his material, we can now proceed to investigate the steps by which he selects and builds the wider framework which encompasses the action.

CHAPTER V

THE SOCIAL FRAMEWORK

SUPPOSE we return to the specific situation mentioned in the previous chapter. Let us assume that the suicide of a faithful wife takes place under conditions which are dramatically ideal—the situation suggests intense possibilities of pity and terror; the social implications are far-reaching. But the system of causation which leads to this event is still untouched; we are dealing *only* with possibilities and implications, because the effect of the event cannot be understood until its causes are dramatized.

The playwright *knows* the meaning of the situation; the potential pity and terror are real to him. But he must prove that his conception of reality is justified; he must show the whole scheme of things which made this event true in the deepest sense.

The playwright is faced by an infinite multiplicity of possible causes. He might very possibly begin by listing a number of questions in connection with the history of the event. Perhaps the most superficial fact is the fact that the husband has fallen in love with another woman. Many women do not kill themselves on this account. We cannot analyze the psychological factors in the case without discovering that far-reaching social and economic problems must be investigated. It is evident that the wife's relationship to her husband is of a special emotional character. This means that her relationship to her environment is also of a special character. We must make a study of the environment, her emotional attitudes toward other persons, her heredity, education and economic status. This in turn forces us to consider the heredity, education and economic status of all the people with whom she is associated. Do they earn their money, or live on income? What has been the amount of their income during the past ten years, where does it come from and how do they spend it? What are their amusements, their cultural experiences? What are their ethical standards and how far do they adhere to these in practice? What is their attitude toward marriage and what events have conditioned this attitude? What has been their sexual experience? Have they any children? If not, why not?

These factors can be traced back through many years. But the woman's personal history, psychologically and physically, is also of great interest: what has been the state of her health? Has she shown any neurotic symptoms? We want to know whether she has shown any previous disposition toward suicide: when, and under what conditions? We want to know about her girlhood, her physical and mental activities as a child.

It may seem necessary to construct a similar personal history of several of the other characters—particularly of the husband and of the other woman. Each personal investigation leads us into a new complex of relationships, involving differences in social and psychological determinants.

This list seems forbidding, but it is only a hasty suggestion of the possible lines of speculation which are open to the dramatist in organizing his material. Aside from its incompleteness, what impression does this list convey? The questions are not very specific, and tend to be psychological rather than factual, static rather than dynamic. But it is precisely objective, factual, dynamic events for which we are searching. The field covered by these questions must be covered—but it cannot be covered *in this way*. The attempt to construct a complete history of everything which led to the moment of climax would lead to the accumulation of a vast amount of unmanageable data. If carried out uncompromisingly, such an undertaking would be more ambitious than the whole life-work of Proust.

The process of selection is not *a narrative process*. The playwright is not looking for illustrative or psychological material, but for a system of actions; just as the final climax sums up a maximum change of equilibrium between individuals and their environment, each of the subordinate crises is a change of equilibrium leading to the maximum change. Each crisis is effective in proportion to its compression and extension. No action of the play can be more significant than the root-action, because in that case it would go beyond the scope of the play.

A more or less narrative list such as the one outlined is only useful as a means of suggesting the sort of events for which we are searching—events which compress the emotional lives of the characters in moments of explosive tension, and which extend as far as possible in their effect on the environment.

In planning the wider framework of the play, the dramatist is organizing material which is obviously less dramatic than the play itself. Events which are assumed to have happened before the opening of the drama, or which are reported during the action, or which take place off-stage or between the acts, cannot be as vital as the visible action behind the footlights. But it must not be supposed that the outer framework is a shadowy fiction, covered by a few vague references to the past lives of the characters and the social forces of the period. Since the larger pattern of events represents the scope of the playwright's conception, it must be dramatized as fully as possible. The playwright who thinks of the ultimate causes underlying his drama in narrative terms, will carry over some of this narrative form into the stage-action. By visualizing these ultimate causes in meaningful and cumulative crises, the playwright establishes the basis for the later and more detailed selection of the stage-action. The reserve of events, behind and around the play, gives sweep and sureness to the action, and gives more meaning to every line of dialogue, every gesture, every situation.

We now have two principles which give us additional guidance in studying the pre-conditions leading to a climactic situation: (1) we are looking only for crises; (2) we are seeking to outline a system of events which not only covers the inner action of the play, but which extends the concept of social necessity (the whole scheme of life in which the climax is placed) to the limit of its possibilities. We find that some of these events show a much greater explosiveness of conscious will than others: these are the most dynamic events, those which cause the most serious changes in the environment and which have the greatest driving force. But these explosive moments are produced by other events, which are less explosive because they involve a more impregnable social necessity opposed to a less awakened conscious will. What is this more impregnable social necessity and where does it come from? It comes from still earlier explosions of conscious will which have been sufficiently powerful to change and crystallize conditions in this fixed form: it is this form of apparently impregnable social necessity which defines the limits of the dramatic scheme. The playwright accepts this necessity as the picture of reality in which the play is framed. He cannot go *beyond* this necessity and investigate the acts of will which created it, because to do so would be to question its ultimate value and to deny the concept of reality as it is embodied in his climax.

The less explosive events are those which constitute the outer framework: these events are dramatic and include the exercise of conscious will; but they are less dynamic; they have less effect on the environment; they show the solidity of the social forces which mold the conscious wills of the characters and which are the ultimate obstacles which the conscious wills must face.

If we return to the list of questions concerning the wife's suicide, and attempt to apply these principles, we find that we must arrange the questions in groups and attempt to create a situation which is the culmination of the social and psychological factors involved. For example: What is the economic status of the family? What has been the amount of their income during the past ten years, where does it come from and how do they spend it? We are not interested in statistics, although statistics may be of value in dramatizing the issue; but we must find an event which has the broadest possible implications; the event need not be a financial crisis; we are interested in the way in which money affects the conscious wills of these people, how it determines their relationship to people of their own class and those of other classes, how it colors their prejudices, illusions, modes of thought. The root-action serves as our reference point: the event must therefore embody the elements of the root-action: the woman's attitude toward suicide or her fear of death, her sentimental attitude toward marriage and love, her emotional dependence and lack of self-confidence. An economic situation will serve to expose the social roots of these attitudes.

The same principle applies in analyzing the childhood of our leading character. We do not wish to find isolated or sensational events which have some psychological connection with the climax; such a connection, isolated from the background, would probably be static rather than dynamic. A woman's childhood is not a set of major and minor incidents to be catalogued, but a process to be considered as a whole. The key to this process is the fact that she ended her life under certain known conditions. We assume that the sum-total of this childhood is revealed in a basic conflict between the child and its environment (in which other persons play a part); we must consider both the other persons and the environment as a whole. We know the final stage of the conflict. We want to crystallize the earlier stages in climactic events.

If the background of the play is English middle-class country life, we must consider the profound changes which have taken place in this life: the heartbreak houses of the gentry shaken by the European war; the armistice celebrated by people drunk with weariness and hope; the breaking down of old social values; the profound economic disturbances.

The plays of Ibsen show a remarkably thorough dramatization of the outer framework. Events which happened in the past, in the childhood of the characters, play a vivid part in the action.

In *Ghosts* Ibsen projects a whole series of crises in the earlier lives of the characters. In the first year of her marriage, Mrs. Alving ran away from her husband and offered herself to Manders, but he forced her to return to her home; when her child was born, she had to "fight doubly hard—fight a desperate fight so that no one should know the sort of a man my child's father was"; she was soon faced with another crisis: her husband had an illegitimate child, by the servant in her own house; then she made another desperate decision: she sent her son away at the age of seven and never permitted him to return during the father's life. On her husband's death, she decided to build and endow an orphanage as a tribute to the memory of the man she hated poisonously.

One is amazed at the concreteness of these events. The construction is powerful and the detailed action is sharply visualized. The limit of the play's outer framework is Mrs. Alving's marriage. Ibsen regarded the family as the basic unit of society. The root-action of *Ghosts,* in which Mrs. Alving must decide whether or not to kill her own son, raises a question which the author cannot answer; it brings us face to face with the social necessity which defines and unifies the action. The marriage marks the beginning, and the ultimate extension, of the whole scheme. The essence of the root-action lies in Oswald's question: "I never asked you for life. And what kind of a life was it that you gave me?"

The concentrated conflict of will which is projected in the stage action begins with Oswald's return from abroad. At this point the wills become conscious and active: the conflict does not involve an attempt to change the fixed structure of the family; it is a conflict with lesser necessities in order to bring them in line with this greater necessity; the family, purged of vice and deceit and disease, is the goal toward which the characters are struggling and the test of the value of their actions.

In *Hamlet* the limit of the action's extension is the poisoning of Hamlet's father, which the author presents in visual action through the device of the play within the play. The problem with which Shakespeare is concerned (and which had immediate social significance in his time) is the *release of the will* in action. The ability to act decisively and without inhibitions was vital to the men of the Renaissance who were challenging the fixed values of feudalism. When Hamlet says, "Thus conscience does make cowards of us all," he expresses the force of ideas and restrictions which are as real as the "ghosts of beliefs" of which Mrs. Alving speaks. The outer framework therefore presents a system of events created by the passion and greed of people of strong wills. This is Hamlet's

world, to the necessities of which he *must* adjust himself. Thus a
deed of violence constitutes both the end and the beginning of the
action and defines its scope.

On the other hand, the stage-action begins with the entry of
the ghost; this is the point at which Hamlet's conscious will is
awakened and directed toward a defined aim. The ghost represents
the justification of the aim; he tells Hamlet that he is free to
commit this act *within* the framework of social necessity. He tells
him that the act is required in order to preserve the integrity of the
family. But the conception of the family is changing; this accounts
for Hamlet's confusion, for his inability to release his will; his
affection for his mother blinds him, he cannot wreak quick vengeance on her, and yet he cannot understand her; he is puzzled by
the "rank corruption, mining all within" which defiles the society
in which he lives. He turns both to his mother and to Ophelia for
help and both of them fail him, because both are dependent, finan-
cially and morally, on the men to whom they are attached. This
too, is part of the "iron framework of fact" which Hamlet must
face. The root-action shows Hamlet conforming to necessity and
dying to accomplish his aim; his last words are devoted solely to
the world of action—

> "I cannot live to hear the news from England;
> But I do prophesy the election lights
> On Fortinbras: he has my dying voice."

The process of selection is fundamentally a process of historical
analysis. There is a direct analogy between the work of the
dramatist and the work of the historian; the playwright cannot
handle his material satisfactorily if his approach is personal or
esthetic; on the other hand, the emphasis on social forces is likely
to be abstract. His work is greatly aided by the study of historical
events and the utilization of an historical method.

The old method of studying history was static and unhistorical
—a series of battles, treaties, the isolated whims and acts of out-
standing individuals. Plekhanov says of the historical views of the
French materialists of the eighteenth century: "Religion, manners,
customs, the whole character of a people is from this point of view
the creation of one or several great persons acting with definite
aims." *

Fifty years ago, biographies of great men showed these heroes
performing noble deeds and thinking high thoughts against a fixed

---

* George Plekhanov, *Essays in Historical Materialism,* translation by
R. Fox (London, 1934).

background. Today the method of history and biography has undergone a great change. It is recognized that a satisfactory biography must show the individual in relation to the whole epoch. The tendency toward scandal and debunking is a minor indication of this trend: as a substitute for making the person real in terms of his time, he is made partially real in terms of his vices.

In dealing with an epoch, the historian (like the playwright) is faced with a problem of selection: he must investigate personal anecdotes, works of imagination and fact, journalistic comment, military and civil records. He must find a pattern of causation in this material. The pattern is dictated by the historian's conception of the meaning of the events; the inter-connection and progression (the view of history as a process rather than as an isolated collection of meaningless incidents) depend on the historian's judgment of values, his idea of the aim of the process.

If one examines an historical event, or group of events, one finds that it is necessary to define the scope of the given action. In order to understand the American revolutionary war, one must coördinate the action in terms of the issue—the victory of the colonies—or in terms of some larger and later issue. If we regard the end of the war as the scope of the action, this throws a certain light upon every incident of the conflict. It gives a key to the logic of events, and also gives them color and texture. Both in a dramatic and in a military sense, Valley Forge gains a special meaning from Yorktown.

One cannot deal with a single incident in the American revolution without considering the complex forces involved: the personalities of the leaders, the aims of the American middle class, the property relations in the colonies, the libertarian ideas of the period, the tactics of the opposing armies. This does not mean that one presents a confusing or over-balanced picture. It means that the selection is made with an understanding of the relation between the parts and the whole.

Suppose one chooses to examine one of the less heroic and more personal aspects of the American war of independence: for instance, Benedict Arnold's personal tragedy. Can one consider his act of treason dramatically without considering the history of his time? One of the most significant things about Benedict Arnold's death is the fact that if he had died a little sooner he would have been the greatest hero of the war; the things which made him a traitor were closely connected with the things which motivated the desperate magnificence of his march to Quebec. This is a fascinating personal conflict, but it is as mad as a tale told by an idiot unless we know the historical background, the social forces which made the revolution, Arnold's relation to these forces, what the revolution meant to him, the culture and morals of his class.

The playwright may properly assume that he is dealing with a segment of history (regardless of whether his story is based on fact or invention). The playwright who feels that his characters are not as *historical* as Benedict Arnold, that they are more detached and less directly entangled in the whirlpool of history, is simply unfair to his characters and the situations in which he places them.

Is one, then, to make no distinction between plays which deal with known facts or famous personages, and those which concern intimate domestic problems? This is exactly my point. In both cases, the playwright must understand his characters in relation to their period.

This does not mean that the play itself must contain references and incidents which cover too wide an area. The whole point of selection is to be selective; the base of the action must be broad and solid—the action itself may involve a meticulous choice of incidents.

In the theatre today, the tendency is toward plays which are built, as it were, on stilts, which have no appreciable base. On the other hand, the younger and more socially-minded dramatists, eager to show us the width and depth of events, go to the other extreme. Herbert Kline comments on this in connection with a review of short plays for working-class audiences: "The result is what may be called *the carry-all plot*. For example, a play will attempt ... to present the plight of oppressed and starving miners, the schemes of the operators to keep wages down and dividends up, the support of the miners' strike by the working class, the working conditions of miners in the Soviet Union, and a number of other details including an appeal to the audience for funds to support the mine strike." *

Peace on Earth, by Albert Maltz and George Sklar, is, to some extent, an example of *the carry-all plot*. The intention in such cases is praiseworthy: the playwrights are endeavoring to enlarge the scope of the action. But since the material is undigested, it remains undramatized. History is not a rummage sale.

One can find many examples of historical method in plays which are not at all sweeping in their action, but which deal with limited domestic situations. For instance two English plays of the early nineteen-hundreds have considerable historical scope; *Chains,* by Elizabeth Baker (1909), and *Hindle Wakes,* by Stanley Houghton

---

* Herbert Kline, "Writing for Workers' Theatre," in *New Theatre* (December, 1934).

(1912). These are not great plays; they lack great depth or insight; nevertheless both are solidly built on a workmanlike understanding of the social forces of the period.

Fanny's independence in *Hindle Wakes,* her flouting of the moral code, has far less social meaning than Nora's declaration of independence in *A Doll's House.* Nevertheless, Fanny is an historic figure; her attitude toward the male, her integrity, her lack of depth, her cheerful assurance that she can defeat the world—these are the qualities of thousands of girls like Fanny; her rebellion, in 1912, foreshadows the widespread rebellion, the brave but futile gestures of the Greenwich Village era. When Fanny refuses to marry Alan, who is the father of the child she is expecting, he says, "I know why you won't marry me." She says, "Do you? Well, spit it out, lad." Alan: "You don't want to spoil my life." Fanny: "Thanks, much obliged for the compliment."

It is interesting to compare this with Shaw's treatment of sex in *Man and Superman,* in which he shows us the "eternal" woman in pursuit of her "eternal" mate. Shaw's discussions, in spite of their brilliance, are always general, and his characterizations are static, because he never achieves historical perspective. *Hindle Wakes* is set realistically against the background of the 1912 era. the weaving industry, the paternalism of the employers, the economic problems, the class relationships.

This is equally true of *Chains,* a carefully documented picture of lower middle-class English life in 1909. The business and home atmosphere, the habits, finances and culture, the futile desire to escape, are exhibited with almost scientific precision.

In Soviet Russia today, there is wide discussion of the method of *socialist realism,* a basic esthetic approach which breaks away from both the romanticism and the mechanistic naturalism of the nineteenth century. I have avoided references to the Soviet theatre, because my knowledge of it is limited; only a few Russian plays, and a few short articles on the theory of the theatre, have been translated.

Socialist realism is a method of historical analysis and selection, designed to gain the greatest dramatic compression and extension. S. Margolin, in a discussion on "The Artist and the Theatre" * describes socialist realism as it affects the work of the scene designer: he must, he says, "look ever deeper into the manifold phenomena of the living realities. . . . The Soviet spectator can be impressed only by a generalized image which sheds light on the

* In *VOKS* (published by the Soviet Union Society for Cultural Relations with Foreign Countries, Moscow), v. 6, 1934.

entire epoch; this alone he considers great art. Naturalism, the heritage of the bourgeoisie, is fundamentally alien to the tendency of the Soviet theatre." The phrase, "a generalized image," is vague; the impression of an epoch is only possible when the action projects the intense operation of the conscious will in relation to the whole environment. This is illustrated by recent Russian motion pictures; *Chapayev* and *The Youth of Maxim* present a personal conflict which has sufficient extension to include "a generalized image which sheds light on the entire epoch."

The scope of the action in *Chapayev* is limited to a particular phase of the Russian revolution: the period of confused heroic awakening of peasants and workers, rushing to the defense of their newly acquired liberty, forging a new consciousness of their world in the heat of conflict. Chapayev's death is selected as the point of highest tension in this system of events.

The historical framework of the action is extremely complicated. It is concerned with: (1) military struggle; (2) political background; (3) the social composition of the opposing forces; (4) the individual psychology and personal conflicts of Chapayev himself; (5) Chapayev's personal function in the military struggle, his merits and faults as a commander; (6) the *moral* problem, which concerns the individual's right to happiness as opposed to his revolutionary duty.

Abstractly, this material seems too elaborate to be organized in a single story. Yet this is exactly what has been done, and done with such uncanny accuracy that the result is a very simple motion picture. The material has been concretized by skilful selection. For instance, the scene in which Chapayev demonstrates military tactics by arranging potatoes on a table shows us more about how he leads his troops than a dozen battles and maneuvers. Chapayev's character combines a violent temper, boisterous good nature, crude appetite for knowledge and childish conceit. All of this is concentrated in a brief scene in which he discusses Alexander the Great with the Commissar. What about the social points of view of the opposing forces? The conflict between Furmanov and Chapayev about looting the peasants furnishes a key to the spirit of the Bolshevik army (at the same time developing Chapayev's character). The atmosphere of the White army, the relationship between soldiers and officers, is shown in a brilliant dramatic incident: Colonel Borozdin's servant pleads for his brother's life; the Colonel pretends to grant the request and cynically confirms the death-sentence. The military struggle is presented in scenes which are unforgettably dramatic; for instance, the "psychological attack," in which the Whites advance nonchalantly smoking cigars. And what about the moral problem? The delicate love story between Anna and Pyetka crystallizes the bitter contradiction between personal happiness and the great task to be performed. This is dramatized with special force in the scene in which he makes love to her and teaches her about the machine gun. The love story is not a side issue. Love and youth are part of the revolution; but there is no time for a sentimental idyl; the struggle must go on. Similarly, there is no time to mourn when Chapayev dies under the raking machine gun fire; the Red Cavalry sweeps across the scene to continue the struggle.

The Sailors of Cattaro, by Friedrich Wolf, tells the story of a revolution in the Austrian fleet at the close of the world war.* The fight is lost because the workers are inadequately prepared for the task. But Franz Rasch goes to his death with a sure hope—the workers are undaunted, they will prepare for future struggles and future victories. Here we have a broad historical framework, covering two main fields of interest: the European war, especially in relation to Austria; and the development of Austro-Marxism and the Austrian labor movement.

The stage-action of *The Sailors of Cattaro*, although it follows a single design, seems diffuse; we do not completely understand the personal conflict of will as it affects Franz Rasch and the other leaders of the rebellion. A great deal of the action happens off-stage; these off-stage events are so closely connected with the immediate action that the description of them seems insufficient. The fault lies in the author's selection of his material (including both the inner action and the wider system): (1) the historical background has not been successfully analyzed in dramatic terms, and, since the background is not fully developed, the revolt tends to be too *universal*—sailors (in general) rebelling against authority (in general). (2) It follows that the conflict tends to express itself in discussion; it is not crystallized in action. (3) Since the author has not dramatized the crises which led to the revolt, the immediate causes of the action (as distinct from the historical background) seem thin and intellectualized. The play deals with workers who are not fully prepared for their task, but we do not know enough about them to know how far this is true. (4) Since the historical forces and prior action are under-developed, there is an *overemphasis* on the personalities of the workers, on petty problems.

---

* The present discussion is based on Michael Blankfort's adaptation of *The Sailors of Cattaro* as presented by the Theatre Union, in New York, in the fall of 1934. I am not familiar with the original, which differs from the adaptation in many respects.

The hero is also over-emphasized; his rôle is not analyzed in relation to events: Franz Rasch is presented abstractly as a noble person rather than a fully understood person.

A comparison between two plays by S. N. Behrman illuminates the question of the historical framework as it affects the technique of the drawing room play. *Biography* and *Rain From Heaven* are identical in theme. Based upon the same conception, the difference lies solely in the process of selection.

Both plays deal with the problem of the liberal in modern society: in both the central figure is a woman of culture, vividly honest, outspoken, tolerant. In both the woman falls in love with a man who is involved in the hate and bitterness of current social struggles. In both the climax is the same: the intense love story comes to a point of inevitable separation. The woman is emotionally torn, but she is true to herself. She cannot relinquish her tolerance, and she cannot change the man she loves.

In *Biography,* the historical groundwork is neglected. The social forces which underlie the action have no dramatic reality. As a result, the scope of the action is so narrow that there can be no progression; the conflict between Marion Froude and Richard Kurt is repetitious because it is based on fixed qualities of character. The basis of the conflict is the same in the last scene as in the first. Marion describes herself as "a big laissez-faire girl." Marion evidently had this attitude in her youth, because she tells Leander Nolan, with whom she had her first affair, "I suspected in myself a—a tendency to explore, a spiritual and physical wanderlust—that I knew would horrify you once you found it out. It horrifies you now when we are no longer anything to each other." Behrman characterizes his heroine very carefully, but it is perfectly evident that he does not view her in process of "becoming." Whatever might have caused Marion's "spiritual and physical wanderlust," and how it might be affected by the world in which Marion lives—these matters are rigorously excluded from the play. During the course of the action, she comes in contact with outside forces, but this contact merely exposes the difference of aims between her and Nolan and the boy with whom she falls in love. In her final scene with Kurt, she says, "You hate my essential quality—the thing that is me." So this core of personality is static; it is in the final analysis mystical, and therefore untouchable. In a stage direction, the author speaks of "the vast, uncrossable deserts between the souls of human beings." Since these imaginary "deserts" are assumed to exist, it follows that the actual contacts of the characters are limited and sentimental.

Kurt's background contains an explanation of his point of view; he tells Marion of the incident in his childhood which motivates his bitterness; since this incident is a genuine dramatization of social forces, it leads to the most moving moment of the play, the love scene which closes the second act. But there is no further development in Kurt's character, nor is the possibility of further development indicated.

Behrman tries to convince us that the social relationships presented in the stage action have more than their apparent extension and meaning. Marion tries to explain Kurt's social point of view: "To you these rather ineffectual blundering people symbolize the forces that have hurt you and you hate them." This shows that the author's intentions are clear. This is what the people ought to do— but they cannot do it as *symbols;* the social forces can only be presented through crucial events.

The selection of events is confusing, and serves to weaken rather than develop the meaning of the root-action. Marion has gained considerable reputation painting the portraits of famous Europeans. Richard Kurt is a young radical who is editor of a weekly magazine, with a circulation of three million. These personal backgrounds do not serve to initiate a serious conflict of wills; Marion's career suggests Bohemianism and courage; it does *not* suggest any great degree of honesty and tolerance which (as we are repeatedly told) are Marion's essential qualities. Kurt presents a much more curious contradiction: how can a man who is an uncompromising radical be the editor of a periodical with three million circulation? This is never explained. It follows that the stage-action resolves itself into the discussion of an incident which has no social extension; Kurt wants to print Marion's autobiography because it will be sensational. The suggestion that the autobiography will serve any social purpose is an absurdity. We are told that Kurt is "only really at home in protest," but in a day of hunger marches, mass unemployment, threats of fascism and war, his protest consists in editing one of the largest magazines in the country and printing the mildly scandalous story of a woman's life.

In *Rain From Heaven,* Behrman attacks the same theme; but he has grown to a more mature consciousness of the social forces which motivate the conflict. The framework is not complete; there remains a tendency toward generalizations, and toward events which are illustrative rather than dramatic. But the root-action goes to the heart of a genuine problem; the concept of social necessity is defined and explored. Lady Wyngate is not an artificial Bohemian; she is a genuine liberal; she knows what is going on in the world and she tries to do something about it. Hugo Willens is a refugee from Hitler's Germany. Lady Wyngate sees that her world is falling in ruins and she faces the fact bravely. There are no "uncrossable deserts" in this play; there are living problems— the threat of fascism, the growing racial prejudice against the Jews, the desperation of capitalism, the drive toward war. When the two lovers face each other, and Hugo decides to return to Germany to enter the struggle against fascism, the decision is an honest act of will.

It is valuable to trace the detailed selection of incidents in these two plays: it is literally true that every line and situation depends on the way in which the social framework has been conceived. Hobart Eldridge, the financier in *Rain From Heaven*, is simply a revision of Orrin Kinnicott in *Biography*. Kinnicott bears a satirical resemblance to Bernarr MacFadden, but his point of view is not clearly presented. In *Rain From Heaven*, the financier ceases to be a caricature and becomes a character, because his activity is meaningful in social terms. Eldridge is doing exactly what men of his sort are doing: he is helping to organize fascism, and is doing it with a great deal of consciousness and will.

In *Biography*, the complication in the love story is furnished by Nolan, who is engaged to Kinnicott's daughter but is in love with Marion: Nolan is in politics and hopes to become a Senator with the aid of the physical culture financier. In *Rain From Heaven*, the other man who is in love with Lady Wyngate is Rand Eldridge. He is a combination of two characters from *Biography*: Nolan, and Tympi Wilson, the handsome young movie actor who appears briefly in the second act of *Biography*. When a character makes what seems to be an entirely pointless appearance in a play, one may be sure that this character represents some unrealized purpose in the back of the playwright's mind. This is the case with Tympi; the dumb popular movie hero turns up in *Rain From Heaven* as the dumb popular hero of aviation; but he has acquired vital meaning: he is the raw material of the Nazi storm troops. In *Biography* Nolan is a stuffy hypocrite. He has no basic connection with the heroine's problem. In *Rain From Heaven*, Behrman has developed and analyzed the character; in combining him with the young movie actor he has given him social meaning; as a result he becomes real, three-dimensional, a person with emotions and with a point of view.

The material in *Rain From Heaven* is not fully realized in terms of action. The construction is not compact. Behrman's remarkable knack for dialogue leads him into discursive discussions and incidents. The fact that the play deals so abstractly with contemporary issues is due to a one-sided approach to these issues; the idea of a destiny which overrides and paralyzes the human will influences Behrman's method, leading him to treat the total environment as an unknown and final power; the decisions of the characters are jerky and incomplete; the impact of social forces is shown in talk rather than in its deeper effect on the consciousness and will. The characters are not fully realized; they have certain qualities which cause them to struggle against the environment, but the roots of these qualities are not exposed. We have noted these tendencies in Shaw; similar modes of thought give a Shavian flavor to Behrman's technique.

Since the theme is not fully thought out, the various actions of the play have only a vague connection with the root-action. The various subsidiary stories are tangential, and are not unified in terms of climax. The final separation of the lovers is genuinely moving, but it is inconclusive. It is not the supreme moment of an inevitable struggle, in which the deepest motives and feelings have been dramatized. Being only partially developed, the situation is only partially effective in terms of theatre.

The tendency to regard external forces (social, moral, political or psychological) as final manifestations of destiny, is characteristic of the modern man's relationship to his environment. Since one cannot dramatize the environment as something which is static or obscure, an abstract treatment of external forces destroys the validity of the play's social framework. One finds this weakness in many plays dealing with the struggles of the working class; social change is viewed mechanically or metaphysically, as if it were accomplished by some rational inevitability or dynamic life force greater than the totality of the wills involved.

In an authors' note to *1931*—Claire and Paul Sifton tell us that the play is "concerned with an individual in the tidal movement of a people caught in a situation which they can neither explain, escape or develop." Perhaps it is unfair to say that this phraseology suggests O'Neill's "conflicting tides in the soul of man." But certainly "the tidal movement of a people" is made up of individual and collective attempts to "explain, escape or develop"; where these attempts are absent there can be no tidal movement at all. The stage directions for the first scene of *1931*— speak of "the ebb of weariness, despair, blind pointless boredom and subconscious desperation." If the authors had attempted to project anything of this sort, their play would be undramatic; but a great deal of the movement of the drama is vibrantly alive and defiant. However the conflict lacks depth; its extension is limited; the framework is too abstract to give the events their proper perspective.

In the first scene, Adam is fired from his job as a trucker in a warehouse. He expresses his conscious strength and will; he flexes his powerful muscles: "Look at that. That's beans, that's ham-and. That's women, that's gasoline. That's *everything.* I got it. I can lift more boxes, more iron, more sacks, load 'em faster, check 'em better, make more trips, do more work, than any of your damn ..." —and he goes to face the world. But as Adam's will breaks, as he and the girl are crushed, the idea of a blind "tidal movement of people" tends to mechanize the action. Since the social forces are not accurately visualized, the psychological pressure is also vague. We are not permitted to see what is going on in the minds of the two central characters; they drift, unable to "explain, escape or develop." At the end, when Adam says, "Might as well see what those guys outside are after. ... Christ, I hope it's something I can get hold of with my hands," we cannot guess what this means in terms of character. The decision is not crucial, because the picture of reality has been documentary rather than fundamental; the decision remains an incident rather than an explosive change of equilibrium.

Yellow Jack, Sidney Howard's most noteworthy contribution to the theatre,* is a remarkable example of historical selection covering a wide field of events. Howard's perspective has definite limitations. But *Yellow Jack* has a scope which is rare in the theatre. This is undoubtedly due in some measure to the character of the subject-matter. Dealing with the development of medical science during a period of its most intensive growth, Howard seems to have been deeply stirred by the possibilities of the material. The greatness of the theme impelled Howard to find an appropriate method of presentation. On the other hand, he might very easily have treated the subject in an unhistorical way: as the struggle of great "detached" individuals; or as a local-color story, drawing heavily upon the atmosphere of Cuba in 1900; or as a story of duty, self-sacrifice and passion, with an intense love affair between Miss Blake and Carroll. These suggestions are not far-fetched; these are the methods of the modern stage. It is amazing that Howard has, in one play, freed himself from these methods, and made some progress toward a broader technique.

In speaking of a broader technique, I am not referring to the physical arrangement of the stage in *Yellow Jack.* Howard explains in a note that "the play flows in a constantly shifting rhythm of

* Written in collaboration with Paul De Kruif.

light." This is an effective way of integrating the movement of the scenes, and was brilliantly realized in Jo Mielziner's set and Guthrie McClintic's production. But a playwright's technical achievement is not measured by whether his play is in one scene or forty, or whether he uses a constructivist set or a drawing room. The emphasis on the exterior trappings of a production is one of the more foolish manifestations of the old form-and-content argument. The number and kind of settings are dictated by the needs of the action; the playwright must also be guided, as Aristotle advised him, by consideration for the limitations of the playhouse. Howard might have restricted the movement of *Yellow Jack* to a single conventional set without restricting the historical scope.

The important thing about *Yellow Jack* is its attempt to treat the fight against yellow fever as a *process,* a conflict in which both individuals and a whole epoch are concerned. Howard's limitation lies in his emphasis on certain factors in the environment, and the neglect of other lines of causation. This springs from the habit of mind which was analyzed in the discussion of *The Silver Cord.* Just as in the former play, the scientific revelations of psychoanalysis are transformed into a "scientific Nemesis," so in *Yellow Jack* the power of medical science is idealized and made cosmic. The author is somewhat dazzled by the idea of "pure" science, detached from the interplay of social and economic forces.

This inability to grasp the whole of his material is evident in the final scene of the play. Here the conception of man's fight for science should be expressed in terms of the deepest and most crucial conflict: yet the last scene is static; Stackpoole, in his laboratory in London in 1929, is *explaining* rather than fighting: "Reed took the disease from monkey to man, Stokes took it from man to monkey. Now we shall be taking it from monkey back to man." It may be said that this is a summing up, that the core of the action concerns the events in Cuba in 1900. But a summing up cannot be less dramatic than the events of which it is the sum.

Yellow Jack reaches its climax in the scene in which the experiment on the four privates is completed. But this climax is sustained and carried over into the short scenes which follow. In the scene of the experiment, the author has been very careful to avoid bringing the action to a moment of maximum tension, thus permitting the action to build through the following scenes, in West Africa and London. One may say that it is the intention of these final scenes to show that the fight for science goes on. But this is the essence of the play. The author does not wish to tell us that the fight for science goes on, but that it grows *less* important and *less* dramatic. The final moments therefore should have been very fully dramatized.

The first scene of exposition takes place in Stackpoole's laboratory in London, in January, 1929, and we return to this same laboratory in the final scene. This opening is the logical point for the beginning of the stage-action. By opening in 1929, the dramatist shows us the *routine* of modern medical research in which mortal danger is treated with heroic unconcern. From this the action progresses to the dramatic struggles of the past; we see the increasing emotional force and meaning of the struggle as men fight slowly to conquer the deadly germ.

But if we examine the first scene carefully, we find that it contains many ideas which are never developed in the course of the play. These ideas are of the utmost importance; they are elements of the social framework which are essential to our complete understanding of the action; since they are introduced in this incomplete form, they constitute mere hints which have no concrete value.

The introductory scene starts with an argument between Stackpoole and a Major of the Royal Air Force and an official of the Kenya Colony. The officials are objecting to the six-day quarantine for plane passengers from West Africa going to Europe. The playwright is aware that Imperialism is in conflict with "pure" science in the year 1929; he is feeling his way toward some use of this conception. But he has not been able to crystallize this problem dramatically. This weakens the framework of causation; it narrows the scope of the events in Cuba in 1900; we cannot understand science in relation to man's life and aspirations unless we understand the social and economic forces which affect the development of science. There is evidently a connection between the British governmental pressure in regard to the Kenya colony and the economic interests of the United States in Cuba. But this remains an association of ideas in the playwright's mind and is never explained.

The climax exposes the conceptual uncertainty: a lonely scientist talks to himself in a vacuum. Stackpoole's final speech casts its shadow over every scene in the play; the action is weakened by the fact that the root-action is not given its full emotional force or extension.

The dominant principle which guides the process of selection is the principle that the play's explosive force can be no greater than the extension, the social implications, of the action. The social framework, however vast it may be, is of no value unless it meets the requirements of dramatic action: it must be concrete, defined, progressive.

The development of the stage-action is a further process of selection and arrangement; the concentrated analysis and projection of events within the social framework. This is a matter of more detailed structural problems; having determined the dynamic forces which underlie the play's movement, the playwright turns to the mechanics of construction.

DRAMATIC COMPOSITION

In dealing with composition, we enter the more familiar realm that has been surveyed and charted by countless volumes on the technique of playwriting. The headings of the chapters, "Exposition," "Dialogue," "Characterization," have the consoling ring of long usage.

But our approach is consistent with the structural analysis developed in Part III, and involves a further inquiry into the social and psychological factors that govern the playwright's selection and arrangement of his material. The parts of the play are subordinate units of action. Each part is related to the whole by the principle of unity in terms of climax, but each part also has its own life and meaning, its inner growth of tension maturing to a crisis.

The study of composition is the study of the detailed organization of scenes and situations, both in their internal structure and in their relationship to the whole system of events.

Chapter I utilizes a term borrowed from the motion picture: it is of interest that there is no word in the technical vocabulary of the theatre that corresponds exactly to continuity; it describes the sequence or linkage of scenes. The absence of such a term in theatre usage may be attributed to the tendency to think of scenes and acts as separate entities, without adequate attention to their fluidity and organic movement. Continuity covers a number of the problems raised at the beginning of the chapter on "The Process of Selection": the heightening and maintaining of tension, the length of various scenes, abrupt and gradual transitions, probability, chance, and coincidence.

At the end of Chapter I, twelve principles of continuity are formulated. Having examined the way in which scenes are arranged and connected in general, we proceed to consider the specific sequence of scenes which constitutes a dramatic structure. Four chapters deal with four essential parts of the structure: exposition, progression, the obligatory scene, and the climax.

Characterization is treated in many theatre textbooks as the portrayal of qualities that are somehow mysteriously assigned to a person whom the dramatist has invented. These qualities have no clear relationship to the play's structure, and the actions in which the individual participates are only incidentally illustrative of the traits that compose his character. Chapter VI seeks to dispel this illusion, and to show that separate study of characterization is misleading. The drama depicts people in action; every moment of the presentation tests and explores the operation of the conscious will; every moment is characterization, and drama can have no other function or purpose.

Chapter VII takes a similar view of dialogue as an indivisible part of the play's structure, which cannot properly be detached from the action of which it is an essential portion. The prosaic and uninspired speech in so many modern plays expresses the befuddled and entangled will of characters who have lost the ability to undertake decisive actions.

Part IV concludes with a brief and necessarily inconclusive chapter on the audience. Since a play derives its life and meaning from the audience, we are here entering a whole new field of inquiry. The chapter is described as a postscript; it might better be regarded as a fragmentary preface to a book that may some time be written.

CHAPTER I

CONTINUITY

SINCE continuity is a matter of detailed sequence, the study of continuity can best be served by the minute analysis of the movement of a particular play. *Yellow Jack* is a solid example of playwriting method, and is of special value because of its historical background, which gives the student an opportunity to compare the playwright's selection of incidents, both with Paul De Kruif's description of the Cuban events (from which Howard drew the plan of his play), and with the wider field of historical source-material which was accessible to the author.

Having already used *Yellow Jack* as an example of historical selection, we can now begin at the point where the previous analysis left off—dissecting each step in the development of the action.

The exposition is divided into three parts: London in 1929, West Africa in 1927, and the first Cuban scenes (1900). What is gained by this triple exposition? Each of these scenes serves a distinct purpose: the action in London shows the scope of the fight against yellow fever and hints at the danger; the West African incident dramatizes the danger, broadens the emotional meaning by going more deeply into the conscious wills of men who are fighting the battle of science; the first Cuban scenes define the problem— the specific conflict between man and his environment took place in Cuba. It is to be noted that the conflict as the playwright conceives it is not *limited* to the Cuban events. Since the action (not the social framework, but the stage-action itself) transcends these events, the exposition must present possibilities of extension which are equal to the extension of the stage-action. For this reason, the scenes in London and West Africa are necessary.

The curtain rises on a scene of direct conflict in regard to the quarantine of passengers from West Africa. The argument is interrupted when Stackpoole's assistant cuts himself on a pipette of yellow fever germs. Quick action: Stackpoole who has had the disease gives him some blood. Thus the danger, the human problem, the unfinished struggle to cope with the disease—all these are dramatically projected. There is a quick shift to West Africa, eighteen months earlier; the transition is cleverly accomplished; tom-toms beat in darkness; the light grows slowly. Here again we have the human equation, the lonely desperate men in the jungle; and the scientific struggle: Dr. Stokes succeeds in giving yellow fever to an Indian Rhesus monkey. Again darkness, and we hear a quartette singing, "There'll be a hot-time in the old town tonight." We are at Columbia Barracks, in Cuba in 1900.

Both these transitions are noteworthy in several ways: (1) The use of sound as an adjunct to dramatic movement; (2) the value of abrupt contrast, the tom-toms breaking in upon the London laboratory, the nostalgic singing breaking into the jungle silence; (3) the value of crystallizing a place and time by means which are unpretentiously simple and clear.

At the opening of the Cuban scene soldiers are crossing in silhouette carrying corpses on stretchers. The sense of death, of an army destroyed by an unknown enemy, is strongly presented, and helps to give the play its social depth. There is no element of metaphysics in this threatening fate; the disease is an enemy to be faced and defeated.

Here we have an interesting problem in selection: at what point does the author pick up the struggle against yellow fever in Cuba? The point which he chooses is a moment of discouragement, when the Yellow Fever Commission is disgusted and hopeless. This is naturally the point which he must select: the cycle of conflict is (a) recognition of difficulties and determination to overcome them; (b) progressive development of struggle; (c) partial achievement; (d) new difficulties and increased determination. The opening scene of *Yellow Jack* shows us a scientist facing a desperate problem; then back to Africa, discouragement and accomplishment; then back to Cuba, the beginning of another cycle.

So far the author has followed a very simple single line: he traces the fight against yellow fever historically, showing its background and historical associations. But in the Cuban scenes he must divide the play into two separate series of events, which merge very much later in the action. Here lies one of the deepest reasons for Howard's setting, for the arrangement of steps and platforms upon which the action can shift with the shifting light. This enables the author to *conceal* the fact that (until the final experiment) the story of the four American privates is only very loosely connected with the story of the American Yellow Fever Commission. The movement on the stage makes the connection appear closer than it is.

The first two scenes in Cuba are a continuation of exposition, introducing the two separate lines of action. We see the fear of the disease among the soldiers. Busch asks Miss Blake to look at his tongue. And above, on the center platform, the Yellow Fever Commission is outlining the problem, "We were sent down here to stop this horror! To isolate a microbe and find a cure! And we've failed." This ends the exposition and begins the rising action, the moment of transition being Reed's statement of the task which must be undertaken; the disease carrier must be found: "What was it crawled or jumped or flew through that guardhouse window, bit that one prisoner, and went back where it came from?"

It is interesting to note that there is no element of surprise in the development of the play. The audience knows what "flew through that guardhouse window." The tension derives from the force of the conflict, not from uncertainty as to its outcome. There is no artificial suspense as far as the story is concerned; the tension is sustained solely by the selection and arrangement of events.

The most serious problem of continuity in "Yellow Jack" is the handling of the two separate lines of action: the group of soldiers and the group of scientists. In this Howard has not been entirely successful. Is this because it is undesirable to have two lines of development which merge at a late point in the play? Not at all. The handling of two (or many) threads of action is one of the most usual problems of continuity.

In *The Children's Hour,* by Lillian Hellman, the construction is disorganized because of the author's inability to handle the two separate (but connected) actions: (1) the conflict between the two women and the malicious child; (2) the triangular situation between the two women and Dr. Cardin. But here again as in *Yellow Jack,* the two lines of action are a necessity: the development and inter-connection of these two series of events is the whole core of the author's meaning. She has been unable to define this meaning and bring it to a decisive head. The root of the trouble is in the climax; the climax exposes the conceptual confusion which splits the play into a dual system.

The difficulty in *Yellow Jack* is of the same sort. Howard has not clarified the activity of the four privates in relation to the theme; their decision to sacrifice themselves in the yellow fever fight is heroic but accidental. What does it mean? Human life must be sacrificed in the great battle for science? To be sure. But is the sacrifice of scientists, who risk their own lives consciously for a conscious end, more, or less heroic, than the somewhat haphazard heroism of the four soldiers? Howard has not taken a decisive stand on this question. The activity of the four privates tends to be diffuse, idle talk. Since their later function is a somewhat passive one, there is really nothing for them to do except talk and wait their turn.

Howard has tried to give the four soldiers depth and meaning. He has tried to show their economic and social point of view. But their points of view are only loosely connected with the dramatic problem. Their opinions are merely comments, which have no driving force. The soldiers are the most static element in the play.

Howard's greatest achievement lies in the dynamic progression of the struggle of the scientists to discover the germ carrier. The characters of Reed and the other doctors are not very subtly or deeply portrayed. Yet each scene has a mounting emotional power. Each scene is a moment of crisis, selected and dramatized with the greatest care; each scene presents a serious human problem, but the human problem is not allowed to obscure the social implications; the conflict is observed, not from a single angle, but in its multiple aspect. The activities involved in the fight against disease are very varied: the man of science must have infinite patience and accuracy, the slightest mistake may undo months of work; he must doubt his own conclusions and test them again and again; he must be willing to give his own life; he must face the moral problem of taking the lives of others when this seems necessary. The scientist is under economic and social pressure; he is interfered with by his superiors; he is often misunderstood by public opinion; he is often laughed at and ignored. These forces constitute the totality of the environment, to which the scientist must adjust himself. In *Yellow Jack,* we see this process of adjustment at its moments of maximum tension.

The first important scene in the rising action is the visit to Finlay whom every one has ignored: "For nineteen years science has laughed at me, Major," says Finlay, "at the cracked old Finlay and his mosquitoes." Reed replies, "I'm no stranger to waiting, Dr. Finlay." One notes that the conflict in this scene is many-sided; Finlay's pride makes him oppose Reed; but it is also clear that he is afraid the others will steal his discovery and take the glory. We see the pathos of Finlay's long wait, but we also see him as grasping and bitter.

The scene with Finlay is the natural starting point of the rising action; his conviction that a female mosquito is the disease carrier forces the doctors to face the problem of experiment on human beings: here the author might easily have side-tracked his drama into a personal conflict in regard to duty and conscience. But he succeeds in presenting these men as men really are; with personal fears and personal ambitions, living in a world whose prejudices and opinions cannot be ignored. Reed says, "They may send their sons to be butchered in battle, but let one of you lift one finger in this war and they will engulf you!"

The need of testing their theory on human beings leads inevitably to the final crisis, the experiment on the four soldiers. What is the structure of the intervening events? (1) The men decide to experiment on themselves. (2) Major Reed is forced to return to Washington; the absence of the leader causes the carelessness which interferes with the certainty of the experiments. (3) The crucial scene in which they realize that Carroll seems to have caught yellow fever. (4) Carelessness makes the experiment uncertain: Carroll had performed an autopsy on a man dead with yellow fever, and thus there is no proof that the mosquito caused the illness. (5) This forces Lazear and Agramonte to take a desperate chance: they invite a passing soldier, Private Dean, into the laboratory; he lets one of the mosquitoes in the test-tubes bite him, without knowing the reason. (6) Carroll seems to be dying. In a very exciting scene, Lazear waits and hopes that Carroll will not die in vain. The only thing that can justify his suffering is news of Dean's illness, which will confirm the fact that the mosquitoes are the source of the plague. The nurse comes in to ask the assistant surgeon to look at a new case.

LAZEAR: What's the soldier's name?
MISS BLAKE: Dean... William H, Troop A, Seventh Cavalry.
LAZEAR (*turns to Carroll*): We know! Do you get that! We know!

But the fact that the doctors know is not sufficient. There is still doubt; Lazear becomes ill without the aid of a mosquito. Now that they have gone so far, they must prove their case in a public, controlled experiment. There is no other way. This leads to (7): the demand for volunteers and the decision of the four soldiers to risk their lives.

It is obvious that, until the final crisis, the four soldiers are shockingly neglected in the action. But the continuity, as it concerns the scientists, is masterly. Let us examine the anatomy of these events: what happens is really a cycle of activity which may be expressed as follows: a decision to follow a certain course of action, tension developed in fulfilling the decision, an unexpected triumph, and a new complication which requires another decision on a higher plane. Each triumph is the culmination of an act of will, which produces a change of equilibrium between individuals and their environment. This change requires new adjustments, and makes the new complications inevitable. The play is laid out in three such cycles. *First cycle:* They decide to experiment on themselves; Major Reed's departure causes a complication; the discovery of Carroll's illness is a moment of triumph; his carelessness in having exposed himself is a new set-back. *Second cycle:* The remaining doctors make a desperate decision—the brutal scene in which they use Dean as an unsuspecting "human guinea pig." This seems unjustified; as we see Carroll apparently dying we feel that the whole thing is hopeless; at the moment of highest tension, the news of Dean's illness brings triumph, followed by new doubts. *Third cycle:* The great decision to make an orderly public experiment; the four privates decide to volunteer; this is followed by the crucial scene in which the four await their fate.

One thing is very clear about these three cycles: each one is shorter than the previous one, the points of tension are more pronounced and the explanatory action *between* the points of tension is cut down. In the third cycle, the events are grouped closely together and each event in the last cycle is itself a first-rate point of crisis, involving a decisive act of will on the part of the characters—the decision of the scientists, and the decision of the four soldiers.

It must not be supposed that the pattern of *Yellow Jack* can be imitated as an arbitrary formula. But the principle which underlies the pattern is basic, and can be applied in all cases. The material arranges itself in certain cycles. If we examine each of the cycles, we find that each one is a small replica of the construction of a play, involving exposition, rising action, clash, and climax. Having selected the high points of the action, the playwright exercises great care in preparing and building the tension, so that these scenes will dominate. The high point of the first cycle is the discovery of Carroll's illness. The high point of the second cycle is the scene at Carroll's bedside. What are the technical means by which the author increases the effect of these crises? First, he continually emphasizes both the danger and importance of the event: we are convinced that everything depends on one of the men being taken ill and that illness will result in death. But telling us this is not enough. The effect is increased by emphasizing the strain on the characters. This may be described as *increasing the emotional load.* Perhaps one can explain the technique by illustrating it in its crudest form. For example, one character says, "I can't stand it," and another character says, "You must..." "I can't, I tell you, I'd rather die," etc., etc. It is done, generally at the wrong time and in the wrong way, in every moving picture.

The most brilliant use of this device may be found in the plays of Clifford Odets. He is extraordinarily skillful in heightening the effect of a scene by underscoring the emotional strain. This is entirely legitimate if the emotion grows out of the inner necessities of the conflict. The only danger lies in the facile use of artificial tension as a substitute for genuine development.

Increasing the emotional load may be accomplished in various ways. It is sometimes done by the repetition of words or movements which create a rhythm. The tom-toms in Eugene O'Neill's *The Emperor Jones,* are an example of the use of mechanical rhythm. The man in the death-house in the first act of John Wexley's *The Last Mile* who keeps repeating the one word "Hol-mes!" creates an increasing physical tension which is also psychological; the repetition exposes the man's diseased conscious will and thus gives him dramatic meaning.

The development of tension must be unified in reference to the point of climax toward which the tension is building. In *Yellow Jack,* as the doctors experiment on themselves, it is clear that they are almost at the breaking point. There are sudden quarrels. Agramonte says: "I have come to the end of my patience now!" When it is Carroll's turn to be bitten by a mosquito, he pushes away the test-tube offered him: "Don't point that thing at me!" (He selects No. 46, which had been fed on a case which had not begun to develop; this is the direct *cause* of his being taken ill. The other mosquitoes had fed on later cases). As we proceed, the men are almost at each other's throats. Carroll shouts furiously, "This damn thing's got me crazy as it is! It's got me all off my feed!" The other two look at the screaming man and they suddenly realize that he has yellow fever. But the end of the scene is suddenly quiet, gaining an effect by a careful unemotional statement of how much is involved: Lazear: "I'm scared to death." Agramonte: "What of? That Carroll's got yellow jack or that he hasn't?" Lazear: "Both."

Thus the developing tension reaches a moment of maximum tension, in which the balance of forces is changed, and a new situation is created which leads to a new series of tensions. This is not a matter of presenting the natural *flow* of events; the activity must be compressed and heightened; the speed of the development and the point of explosion must be determined in reference to the climax of the cycle and the climax of the whole play. The end of the scene quoted shows the value of a sudden contrast of mood and tempo—the moment of climax is marked by the abrupt cutting off of the emotion and the use of understatement. The clarity of

Howard's lines should also be noted. He states the essential issues with workmanlike precision.

Transitions (both physical and emotional) are a difficult technical problem. In *Yellow Jack* the soldiers are of great service to the playwright in this connection. Although he has failed to give them an organized part in the developing action, he uses them effectively as a way of maintaining the movement of scenes—the singing of old songs, the silhouette of men carrying stretchers, the bits of conversation. These transitions illustrate two very important features of continuity: (1) abrupt contrast, cutting a scene short at a high point and sharply projecting activity of an entirely different sort, preserving unity by the very vigor of the contrast; (2) overlapping, the simultaneous presentation of two sorts of activity, the second action being projected before the first action is completed. Both of these devices are very clearly illustrated in *Yellow Jack;* both (in various forms and with various modifications) will be found in the great majority of plays.

In the matter of transitions (and in other problems of continuity), the playwright can learn a great deal from a study of motion picture technique. Arthur Edwin Krows points out that the cinema makes extensive use of what he describes as the "cut-and-flash" method: "The guiding principle is to 'cut' the main line of interest and to 'flash' the lesser.... The principle of cut-and-flash is a principle of the human mind itself. A person's brain is always cutting and flashing ideas, one suggesting and strengthening the other." *

The psychological value of contrast, and the use of subordinate events in strengthening the main line of interest, suggests a very wide field of inquiry, for which the motion picture offers invaluable material. An important beginning in the analysis of motion picture continuity has been made by V. I. Pudovkin, whose *Film Technique* is required reading for any student of the theatre. Pudovkin uses the scene of the massacre of the mob on the great flight of steps in Odessa, in *The Battleship Potemkin,* as an example of Eisenstein's arrangement of incident: "The running of the mob down the steps is rendered rather sparingly and is not especially expressive, but the perambulator with the baby, which, loosed from the grip of the shot mother, rolls down the steps, is poignant in its tragic intensity and strikes with the force of a blow." † In this, and similar instances of cutting, the effect is achieved by the

* *Opus cit.*
† V. I. Pudovkin, *Film Technique,* translation by Ivor Montagu (London, 1929).

precise analysis of the relationship of the incidents and the precise timing of the transitions. Pudovkin says: "For every event, a process has to be carried out comparable to the process in mathematics termed 'differentiation'—that is to say, dissection into parts or elements." The incident of the perambulator is the root-action of the events on the Odessa steps: it concentrates a maximum of emotional compression and generates the greatest extension of meaning.

A great deal of technical discussion is devoted to probability and coincidence. Since there is no abstract probability, the test of the probability of any incident lies in its relation to the social concept embodied in the root-action. Viewed in this light, the question of what is and is not plausible ceases to be subject to variable and inconclusive judgments, and becomes a matter of structural integrity. Whether or not the audience accepts or rejects the social concept underlying the play depends on whether or not the author's consciousness of social necessity meets their own needs and expectations. This is also true of any scene or character in the play. But the validity of the scene or character in the dramatic scheme does not depend on its relation to events in general, but on its use-value in relation to the root-action. The purpose of the play is to prove that the root-action is probable and necessary. Therefore nothing in the play which is essential to the development of the climax can be improbable—unless the climax itself is improbable.

The element of coincidence enters into any event: to assume that we can eliminate coincidence in the presentation of an action is to assume that we can attain knowledge of *all* the pre-conditions of the action. A coincidence passes unnoticed if it conforms to our idea of probability. The action of *Yellow Jack* is both historical and probable. But even if every event were a direct transcription from reliable historical sources, the believability of the combination of events would depend, not on the accuracy of the transcription, but upon the author's purpose and point of view.

Coincidence is to be found in every scene of *Yellow Jack*. Carroll *happens* to select a certain test-tube; Dean *happens* to be dumb enough to allow himself to be bitten by the mosquito in the laboratory. Lazear *happens* to catch yellow fever at an opportune moment. These events are both plausible and necessary, because they contribute to the inevitability of the scheme of events.

There is an important distinction between physical improbability and psychological improbability. We have repeatedly emphasized the fact that a play embodies both the author's consciousness and will. The resulting picture of reality is volitional and not photographic. Our visions and hopes are based on our experience; when men imagine a strange place or a future paradise with hierarchies of angels, they draw the picture in the colors and shapes of reality as they know it. In the middle ages, the picture of heaven corresponded to psychological probability; Dante filled heaven and purgatory and hell with the citizens of Florence. The test of the *Divine Comedy* is its psychological truth; it would be absurd to question this truth on the ground that the events are physically impossible.

The laws of thought enable us to intensify and extend our picture of reality. A play, conforming to the laws of thought, creates conventions which violate physical plausibility without a qualm: we accept actors as being imaginary persons; we accept scenery as being what it obviously is not; we accept a series of events which begin at eight-forty-five and end at eleven and which are repeated nightly at the same time and place.

Many events appear implausible in the theatre of the past because they represent conventions which have become outmoded. These conventions are not merely technical. Theatrical conventions are the product of social conventions. We cannot judge these devices by their physical probability, but by their meaning and purpose. The potion which Friar Lawrence gives to Juliet so that she may appear to be dead is the classic example of a device which is described by technical writers as being inherently implausible. Conventions of this sort were common in the Elizabethan theatre. What really disturbs us about the incident today is our inability to understand the social necessity which justified the friar's use of the potion. We have the same difficulty in understanding the root-action of *Romeo and Juliet;* the deaths at Juliet's tomb seem excessive and coincidental, because in our society these deaths would happen for different reasons. If we examine the play historically, if we endeavor to see it as it would have been seen by the audiences of the period, we find that the web of causation is sure and inevitable.

The ghost in *Hamlet* is another convention of the same kind. In a recent production of *Hamlet,* the melancholy Dane spoke the lines which are attributed to the ghost, thus giving the impression that the apparition is the voice of Hamlet's subconscious. This distorts Shakespeare's meaning, and obscures the valid rôle which the ghost plays in the drama. By making the vision more natural, it is made less real. A modern dramatist might very properly introduce a ghost into a realistic play. He would not be so foolhardy as to ask us to believe in the *naturalness* of the ghost; but an actor in the rôle of a dead man may serve a real and understandable purpose; we must know what the dead man means, not as a symbol, but as a factor in the living action; if the effect on the action corresponds to reality as we know it, we accept the psychological truth of the convention by which the effect is produced. (For example, the purpose of the masks in *The Great God Brown* is instantly understandable; we are all in the habit of hiding behind an imaginary mask on certain occasions, while at other times we speak frankly and unmask ourselves. We accept the masks the moment we see them; the difficulty in *The Great God Brown* lies in the author's own confusion in regard to the end served by the use of the masks; we become gradually more confused, because he tries to make them mean more than they *do* mean.)

The playwright who misunderstands the question of plausibility will generally over-simplify and over-emphasize the immediate link of cause and effect between events. He will be so anxious to invent probable causes that he will neglect the scope of the action. If we examine the coincidences in *Yellow Jack,* we find that the play derives a great deal of its driving force from the directness of the action and the disregard of explanatory detail. Major Reed's return to Washington is an important incident in the early part of the play; an inept playwright might worry about the reasons for the Major's departure, and would interrupt the action to offer explanations. He might also introduce an entire scene to explain Private Dean's character, so as to increase the plausibility of the scene in which Dean is used for the experiment. This would be unnecessary because the essential causal relation is the relation between the event and the root-action of the play. The thing which builds drama is the introduction of *new* causes which may or may not grow out of the preceding action, but which change the conflict, which introduce new obstacles, thus delaying and intensifying the final conclusion. The notion that a play is an unbroken line of cause and effect is a dangerous one, because it prevents the piling up of diverse forces driving toward the climax. If *Yellow Jack* consisted of a simple arrangement of direct cause and effect, it would be far less complex and exciting.

One is apt to assume that Howard's treatment of the four privates would be more effective if they were tied more closely to the work of the doctors: the fault in the handling of the soldiers lies in their connection with the root-action, and not in their contacts with the doctors. Two or more lines of causation can be entirely separate, provided they move toward a common goal. If the activity of the soldiers were meaningful in relation to the theme, their connection with the doctors would be clear even though there were no inter-play of cause and effect between the two groups until the moment of climax.

The complex action in Shakespeare's plays never fails to drive forward toward a point of maximum tension. When these plays appear diffuse to modern audiences, it is due to inadequate productions and failure to understand the conceptions on which the plays are based. Shakespeare does not hesitate to introduce new elements and separate lines of causation. The conflict is not a matter of "one thing leading to another," but a great battle in which many forces are martialed to a final test of strength. In *Hamlet* the killing of the King comes only after Hamlet has made the most desperate effort, has literally exhausted his mind and heart, in an effort to find another solution. The introduction of Rosencrantz and Guildenstern introduces an entirely new factor; the arrival of the players is not caused by the preceding action, and turns the play in another direction. The sending of Hamlet abroad, his return and the scene at Ophelia's grave, are ways of developing unexpected possibilities of the action, delaying and intensifying the result.

"Retardation," says Krows, "should always add something to the action proper." The playwright, he continues, can achieve "power in delay." * This is true, but the real power lies, not in the delay, but in the introduction of new forces which create a new balance of power and thus make the delay necessary and progressive. This increases the tension, because it increases the possibilities of explosion which are inherent in the situation and which *will* explode at the moment of climax.

It is customary to speak of tension as a somewhat mystic bond across the footlights, a psychic identification between audience and actors. It is far more enlightening to consider the word in its scientific sense. In electricity it means a difference of potential; in engineering it applies to the amount of stress and strain, which may be carefully calculated.

In play-construction, tension depends on the tensile strength of the elements of the drama, the degree of stress and strain which can be withstood before the final explosion.

The principles of continuity may be summed up as follows: (1) the exposition must be fully dramatized in terms of action; (2) the exposition must present possibilities of extension which are equal to the extension of the stage action; (3) two or more lines of causation may be followed if they find their solution in the root-action;

* *Opus cit.*

(4) the rising action is divided into an indeterminate number of cycles; (5) each cycle is an action and has the characteristic progression of an action—exposition, rise, clash and climax; (6) the heightening of the tension as each cycle approaches its climax is accomplished by *increasing the emotional load;* this can be done by emphasizing the importance of what is happening, by underlining fear, courage, anger, hysteria, hope; (7) tempo and rhythm are important in maintaining and increasing tension: (8) the linking of scenes is accomplished by abrupt contrast or by overlapping of interest; (9) as the cycles approach the root-action, the tempo is increased, the subsidiary climaxes are more intense and grouped more closely together, and the action between the points is cut down; (10) probability and coincidence do not depend on physical probability, but on the value of the incident in relation to the root-action; (11) the play is not a simple continuity of cause and effect, but the inter-play of complex forces; new forces may be introduced without preparation provided their *effect* on the action is manifest; (12) tension depends on the emotional load which the action will bear before the moment of explosion is reached.

CHAPTER II

EXPOSITION

SINCE exposition is regarded as a matter of preparation, it is frequently considered sufficient if the dramatist offers necessary information as quickly and clearly as possible. "There are certain things," says Pinero, "which must be told the audience, as quickly and conveniently as possible, at the outset of any play. Why not tell these things quite frankly and get them over with?" Pinero is as good as his word; in *The Second Mrs. Tanqueray,* we see Aubrey Tanqueray having a little bachelor dinner with two of his old friends, discussing himself and his approaching marriage with wooden frankness.

Theatre textbooks recognize the dangers of static or unimaginative exposition; but it is suggested that the dramatist must overcome these dangers by his skill in handling undramatic material. Baker says that the playwright "is writing supposedly for people who, except on a few historical subjects, know nothing of his material. If so, as soon as possible, he must make them understand: (1) who his people are; (2) where his people are; (3) the time of the play; and (4) what in the present and past relations of his characters causes the story." * It is true that this information must be conveyed; since the exposition is part of the play and is subject to the rules of dramatic conflict, the information must be dramatized. Baker's points—the questions, *who, where* and *when*—are included in the present and past relationships which cause the story. If the dramatist is interested only in the story as he intends to tell it in stage-action, and if he has failed to analyze the social framework, he is sure to present the expository material in its most static form. If one regards the beginning of the drama as an absolute beginning, one cannot give dramatic vitality to the presentation of preliminary facts, however useful the facts may be. Explanations are explanations, no matter how shrewdly they may be concealed. As long as the opening scenes are regarded as explanatory, they are sure to be dull or undeveloped; the playwright is looking ahead; he is anxious to clear the ground and get down to the serious business of the play.

But the beginning of a play is not absolute; it is a point in a larger story; it is a point which can be clearly defined, and which is necessarily a very exciting point in the development of the story —because it is the point at which a dangerous decision is made. This point was earlier described as the arousing of the conscious will to concentrated conflict with a defined aim. Such a decision is itself a climax of magnitude and cannot be covered by explanations. On the contrary, anything which is descriptive reduces the significance of the decision and obscures its meaning. Since this situation is the key to the play, a static or undeveloped opening will infect the movement of the whole play.

In order to understand this decision, we must know its circumstances. The curtain cannot rise on a man making up his mind concerning something we know nothing about. The term, exposition, as applied to the first cycle of the action is not altogether a misnomer; all action contains expository elements; the climax of the play is expository, because it exposes additional facets of the situation, additional information and possibilities. The opening of a play presents an individual or group of individuals who are undertaking a momentous conflict which is forced on them by circumstances. It is apparent that these circumstances must be dramatic; since the decision is so important that it covers all the possibilities of the play, it must be the result of considerable changes of equilibrium between the individuals and their environment. These disturbances cannot be described, but must be seen and felt

* *Opus cit.*

at the moment when their impact on the conscious will causes a
change or intensification of the individual's needs and purposes.

Since the exposition covers the possibilities of the drama, it must
be more closely connected with the root-action than any other part
of the play.

It is this connection which holds the play together; as the scope
of the action is defined in the climax, so its scope is visioned in the
exposition. The unity of cause and effect which operates throughout
the play is essentially the unity between the exposition and the
climax. This leads us to a more exact understanding of the way in
which the selection of the play's point of departure is determined.
Having selected the climax as the embodiment of his conception of
necessity, the playwright will select for his opening, the event which
seems to him to embody the most direct and most real cause of this
necessity. Since the playwright's idea of causation is based on his
attitude toward his environment, the point at which he opens his
story reveals his social judgment. The climax shows what he wants
society to be within the limits of what he regards as its possibilities.
The exposition shows *why* he believes that these limitations are
final. This does not mean that the inevitability of the climax is
exposed in the first scenes; if this were the case, there would be no
occasion for continuing the play. The opening scenes show the
setting up of a goal under conditions which make the setting up of
such a goal seem necessary. New information is presented and new
difficulties are added in the course of the play; there are progressive
changes both in the characters and the environment. But at the
moment of climax, we must be able to refer directly back to the
first scene; the social causes which are manifest in the climax must
have been present in the original conditions; the action is motivated
by a picture of reality which is proved more or less true or false
at the end; but however false the original picture of reality may
have been, it must have been framed in the same reality which is
made manifest at the end. The setting up of a goal at the beginning
of the play must have been caused by the same *real* forces which
dominate the climax. At the beginning of the play, we wish to
understand as fully as possible why the conflict of will is necessary:
the past and present experience of the characters makes it necessary;
the opening action sums up this experience; this creates the environment; the environment is enlarged as the play proceeds; but it is
the same environment; the forces which determine the original act
of will are the forces which determine its conclusions. The opening
of the play is the point at which these forces have their maximum
effect on the will giving it the direction which is sustained through-

out the play. Causes introduced later are subordinate, because the introduction of a stronger cause would change the conditions of the action and would destroy the play's unity.

The arrangement of *Yellow Jack,* returning in the final scene to the London laboratory which initiated the action, illustrates the logical link of direct cause and effect between exposition and climax. Howard embodies his idea of social causation (the motivations of the men of science and the social and economic conditions under which they work) in the three scenes of exposition. But his idea of social necessity (the inevitability of scientific conquest) is less clear and therefore less dramatically projected.

This principle is not an abstraction; like the principle of unity in terms of climax, it applies directly to the practical tasks of the playwright. The direct link between the climax and the exposition is not a matter of what the author wishes and plans; however confused or disorganized the play may be, the link will be present and can be analyzed.

The proof that this is the way one's mind works lies in thinking about any event and noting the course of one's thoughts. If one considers a murder, one visualizes the crime itself; one immediately asks why the crime was committed; one turns back to find the most fundamental cause of the act; having discovered this, one reconstructs the intermediate lines of causation. Suppose one moves forward and chooses a later moment of climax; the execution of a murderer. In this case, the cause is self-evident; one's mind jumps back from the picture of the man about to pay the penalty to the picture of the act for which the penalty is being paid. These are the two poles of an action, and the intervening events form a unit of movement within these limits. Of course the killing is merely the most obvious cause of the execution; one might select many other events before or after the murder as being the basic reason for the execution. This depends on one's attitude toward the final situation, on the lesson one draws from it—which determines one's opinion in regard to its social cause.

The first cause (not first in time, but first in importance) may be very close to the event in point of time, or very far from it. George O'Neil's play, *American Dream,* ends with the suicide of the wealthy intellectual, Daniel Pingree. The author believes that this event is historically motivated; he turns back to the early history of the family, and opens his play in 1650.

In *Hedda Gabler,* the cause of Hedda's tragedy is the community in which she lives. The play begins with the return to the community. The first lines are Miss Tesman's: "Upon my word, I don't believe they are stirring yet!" And Berta's: "Remember how late the steamboat got in last night. And then, when they got home!—Good Lord, what a lot the young mistress had to unpack before she could go to bed."

The exposition is less dramatic than in most of Ibsen's plays; the conversation between Tesman and his aunt Julia is descriptive and awkward. This is probably due to his intense concentration on the character of Hedda, and his tendency to see every element of the environment through her consciousness and will. But the opening shows us that neither her marriage nor her renewed friendship with Lövborg can be regarded as the direct causes of her suicide. If Ibsen regarded Judge Brack's threats in the final scene as being responsible for her death, the play would begin with a scene indicating the relationship between Hedda and the Judge. But Hedda's "want of an object in life" is conditioned by the community; Miss Juliana Tesman typifies the community, and the action must commence with her.

The end of *Strange Interlude* shows Nina and Marsden together, ready at last "to die in peace!" The social cause of this situation is Nina's father complex which she has transferred to Marsden. The play opens with Marsden waiting for Nina in the library of her father's home. In a long soliloquy, Marsden expresses his feeling for Nina; then Professor Leeds enters and the two men discuss the problem. All the causes, the sexual relationships and emotions, which O'Neill regards as basic, are compactly presented in this scene, and lead directly to the conclusion.

In John Wexley's *They Shall Not Die,* the closing courtroom scene ends with a stirring attack upon the prejudice of the Alabama court. Rokoff says: "There are hundreds of thousands of men and women meeting in a thousand cities of the world in mass protest against oppression and ownership of man by man ... and over them, you have no jurisdiction..." Nathan Rubin, the New York lawyer, makes the final speech: "And if I do nothing else in my life, I'll make the fair name of this state stink to high heaven with its lynch justice... these boys, *they shall not die!*" Idiot laughter is heard from the jury room as the curtain descends. The dramatic power of this ending is unquestionable. But there is a double conception in these two speeches. We are told that the final word lies with the men and women who are raising their voices in protest in a thousand cities. But we are also told that the lawyer will devote his life to exposing the rottenness of Alabama justice. These two conceptions are not contradictory; but Wexley ends with the lawyer's defiance and has so built the scene that the moment of supreme tension lies in his declaration coupled with the horrible laughter of the jurors. Dramatically this would be sound, if it were completely realized in terms of the lawyer's character. But the juxtaposition of the ideas shows that the relationship between the individual and the social forces is not clearly conceived. If the mass protest of vast numbers of people is the ultimate social force which can defeat the lynchers, this balance of forces must be the highest climactic moment which the play can reach, and the lawyer must be placed within this scheme.

If we turn to the opening of *They Shall Not Die,* we find that the first scene shows the flaw in the system of causation. The play opens in the jail. On one side of the stage, three white prisoners, Red, Blackie and the St. Louis Kid, are talking. On the other side, we see the office, in which two deputy sheriffs, Cooley and Henderson, are talking lazily. We are shown the atmosphere of the South, the laziness, corruption, hatred and fear of Negroes; thus the basic cause of the action is localized. The South which we see in the first scene is the South of the idiot laughter; the South whose fair name will "stink to high heaven," according to Rubin's final speech. This is valid as far as it goes; but it neglects the larger issues which are implicit in the case and which the play touches in its strongest moments.

For this reason, the two lines of action in *They Shall Not Die* lack any deep connection. The second act is in three scenes, the first in Lucy Wells' home, the second in the Negro death cells in Pembroke prison, and the third is again in Lucy's home.

The visit of Rokoff to the condemned Negroes and his promise to help them is one of the best examples of scene-construction in the modern theatre. But this event is not integrally linked to the preceding and following scenes; the progression is casual rather than inevitable. The necessity which ought to bind the separate events is the goal toward which both are moving. The connection between Lucy and the social forces which are battling for the lives of the nine boys is personal and unclear, just as, in the root-action, the lawyer's connection with these social forces is unclear. The difficulty is reflected in the exposition, and affects every part of the play.

The exposition is an action: the preparatory movement, like other parts of the drama, is a cycle of events which has its inner unity and defined limits. It exhibits the characteristic form of an action, containing within itself exposition, rising action, clash and climax.

The first lines of a play are expository, not only of the action of the play, but of the expository situation within the play, which quickly develops in tempo and intensity. Since the exposition deals with the setting up of a conscious aim, the moment of highest tension is the moment at which the decision is made. The decision may be spoken or implied; it may be due to the immediate circumstances, or it may have been previously made; a play does not always begin with the forming of a brand-new line of conduct. The purpose may have existed previously; but it is forced into the open in the expository conflict; the climax of the exposition exposes the meaning and scope of the decision, and thus creates a change of equilibrium between the individuals and their environment. The first cycle of the rising action develops out of this changed balance of forces.

The exposition may also be sub-divided into subordinate actions which develop to subordinate climaxes. This division is especially clear in plays in which the exposition covers several scenes or several lines of causation. *Yellow Jack* is a case in point. *Stevedore,* by Paul Peters and George Sklar, is another example of an exposition which is both complex and vivid. The play ends with the united struggle of Negro and white workers against their oppressors. The three opening scenes expose three lines of causation which underlie the necessity of the root-action. Since the play's climax shows the overcoming of the prejudice against the Negro which is ingrained in Southern whites, the authors regard this prejudice as the cause of the action. The play opens on a moment of intense conflict which reaches its climax in an hysterical outburst of race prejudice. The curtain rises on a quarrel between a white woman and her lover in a backyard in a poor district. There is a physical struggle; the man knocks the woman down and runs away. In answer to her cries, figures creep out from neighboring buildings, asking who did it. Florrie, weeping desperately, answers, "It was...a nigger!" Blackout. This is not the end of the exposition, but only the first cycle of action *within* the exposition. The second scene is the police line-up; Florrie is trying to identify her alleged assailant. In the line of Negroes, who are threatened and brow-beaten, stands Lonnie Thompson who works for the Oceanic Stevedore Company. Here we are introduced to a central character; Lonnie's relationship to his environment is undergoing a serious change as a result of the event which took place in the previous scene. We see this change as it affects his conscious will and forces him to a decision.

It may be claimed that the second scene, exposing the attitude of the police and the social and economic roots of the action, is more fundamental than the first scene. This shows that the authors' conception of social causation is not fully defined. This accounts for the looseness of the connection between the first scene and the later action of the play. Florrie and her lover do not appear again. In watching the later struggle with the lynch mob, we tend to forget the event which motivated the action. The event, in spite of its emotional effectiveness, has neither the compression nor extension required. The weakness is evident in the climax, which has abundant physical vigor and excitement, but which shares the fault of the opening scene in being abrupt and underdeveloped.

The third scene, in Binnie's lunchroom, introduces the Negro background, the other important characters, and the question of wages and organization among the stevedores. This brings the action to a point of issue. Lonnie's words, "Well here's one black man ain't satisfied being just a good Nigger," are the firing of the fuse, the declaration of purpose.

These opening scenes, in spite of their structural imperfection, prove the value of dramatic conflict as a means of conveying actual information. Data which is presented statically can have no meaning in terms of action. In *Stevedore* the curtain rises on a moment of intense struggle; the development is objective, progressive and meaningful. An unusual amount of factual information is conveyed, both as to characters, theme and social background. If one classifies this information, and attempts to imagine a dialogue designed to include all the necessary facts, one finds that such a dialogue would be extremely long, difficult and dull.

We find an illustration of just such a dialogue in the opening scenes of *Peace on Earth*. The arrest of Bobbie Peters, the strike against war, the liberal atmosphere of the Owens' home, are the materials of drama, but the situations have not been dramatized. The exposition is static, and therefore necessitates such naïve questions as Jo's: "Mac, don't tell me that longshoremen are idealistic enough to go out and strike against war?"

Hindle Wakes is a play of a very different sort which opens on a direct conflict. The conditions of the action are exposed in the conflict itself and lead to a declaration of will made necessary by the accumulated experience of the character. Fanny Hawthorne's parents accuse her of spending the week-end with a man. Her mother says, "As certain as there's a God in Heaven, we know it!" Fanny answers, "Well that's not so certain after all"— thus giving us a flash of insight into her character and her attitude toward her parents. She then says she spent the week-end with

Mary Hollins, and the two of them returned together. The answer furnishes a dramatic shock which constitutes the first moment of climax in the inner movement of the exposition: "Mary Hollins was drowned yesterday afternoon." Fanny's response is a break in the mood, showing the changed condition and indicating the way in which her conscious will adapts itself to the change: "Ah! My poor Mary!" Fanny is not forced to change her line of conduct, but she is forced to declare herself, and to intensify her determination to follow her own will.

Modern playwrights are adept at tricks which gloss over the explanatory character of exposition, giving the appearance of movement without achieving meaningful or progressive action. For instance, in A. E. Thomas' comedy, *No More Ladies,* the hero has lost the heroine on a round of night-clubs and comes back to her home without her. Sherry Warren's good-natured comments on having mislaid Marcia give us a lively insight into their characters and the relationship between them. But this conversation is really static, because it is a summing up of certain experiences and certain possibilities rather than an actual conflict. It is instructive to compare this scene with the opening of *Hindle Wakes.* In the earlier play, the dynamic activity is inevitable under the given conditions. In *No More Ladies* the playwright has simply devised a natural incident through which to tell the audience what he thinks they ought to know.

The opening scene of Francis Edwards Faragoh's *Pinwheel* shows the remarkable compression and extension made possible by the proper use of what may be called an expressionistic method. Faragoh's treatment is non-naturalistic, but the scene is a dramatization of reality as we know it.

Expressionism often seeks to create symbols as substitutes for reality; this is invariably undramatic because it springs from a subjective mode of thought, a tendency to regard the image of a thing as more real than the thing itself. There are examples of this tendency in the later action of *Pinwheel.* But the opening scene projects individual wills in relation to complex social forces with sharp clarity, and without subjective distortion. The curtain rises on "a breathless process. A hurrying mob that has obscured its component individuals. A whirlwind just now actuated by the alarm-clock,—for it is morning." The people are rushing in and out of subway booths at the rear of the stage. The confused voices convey a wealth of meaning: "My radio set...the landlord... she's a peach...Them Russians...Two weeks at the seashore... Fifty dollars...A hundred dollars...Two hundred dollars

...No real man wears suspenders," etc.... The action quickly concentrates on the two girls hurrying to the office, and the Jane meets the Guy.

> THE JANE: I gotta hurry...to work...(*throws herself against the wall of people, trying to break through. The wall resists her*).
>
> THE GUY (*is almost glued to her, takes hold of her arms now*): Nobody can make you go to work when you don't feel like it. You don't see *me* slavin', do you? You don't have to go to work!

This touches the core of her will, and forces her to make a decision which changes her adjustment to her whole environment; she leaves her job and goes to Coney Island with the Guy.

Since each part of the play is an action, each cycle of movement includes expository material. It would be impossible to include *all* the conditions of the action in the early scenes. At any point it may be necessary to set a fuse which will explode at a later point. Since the new forces which are introduced must be tested in terms of the root-action, it follows that the conditions under which these forces appear must be tested in terms of the conditions which motivate the play as a whole. The introduction of persons, or incidents, or objects, may be completely unexpected, but it must conform to, and be subordinate to, the conditions embodied in the exposition.

If we return to *Stevedore*, we find illustrations of both the proper, and improper, introduction of new elements. In the fourth scene of the first act, a new character, the dock boss, is introduced. The exposition has shown us that the Negroes work on the docks, and anything introduced in relation to this activity is natural and expected. However, another new character is introduced in Act II: we suddenly meet the white union organizer. This brings in an entirely new factor, for which we are not sufficiently prepared. Here again, the detailed defect is related to a more serious weakness in the structure of the play: since the white organizer plays an essential role in the conflict, the authors are at fault in introducing him casually, and without earlier preparation. This affects the latter part of the action: we never fully understand the white organizer's relationship to the other characters, because no groundwork for this relationship has been laid.

In Sidney Howard's *Alien Corn,* the second-act curtain rises on Stockton cleaning a revolver. This activity is artificial; we know that the gun is not being cleaned for its own sake, but that the dramatist has an ulterior (and transparent) motive. Certainly there is nothing improbable in a man cleaning a gun; but the incident is dramatically implausible because the conditions of the action are not such as to make the introduction of the gun *just what we might expect* under the circumstances. If the purpose which the gun serves were inevitable in terms of the root-action, and if the play's opening properly dramatized the basic causes of the root-action, we would regard the gun as *just what we might expect.*

The great dramas of the past have invariably presented exposition in the form of active conflict. Greek tragedy opens with a formal prologue, in which the historical events of which the play is the culmination are outlined. This is descriptive but it is not static; it is a record of actions which defines the scope of the drama, and which leads to a point which concentrates the experience of the past in a decisive event. Donald Clive Stuart says: "The Greek dramatist often opened his play with a scene which, as in *Antigone,* would form the climax of the first act in modern drama." * In Euripides, we find a tendency to dramatize the prologue. In the *Electra* of Euripides, the prologue is spoken by a peasant, coming out of his cottage at dawn on his way to work—in marked contrast to the more heroic manner of Aeschylus and Sophocles.

Aristophanes discards the formal recitation and defines the action in a comic dialogue. Some of the more expository material is aimed directly at the audience. A character says, "Come, I must explain the matter to the spectators," and proceeds to do so. But this is always accompanied by concentrated and meaningful activity. In *The Birds,* two men appear carrying a jackdaw and a raven. They are trying to find the realm of the birds, but the creatures are giving them hopelessly contradictory directions.

> EUELPIDES (*to his jay*) : Do you think I should walk straight for yon tree?
> PISTHETAERUS (*to his crow*) : Cursed beast, what are you croaking to me?...to retrace my steps?
> EUELPIDES: Why, you wretch, we are wandering at random, we are exerting ourselves to return to the same spot; 'tis labor lost.
> PISTHETAERUS: To think that I should trust to this crow, which has made me cover more than a thousand furloughs!
> EUELPIDES: And I to this jay, who has torn every nail from my fingers!

The will is here being exerted in relation to the environment; conditions are presented which force the characters to re-examine and intensify their purpose.

* *Opus cit.*

Shakespeare's plays are unequalled in the use of objective conflict in establishing the causes of the action. *Macbeth* begins with the eerie scene of the witches, followed by the news that Macbeth has won a great victory. *Hamlet* opens with the tableau of the silent transit of the ghost. In both these cases, the extent of the information conveyed is in proportion to the intensity of the tension created. Shakespeare's use of the supernatural is an important aspect of his conception of social causation: the supernatural forces do not inhibit the will, but encourage the characters to *act,* stimulating their passions and desires. The ghosts and witches dramatize the social pressures which drive men to exercise their will.

Many of Molière's comedies begin with a violent quarrel. *The Doctor in Spite of Himself* opens with husband and wife screaming at each other: "Plague take the arrant ass".. "Plague take the trollop"..."Traitor...Swaggerer...Deceiver...Coward... Scamp...Rascal...." Whereupon the man starts to beat her with a stick. At the beginning of *Tartuffe,* old Madame Fernelle is leaving her daughter-in-law's house forever; as the curtain rises, she is shouting her opinion of every one in the house in unbridled language.

The introductory comments in *Hedda Gabler* are not fully dramatized. But most of Ibsen's plays begin at a moment of conflict which develops rapidly to a preliminary crisis. *Ghosts* begins with the curious struggle between Regina and her supposed father. Ibsen selects this point of departure because Alving's sexual depravity is the aspect of the marriage which directly causes the root-action. The social meaning of this aspect is concentrated in the secret of Regina's birth; her relationship to the family is the condition of the play's development. *Ghosts* could not begin, as *Hedda Gabler* does, with the excitement attending the return of the leading character to the community; this would give the community a weight which is not required for the climax of *Ghosts.*

CHAPTER III

PROGRESSION

SO far we have referred to the elements of an action as exposition, rising action, clash and climax. In order to understand the play's movement, we must examine these elements a little more carefully.

It is evident that the rising action is more extended and more complex than the other parts of the play. We have dealt so far with the meaning of the play, the basic cause and effect which are outlined at the beginning and realized at the conclusion. But the changes in character and environment which constitute the play's progression lie in the rising action. This means that there are more cycles of movement in the rising action; the cycles are not only consecutive; they over-lap and have varying degrees of extension. The progression depends on the movement of these subsidiary actions.

If we observe an action as we actually perform it in our daily experience, we find that any action (regardless of its scope) consists in (a) the *decision* (which includes the consciousness of the aim and of the possibilities of its accomplishment); (b) the *grappling with difficulties* (which are more or less expected, because the decision has included a consideration of possibilities); (c) *the test of strength* (the moment toward which we have been heading, when, having done our best to evade or overcome the difficulties, we face the success or failure of the action); (d) the *climax* (the moment of maximum effort and realization).

In a technical sense, the third of these divisions is the obligatory scene. It may appear, at first glance, that the obligatory scene is the same as the climax; but there is a very important difference between the *expected clash* and the *final clash*. The former is the point upon which we concentrate our efforts, and which we believe will be the point of maximum tension. This belief is based on our judgment of our environment; but our judgment is not one hundred percent correct. We find that our expectation has been tricked, and that the clash toward which we have been working reveals a balance of forces which does not correspond to our former picture of the situation. This leads to redoubled effort, to a new and final test of possibilities.

The obligatory scene may, in certain instances, be almost identical with the climax in time and place; but there is a great difference in its function; the difference is essential to our understanding of an action, because it is this contradiction between the thing we do and the result of the thing we do which energizes the dramatic movement. This contradiction exists in all the subordinate cycles of action, and creates the progression. This is not a matter of cause and effect—it is rather a sharp break between cause as it seemed and effect as it turns out. This happens, in a minor degree, throughout the course of the drama: the characters are *continually* realizing differences between what they intended and what is actually going on; they are thus forced to revise their consciousness of reality and increase their effort; this is what, literally, keeps them *moving;* the more important moments at which such a recognition occurs are the obligatory scenes of the various cycles of action. The break between cause and effect leads to the *actual* effect, the culmination of the action. For this reason, the climax invariably contains the element of surprise; it is beyond our expectation, and is the result of a break in the expected development of the action.

This is the *dramatic* element in any situation, and constitutes the most essential difference between dramatic action and human activity in general. In the more prosaic activities of our daily lives, there are no obligatory scenes; we do not pause to recognize any sharp break between cause and effect; we simply adjust ourselves and proceed to get the thing done, as best we can. We are interested in the results, rather than in the significance, of events. It is only when we undertake actions of unusual scope that the sequence is broken by the recognition of the difference between the probabilities as we had estimated them and the necessities as they loom ahead of us. When this happens, events become dramatic.

The action of a play intensifies reality, because even the more minor breaks between cause and effect are emphasized in order to maintain the play's movement. The degree to which the dramatist projects recognition and culmination in the subordinate crises of the play, is the degree to which he makes the subordinate scenes dramatic.

A play may contain any number of lesser cycles of action, but these can invariably be grouped in four divisions; since the rising action is the longest of the divisions and includes a larger number of sub-divisions, the movement of the play is somewhat as follows:

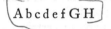

AbcdefGH

A is the exposition; b c d e f are the cycles of the rising action; G is the obligatory scene; H is the climax. A may contain two or more cycles of action. G and H are more concentrated, but may also include several cycles. Since an action is our *unit of movement,* we are able to divide any of the subordinate actions in the same way. For example, c reaches a climax which is the culmination of a system of action of which the exposition, rising action, and obligatory scene may be traced. The whole group, b c d e f also constitutes a system, of which b may be the exposition, c and d the rising action, e the obligatory scene and f the climax.

This would be comparatively simple if it were a matter of direct sequence, if each division and cycle were complete in itself, beginning where the other left off and proceeding to a climax. But the action is woven of a multiplicity of threads which are unified in terms of the play's root-action. The threads leading to any subordinate climax are also unified in terms of this climax, but these threads are woven through the other parts of the play.

Each subordinate climax has a certain compression and extension; it has enough explosiveness to affect the root-action of the play; this means that it has enough extension to affect the final picture of reality embodied in the root-action; its causes may therefore extend to any point within the limits of the play's framework. If this were not the case, it would be impossible to introduce prior or off-stage events, and each situation would be limited to an immediate decision and unconditional results.

We therefore find that the culminating moment of any event is the result of two separate systems of action: one represents its compression, and is the result of the exposition, rising action, obligatory scene and climax within the cycle; the extension is the result of a wider system of a similar character. The play itself is a compression of events in the stage-action; and an extension of events to the limits of the social frame-work.

The first act of *Ghosts* is a remarkable piece of construction which may serve to clarify the way in which threads of action culminate in a subordinate climax. The first act ends with the climax of the exposition; the climax is closely juxtaposed to the moment of the break between cause and effect (which may be called the obligatory scene), but the two points are clearly differentiated. If we turn back and examine the exposition as a separate and complete action, we see that it may be sub-divided as follows:

(1) SUBORDINATE EXPOSITION, which concerns Regina and is divided into three cycles:

(a) Regina's conflict with her father; (b) Regina's discussion with Manders; (c) Manders and Mrs. Alving express their conflicting opinions in regard to Regina's future, ending with her *decision:* "I have taken Regina into my charge, and in my charge she remains. Hush, dear Mr. Manders, don't say any more about it. Listen! Oswald is coming downstairs. We will only think of him now."

(2) SUBORDINATE RISING ACTION, which develops the conflict between Mrs. Alving and Manders, and which is also divided into three cycles:

(a) the discussion of Oswald's life abroad, in which he speaks of "the glorious freedom of the beautiful life over there"; (b) this leads to the more direct conflict between Manders and Mrs. Alving, in which he accuses her of "a disastrous spirit of wilfulness," and which ends in his telling her that she is "a guilty mother!" (c) Mrs. Alving's confession, building to her declaration that the "purchase money" with which she was bought is being put into the orphanage so that it shall not contaminate her son.

(3) This brings us to the SUBORDINATE OBLIGATORY SCENE: Mrs. Alving faces the split between her purpose and the possibility of its accomplishment. She says: "After tomorrow, I shall feel as if my dead husband had never lived in this house. There will be no one else here but my boy and his mother"—and in the dining room she hears Oswald making love to Regina, and Regina's whispers, "Are you mad? Let me go!" *

(4) This forces Mrs. Alving to revise her judgment and re-inforce her will. The MOMENT OF SUBORDINATE CLIMAX reveals the necessity which underlies this preliminary system of events. Regina is Alving's illegitimate child. From Mrs. Alving's point of view, there is nothing *ultimate* about this necessity; it is what she has long known and faced; but the conditions are now changed, and her aroused decision under these new conditions is the basis of the whole action of the play.

It is evident that this system of events reveals all the characteristics which we have described as characteristic of an action; the subordinate exposition is closely linked to the subordinate climax; every incident in the scheme is unified in terms of climax; the rising action is more complex than the other parts; as the rising action develops, the compression and extension increase; the development is based on a decision as to possibilities which leads to facing these possibilities, which in turn produces a point of maximum tension.

This is equally true of the subordinate divisions and cycles of action: each is a unit which includes exposition, rising action, clash and climax. But each also has an extension which goes beyond the limits of the stage action: the second cycle of the rising action, (in which Manders and Mrs. Alving come into direct conflict), goes *back* to her visit to Manders in the first year of her married life; this extension may also be analyzed as a system of

---

* The fact that the scene between Oswald and Regina takes place offstage is absurdly awkward and constitutes a serious artistic blemish. There is a reason for this: throughout the play, Ibsen evades the dramatization of Regina's problem; an analysis of Regina's case would involve class relationships which are outside the scope of the family situation as Ibsen sees it.

action, which centers around Manders and is motivated by his *decision* long ago to force her to return to her husband, and develops the results of that decision to the culminating moment in the present.

The third cycle of the rising action has a greater extension, covering Mrs. Alving's marriage, the birth of her son, and the story of her husband's profligacy. It therefore has a greater explosive force, and a more direct connection, both with the climax of the exposition as a whole, and with the climax of the play as a whole.

The modern playwright is especially weak in the handling of progression. The use of patterns of repetition growing out of retrospective modes of thought, has been discussed at some length. Even such a brilliant dramatist as Clifford Odets has difficulty in giving his plays enough extension and drive to establish genuine progression. The scenes of his plays are more dynamic than the movement of the play as a whole. In spite of his deep social awareness, Odets fails to think out the full causal relationship between the social forces as they exist in the environment and the decisions of individuals as they come in conflict with these social forces.

Odets' awareness of his material is still instinctive, and as yet insufficiently clear in terms of rational understanding. His most emotional and highly colored passages are often those which are most unsound dramatically. The root-actions of his plays expose this weakness: the lyric escape of the lovers at the end of *Awake and Sing,* and the call to strike at the close of *Waiting for Lefty.*

Odets deals with characters who think pragmatically. But his approach to these people is somewhat unclear because he has not overcome *his own tendency to think pragmatically.* In the exposition of *Awake and Sing,* the social maladjustments of each character are indicated by a wealth of detail in regard to the character's background. Much of this is humorous, relating to minor feelings and complaints; this conveys a sense of oblique, half-realized emotional protest. For instance, Ralph says: "All my life I want a pair of black and white shoes and can't get them. It's crazy!" Abrupt contrasts of ideas are used effectively: Jacob: "By money men the interests must be protected. Who gave you such a rotten haircut?"

None of this material is extraneous. It enlarges the social framework and gives us a carefully documented picture of character in relation to environment. We learn that Ralph Berger was never given skates as a child, but when he was ill at the age of twelve, his mother spent the last twenty-five dollars she had in the world to get a specialist. This is an example of a prior event which is realized in dramatic terms and which is closely linked to the root-action—the escape of Ralph and Hennie from their mother's influence. But in general the social framework of *Awake and Sing* is not fully dramatized; the reason for this is that the incidents are detached bits of action which are not organized in cycles of movement; we get the *intuitive* reactions of the characters to the needs and pressures of the environment, but we do not get *inside* the characters.

Having exposed the possibilities of the action in the first act, the author leaves his people exactly where he found them, in a state of suspended animation. The events of the play are illustrative rather than progressive. The contradiction between cause and effect is not dramatized as it strikes the conscious wills of the characters and drives them to revise and intensify their decisions. Perhaps the most pivotal event of the play is Old Jacob's suicide. If we trace the development of this action, we find that it has its beginnings in the scene in the first act in which Jacob plays his phonograph records to Moe; the rising action building toward the suicide is the series of conflicts between Jacob and Bessie, culminating in the obligatory scene, the breaking of the phonograph records. This is the most progressive movement of events in the play, because it leads to a defined act; but it has no organic connection with the play as a whole, as it is summed up in the root-action. The grandfather's death does not make Hennie's running away inevitable, nor does it clearly motivate Ralph's new courage and understanding.

In the final act, Ralph says: "I grew up these last few weeks." But how has he grown? His growth is not dramatized in any specific conflict. He faces two problems (which have existed in just the same form throughout the play) : his relationship with his mother, and with the girl he loves. How does he solve these questions? He remains in the house and gives up the girl, simply telling us that everything is different.

Hennie's struggle against her mother's domination, her relationship with her husband, her love for Moe, are not developed dramatically. She seems to take no responsibility for the pitiful deceit of marrying a man whom she does not love and deceiving him in regard to her child. She simply ignores this problem, or that she has any part in it. Her last lines to her husband (in the final act) are curiously insensitive: "I love you .. I mean it." Sam replies: "I would die for you ..." and leaves. It is clear that Hennie is trying to comfort him; but the sentiment of these two lines is false, closing a situation which is meaningless because it has never been faced. Her relationship with Moe is also unclear, based on no logical progression. Why does she decide to run away with him at this point? Has anything happened to make her understand him or herself better? What separated her from Moe in the first act? She explains this as being due to her "pride." Are we to believe that this pride (which is never dramatized or made factual) is stronger than the sexual and economic pressures which would drive her to Moe the moment she realized she was to have a child by him? Certainly other factors might have prevented this, but these factors must be grounded in social reality, as dramatized in the framework of the action. Action cannot be motivated by "abstract" sentiments, such as pride.

This is due to failure to analyze the conscious wills of the characters and to build a system of causes which underlies the acts of will. This in turn is due to a mode of thought which accepts *emotional drift* as a substitute for rational causation. Instead of basing his dramatic logic on the theory that "contradiction is the power that moves things," the author shows a tendency to show us what William James calls a "series of activity situations," in which the immediacy of sensation, the fleeting feeling of frustration or anger or desire, takes precedence over the testing and carrying out of decisions. We understand that Hennie lives in a pragmatic world, that she plans nothing beyond the immediate moment, that she is confused, desperate, irresponsible. But her drama lies in the way in which her "pure experience" is continually tested and wounded; we cannot *know* Hennie through her moods; we can only know her through her attempts, however fleeting and unsatisfactory, to reach decisions. Insofar as we see only her moods, we see her as a person who is rootless, driven blindly by social forces which are mysterious and fateful.

Thus there is a contradiction between the immediate sensation (the projection of each event) which is unsparingly real, and the whole scheme which is blurred. The root-action dissolves in sex-mysticism, which contains the double idea of love and force. Moe's pragmatic ability to cope with immediate difficulties is violent, sentimental, irrational, the emotional drive of a man who follows the dictates of his "blood and nerves": Moe: "You won't forget me to your dyin' day—I was the first guy. Part of your insides. You won't forget. I wrote my name on you in indelible ink!" And again: "Nobody knows, but you do it and find out. When you're scared the answer is zero."

One can well understand that Moe feels this way: but this scene contains the solution of the action; Moe's appeal, and the departure of the lovers which follows it, is as clearly the answer to the problem of the middle class family in the Bronx, as Nora's departure is the answer to the problem presented in *A Doll's House*. But while Nora's escape is an act of will, the romantic escape of Moe and Hennie is an act of faith. It is not conflict, but the denial of conflict.

In *Waiting for Lefty,* Odets has made a tremendous advance. Here there are no overtones of unresolved mysticism. But can it be said that he has solved the structural fault, the lack of progression, which mars the previous play? On the contrary, he has created a device which makes structural development to some extent unnecessary. There can be no question that the device is admirably suited to the needs of the play. But there can also be no question that the unity thus achieved is superficial. Each scene crystallizes a moment of sharp protest, of crucial social anger. But the arrangement of the scenes is somewhat fortuitous. The first scene, Joe and Edna, may be regarded as the most significant, because it concerns the fundamental problems of the worker's family, food and clothes for his children. The third episode (the young hack and his girl) is also basic. The later scenes (the young actor in the manager's office, the interne in the hospital) are of a more special character, less closely related to the workers' struggle. The emotional tension mounts as the play proceeds: this intensity does not spring from the action, but from the increasingly explicit statement of revolutionary protest, which therefore tends to be romantic rather than logical, sloganized rather than growing out of the deepest needs of the characters. The stenographer says: "Come out into the light, Comrade." Dr. Barnes says: "When you fire the first shot say, 'This one's for old Doc Barnes!'" This is exciting, so exciting that it is impossible, at the time, to stop and analyze it. One is swept along, swept by Agate's call to action at the end: "Stormbirds of the working-class." But the development which leads to this speech is not cumulatively logical, not based on flesh-and-blood realities.

It is true that the depression has forced many technicians, actors, doctors, to become taxi-drivers. But here we have a militant strike committee made up largely of declassed members of the middle class. One cannot reasonably call these people "stormbirds of the working class."

The difficulty in *Waiting for Lefty* springs from the gap between the immediate impulses of the characters and the wider frame-work of events. In each scene, the decision is impulsive; it is assumed that the social forces which create the decision are absolute, and that the intuitive recognition of these forces is a moment of supreme climax. Thus the moment of clash, of the break between cause and effect, is neglected.

One thing shows that the author is aware of this problem and is feeling for a solution of it. The key to the problem lies in the incident which breaks Agate's final speech—the flash of news that Lefty has been found "behind the car barns with a bullet in his head." Thus the title of the play is a stroke of genius, which indicates Odets' instinctive flare for dramatic truth. It suggests the need for a deep unity which is merely hinted at in the action. Lefty's death is unprepared, undramatized. Yet it seems to be the culmination of a series of relationships which are the core of the action, the essence of the social conflicts around which the play is organized.

Waiting for Lefty is smashingly effective without this fundamental progression. *Till the Day I Die* is a different matter: here the playwright projects a personal conflict. Ernst Tausig's struggle with his environment is not a moment of protest; it is a long agony, in which his revolutionary will is strained to the breaking point. The choice of this theme is significant, showing Odets' progress. But he fails to develop the theme fully. With great clarity, he shows us brief flashes of individuals. The method is the same as in *Awake and Sing,* the emphasis on small fears, hopes, memories. In the first scene Baum says: "I used to be a peaceful man who planted tulips." Tilly speaks of her girlhood: "In summer I ate mulberries from our own trees. In late summer the ground was rotten where they fell."

But the figure of Ernst Tausig is pale against the background of minor characters and startling scenes. The first four scenes deal with the capture and torture of Ernst. In the fourth scene, the Major tells him of the horrible plan to make his friends think he is a stool pigeon. The fifth scene deals with his return to Tilly, and the melodramatic incident of the detectives breaking in. The sixth scene shows a Communist meeting at which it is decided to blacklist Ernst. In the seventh scene, he returns to Tilly broken in body and mind, and kills himself. Thus the sustained conflict, the conscious will of man pitted against terrible odds, is omitted. We see him only *before* and *after.* The crucial stage, in which his will is tested and broken, occurs between scenes five and seven.

One of the most moving moments in the play is that in the sixth scene: the vote is taken, Tilly raises her hand, agreeing with the others to make an outcast, a traitor, of the man she loves. But here too the playwright fails to dramatize a *progressive* struggle which gives meaning to Tilly's decision. We do not see the conflict of will which leads to the raising of her hand. We know she believes in his innocence, but we do not see this belief tested, opposed to her party-loyalty, assailed by doubts. Therefore, the raising of the hand is not really a decision, but a gesture.

|Odets remains more of a *scenewright* than a playwright. In the creation of scenes he is unequalled in the modern theatre. One more example: the unforgettable portrait of the liberal Major, his struggle with his subordinate and his suicide, in scene four of *Till the Day I Die*. But here again he dramatizes a moment of maximum maladjustment, the quick breaking of an unbearable strain. The progression within the scene is effective, because the scene is unified in terms of its climax—of a complete change of equilibrium between the individual and his environment. The quick drive to the realization of such a change, the quick impact of social necessity, is powerfully projected. But since this is not the result of previous decisions and does not involve the making and testing of new decisions, there is nothing to carry over, to develop a broader meaning and a deeper test of consciousness and will.

Odets' conception of social change is still somewhat romantic; it is seen as a vast force, the recognition of which constitutes a personal regeneration. Thus he perceives the moment of explosive anger, of realization and conversion. Indeed *Waiting for Lefty* is a study in conversions. This is the source of its power. But Odets will undoubtedly go beyond this to mastery of more profound and more sustained conflict.

The neglect of progression in the contemporary theatre creates a practical problem which the craftsman cannot ignore. The genuine dramatic force of separate scenes, which makes the plays of Odets continually exciting, is absent in many modern plays. The essential moments of conflict exist only in embryo, in a delayed or diluted form, or are missing altogether. Since tension depends on the balance of forces in conflict, it seems reasonable to conclude that if conflict is avoided, tension will be fatally relaxed. But the interest of the spectators *must* be sustained. It follows that the drama of today has developed extraordinary facility in maintaining fictitious tension. The most common method of sustaining audience-interest without progression is the use of *surprise*. This device is employed unsparingly; it has, in fact, become the basic technique of the modern drama.

In the Greek theatre the "reversal of fortune" was a vital part of the tragic technique. Aristotle used *Oedipus Rex* as an example: "Thus, in the Oedipus, the messenger comes to cheer Oedipus and free him from his alarms about his mother, but by revealing who he is, he produces the opposite effect." This turn of events is linked directly to the climax of the drama.

Surprise by artifice, by consciously misleading the spectators, is a very different matter. Lessing points out that surprises which are easily achieved "will never give rise to anything great." He describes the sort of play which is "a collection of little artistic tricks by means of which we effect nothing more than a short surprise." * Archer makes a similar comment: "We feel that the author has been trifling with us in inflicting on us this purely mechanical and momentary scare." †

One must bear in mind the distinction between surprise which *legitimately carries the action forward,* and surprise which *negates the action.* The distinction is not difficult to make: we recall that one of the forms of reversal of fortune to which Aristotle referred was the "anagnorisis" or recognition scene, the finding of friends or enemies unexpectedly. Aristotle used this as a rather mechanical formula, but when we examine Greek tragedy we find that the reversal of fortune is invariably accompanied by *recognition* of the persons or forces which bring about the change. The messenger reveals himself, the effect is the opposite of what was expected, forcing Oedipus to recognize a change and to face a new problem. We have already pointed out that it is this *recognition* of the difference between what was expected and what takes place which drives the action forward. In this sense, surprise is the essence of drama, and is present in every movement of the action.

But recognition of the break between cause and effect is very different from ignoring or evading the logic of events. "Nothing," says Lessing, "is more offensive than that of which we do not know the cause." ‡

Surprise, employed without recognition of its cause or significance, is used in two ways: one of these is the *direct shock,* which consists in breaking off the action when a moment of conflict is impending, leaving the audience to imagine the crisis which the dramatist has avoided. The author then diverts attention by creating another series of promising events which are again broken off. The other method is that of *suspense by concealment:* instead of making open preparations which lead to nothing, the playwright

* *Opus cit.*
† Archer, *Playmaking, a Manual of Craftsmanship.*
‡ *Opus cit.*

makes secret preparations which lead to something unexpected. But since the audience has been consciously misled, the unexpected event has no real significance and is merely a mechanical means of shocking or diverting us.

The most famous example of a play in which the outcome is concealed is Henri Bernstein's *The Secret*. Bernstein was a remarkable craftsman, and this play is still of great interest as an example of ingenious deception. The technique of *The Secret* was a new and important thing at its time. Clayton Hamilton (writing in 1917) says of it, "Bernstein has brushed aside one of the most commonly accepted dogmas of the theatre—the dogma that a dramatist must never keep a secret from his audience." * There can be no question that the mechanical methods of Bernstein and some of his contemporaries have had much more influence than is generally realized. The connection between Bernstein and George S. Kaufman is surprisingly close.

The most mechanical form of keeping a secret is that which may be observed in crime melodrama and sex farces. In the crime play, the finger of suspicion is pointed at all the characters in turn, so that the audience may be illogically amazed by the revelation of the real criminal. In the sex play, the question of who will go to bed with whom, and who will find out about it, furnishes exciting, if somewhat trivial, "straining forward of interest."

Misleading the audience may be very delicately done. The playwright cannot be accused of crude deception; but he offers hints which give a wrong impression; he sustains his action by false promises. *Strictly Dishonorable,* by Preston Sturges, relates the adventure of an innocent Southern girl who meets an opera singer in a speakeasy and spends the night in his apartment. At the end of the first act, the hero assures his visitor that his intentions are "strictly dishonorable." Since the play proceeds directly to the realization of this aim, without other obstacles than the whims of the characters, the second act is an artificially extended obligatory scene. There are excellent comic possibilities in the situation; but the comic elements lie in a genuine conflict, in which the social points of view, personalities and habits of the two opponents would be exposed in the course of a lively struggle. Sturges has not developed these comic possibilities. The hero's declaration of purpose at the end of the first act is misleading; suspense is sustained by a series of twists: first surprise, the singer gets an attack of conscience; second surprise, the innocent heroine feels that she has been duped and insists on being betrayed. The dramatist is at

* *Opus cit.*

liberty to repeat the trick ad nauseam; the hero can change his mind; the heroine can change her mind. This may be called a conflict. Provided the vaccilation of the characters is skillfully presented, it is not unnatural. But it contains no suspense in the real sense, because it is a struggle of whims and not of wills.

The most serious technical use of surprise in the modern theatre is not revealed in the more or less mechanical trick of concealment. The method of breaking off the action in order to avoid its culmination is far more significant. The great master of this use of surprise is George S. Kaufman. Kaufman is an expert technician, but the key to his method lies in his constant employment of the melodramatic twist. This device serves him exactly as the asides in *Strange Interlude* serve O'Neill—to avoid conflict, to give the action effectiveness without progression.

Merrily We Roll Along (written in collaboration with Moss Hart) is by far the most interesting play in which Kaufman has been concerned. There has been a great deal of comment on the fact that this drama is written backward, beginning in 1934 and ending in 1916. This has been described as a trick, a seeking after sensation, an effort to conceal the play's weakness. It seems to me that the backward method is an honest and necessary way of telling this particular story. In fact, I venture to surmise that it would be impossible to tell the story properly in any other way. The basic theme of *Merrily We Roll Along* is an ironic looking backward over the years since the European war. The reverse action is a natural way of handling this theme—nor does it at all change the principles of construction.

The selection of the climactic event in *Merrily We Roll Along* is confusing. The action of the play shows the search for something vital which has been lost; the thing lost (the ultimate necessity which determines the action) must be revealed in the climax. Instead we find a young man on a platform, delivering platitudes about friendship and service. There may be considerable disagreement as to what is and what is not idealism; most people will agree that it manifests itself in courage, a willingness to face danger, to oppose accepted standards. But whatever idealism may mean abstractly, it can have no dramatic meaning unless it is crystallized in a moment of extreme tension which reveals the scope of the conception. Since we never see Richard Niles express his idealism in conduct, we have no way of knowing what sort of conduct it would involve; there is no way of testing any of the decisions in the play in relation to the system of events in which they are placed.

Since the decisions cannot be tested, we cannot see the clash between expectation and fulfillment, and the action cannot progress. The fact that the plan of the play is a backward progression does not affect this problem, but would intensify the irony of each partial recognition of necessity in relation to events with which we are already familiar.

The exposition shows Richard Niles (in 1934) at the height of his success. The theme is cleverly introduced in a scene of dramatic conflict: Julia Glenn, who has known Richard since the days of his poverty, insults his guests and tells him that his material success has destroyed him. We then proceed to an intense scene between Richard and his wife, Althea. She is bitterly jealous. She knows that he is having an affair with the leading woman in his new play. The conflict between husband and wife is important, and essential to our knowledge of the theme. However, instead of developing this conflict, it is cut short by a melodramatic shock— Althea throws acid in the other woman's eyes.

Thus the relationship between husband and wife in 1934 is cut short, and we go back to the earlier stages of this relationship. The play is constructed around the conflict between Richard and Althea. She is used as the symbol of the luxury and cheap ambition which gradually destroy Richard's integrity. We follow this process back into the past as the play develops: in the final scene of the first act (in Richard Niles' apartment in 1926), Richard is in the earlier stages of his affairs with Althea. She is married to another man. In this scene, Jonathan Crale, Richard's closest friend, warns him against Althea, begs him to give her up. Crale leaves and Althea comes to the apartment; here again is the beginning of an emotional scene, in which the conflict between Richard and Althea may be analyzed and dramatized. The scene is cut short, almost before it has begun, by a melodramatic surprise—the news that Althea's husband has shot himself.

Another line of causation is undertaken in the first act: the conflict between Crale and Richard, the idealist and the opportunist. The first act shows us an interesting clash between the two friends, and we are led to believe that we shall see the earlier stages of this conflict. But in the following acts, they meet only for brief moments and never in a dramatic scene. Thus the relationship between the two men is also a false lead.

What is the obligatory scene in *Merrily We Roll Along,* and how is it handled? The *decision* which is presented in the exposition, and upon which the play is based, is Richard's falling in love with Althea. The climax of the exposition (the throwing of the acid) concentrates our attention on the events which led to this disastrous result. The expected clash toward which the action moves is the beginning of the emotional entanglement with Althea; this is the point at which the possibilities of the action (the disappointment and bitterness of Richard's later life) are revised in accordance with a new vista of necessity (the ideals of his youth).

A great deal of skill is used in building up audience-expectation in regard to this key-situation. The preparation leads us to expect the scene at the end of Act II—in Althea's apartment in 1923, on the night of the opening of Richard's first successful play. The beginning of the love story is closely interwoven with the beginning of Richard's successful career. Althea is the star of the play. So far the authors have avoided any fully developed contact between Richard and Althea. But at this point the love scene seems inevitable.

The scene opens on the arrangements for the party which will celebrate the first night of the play. There is a great deal of diverting detail. The exits and entrances, the bits of characterization, the movement of crowds, are skillfully conceived and directed. We especially notice a tiger skin which is prominently placed on the couch in Althea's apartment. In a previous scene we have been told about this tiger skin; it was used as evidence in the sensational divorce in 1924; Richard's first wife found him making love to Althea on the tiger skin.

The tiger skin is amusingly characteristic of the Kaufman and Hart method. The playwrights pique our curiosity, they indicate the approaching scene, they show us the exact spot where the love affair will take place—but they bring down the curtain at a noisy moment of Althea's party, the stage crowded with chattering people in evening dress. The effect is a shock; the cutting off of the action on the noisy crowd is undeniably effective; but the obligatory scene is omitted.

The use of crowds in *Merrily We Roll Along* is of special interest; the first act begins with a party in full swing, showing, according to the principle of selection which governs the choice of expository events, that the authors regard the people who come to parties—the wealthy cynical upper-crust of New York professional people—as the fundamental social cause of the action. This accounts for the substitution of the crowd-scene for the necessary conflict of will at the close of the second act.

It is curious that a play which moves backward, and in which we are told about events before we see them happen, should depend for its effectiveness solely on surprise. By relying on this device,

Kaufman and Hart have missed the greatest value to be derived from the use of the backward method: the reversal of the life process, enabling us to observe acts of will of which we know the effects. Since the acts of will are omitted, the irony is sadly diluted.

Kaufman's brilliant superficiality is sometimes blamed on a cynical approach to the art of the theatre, a willingness to sacrifice serious meaning for effective showmanship. But his method goes much deeper than this; the question is not one of integrity, but of the author's mode of thought which reflects his relationship to the totality of his environment. There is no mysticism in *Merrily We Roll Along,* but the mood is fatalistic: here the Nemesis which afflicts the will is more mechanical than psychological. The treatment suggests the stimuli and responses of behaviorism. The material environment is so much stronger than the characters that their actions are no more than a series of reflexes. A feeling of irresponsibility is created, because whenever the characters undertake an action, something outside themselves prevents its completion. Events happen to them, suddenly, unaccountably, *against their will*.

The cutting of the action before it has come to a head is more extensively used in comedy and farce than in other departments of the drama. We touched on the question of comic progression in dealing with *Strictly Dishonorable;* there seems to be considerable misunderstanding as to the technique of comedy; it is often thought that comedy deals only with surfaces, and is less analytical than the serious drama. But the essence of humor lies in exposing the maladjustments between people and their environment. Allardyce Nicoll says, "The fundamental assumption of comedy is that it does not deal with isolated individuals." It deals, as George Meredith points out in his essay "On the Idea of Comedy," with men "whenever they wax out of proportion, overblown, affected, pretentious, bombastical, hypocritical, pedantic, fantastically delicate; whenever it sees them self-deceived or hoodwinked, given to run riot in idolatries, drifting into vanities, congregating in absurdities, planning short-sightedly, plotting dementedly; whenever they are at variance with their professions, and violate the unwritten but perceptible laws binding them in consideration one to another; whenever they offend sound reason, fair justice; are false in humility or mined in conceit, individually, or in the bulk." *

Personal Appearance, by Lawrence Riley, is a frothy burlesque about a glamour girl from Hollywood. Carole Arden invades the Struthers' farmhouse on the road between Scranton and Wilkesbarre: since sex is her specialty, she attempts to have an affair

* George Meredith, *An Essay On Comedy* (New York, 1918).

with the handsome young automobile mechanic who is engaged to Joyce Struthers. The obligatory scene is the scene in which the seduction is attempted. The situation is similar to that in *Strictly Dishonorable,* but here the woman is the aggressor and the man is the defender of his virtue. This is a rich occasion for comic analysis of character and social viewpoint.

We want to know how the man will react to Carole's blandishments. We want to see him definitely resist or definitely give in. We want to see the clash between the social standards of Hollywood and those of a Pennsylvania farm. This means that the root-action must embody a defined point of view, which must achieve the maximum extension and compression. We cannot derive sustained laughter from consideration of these people as "isolated individuals." Their "planning short-sightedly, plotting dementedly," can only be judged in relation to "the unwritten but perceptible laws" of conduct.

The root-action of *Personal Appearance* is merely a repetition of the opening situation—the actress leaves the farm exactly as she found it. There has been no progression; the attempted seduction has been avoided.

The obligatory scene is therefore not dramatically humorous; it contains no genuine action; the comedy derives solely from the fact that the *idea* that the actress wants to seduce the man and that he is unwilling, is itself amusing. But this idea has already been outlined in the first act. The obligatory scene arouses expectation, because we wish to see the possibilities of the idea explored; we wish to see the characters test and revise their purpose as they recognize the break between their expectation and reality. Failure to develop the conflict to this point is a betrayal of the comic spirit.

The second act builds to the moment when the two are left alone together. But there is only a little preliminary sparring between the movie queen and her intended victim. Then the situation is cut short by the abrupt entrance of old lady Barnaby, Joyce's aunt. Thus the playwright avoids a troublesome dilemma; if the man gives in, a series of difficult complications must ensue. If he fails to give in, under continued pressure, he must appear (at least in the eyes of a majority of the audience) as something of a sap. But this contradiction is the core of the play, exposing its social meaning and dramatic possibilities. The playwright should pay special attention to the difficulties inherent in his material, the complications which seem to defy solution. These contradictions expose the difference between expectation and fulfillment, and furnish the motive-power for the play's progression.

Aristotle covered the question of progression simply and thoroughly. He spoke of tragedy, but his words apply to all dramatic action—both to the play as a whole and to all its parts: "To be about to act . . . and not to act, is the worst. It is shocking without being tragic, for no disaster follows."

CHAPTER IV

THE OBLIGATORY SCENE

THE function of the obligatory scene has been discussed in dealing with progression. Francisque Sarcey deserves credit for the theory of the obligatory scene; but he failed to develop the idea in relation to any organic conception of technique. Archer defines the obligatory scene as "one which the audience (more or less clearly and consciously) foresees and desires, and the absence of which it may with reason resent." * Sarcey says, "It is precisely this expectation mingled with uncertainty which is one of the charms of the theatre."

These comments are important, because they both stress the principle of expectation as it affects the *audience*. The sustained interest with which the spectators follow the action may undoubtedly be described as "expectation mingled with uncertainty." The degree of expectation and uncertainty are variable. But the decisive point toward which the action seems to be driving must be the point concerning which there is the greatest expectation and the smallest uncertainty. The characters of the play have made a decision; the audience must understand this decision and must be aware of its possibilities.

Spectators look forward to the realization of the possibilities, to the *expected* clash. The judgment of the audience as to the possibilities and necessities of the situation may differ from the judgment of the characters. The playwright strives to make the action appear inevitable. We assume that he does this by carrying the audience with him, by stirring their emotions. But the spectators are moved by the progression of the action only insofar as they

* Archer, *Playmaking, a Manual of Craftsmanship.*

accept the truth of each revelation of reality as it affects the aims of the characters.

Since the spectators do not know what the climax will be, they cannot test the action in terms of climax. They *do* test it in terms of their expectation, which is concentrated on what they believe to be the necessary outcome of the action—the obligatory scene.

Archer feels that the obligatory scene is not really obligatory: he warns us against the assumption "that there can be no good play without a *scène à faire.*" To be sure, he is using the term in a narrow and somewhat mechanical sense. But no play can fail to provide a point of concentration toward which the maximum expectation is aroused. The audience requires such a point of concentration in order to define its attitude toward the events. The dramatist must analyze this quality of expectation; since the obligatory scene is not the final outcome of events, he must convince the audience that the break between cause and effect as revealed in the obligatory scene is inevitable.

Just as the climax furnishes us with a test by which we can analyze the action *backward,* the obligatory scene offers us an additional check on the *forward* movement of the action. The climax is the basic event, which causes the rising action to grow and flower. The obligatory scene is the immediate goal toward which the play is driving. The climax has its roots in the social conception. The obligatory scene is rooted in activity; it is the physical outgrowth of the conflict.

Where do we find the obligatory scene in *Yellow Jack?* What is the expected clash in this play? It is the point at which the four soldiers face the issue, the possibility of sacrificing themselves for science. This scene is handled far less effectively than the earlier scenes of *Yellow Jack.* It does not drive the action forward, because it does not involve a break between expectation and fulfillment. It cannot do so, because the soldiers have made no previous decision or effort. They are unprepared for the act of will which they are called upon to perform. Furthermore, since the play has followed two separate lines of action, it would seem inevitable that these two lines merge completely at this point: this would mean that the scientists play an active part in the decision of the four privates. The fact that the doctors are only indirectly involved in the decision, and that Miss Blake, the nurse, acts as a rather awkward connecting link, serves to weaken the emotional impact.

In *The Children's Hour,* by Lillian Hellman, we have a weak climax (Martha Dobie's suicide) which is preceded by a strong obligatory scene (the close of the second act, when the demoniac child is brought face to face with her two victims).

If we examine the climax of *The Children's Hour,* we find that it ends in a fog. It is impossible to find emotional or dramatic meaning in the final crisis. The two women are broken in spirit when the last act opens. Their lives are ruined because a lying child has convinced the world that their relationship is abnormal. Martha confesses that there is really a psychological basis for the charge: she has always felt a desperate physical love for Karen. Dr. Cardin, Karen's fiancé, who has loyally defended the two women, talks over the problem with Karen and she insists that they must break their engagement. But all of this is *acceptance* of a situation: their conscious wills are not directed toward any solution of the difficulty—it is assumed that no solution exists. Martha's suicide is not an act which breaks an unbearable tension, but an act which grows out of drifting futility. There is a feeling of acid bitterness in these scenes which indicates that the author is trying to find expression for something which she feels deeply. But she has not dramatized her meaning.

The rising action of *The Children's Hour* is far more vital than its conclusion. But the weakness of the climax infects every minute of the play. The scenes between the two women and Dr. Cardin in the first act are designed to indicate Martha's jealousy, her abnormal feeling for Karen. But the idea is planted awkwardly; the scenes are artificial and passive because they have no inner meaning. The relationship between Martha and Karen cannot be vital because it has no direction; it leads only to defeat.

The rumor started by the neurotic child constitutes a separate (and much stronger) story. The child, Mary Tilford, hates the two teachers. In revenge for being punished, she runs away to her grandmother. Not wishing to return to the school, she invents the yarn about the two women. They deny the story, but it is believed. Now the first thing we notice about this series of events is that it is *too* simple. Several critics have asked whether it is plausible for the child's grandmother, and other witnesses, to so quickly accept her testimony. Certainly there is nothing fundamentally impossible in two lives being ruined by a child's gossip. The situation gives us the impression of being implausible because it is not placed in any solid social framework. This is evident in the inconsequentiality of the suicide at the end. The root-action lacks adequate compression and extension. Without a social framework, we cannot gauge the effect of the child's gossip on the community: we do not know the conditions within the community; we have no data as to the steps by which the scandal is spread and accepted. Therefore the psychological effect on the two women is also vague, and is taken for granted instead of being dramatized.

What would be the effect on the construction of *The Children's Hour* if Martha's confession had been placed in the first act instead of the third? This would permit unified development of the psychological and social conflict; *both* lines of action would be strengthened. The confession would have the character of a decision (the only decision which gets the action under way at present is the child's act of will in running away from school). A decision involving the two women would clarify the exposition; it would enlarge the possibilities of the action; the conflict of will engendered by the confession would lead directly to the struggle against the malicious rumors in the community. The inner tension created by the confession would make their fight against the child's gossip more difficult, would add psychological weight to the child's story, and greatly increase its plausibility. This suggestion is based on the principle of unity in terms of climax: if Martha's suicide had been correctly selected as the climax, the exposition must be directly linked to this event and every part of the action must be unified in its connection with the root-action. Martha's emotional problem will thus be dramatized and woven through the action. In order to accomplish this, her confession must be the premise, not the conclusion.

The rising action of *The Children's Hour* shows the danger of following a line of cause and effect which is so simple that it is not believable. The indirect causes, the deeper meanings, are lacking—these deeper meanings are hidden (so successfully hidden that it is impossible to find them) in the final scene.

In spite of this, the play has a great deal of forward drive. The author's sincere way of telling her story brings her directly (without serious preparation but with a good deal of emotional impact) to the obligatory scene: Mrs. Tilford is shocked by her granddaughter's story. She telephones to all the parents to withdraw all the children from the school. Martha and Karen come to protest. They demand to be confronted with the child. Mrs. Tilford at first refuses. (Here it almost seems as if the author were hesitating, trying to build the event more solidly). When she is pressed, Mrs. Tilford says that being honest, she cannot refuse. One senses that the author's honesty is also compelling her (a little against her will) to face the obligatory scene. The drive toward the obligatory scene is over-simplified, but effective, because it shows the child's conscious will setting up a goal and striving to bring everything in line with it; the second act progresses by projecting a series of breaks between the possibilities of the child's decision and the actual results of it. Our expectation is concentrated on the obligatory scene, which embodies the maximum possibilities as they can be foreseen.

But the author cannot show us any rational result of this event, because she has achieved no rational picture of the social necessity within which the play is framed. The last act turns to the familiar pattern of neurotic futility, faced with an eternal destiny which can neither be understood nor opposed. One is reminded of the lines in Sherwood's *The Petrified Forest:* Nature is "fighting back with strange instruments called neuroses. She's deliberately afflicting mankind with the jitters." The attitudes of the characters in the closing scenes of *The Children's Hour,* and particularly Martha's confession of feeling, are based on the acceptance of "the jitters" as man's inexorable fate.

The play ignores time and place. The prejudice against sexual abnormality varies in different localities and under different social conditions. We are given no data on this point. Only the most meager and undramatic information is conveyed concerning the past lives of the characters. This is especially true of the neurotic child. The figure of the little girl burning with hate, consumed with malice, would be memorable if we knew *why* she has become what she is. Lacking this information, we must conclude that she too is a victim of fate, that she was born evil, and will die evil.

But the detailed activity, especially in the first two acts, shows that the playwright is not satisfied with this negative view of life. The scheme of the play is static, but the scenes move. In the relationship between Karen and Martha, the author strains to find some meaning, some growth in the story of the two women. She wants something to *happen* to her people; she wants them to learn and change. She fails; her failure is pitilessly exposed in the climax. But in this failure lies Miss Hellman's great promise as a playwright.

The Children's Hour illustrates the importance of a thorough analysis of the connection between the obligatory scene and the climax. The root-action is the test of the play's unity; the forward drive and the arousing of expectation are vital; but the concentration of interest on an expected event cannot serve as a substitute for the thematic clarity which gives the play its unity.

Wherever the link between the obligatory scene and the climax is weak, or where there is a direct break between them, we find that the forward movement (the physical activity of the characters) is thwarted and denied by the conception which underlies the play as a whole.

CHAPTER V

CLIMAX

I HAVE constantly referred to the climax as the controlling point in the unification of the dramatic movement. I have assumed that this event is the *end* of the action, and have given no consideration to the idea of *falling action,* wherein the cycle of events is concluded through catastrophe or solution. For instance, what is the logic of saying that Hedda's suicide is the climax of *Hedda Gabler?* This seems to confuse the climax with the catastrophe; far from being generally accepted, the assumption that the final scene is the climax is contradicted by a large body of technical theory. It is customary to place the climax at the beginning—not the end—of the final cycle of activity; it presumably occurs at the end of the second act of a three-act play, and may frequently be identified with the event which I have defined as the obligatory scene. Furthermore, I seem to have been guilty of certain inconsistencies: in *The Shining Hour,* the suicide of the wife occurs at the end of the second act—why should this be termed the climax of *The Shining Hour?* If this is true of Keith Winter's play, why is it not equally true of other plays?

Freytag's famous pyramid has had a great (and unfortunate) influence on dramatic theory. According to Freytag, the action of a play is divided into five parts: "(a) introduction; (b) rise; (c) climax; (d) return or fall; (e) catastrophe." The falling action includes "the beginning of counter-action" and "the moment of last suspense." The rising action and the falling action are of equal importance. "These two chief parts of the drama are firmly united by a point of the action which lies directly in the middle. The middle, the climax of the play, is the most important place of the structure; the action rises to this; the action falls away from this." *

Freytag makes an interesting analysis of the structure of *Romeo and Juliet.* He divides the rising action into four stages: (1) the

* *Opus cit.*

masked ball; (2) the garden scene; (3) the marriage; (4) the death of Tybalt. He says that "Tybalt's death is the strong break which separates the aggregate rise from the climax." The climax, he tells us, is the group of scenes beginning with Juliet's words, "Gallop apace you fiery footed steeds," and extending to Romeo's farewell, "It were a grief, so brief to part with thee; farewell." This includes the scene in which the Nurse brings Juliet news that Tybalt has been killed, and the scene in Friar Lawrence's cell in which Romeo laments "with his own tears made drunk," and the Friar chides him:

> What, rouse thee, man! thy Juliet is alive...
> Go, get thee to thy love as was decreed,
> Ascend her chamber, hence and comfort her.

After seeing Juliet, Romeo is to escape to Mantua and await further word from the Friar.

It is very curious that these two scenes should be termed the climax of the play. To be sure, there has been a marked *reversal of fortune* in the story of the lovers, but this reversal has already happened—in the scene in which Tybalt is killed and the Prince pronounces his sentence of banishment against Romeo. The two scenes which Freytag calls the climax show the emotional reaction of the lovers to what has already taken place. These two scenes are comparatively passive; they do not show the intensification of decision with which the lovers meet the changed conditions; this intensification occurs in the scene which follows, the parting of the lovers. Far from indicating a point of supreme tension, the two scenes are really an *interlude,* preparing for the greatly increased momentum of the coming action: Romeo's departure and the plans for Juliet's marriage to Paris.

What is the essential conflict in *Romeo and Juliet?* It is the struggle of two lovers for the fulfillment of their love. Can the killing of Tybalt be regarded as the high point of this conflict? On the contrary this event is the introduction of a new factor, which makes the struggle more difficult. The inevitable drive of the action is toward the open fight between Juliet and her parents, the attempt to force her to marry Paris. Tybalt's death has not changed this situation; it simply creates an additional obstacle. The fact that Romeo is banished and the marriage with Paris is so close, brings the conflict to a new level. But the tension is not relaxed. Even when Romeo fights with Paris outside Juliet's tomb, the outcome of the action is uncertain.

in an earlier version, Hedda separates the manuscript and burns only part of it: she "opens the packet and sorts the blue and white quires separately, lays the white quires in the wrapper again and keeps the blue ones in her lap." * Then she "opens the stove door; presently she throws one of the blue quires into the fire." Then she throws the rest of the blue quires into the flames. There is no indication of what Ibsen intended by the blue and white quires, or why he discarded the idea. But it shows that he did not regard this situation as the culmination of an unbearable emotional crisis, which sealed Hedda's doom. He felt for certain meanings and overtones in the scene. He imagined his heroine as dividing the manuscript and deliberately choosing certain pages.

Hedda Gabler shows us a constantly ascending series of crises. Hedda fights for her life until she cracks under the increasing strain. To divide the climax and the denouement is to give the play dual roots and destroy the unity of the design.

Every conflict contains in itself the germs of solution, the creation of a new balance of forces which will in turn lead to further conflict. The point of highest tension is necessarily the point at which the new balance of forces is created. This is the end of the development of any given system of events. The new balance of forces, new problems, new conflicts, which follow, are not within the scope of the theme which the playwright has selected.

The idea of continuing an action *beyond its scope* is a violation of the principles of dramatic action. If this is done, the solution must be passive and explanatory, in which case it has no value in terms of action; or else the balance of new forces must involve new elements of conflict: new forces are brought into play, in which case the continued conflict would require development in order to give it meaning, thus leading to another climax—which involves a different theme and a different play.

The idea of "falling action" has meaning only if we regard the system of dramatic events as *absolute,* an arrangement of emotions detached from life, governed by its own laws, and moving from a fixed premise to a fixed conclusion. The base of Freytag's pyramid is idealist philosophy: the action rises from the categorical imperative of ethical and social law, and descends at another point in the same line of conduct. The conclusion can be complete, because the principles of conduct revealed in the conclusion are final. The action requires no social extension; in the end, the threads of causation are tied together, and the system of events is *closed.*

This cannot be the case if we accept Lessing's statement that

* Ibsen, *opus cit.,* v. 12.

"in nature everything is connected, everything is interwoven, everything changes with everything, everything merges from one to another." To be sure, the playwright, as Lessing says, "must have the power to set up arbitrary limits." But it is the purpose of his art to achieve the maximum extension within these limits. He is dealing with the stuff of life. He molds this stuff according to his consciousness and will. But he defeats his purpose if he detaches this material from the movement of life of which he himself is a part. This movement is continuous, a movement of endless crises, of endless changes of equilibrium. The point of highest tension which the dramatist selects is the point which is most vital *to him;* but this does not mean that the life process is arrested at this point.

If we view the drama historically, we find that the choice of the point of climax is historically conditioned. For instance, Ibsen saw the structure of the bourgeois family breaking and going to pieces at a certain point; this point was the ultimate significance of the situation to him, and he necessarily used this as the point of reference in his dramas. But history moves; today it is fairly evident that what Ibsen saw as the end of the process is not the end; thus, Nora's defiance and Hedda's suicide seem far less conclusive today than under the social conditions with which Ibsen dealt. Nora's departure is historical, not contemporary, just as Romeo and Juliet in their marble tomb are historical, not contemporary.

At the end of Marlowe's *Tamburlaine the Great,* are the lines: "Meet Heaven and Earth, and here let all things end." But all things do not end. All things are in process of growth and solution, decay and renewal. A conflict may involve increasing tension or decreasing tension. But since the life process is continuous, decreasing tension is a period of preparation, the germination of new stages of conflict.

The principle that the limit of dramatic conflict is the limit of increasing tension does not imply that the climax must occur at a precise moment in relation to the end of the play.

It is natural to speak of the climax as a *point* of action. This gives the correct impression that it is closely knit and sharply defined. But it is not necessarily a point of time. It may be a complex event; it may combine several threads of action; it may be divided into several scenes; it may take a very abrupt or a very extended form.

It is also obvious that many plays violate the principle that the action cannot "fall" or move in any direction beyond the climax. There are many borderline cases, in which several events might be regarded as the climax. It is generally safe to assume that the final situation constitutes the root-action, even though it may be obviously weaker in a dramatic sense than earlier crises. However, in such cases, we must also consider that the lack of a defined climax springs from lack of a defined meaning, and that the author may have misplaced the root-action at some earlier point in the play.

A special question arises in regard to classical comedy. In the great comedies of Shakespeare and Molière, the complications reach a point of crisis which is often followed by formal explanations in the closing scenes. This unravelling is of a purely mechanical nature, and there can be no question that it is undramatic. It cannot be described as "falling action" because it is not action at all. The structure of classical comedy is based on a series of involvements which become more and more hopeless, but which contain the seed of their own solution. At the point of highest complication the knot is cut. This is the end of the conflict. The artificial conclusion, the extended discussion of previous mistakes and disguises, is often unnecessary and always undesirable. Modern comedy has fortunately escaped from this awkward convention (although there are vestiges of it in the farce and the mystery play).

In *The Shining Hour,* the climax comes in the middle of the play and is followed by a series of negative scenes. One is forced to regard the wife's suicide as the limit of the action: if one attempts to place the climax in the final act, one finds that every event in this act refers *back* to the suicide and is really a part of it. We are dealing here with a resumé of what has happened—like the explanatory scenes in the old comedies.

However, a climax which is extended over an entire act may be quite legitimate. *Dodsworth,* dramatized by Sidney Howard from the novel by Sinclair Lewis, is an example. It concerns the dissolution of a marriage. At the opening, Dodsworth and his wife start for Europe, leaving the successful mediocrity of the manufacturing town of Zenith. Differences of character and point of view develop. Fran, the wife, is neurotic, dissatisfied, looking for something she can't define. The "setting of the fuse" occurs at the end of Act I: in London, Fran has an innocent flirtation with Clyde Lockert. She tells Dodsworth about it and he is amused; but she is frightened; she no longer feels sure of herself. The adventure forces her to reconsider her adjustment to her environment, and to make the decisions on which the play is based.

In Act II, the conflict between Fran and her husband develops. Her psychological stress is shown in an effective line: "You're rushing at old age, Sammy, and I'm not ready for old age yet."

So she sends him back to America, and she gets entangled in a serious love affair. The play gathers momentum as it moves toward the obligatory scene—Dodsworth confronts his wife and her lover. He wants a show-down; he wants to know whether she wishes a divorce; he lays down the conditions on which they can continue to live together.

In the beginning of the third act, Dodsworth is making an effort to win his wife back; but she becomes involved in another affair, with Kurt von Obersdorf. In this scene the maximum tension is developed; she tells Dodsworth she wants a divorce and will marry Kurt. Dodsworth leaves her. This separation is really the limit of the action; however, the playwright, with remarkable technical virtuosity, succeeds in stretching this event over four substantial scenes. Dodsworth goes to Naples; he meets Edith Cortwright, he becomes devoted to her; back in Berlin, Kurt's mother prevents his marriage to Fran; she desperately telephones to Dodsworth, who reluctantly agrees to meet her and sail for New York, although he is in love with Edith. When he meets Fran at the steamer, he reaches the decision which has been inevitable throughout the act, and leaves her as the boat is about to sail. Thus the suspense is maintained until the last five seconds of the play.

The separation at the end of the play is a repetition of the separation in the first scene of the last act. In the intervening scenes, two entirely new elements are introduced: Kurt's mother, and the relationship between Dodsworth and Edith Cortwright. But do these elements affect the basic conflict between Fran and her husband? No, because everything which genuinely concerns this conflict has already been told. The fact that her lover has a mother gives Fran a new problem, but it does not affect her fundamental conflict with her environment. She will undoubtedly fall in love with someone else of the same sort. The fact that Dodsworth finds another woman is convenient, but it does not motivate his leaving his wife. He leaves her because it is impossible for them to live together, which is abundantly clear in the first scene of the third act.

The whole third act might have been compressed in a single scene; all the elements of the act, Kurt's mother, Edith Cortwright's honest affection, Dodsworth's realization of his wife's shallowness, his feeling that he must stick by her and his decision to leave her—these elements are aspects of a single situation. The author takes a single scene of separation, breaks it to show the various issues involved, and comes back to finish the scene.

One cannot say with finality that Howard's method is unjustified. The arrangement of the last act in five scenes has certain advantages. The form is more narrative than dramatic, but suspense is maintained; the fact that the new love story (with Edith Cortwright) is introduced almost as a separate plot gives it a certain substance which it might otherwise lack.

On the other hand the bringing in of new elements diffuses the final tension between husband and wife; the situation has less compression and less extension; their separation becomes more personal and less significant.

Stevedore, on the other hand, offers an example of a climax which is treated literally as a *point* of time. The point of supreme tension is the moment in which the white workers come to fight side by side with the Negroes against the lynch mob. This raises the struggle to its highest level and also contains the solution of this phase of the struggle. The coming of the white workers is introduced as a melodramatic punch just as the curtain is descending.

Is this abbreviated treatment of the climax a fault? Since the climax is the core of the social meaning, it is obvious that this meaning cannot be expressed in the form of a single shout of triumph at the close of a play.

The authors have insufficiently analyzed and developed the root-action. John Gassner * speaks of "the assumption in *Stevedore* that the union of white and Negro workers in the South is child's play. ... I submit that this is not only an unjustifiable over-simplification of a problem but that this weakness affects the very roots of the drama."

The over-simplification of the root-action means that the system of causation leading to it is not fully developed. Much of the action of *Stevedore* consists in the repetition and stretching out of the obligatory scene. The decision which motivates the conflict occurs in Lonnie's statement in the third scene of the first act: "Well here's one black man ain't satisfied being just a good Nigger." The next phase of the action is clear-cut; Lonnie's defiance of the white bosses gets him into immediate trouble. The obligatory scene is therefore sharply indicated: we foresee that Lonnie's plight will force the Negro workers to face the issue— they must either be slaves or fight for their rights. This in turn leads to the intensification of their will and the final clash—the coming of the white workers—which is both unexpected and inevitable. There are very complex forces involved in this situation: in

* John Gassner, "A Playreader on Playwrights," in *New Theatre* (October, 1934).

order to realize the full possibilities of the theme, it would be necessary to dramatize these complex forces in all their emotional and social richness. But the playwrights have chosen to emphasize one phase of the problem, and to repeat it with increasing intensity, but *without* development. In the first act, Lonnie calls directly on the workers to fight: "Lawd, when de black man gwine stand up? When he gwine stand up proud like a man?" The demand is repeated in the same terms in the second act, and the reaction of the workers is exactly the same. Since the theme is repeated, the physical activity is also repeated: in the second scene of Act II, Lonnie is hiding; he is almost caught and escapes. In the next scene (in Binnie's lunch-room), he is hiding again; again he is almost caught and again he escapes. The situation is repeated in the first scene of Act III.

These recurring scenes are effective because the subject matter is poignant, and the social meaning is direct. The playwrights also make skillful use of the device of increasing the emotional load. For instance, in the first scene of Act III, Ruby becomes hysterical, refusing to believe that Lonnie is still alive: "He's dead.... They killed him.... You just trying to fool me, that's all." Her hysteria has no meaning in the development of the story; it happens artificially at a convenient moment, in order to give emotional value to Lonnie's entrance.

The final decision of the black workers to "stand up and fight" comes in the third act. Here the obligatory scene (which has been stretched out over the entire play) comes to a head. Lonnie tells the preacher that it's no time to depend on religion; he tells the cowardly Jim Veal that there's no alternative, no use in running away. This is a strong scene; but its force is diluted by the fact that it has already been offered to us piece-meal.

Stevedore is an epoch-making play, sounding a new note of vitality and honesty in the American theatre, and exploring important contemporary material. Yet the structure of *Stevedore* reveals that the authors have not completely freed themselves from a static point of view. Instead of showing growth through struggle, the struggle is shown within fixed limits. The union of white and Negro workers seems *easy* because it is the result of social forces which are not concretized—and which therefore seem mechanical. The characters seem thin and two-dimensional; we do not see the impact of the environment on their conscious wills. The play abounds in homely, telling details of character. But the people do not *change;* they follow a pre-determined line of conduct.

The climaxes of two recent plays by Elmer Rice offer a valuable index of the playwright's development. The root-action of *We the People* lacks dramatic realization. The scene presents a lecture platform from which people are delivering speeches. The speakers make an appeal to our social conscience; *we the people* must make our country a land of freedom: "Let us cleanse it and put it in order and make it a decent place to live in." This is a stirring appeal; but since it does not show us any principle of action which corresponds to the abstract statement, we cannot test its value as a guide to action. The climax does not define the scope of the system of events, because it leaves us completely at a loss as to *how* the characters in the play will react to this appeal. Since there is no tension, there is also no solution.

The development of *We the People* consists of a series of scenes which are effective as separate events, but which are illustrative rather than progressive. Since the climax is an intellectual statement of a problem, the play consists of an intellectual exposition of the various phases of the problem. More than two-thirds of the play may properly be regarded as expository. Again and again, we go back to the lower middle-class Davis home; in the seventh scene, things are getting worse; in the ninth scene, they have taken a boarder and the bank holding their investments has closed; in the eleventh scene, things are still worse. Finally, in the thirteenth scene, there is definite activity, a reaction to the necessities of the environment—the father is asked to lead a march of the unemployed. Davis' decision to lead the march is believable, because we have seen the hunger and misery of the family. But the decision lacks depth, because the man's conscious will is not exposed. And once Davis becomes active, we never see him again!

The use of *ideas* as substitutes for events is illustrated in the eighth scene. Steve, the Negro servant, says that he has been reading H. G. Wells *Modern Utopia,* and talks about Negro oppression in general terms. This is a minor incident, but it is a striking instance of the author's method. The Negro has no value as a person beyond his comment on a book he has read.

On the other hand, the root-action of Rice's later play, *Judgment Day,* is violent, abrupt, vital. The structure of this play is also in sharp contrast to that of *We the People.* The most significant thing about the final situation in *Judgment Day* is its dual character: the great revolutionist, who is supposed to be dead, appears suddenly in what is obviously intended to be a court room in Hitlerized Germany, although the play is set in a fictitious country. *At the same time,* the liberal judge shoots the dictator. This double climax reflects a contradiction in Rice's social point of view: he recognizes the deadly nature of the conflict in the courtroom; he sees that the working-class leader plays an important part in this struggle; he sees the weakness of the liberal position, but he has an abiding faith in the liberal's ability to think and act. He therefore introduces the working class leader as a dominating figure—while at the same moment the honest liberal destroys the dictator.

This contradiction permeates the play. The two threads of action which lead to the double climax are not clearly followed. The action of the judge in shooting the dictator is almost totally unprepared. It is hinted at during the deliberations of the five judges at the beginning of Act III: the liberal Judge Slatarski says: "Gentlemen, I am an old man—older than any of you. . . . But while there is the breath of life in me, I shall continue to uphold my honor and the honor of my country." This brief rhetorical formulation gives no insight into the man's character, or the mental struggle which could possibly lead him to the commission of such an act.

Rice's approach to his material is unclear, and his historical perspective is limited. But his eyes are open, and his work shows constant growth. His characters possess will power and are able to use it. The difficulty, in *Judgment Day,* lies in the fact that Rice is still unable to see history as a process: he sees it as the work of individuals, who possess varying degrees of integrity, honor and patriotism. He regards these qualities as immutable; the dictator is a "bad" man who is opposed by "good" men. Thus the action is limited and thrown out of focus. The courtroom is removed from *our* world, placed in an imaginary country. The characters are given queer names. Dr. Panayot Tsankov, Dr. Michael Vlora, Colonel Jon Sturdza, etc. This creates an effect of artificial remoteness: when Lydia's brother says he comes from Illinois, he is asked: "Do they hang people there from the limbs of trees as they do in the streets of New York?" Instead of bringing the drama close to us, the playwright deliberately sets it apart.

Rice has been much influenced by prevailing modes of social thought. He emphasizes immutable qualities of character; he believes that these qualities are stronger than the social forces to which they are opposed. Since *Judgment Day* is a conflict of qualities, it has no developed social framework.

Nevertheless *Judgment Day* possesses an abounding vitality. There is no avoidance of conflict, but rather a succession of crises which are more violent than logical. The lack of preparation, the violence of the action, give the impression that the author is straining for concreteness, for a sharper meaning which he is as yet unable to unify and define. This accounts for the abrupt but illogical vigor of the dual climax.

The climaxes of Ibsen's plays illustrate the remarkable clarity and force which can be compressed in the final moment of breaking tension. Just before Oswald's insane cry, "Give me the sun," at the end of *Ghosts*, Mrs. Alving has said, "Now you will get some rest, at home with your own mother, my darling boy. You shall have everything you want, just as you did when you were a little child." The *recognition* of his insanity which follows this, compresses Mrs. Alving's whole life—all she has lived for and is ready to die for—in a moment of unbearable decision.

The ends of Shakespeare's plays have a similar compression and extension. Othello's magnificent final speech reviews his life as a man of action and builds to its inevitable culmination:

> Soft you; a word or two before you go.
> I have done the state some service, and they know't—
> No more of that.—I pray you, in your letters,
> When you shall these unlucky deeds relate,
> Speak of me as I am; nothing extenuate,
> Nor set down aught in malice; then must you speak
> Of one that lov'd not wisely, but too well;
> Of one not easily jealous, but, being wrought,
> Perplex'd in the extreme; of one whose hand,
> Like the base Judean, threw a pearl away
> Richer than all his tribe; of one whose subdu'd eyes,
> Albeit unused to the melting mood,
> Drop tears as fast as the Arabian trees
> Their medicinal gum. Set you down this;
> And say, besides,—that in Aleppo once,
> Where a malignant and a turban'd Turk
> Beat a Venetian and traduc'd the state,
> I took by the throat the circumcised dog,
> And smote him,—thus.

He strikes the dagger into his own heart.

CHAPTER VI

CHARACTERIZATION

THE theatre is haunted by the supposition that character is an independent entity which can be projected in some mysterious way.

The modern dramatist continues to do homage to the unique soul; he feels that the events on the stage serve to expose the inner being of the people concerned, which somehow transcends the sum of the events themselves.

The only thing which can go beyond the system of action on the stage is a wider system of events which is inferred or described. Not only is character, as Aristotle said, "subsidiary to the actions," but the *only* way in which we can understand character is *through the actions to which it is subsidiary*. This accounts for the necessity of a solid social framework; the more thoroughly the environment is realized, the more deeply we understand the character. A character which stands alone is not a character at all.

W. T. Price says: "Character can be brought out in no other way than by throwing people into given relations. Mere character is nothing, pile it on as you may."* One may also point out that mere action is nothing, pile it on as you may. But character is subordinate to the action, because the action, however limited it may be, represents a sum of "given relations" which is wider than the actions of any individual, and which determines the individual actions.

Baker distinguishes between *illustrative action* and *plot action*. This is the essential problem in regard to characterization: can illustrative action exhibit aspects of character apart from the main line of the play's development?

In the dock scene in the first act of *Stevedore,* a great deal of the activity seems to illustrate character rather than carry forward the plot: Rag Williams shadow-boxes with a mythical opponent; Bobo Williams dances and sings. In *Ode to Liberty* (adapted by Sidney Howard from the French of Michael Duran), we find another typical case of apparently illustrative action: the end of the first act shows the Communist who is hiding in Madeleine's apartment settling down to mend a broken clock. A man mending a clock is performing an act. The act exhibits character. But the incident seems to stand alone. Mending a clock does not necessarily involve conflict. It does not necessarily throw the man "into given relations" with other people.

A play is a pattern involving more than one character. The conduct of every character, even though he is alone on the stage, even though his activity seems to be unrelated to other events, has meaning only in relation to the whole pattern of activity.

When the Communist mends the clock in *Ode to Liberty,* the significance of the act lies in his relationship with a number of

* *Opus cit.*

people: he is hiding from the police, he is in the apartment of a
beautiful woman. Detached from these relationships, performed
as a bit of vaudeville without explanation, his act would have no
meaning at all. But one must still ask whether the act is illustrative
or progressive? Would the plot move on just as well if the man
did *not* mend the clock? And if so, is the action permissible as a
bit of characterization?

If one considers the principle of unity, it is obvious that illustrative action as an independent commentary on character is a
violation of unity. How can one introduce anything (however
small) "whose presence or absence makes no visible difference" in
relation to the whole structure? If this were possible, we would
be compelled to throw away the theory of the theatre which has
here been developed—and begin all over again.

One may apply the test of unity to any example of so-called
illustrative action. The mending of the clock in *Ode to Liberty*
involves decision and carries the action forward. The incident
defines and changes the intruder's relationship to Madeleine; this
is absolutely necessary in order to build the events of the second
act. Furthermore the clock, as an object, plays an important part
in the story; Madeleine later breaks it to prevent the Communist
from leaving.

The attempt to deal with characterization as a separate department of technique has resulted in endless confusion in the theory
and practice of the theatre. The playwright who follows Galsworthy's advice in endeavoring to make his plot dependent on his
characters invariably defeats his own purpose; the illustrative
material, introduced with a view to character delineation, obstructs
the characters—instead of being character-material it turns out to
be unwieldy plot-material.

Since the rôle of the conscious will and its actual operation in
the mechanics of the action have been exhaustively analyzed, we
can here limit ourselves to a brief survey of some of the more
usual forms of illustrative action: these are: (1) the attempt to
build character by excessive use of naturalistic detail; (2) the use
of historical or local color without social perspective; (3) the
heroic, or declarative, style of characterization; (4) the use of
minor characters as feeders whose only function is to contribute to
the effectiveness of one or more leading characters; (5) the illustration of character solely in terms of social responsibility to the
neglect of other emotional and environmental factors; (6) the
attempt to create audience sympathy by illustrative events.

(1) George Kelly, who is a skillful craftsman, tries to bring

character to life by showing us a multiplicity of detail which is unified only in terms of the author's conception of the character. *Craig's Wife,* the most interesting of Kelly's plays, projects a portrait against a background which is observed with the utmost care; but both the social framework and the stage-action serve only to pile up unrelated minutiae of information; instead of increasing the livingness of the character, the illustrative events prevent decision and therefore prevent the meaningful development of the individual.

(2) *Gold Eagle Guy,* by Melvin Levy, is a play of a very different sort; the action is robust and highly colored; but the social framework is designed only as an ornamentation around the personality of Guy Button. As a result, the passions and desires of the character are diluted; we see an environment and we see a man, but we fail to see the inter-action between them; the character is conceived as something which is seen through the events, as stars are seen through a telescope.

(3) Archibald MacLeish's *Panic* attempts a portrait on an heroic scale. But here again the supposedly titanic figure of the central character is ineffective because the events are illustrative, and are intended as an abstract background for McGafferty's conflict of will. MacLeish deals directly with contemporary social forces. But he sees these forces in terms of time and eternity:

> It is not we who threaten you! Your ill is
> Time—and there's no cure for time but dying!

The influence of the Bergsonian conception of the *flow of time* is evident. MacLeish says that he attempts to "arrest, fix, make expressive the flowing away of the world." At the same time, his emphasis on the will as man's ultimate salvation is as emphatic as Ibsen's. In *Panic,* as in Ibsen's last plays, the individual will is merged in the universal will.

MacLeish describes McGafferty as "a man of will; who lives by the will and dies by the will." But McGafferty's actions are limited and chaotic, and exhibit no sustained purpose. He chides his business associates; he argues with the woman he loves. He kills himself. His self-destruction is caused by something outside himself; he is forced to die because a blind man predicts his doom. This is not the result of a struggle of wills. The blind man's power is itself mystic, expressive of the flow of time. The action has no unifying principle, because it is simply illustrative of "the flowing away of the world."

(4) The law that progression must spring from the decisions of the characters applies not only to the leading figures, but to all the subordinate persons in the drama. The neglect of this law often leads the playwright to make a curious distinction between the leading characters and the subordinate persons in the story: two or three central figures are seen purely in terms of character, the attempt being made to subordinate the action to the presentation of what are supposed to be their qualities and emotions. But all the minor characters are treated in exactly the opposite way, being used as automatons who are shuffled about to suit the needs of the leading persons.

A minor character must play an essential part in the action; his life must be bound up in the unified development of the play. Even if a few lines are spoken in a crowd, the effectiveness of these lines depends on the extent to which the individual is a part of the action. This means that he must make decisions. His decisions must affect the movement of the play; if this is the case, the events react upon the character, causing him to grow and change.

In *Stevedore,* the members of the group of Negroes are individualized by dialogue and bits of action. But their emotional range is very limited. Their actions are to some extent illustrative. One cannot say that the development of the play would be inconceivable without each of these characters, that the presence or absence of each would make a "visible difference" in the outcome. Thus the action as a whole is limited; if the emotions of the minor characters were more fully explored in terms of will, the plot-structure would have a greater extension; the emotional life of the leading characters would then be deeper and less one-sided.

In *The Front Page,* Ben Hecht and Charles MacArthur have created a lively group of reporters; but they have only two dimensions, because they are not deeply involved in a unified plot. Therefore, in spite of the apparent commotion, there is no movement; the reporters are simply a fresco of persons painted in the acts of swearing, cracking jokes, squabbling.

(5) The over-simplifying of the characters, which is to be noted in *Stevedore,* is a defect which may be observed in the majority of plays dealing with working-class themes. The heart of the trouble is an inadequate analysis of the conscious will; although the social forces are seen clearly and concretely, the actual activity of the characters is illustrative of these forces, because it fails to dramatize the relationship between the individual and the whole environment. *Black Pit,* by Albert Maltz, shows that the author is

aware of this problem, and is making an effort to achieve a wider range of characterization and emotion. For this reason, *Black Pit* is the most important effort that has yet been made in the field of proletarian drama. The play tells the story of a coal miner who betrays his fellow-workers and becomes a stool-pigeon. The web of causation in which Joe Kovarsky is caught is fully presented; but the events lack their full meaning and progression because the *decisions* which drive the action forward are not dramatized.

The exposition shows Joe Kovarsky's marriage; he is immediately dragged to prison on a charge growing out of his militancy in a strike. He returns to his wife three years later. One naturally asks: how has he changed? What has this ordeal done to him? There is no indication that prison has had any effect on him at all. Thus there is no preparation for any later change.

Throughout the play, Joe is driven by events. He is a weak man, but his weakness is not made poignant. Even a weak man is driven to a point where he is forced to make a decision. This moment of the weak man's decision, when circumstances trap him and he cannot avoid *committing* an act is, both dramatically and psychologically, the key to progression—it is therefore also the key to the character. A weak man fights under pressure—and unless he fights, according to his own powers and in his own way, there is no conflict.

The two most important scenes in the play are the last scene of Act I (in which the mine superintendent first gains control of Joe), and the end of Act II (in which the superintendent forces Joe to tell the name of the union organizer). In both these decisive moments, Joe is passive; the author is careful to tell us that the character is irresponsible, that circumstances are too much for him. Thus the character seems less real, and the circumstances seem less inevitable.

The root-action of *Black Pit* shows Joe disgraced, cursed by his own brother, leaving his wife and child. But the scope of this situation lies in Joe's coming face to face with the meaning of his own acts. His recognition of what he has done is essential: this recognition must also be an act of will, a heart-wrenching decision forced by the increasing tension between the man and the social conflict in which he is involved. Even if a man's character is disintegrating, he is capable of passionate realization of what he has become; perhaps this is the last act of will of which he is capable. Without it, recognition of the dramatic and social meaning is slurred.

His brother's recognition is not enough. Joe's admission that he "feel like to die" is not enough. He simply admits his fault like a small child and asks his brother what to do: Tony tells him he must go away. If Tony is the only one who understands and feels what has happened, then the play should be about Tony. Joe's separation from his wife and child lacks tragic depth because here again the conscious will is untouched; we have no idea what Joe is going through because he takes no part in the decision. Instead of emphasizing the horror of Joe's crime, this tends to mitigate it. To tell a man to leave the wife and child whom he loves is unimpressive, and implausible. To have him decide to do so, to have the decision torn from his broken mind, might be vitally dramatic.

(6) We now come to the most widespread, and most pernicious, form of illustrative action—the substitution of a sentimental appeal for sympathy for the logical development of the action.

The idea that the playwright's main task is to gain sympathy for his leading characters (by fair means or foul), is a vulgarization of a genuine psychological truth: the emotional participation which unites the audience with the events on the stage is an important aspect of audience psychology. "For the time being," says Michael Blankfort,* "the audience places its bets on some person in the play. *Identification* is more than sympathy with that character; it is a 'living in the character'—what writers on esthetics call 'empathy.'" The principle of "empathy" is obscure, but there can be no question that the emotional experience of the audience is a sort of identification. However, the dramatist cannot induce this experience by an appeal to the sentiments and prejudices of the audience. Identification not only means "more than sympathy," but something which is essentially *different* from sympathy. To show us a distorted view of a character, to convince us that he is kind to his mother and gives candy to little children, does not cause us to live *in* the character. Identification means sharing the character's *purpose,* not his virtues.

In Elmer Rice's *Counselor-at-Law* and in Sidney Howard's *Dodsworth,* the insistence on sympathetic traits devitalizes the leading characters. In *Dodsworth* the cards are stacked in favor of the husband and against the wife. There is a great deal to be said on Fran's side, but the dramatist invariably places her in a bad light. Dodsworth moves in a glow of kindness and good-nature, which is created by activity which is only incidental to the action. Even when he exhibits a strain of bad temper (in the fourth scene of Act II) a bit of charm is immediately introduced as a counter-weight.

* *New Theatre,* November, 1934.

The factors which give Fran an excuse for her conduct are ignored. Her desire to live, to run away from old age, may be cheap and absurd, but it is also tragic. For instance, there is a sexual side to the problem: In the final scene of Act II, Fran (in her lover's presence) tells her husband that he has never been a satisfactory lover. Thus something which is a justification of her conduct is introduced in such a way that it makes her appear additionally cruel. Let us assume that her cruelty is itself characteristic. Then one may demand that the playwright go more deeply into the causes for this cruelty, that he show us how she has become what she is. In doing this, he would both explain and justify the character.

The one-sidedness of *Dodsworth* dilutes the conflict and weakens the construction. The immediate cause of this is the conscious attempt to win sympathy. But the deeper cause is the dramatist's belief that qualities of character are detachable, and that charm or kindliness can be superimposed on actions that are not intrinsically charming or kindly. Sometimes the charm is supplied by the actor, whose consciousness and will may make up for the deficiencies of authorship.

It is generally admitted that the main problem of characterization is progression. "The complaint that a character maintains the same attitude throughout," says Archer, "means that it is not a human being at all, but a mere embodiment of two or three characteristic which are fully displayed within the first ten minutes and then keep on repeating themselves, like a recurrent decimal." * Baker remarks that "the favorite place of many so-called dramatists for a change of character is in their vast silences between the acts."

Baker says: "To 'hold the situation,' to get from it the full dramatic possibilities the characters involved offer, a dramatist must study his characters in it till he has discovered the entire range of their emotion in the scene." † It is undeniable that the dramatist must discover the entire range of emotion under the given circumstances. This applies not only to each situation, but to the whole structure of the play. But if emotion is viewed simply as a vague *capacity for feeling* which the character may possess, it follows that the range is limitless; it also follows that the emotion projected may be illustrative or poetic, and have no meaning in the unified development of the play.

The scope of emotion within the dramatic scheme is limited by the scope of the events: the characters can have neither depth nor

* Archer, *Playmaking, a Manual of Craftsmanship.*
† *Opus cit.*

progression except insofar as they make and carry out decisions
which have a definite place in the system of events and which
drive toward the root-action which unifies the system.

CHAPTER VII

DIALOGUE

LEE SIMONSON, in his entertaining book, *The Stage is Set,*
complains of the lack of poetry in the modern theatre. The playwright fails, he says, to make his characters "incandescent and
illuminating at their climactic moments because of his inability or
unwillingness, to employ the intensifications of poetic speech." *

This is largely true. But one cannot suppose that it is due entirely to the perversity or sterility of contemporary playwrights.
The mood and temper of the modern stage are reflected in the dry
phrasing and conventionality of the dialogue. The material with
which the middle-class theatre deals is of such a nature that "the
intensifications of poetic speech" would be an impertinence. One
cannot graft living fruit on a dead tree. If a playwright believes
that the ideals of youth find their full expression in a speech at a
college graduation (in *Merrily We Roll Along*) one may be quite
sure that the words used to express these ideals will not be
"incandescent and illuminating."

Simonson notes the symptoms of the disease, but he ignores the
cause and cure. He also assumes that the American theatre is completely destitute of poetry. This is far from true. One need only
mention the early plays of Eugene O'Neill, the work of John Dos
Passos, Em Jo Basshe, Paul Green, George O'Neil, Dan
Totheroh; *Children of Darkness* by Edwin Justus Mayer; *Pinwheel* by Francis Edwards Faragoh. In approaching the question
of style in dramatic speech, one must give due consideration to
what has already been accomplished.

It must be understood that we are not here dealing with poetry
in the narrow sense. MacLeish says of blank verse that "as a
vehicle for contemporary expression it is pure anachronism." †
Maxwell Anderson has failed sadly in attempts to breathe life into

---

* New York, 1932.
† Introduction to Archibald MacLeish, *Panic* (New York, 1935).

Elizabethan verse forms; the result is dignified, fluent, uninspired.

If poetic forms are to develop in the modern theatre, these forms must evolve out of the richness and imagery of contemporary speech. The first step in this direction is to clarify the nature of dramatic dialogue. There is a general tendency to regard speech as a decorative design which serves to embellish the action. In many plays, the words and the events seem to run parallel to each other, and never meet. However "decorative" the words may be, they are valueless unless they serve to drive the action forward.

Speech is a kind of action, *a compression and extension of action.* When a man speaks he performs an act. Talk is often called a substitute for action, but this is only true insofar as it is a weaker, less dangerous and more comfortable kind of action. It is obvious that speech requires physical effort; it comes from energy and not from inertia.

Speech has enormously broadened the scope of man's activity. In fact, without it, organized activity would be impossible. By speech man is able to accomplish more, to act more extensively. This is elementary—but it enables us to realize the function of speech in the drama. It serves, as it does in life, to broaden the scope of action; it organizes and extends what people do. It also intensifies the action. The emotion which people feel in a situation grows out of their sense of its scope and meaning. They are conscious of the possibilities and dangers which are inherent in the situation. Animals are apparently incapable of any considerable emotion because they do not grasp the scope of their acts.

The crises of which a drama is composed grow out of a complex series of events. Dialogue enables the playwright to extend the action over the wide range of events which constitutes the play's framework. The awareness of these other events (derived from speech and expressed in speech) increases the emotional stress of the characters, achieving the compression and explosion which is action.

To realize this intensity and scope, poetic richness is a necessity. For this reason, I begin this chapter with a reference to poetry. Poetry is not simply an attribute of dialogue, which may be present or absent. It is a quality which is indispensable, if dialogue is to fulfill its real purpose. Speech puts the actual impact of events into words: it dramatizes forces which are not seen. To do this effectively, to make these other events visible, requires language which is incandescent. This is not a matter of "beauty" in general; but of achieving the color and feel of reality. Genuinely poetic speech produces a physical sensation in the listener.

The structural limitations of a play bear a close relationship to the style of dialogue. For example, in *Stevedore* the language is honest and vigorous, but it lacks richness; it fails to sufficiently extend the action. This is also a structural defect. The emotions of the characters, the fullness of the story, are also limited.

Those modern dramatists who have achieved a degree of poetic quality are those who have attempted to bring substance and social meaning into the theatre. If one examines the work of some of the men I have mentioned, one finds that their plays (particularly in the case of Dos Passos and Basshe) lack structural unity. Critics often assume that there is a natural opposition between poetic license and the prosaic neatness of the "well-made play." Many of these so-called "well-made plays" are not well-made at all, but are as weak in construction as in language. On the other hand, the work of Dos Passos and Basshe, in spite of its faults, is tremendously alive; the story-telling is diffuse, but it attains isolated moments of great compression and extension. The style of writing reflects the uncertainty of the action. In *The Garbage Man,* Dos Passos tries to dramatize the economic and social forces of the world around him and ends up, literally, in eternal space. These are the closing lines of the play:

> TOM: Where are we going?
> JANE: Somewhere very high. Where the wind is sheer whiteness.
> TOM: With nothing but the whirl of space in our faces.

One finds throughout Dos Passos' work the contrast between his extraordinary physical perception and his unresolved mysticism. The ending of *The Garbage Man* is a denial of reality; people "with nothing but the whirl of space" in their faces can have little meaning for us who remain (whether we like it or not) among the sights and sounds and smells of the visible world. This ending is accompanied by the double pattern of escape and repetition which we have traced in so many modern plays: Tom becomes free by an act of intuitive emotion: he *drums on the moon.* Thus he transcends his environment; he goes beyond reason, he enters the starry world of infinite time and space. At the same time, we find the statement that life is an endless and dull repetition.

Jane asks: "Will it always be the same old treadmill?" Again she says: "But the creaking merry-go-round of our lives has started again, Tom. We're on the wooden horse together. The old steam piano is wheezing out its tune and the nine painted ladies are all beating time. Faster and faster, Tom. Ahead of us the dragon, behind us the pink pig." This illustrates the contradiction between the realistic trimmings ("ahead of us the dragon, behind us the pink pig") with which Dos Passos decks his thought, and the retrospective quality of the thought itself.

We find this idea of repetition again in the root-action of *Fortune Heights:* Owen and Florence have lost everything; he says: "All we want to do's to dope out some way to live decent, live, you and me and the kid. Gettin' rich is a hophead's dream. We got to find the United States." As they go down the road, a car drives up, the real estate agent "steps out of the office, and a man and woman who look as much as possible like Owen and Florence without being mistaken for them step out of the car."

There are traces of this repetition-idea throughout the action of *Fortune Heights;* but there are many scenes in the play which attain depth and insight, which break through the conceptual confusion and drive the action forward with desperate energy. As a result of this contradiction, Dos Passos is a playwright whose work shows unequalled dramatic potentialities and who has never written an integrated play.

It is in dealing with factual experience, with sights and sounds and smells, that Dos Passos' dialogue attains genuine poetic value: for example, the Old Bum in Union Square in *The Garbage Man:* "I been in Athabasco an' the Klondike, an' Guatemala an' Yucatan, an' places I never knowed the names of. I was a year on the beach at Valparaiso, till the earthquake shook the rotten town down round my ears, an' I've picked fruit along the Eastern Shore, an' run a buzzsaw up on the Columbia River." One need hardly point out that this speech is an extension of action. So is this, when the Old Bum talks about the "guys on the inside track": "They set each other up to banquets in rooms where everything's velvet an' soft an' sit there eatin' pheasants an' French peas an' Philadelphia poultry, an' beautiful young actresses come up out o' pies like the blackbirds an' dance all naked round the table."

George O'Neil's work is bleaker and less exuberant than that of Dos Passos, but one finds the same inner conflict. The lines are compressed, beautifully worded—but blurred by a large vagueness. For instance, in *American Dream:* "Can't you hear the earth? It goes on and on—in the dark, like the sea—like our hearts." Or, "There's bread here, but no breath, and that is the evil of the world."

One also finds this dallying with infinity in Basshe. For example, in *The Centuries;* "On your brow are impressed the memories that

ding to earth"... or... "Your head is a planet searching for a
hiding place."

If mysticism were the whole content of these playwrights'
thought, their work would be as remote as the fog-drenched dramas
of Maeterlinck. But the remarkable thing about these American
authors is their confused but intent awareness of reality: they fight
their way toward a knowledge of the living world; they fight
against their own limitation.

Poetry is too often regarded as an obstruction between the writer
and reality, rather than a sharper perception of reality. Shakespeare's poetry soars, but it never escapes. In recent years, only
the plays of J. M. Synge have attained the turbulent realism of the
Elizabethans. Synge says: "On the stage one must have reality
and one must have joy; and that is why the intellectual modern
drama has failed, and people have grown sick of the false joy of
the musical comedy, that has been given them in place of the rich
joy found only in what is superb and wild in reality. In a good
play every speech should be as fully flavored as a nut or an apple,
and such speech cannot be written by any one who works among
people who have shut their lips on poetry." *

Synge refers to the highly-colored speech of the Irish peasants
about whom he wrote. Are we to conclude that joy has died and
that we live "among people who have shut their lips on poetry"?
To any one who has opened his ears to the cadences of American
speech, the question is absurd. Dos Passos has been very successful
in catching what is "superb and wild" in the reality of American
talk. Basshe has given us the full flavor of the East Side in *The
Centuries*. More recently, Odets has found gaiety and warmth and
singing beauty in American speech.

The only speech which lacks color is that of people who have
nothing to say. People whose contact with reality is direct and
varied must create a mode of speech which expresses that contact.
Since language grows out of events, it follows that those whose
talk is thin are those whose impression of events is pale and abstract. Then what about the popular myth of the "strong, silent
man of action"? Such a man (if and when he exists) is the ideal
of the upper-class leader, not emotionally involved in the events
which he controls.

"Good dialogue," says Baker, "must be kindled by feeling, made
alive by the emotion of the speaker." † Emotion divorced from reality is *inhibited* emotion, which therefore cannot be expressed. Freud

* Preface to *The Playboy of the Western World* (New York, 1907).
† *Opus cit.*

and others maintain that inhibited emotion finds inverted expression in dreams and fantasies. These fantasies are also a form of action. It is conceivable that this material may be used in literature and drama (for instance, the dramatic nightmare in James Joyce's *Ulysses*). However, when we analyze fantasies of this type, we find that what makes them intelligible is what connects them with reality. An individual's dream of escape may be satisfactory to *him,* but its social meaning lies in knowledge of what he is *escaping from.* As soon as this knowledge is supplied, we are back in the field of known events. The theatre must deal with emotion which can be expressed—the fullest expression of emotion comes from men and women who are aware of their environment, uninhibited in their perceptions.

The stage today is largely concerned with people whose main interest is escape from reality. The language is therefore thin and lifeless. When the middle-class playwright attempts to achieve poetic handling of mythical or fantastic subjects, his speech remains colorless: he is afraid to let himself go; he is trying to hide the link between fantasy and reality.

In the past fifteen years, the theatre has made a desperate effort to find more colorful material, more vibrant speech. Playwrights have discovered the lively talk of soldiers, gangsters, jockeys, chorus girls, prizefighters. The stage has gained tremendously by this— but the approach to this material has been limited and one sided; dramatists have looked only for sensation and cheap effects, slang and tough phrases, and they have found exactly what they were looking for. There is also singing poetry in common speech; it grows out of moments of deeper contact with reality, moments that are "kindled with feeling."

Today, in a period of intense social conflict, emotions are correspondingly intense. These emotions, which grow out of daily struggle, are not inhibited. They find expression in language which is heroic and picturesque. To be sure, this is not a world of the "rich joy" of which Synge speaks. There is exaltation in conflict; there is also fierce sorrow. This is equally true of the plays of Synge: *Riders to the Sea* and *The Playboy of the Western World* can hardly be described as happy plays.

Among "refined" people (including "refined" playwrights) there seems to be an idea that all workers talk alike—just as all prizefighters, or all chorus girls, are supposed to talk alike. The speech of American workers and farmers is very personal and varied. It ranges all the way from repetitious slang to moments of startling beauty. No dramatist can ignore the task of capturing the richness, the unrivalled dramatic possibilities of this speech.

In *Panic,* MacLeish uses poetry as something quite apart from action. MacLeish (like Dos Passos and so many others) is at war with his own mysticism. He seeks the visible world with an emotion which illuminates his poetry. Thus, although he is unable to project conflict in dramatic terms, his poetry is so dynamic that it serves as a substitute for action; it contains a life of its own which is objectively real, and separate from the actions on the stage.

In his preface to *Panic,* MacLeish explains that blank verse is too "spacious, slow, noble, and elevated" for an American theme; that our rhythms are "nervous, not muscular; excited, not deliberate; vivid, not proud." He has therefore evolved "a line of five accents but unlimited syllables." In the choruses he uses a line of three accents. The result is noteworthy. MacLeish points the way to a new and freer use of dramatic poetry. All that stands in the way is the barrier (which he himself has erected) between speech and action.

In discussing poetry, we have neglected the usual technical qualities of dialogue: clarity, compression, naturalness. Are we to ignore Baker's advice that "the chief purpose of dialogue is to convey necessary information clearly"? This depends on what we mean by "necessary information." Information can be very accurately and tersely conveyed by a set of statistics. But the facts with which a play deals are not statistics, but the complex forces which are behind statistics. Baker also speaks of the need of emotion in dialogue, but he fails to analyze the relationship between emotion and information. Indeed, as long as emotion is regarded abstractly, there is bound to be a gap between the conveying of facts and the expression of feeling. This is the gap between action and character which has already been noticed.

When we understand the complexity and emotional depth of the information which must be conveyed in dialogue, "the intensifications of poetic speech" become a necessity. The fullness of reality must be compressed without losing color or clarity. To do this requires a great poetic gift. Poetry is not undisciplined: it is a very precise form of expression. It is, in fact, the prosiness of O'Neill's later plays that causes them to be over-written. The early sea plays are far more poetic—and also possess more clarity and conciseness.

Ibsen's mastery of free flights of poetry is shown in *Peer Gynt.* In the prose plays, he consciously compresses and restricts the language. The dialogue lacks rich images and brilliant color, because the people are inhibited and unimaginative. Yet the speech is never thin; some of the quality of *Peer Gynt* is found in all the plays—a poetic concentration of meaning, as in Oswald's cry for the sun. In examining Ibsen's notebooks, one finds that his revision of lines was always intended to sharpen clarity, and at the same time to deepen the meaning. In an earlier version of *A Doll's House,* the lines between Nora and her husband, when she discovers that he has no intention of sacrificing himself to save her, are as follows:

> NORA: I so firmly believed that you would ruin yourself to save me. That is what I dreaded, and therefor I wanted to die!
> HELMER: Oh, Nora, Nora!
> NORA: And how did it turn out? No thanks, no outburst of affection, not a shred of a thought of saving me.*

In the final version, Ibsen has wrought a remarkable change:

> NORA: That was the miracle that I hoped for and dreaded. And it was to hinder that that I wanted to die.
> HELMER: I would gladly work for you day and night, Nora— bear sorrow and want for your sake—but no man sacrifices his honor, even for one he loves.
> NORA: Millions of women have done so.

It is evident that the revision has accomplished several things: the conflict is better balanced, because Helmer defends his point of view. Instead of crying, "Oh, Nora, Nora!" he tells us what he wants and believes. Nora's answer, which in the earlier version is personal and peevish, becomes a deep expression of emotion; it shows her growing realization of her problem as a woman; it extends the conflict to include the problems of "millions of women."

Although the language of the Broadway theatre is unpoetic, it often exhibits remarkable technical dexterity. It excels in naturalness and hard-boiled brassy humor. The dialogue in Maxwell Anderson's modern plays is full of pith, hardness, derision. But when Anderson turns to history, his blank verse ignores reality and deals in noble generalities. In *Elizabeth the Queen,* Essex says:

> The God who searches heaven and earth and hell
> For two who are perfect lovers, could end his search
> With you and me...

This reflects Anderson's conception of history; events are pale compared to the feelings of great individuals. He reaches the conclusion that events hardly exist. In *Mary of Scotland,* Elizabeth says:

* Ibsen, *opus cit.*, v. 12.

'It's not what happens
That matters, no, not even what happens that's true,
But what men believe to have happened.

But when Anderson deals with contemporary themes, we find phrases like these in *Both Your Houses:* "Of course illicit passion may have raised its pretty tousled head" ... or ... "The girls are a hell of a lot fresher on Long Island than down there at the naval base where the gobs have been chasing them since 1812."

Anderson's work exposes the inner contradiction which has been discussed in regard to Dos Passos and MacLeish. However MacLeish and Dos Passos endeavor to solve the contradiction, and therefore offer a chaotic but emotional view of the modern world. In Anderson the split is much wider and the conflict is concealed. He finds a comfortable escape in the past, satisfied with what he may "believe to have happened." When he views the present, he sees only the surface of events; his idealism makes him harsh and bitter; but his irony is not deeply emotional.*

The Front Page is a masterpiece of rough-and-tumble dialogue. A reporter asks over the telephone: "Is it true, Madame, that you were the victim of a peeping Tom?" The dialogue is *all* action: "Drowned by God! Drowned in the river! With their automobile, their affidavits and their God damn law books!" ... "Get him to tell you sometime about how we stole old lady Haggerty's stomach ... off the coroner's physician." The flow of events is astonishing: a car ran into the patrol wagon and the cops came "rolling out like oranges." A Negro baby was born in the patrol wagon. The Reverend J. B. Godolphin is suing *The Examiner* for one hundred thousand dollars for calling him a fairy. This is action with a vengeance. But there is neither emotion nor unity. The information conveyed is exhaustive; but one has no test of whether or not it is necessary. Instead of showing us the connection of events, Hecht and MacArthur are endeavoring to impress us with their lack of connection.

The vitality of the lines in *The Front Page* derives both from their inventiveness and their suddenness. The technique is a very special one: the characters do not so much answer each other as talk in opposition to each other. Violent contrasts are stressed, and at several points the lines are scrambled in a very effective way:

WOODENSHOES: Earl Williams is with that girl, Mollie Malloy! That's where he is!

* Anderson has attempted to resolve this contradiction in *Winterset.*

HILDY: Can you imagine—this time tomorrow I'd have been a gentleman. (*Diamond Louie enters.*)
LOUIE: Huh?
WOODENSHOES: She sent him a lot of roses, didn't she?
HILDY: God damn it, the hell with your roses. Gimme the dough. I'm in a hell of a hurry, Louie.
LOUIE: What are you talkin' about?
WOODENSHOES: I'll betcha I'm right.

One finds the same dialogue method employed to express the confusion of the bourgeoisie in the Soviet drama, *Armored Train 16-49,* by Vsevolod Ivanov.* Uncle Simon is talking about the office where he has been promised a job. The room has a seismograph in it:

SIMON: A seismograph for measuring earthquakes. There must be some reason for it.
NIZELASOV: Varia, I was down by the sea just now thinking of you. There were two corks tossing about in the breakers and as I watched them I thought they might be us.
VARIA: What queer ideas you get. Haven't the furnishing men arrived yet.... Aunt Nadia, haven't the furnishers arrived yet?
NADIA: They're coming today. I am going to have all the walls hung with Chinese silk.

The importance of both the above examples lies in the fact that the characters express their *will* toward their environment in concrete terms. The confusion comes from the intentness with which each pursues the line of potential action which occupies his consciousness. This also accounts for the dramatic quality of the scenes.

A speech or group of speeches is a subordinate unit of action, and exhibits the form of an action: exposition, rising action, clash and climax. The decision which motivates the action may relate to a past, present or potential event; but it must rise to a point of clash which exposes the break between expectation and fulfillment, and which leads to a further decision. The first act of John Wexley's *The Last Mile* takes places in the death-house of a prison; the men in the cells are all condemned to death; Walters, in cell number seven must pay the penalty immediately, while Red Kirby has thirty-five days to live:

KIRBY: Seven, if it was possible for me to do it, I'd give you half of mine, and we'd both have seventeen and a half days each. I wish I could do it.

---

* Translated by W. L. Gibson-Cowan and A. T. K. Grant (London, 1933).

WALTERS: You wouldn't fool me, would you, Red? This ain't no time to do that.

KIRBY: Not right here in town with my shirt on. Of course I got no way to prove my statement to you. I can see why you find it hard to believe; but just the same, I would do it. I wish it was only possible, because I hate like Hell to see you go, Seven.

WALTERS: I wish you could do it, Red, if you ain't kidding me?

MAYOR: He ain't, he'd do it. I believe him.

WALTERS: Ya all think so, guys?

D'AMORO: Seven, we all think he means what he says.

WALTERS (*Breathing deeply*): Well, thanks a lot, Red.

In this scene the declaration of will is potential: but the dramatist has made this potentiality intensely moving because he has shown the straining of the characters toward some realization, some means of testing the decision: the exposition is Kirby's first statement; the rising action develops from Walter's desperate need of proving the validity of the offer. When Walters asks: "You all think so, guys?" he is testing the decision in terms of reality as it exists within the narrow confines of the death-house. This reaffirms his own decision, his attitude toward his approaching death.

The problems of dialogue technique are identical with the problems of continuity. The units of action (single speeches or unified groups of speeches) may be tested in relation to the root-action of each unit; the decision and progression may be analyzed.

Compression is not only achieved by hot violent words, but by sudden contrasts, by breaks, pauses, moments of unexpected calm. For instance, in *We the People,* the scene in which Bert and Helen have gone to Senator Gregg to plead for help for Helen's brother ends with a bit of commonplace conversation:

BERT (*To Weeks, the Senator's Secretary*): I wonder if you could tell us how to get out to Mount Vernon.

WEEKS: Why no I really couldn't. I've never been out there myself.

BERT: You haven't?

WEEKS: No, but I'm sure any policeman can tell you how to go.

BERT: Well, thanks, goodbye.

HELEN: Good day.

WEEKS: Good day. (*They go out*). Curtain.

The same mode of understatement is used in *Peace on Earth.* At the end of Scene 3, in the first act, when Owens goes out with

Mac to investigate the strike, Jo, his wife, tries to prevent his going. In this case, Owens' decision is the basic decision which leads to the play's climax:

> JO: Pete, you listen to me— (*He puts his hands over his ears. She pulls them away. He kisses her.*)
> OWENS: So long.
> JO: Pete, if you get hit with a club I'll divorce you.
> OWENS: All right, see if I care. Come on, Mac. Be back soon, Josie.
> MAC: See you in church, Jo.
> JO: See you in church.

The lines quoted from *We the People* and *Peace on Earth* are dramatically effective, and the use of the unexpected understatement is justified. But both quotations illustrate the peculiarly pedestrian quality of American stage speech. There is not a hint of illumination in the lines. The same effect of sudden calm might have been achieved in sharply poetic phrases. This would not affect the *naturalness* of the words. In fact, the poet would endeavor to heighten the naturalness, to enforce the commonplace simplicity which is the purpose of the scenes. For instance, in *We the People,* the fact that Bert and Helen want to go to Mount Vernon has far more possibilities of compression and extension than have been indicated. In the scene in *Peace on Earth,* Jo's line, "See you in church," is commonplace without being characteristic or imaginative. In order to dramatize the commonplaceness of this moment, with all the potentialities and dangers which are inherent in its commonplaceness, one would require a line so poignant in its simplicity that it would awaken our pity and terror. Yet the quality of the scene, the good-natured uneventful leave-taking, would be preserved.

Dialogue without poetry is only half-alive. The dramatist who is not a poet is only half a dramatist.

CHAPTER VIII

THE AUDIENCE

THIS chapter is a postscript. During the course of this book, I have restricted myself to the analysis of the playwriting process, and have referred to the production process rarely and briefly. It has seemed to me that my method required this limitation; the problems of audience response have been hinted at only obliquely, because these problems go beyond the scope of the present investigation.

The audience is the ultimate necessity which gives the playwright's work its purpose and meaning. The laws by which the dramatist creates his product are determined by the use to which the product is to be put. The purpose of the drama is *communication:* the audience plays, not a passive, but an active part, in the life of a play. Dramatic technique is designed to achieve a maximum response. If a playwright is not seeking to communicate with his fellow men, he need not be bound by unity or logic or any other principle, because he is talking to himself, and is limited only by his own reaction to his own performance.

The laws of volitional thinking are binding upon the audience as well as the dramatist; the audience thinks and feels about the imaginary events in terms of its own experience, just as the dramatist has created the events in terms of *his* experience. But the audience approaches the events from a different angle: the play is the concentrated essence of the playwright's consciousness and will; he tries to persuade the audience to share his intense feeling in regard to the significance of the action. Identification is not a psychic bridge across the footlights; identification is acceptance, not only of the reality of the action, but of its meaning.

I have chosen to analyze the dramatic process by beginning with the playwright; one could reach many of the same conclusions by *beginning with the audience.* But an attempt to define dramatic theory by an analysis of audience response would be a far more difficult task, because it would involve many additional problems. The attitudes and preoccupations of the audience in observing a play are far more difficult to gauge than those of the playwright in creating the play. At every moment of the production, the various members of the audience are subject to an infinite variety of contradictory influences, depending on the architecture of the playhouse, the personalities of the players, the persons in the surrounding seats, the reports which have been circulated about the play, and a thousand other factors which vary from one performance to the next.

All the factors mentioned are social and psychological determinants. The playwright is also subject to all these variable factors in writing the play—indigestion, love, an automobile accident, an altercation over a debt, affect his relationship to his material. But the result, the play as it is written or produced, is a comparatively fixed object; the production involves the work of many persons besides the playwright; the production is never the same, and each performance is to some extent a new event. Nevertheless, the play itself, as a unified conception, is sharply enough defined to furnish reliable data concerning its function and the process by which it is created. The psychological and social determinants can be checked and tabulated.

Suppose we consider the one question of *attention*. The degree to which the playwright has been preoccupied with other matters during the preparation of the drama may or may not disturb the unity of the finished product; but we can judge the product accurately as a summary of the playwright's thought, without worrying about the author's day-to-day moods during its composition. But the preoccupations of the individual members of the audience, the degree to which their attention is concentrated or diffused, determines their participation in the dramatic events.

There are no data on which to base a study of audience response under various conditions. The extent to which the participation is active or passive, the responsiveness to different sorts of stimulation, the inter-connection between group and individual reactions, the way in which the emotional response affects the conduct and habits of the spectators—all of these are social and psychological problems concerning which almost nothing is known.

Professor Harold Burris-Meyer, of Stevens Institute of Technology, has been carrying on experiments for four years in order to determine the physiological reactions produced by the "dramatic use of controlled sound." It has been discovered that the varying pitch and intensity of an arbitrarily chosen sound can "stimulate physiological reactions so violent as to be definitely pathological." *

To attempt a premature appraisal of audience psychology without the necessary scientific groundwork is likely to lead one to assume that the contact between the audience and the stage is established from above, like Communion in church.

Most theories of dramatic art begin with the statement that the audience is the dominant factor. Having established this truth (which is so self-evident that it needs no elaboration), the theorist frequently finds himself unable to proceed: since he has made no investigation of the audience, he accepts it as an *absolute*—he pictures a final and changeless audience, to be accepted and feared, to be appealed to, flattered or cajoled. This leads to vulgar commercialism or to extreme estheticism. "It is an indisputable fact,"

* *New York Times,* April 30, 1935.

wrote Francisque Sarcey, "that a dramatic work, whatever it may be, is designed to be listened to by a number of persons united and forming an audience, that this is its very essence, that this is a necessary condition of its existence." * Sarcey's emphasis on the audience led him to develop the theory of the obligatory scene, which has a special bearing on audience psychology. But since Sarcey regarded the Parisian audience of the eighteen-seventies and eighties as the perfect image of an absolute audience, he accepted Scribe and Sardou as *absolute* dramatists. Modern criticism has followed Sarcey in the categorical acceptance of the audience and the consequent negation of dramatic values.

Gordon Craig goes to the opposite extreme, and wants to ignore the audience completely: "Once let the meaning of the word *Beauty* begin to be thoroughly felt once more in the Theatre, and we may say that the awakening day of the Theatre is near. Once let the word *effective* be wiped off our lips, and they will be ready to speak the word Beauty. When we speak about the effective, we in the Theatre mean something which will reach across the foot-lights." † Here we have in capsule form the whole history of the esthete in the theatre: he starts with beauty, and ends, unintentionally and probably against his will, without an audience.

H. Granville-Barker comes nearer to the heart of the matter—because he recognizes the social function of the drama. His book on *The Exemplary Theatre* is one of the few modern works which sees "the drama as a microcosm of society": "Dramatic art, fully developed in the form of the acted play, is the working out—in terms of make-believe, no doubt, and patchily, biasedly, with much over-emphasis and suppression, but still in the veritable human medium—not of the self-realization of the individual but of society itself." ‡ This points to an understanding of the way in which the audience functions: "If the audience is a completing part of the play's performance obviously its quality and its constitution matter. Not the least of the tasks of any theatre is to develop out of the haphazard, cash-yielding crowd a body of opinion that will be sensitive, appreciative, and critical."

Thus the audience is a variable factor; and since it plays a part in the play, its composition must be considered. The playwright is not only concerned with the opinions of the audience; he is also concerned with its *unity and arrangement*.

* Sarcey, *A Theory of the Theatre,* translated by H. H. Hughes (New York, 1916).

† *Opus cit.*

‡ H. Granville-Barker, *The Exemplary Theatre* (London, 1922).

Being so clear about the audience, Granville-Barker is also led to a realization of its class character. Since he is himself a representative of the middle class, he sees the theatre as part of the machinery of capitalist democracy, doing work which is similar to that of "press, pulpit, politics—there are powers these lack that the theatre can well wield." Since the theatre performs these responsible functions, he believes that the class line must be strictly drawn in the selection of audiences; "There is indeed a social distinction which the good theatre must rely on: it can only appeal to a leisure class."

We cannot consider the audience without considering its social composition: this determines its response, and the degree to which its response is unified.

The playwright's interest in his audience is not only commercial, but creative: the unity which he seeks can only be achieved through the collaboration of an audience which is itself unified and creative.

In the early nineteen-twenties, the more rebellious spirits in the theatre talked of breaking down the walls of the playhouse; the moldy conventions of the drawing room play must be destroyed; the drama must be created anew in the image of the living world. These declarations were vitally important; but those who attempted to carry out the task had only an emotional and confused conception of the living world of which they spoke. They succeeded in making a crack in the playhouse walls, through which one caught a glimpse of the brightness and wonder which lay beyond.

This was a beginning: the serious artist who caught a fleeting glimpse of the free world knew, as Ibsen knew in 1866, that he must *"live* what until now I *dreamt,"* that he must leave the mist of dreams and see reality "free and awake." This could not be done by selecting bits of reality piecemeal or by building a dramatic patchwork of fragmentary impressions. Since the drama is based on unity and logic, the artist must understand the unity and logic of events. This is an enormously difficult task. But it is also an enormously rewarding task: because the real world which the artist seeks is also the audience of which he dreams. The artist who follows Emerson's advice to look for "beauty and holiness in new and necessary facts, in the field and roadside, in the shop and mill," finds that the men and women who are the stuff of drama are the men and women who demand a creative theatre in which they may play a creative part.

A living theatre is a theatre of the people.

INDEX

Index